THE LIBRARY OF CONGRESS
ILLUSTRATED TIMELINE OF THE
CIVIL WAR

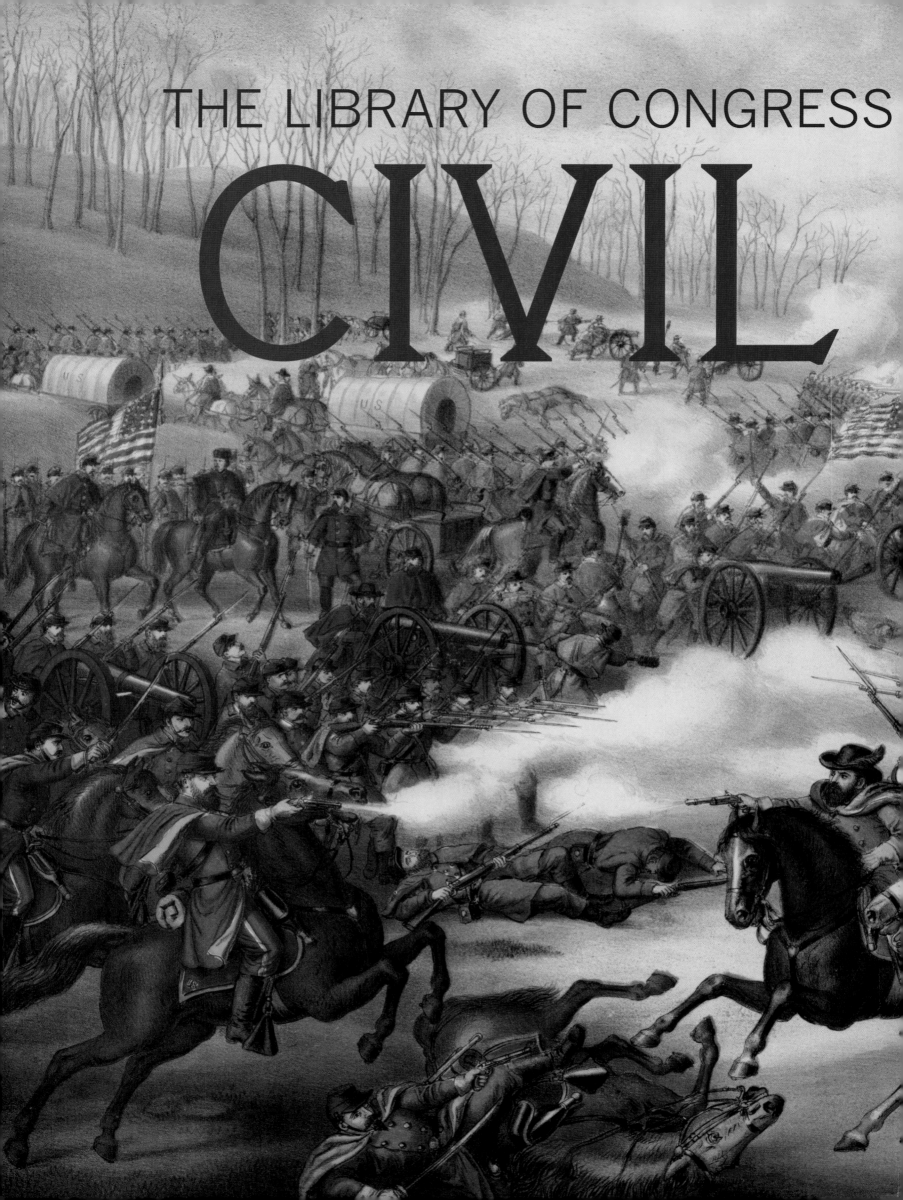

THE LIBRARY OF CONGRESS

CIVIL

ILLUSTRATED TIMELINE OF THE

WAR

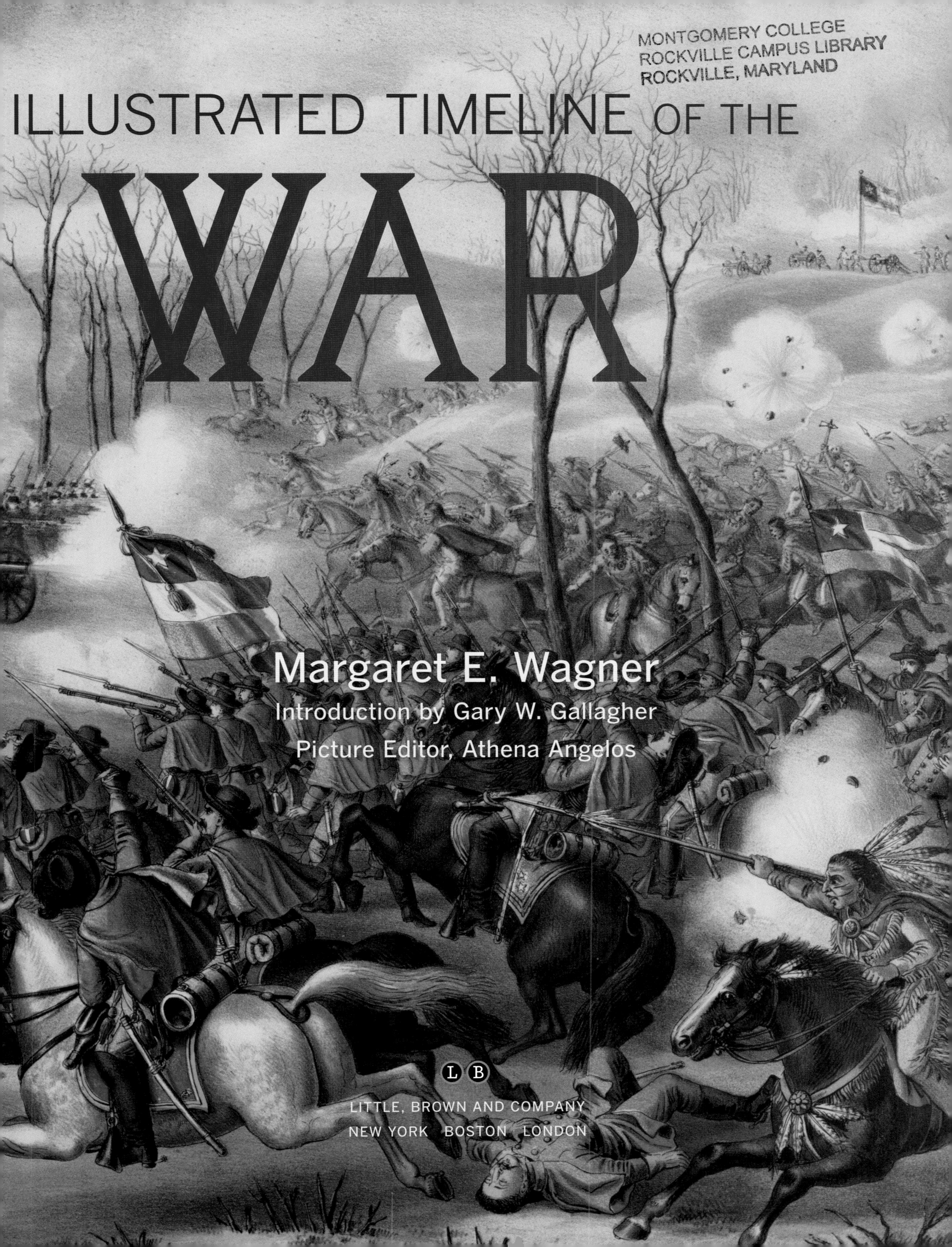

Margaret E. Wagner
Introduction by Gary W. Gallagher
Picture Editor, Athena Angelos

L B

LITTLE, BROWN AND COMPANY

NEW YORK BOSTON LONDON

To the millions of Americans and aspiring Americans, sung and unsung,
who have sacrificed to create and maintain the United States;
and to all those who honor them by exploring and preserving the nation's history.

Little, Brown and Company
Hachette Book Group
237 Park Avenue, New York, NY 10017
www.hachettebookgroup.com

Designed by Laura Lindgren

First Edition: October 2011

case binding: *Federal Encampment on the Pamunkey River* (p. 173)
page i: *The Confederate Army* (p. 37)
pages ii–iii: *Battle of Pea Ridge, Ark.* (p. 53)
pages iv–v: *Military Map of America,* 1862 (p. 6)
page 1: *Seeking for the Wounded, by Torch-light, After the Battle.*
Wood engraving in *Harper's Weekly,* March 8, 1862.

Little, Brown and Company is a division of Hachette Book Group, Inc. The Little, Brown name and logo are trademarks of Hachette Book Group, Inc.

The publisher is not responsible for websites (or their content) that are not owned by the publisher.

Library of Congress Cataloging-in-Publication Data
Wagner, Margaret E.
   The Library of Congress illustrated timeline of the Civil War / Margaret E. Wagner and the Library of Congress. — 1st ed.
    p. cm.
   Includes bibliographical references and index.
   ISBN 978-0-316-12068-5
   1. United States — History — Civil War, 1861–1865 — Chronology.
   2. United States — History — Civil War, 1861–1865 — Pictorial works. I. Library of Congress. II. Title.
   E468.3.W34 2011
   973.7 — dc22   2011008112

10 9 8 7 6 5 4 3 2 1

SC

Printed in China

CONTENTS

PREFACE

On July 4, 1860, Americans at home and abroad sang, marched, recited the Declaration of Independence, and raised glasses to toast the eighty-fourth birthday of the United States of America — an unprecedented, if greatly flawed, democratic republic established by people determined to forge a future untainted by the tyrannies of the past. Yet only a few months after these grand celebrations, Southern states — whose economies rested heavily upon the backs of four million people held in slavery — began seceding from the Union. By February 1861, the American experiment in representative democracy trembled on the verge of failure.

Two weeks after the artillery barrages in Charleston Harbor ignited the Civil War, the Library of Congress celebrated its sixty-first birthday. Then located in the U.S. Capitol, the Library held seventy thousand volumes and a small collection of maps that members of Congress consulted as they addressed the increasingly complex issues confronting the troubled nation. Southern legislators who had withdrawn from Congress and returned to their states still had some 276 volumes charged out to them that historic April; and Commander in Chief Lincoln would soon be borrowing books from the Library's collections as he schooled himself in military strategy during the first years of the war. In May 1861, President Lincoln appointed a political supporter, Indiana physician John G. Stephenson, as the fifth Librarian of Congress. This proved to be beneficial for many of the soldiers who garrisoned the nation's capital, for, in addition to heading the small Library staff, Stephenson volunteered his medical services in some of Washington's hospitals and makeshift infirmaries. In 1863, he served as a volunteer aide-de-camp during the battles of Chancellorsville and Gettysburg.

Stephenson and the assistant librarian, Ainsworth Rand Spofford, who became the sixth Librarian of Congress in 1864, also began acquiring material pertaining to the Civil War, a process that continues to the present day. Among the more than 145 million items that the Library now holds for Congress, the nation, and the world are well over a thousand discrete manuscript collections, including the papers of Abraham Lincoln, "Angel of the Battlefield" Clara Barton, abolitionist and former slave Frederick Douglass, and Confederate general Jubal A. Early, as well as letters and diaries of many less well-known soldiers and civilians on both sides.

Our Civil War collections also include military maps created by both Confederate and Union topographical engineers; photographs by Mathew Brady, George Barnard, Timothy O'Sullivan, and others; original drawings made by Alfred R. Waud and other Union special artist-correspondents and by soldier-artists such as William McIlvaine, James Fuller Queen, and Charles Wellington Reed; sheet music written and sung during the war; envelopes decorated with Union and Confederate political messages; law books and other administrative publications of the Confederate and United States; color and black-and-white lithographs depicting battles, leaders, and patriotic wartime themes; political cartoons, newspapers, and broadsides; dime novels, poetry, and memoirs published during the war; and thousands upon thousands of postwar memoirs and histories, including contemplations of the war and its reverberations published during the fiftieth, seventy-fifth, and one hundredth anniversaries of our nation's most rending conflict.

Published as the sesquicentennial commemoration of the war begins, *The Library of Congress Illustrated Timeline of the Civil War* includes more than 350 illustrations as well as a rich compendium of facts and quotations drawn from this unparalleled wealth of material. Starting with the journeys that presidents-elect Lincoln and Davis began on February 11, 1861, departing their homes to travel to their inaugurations, and concluding with a brief survey of postwar changes and challenges, this absorbing outline of four of the most difficult years in American history reflects the complexity, anguish, stubborn determination, and valor that characterized both sides of this bitter, fratricidal war. More than a history, the *Illustrated Timeline* is also an invitation to delve more deeply into Civil War history by visiting the Library — online at www.loc.gov, in person, and via the Library's other print and electronic publications. To begin your investigation, see "Civil War Collections in the Library of Congress," on page 244 of this book.

Emerging from the war terribly wounded but still very much intact, with slavery finally and forever outlawed within its borders, the United States has gone on to celebrate 146 birthdays since 1865. Each year of the country's existence brings stunning accomplishments and formidable challenges; each challenge underlines the importance of moving into the future armed with the best possible understanding of the past. In the Library of Congress, so often and aptly called the "Nation's Memory," history is alive and accessible in media from books to movies, from manuscripts to "tweets." I hope you will accept this invitation to explore our collections. You will be amazed, moved, stimulated, and enlightened by what you will find.

James H. Billington
The Librarian of Congress

The Grand Review of the Army. General Henry W. Slocum (Army of Georgia) and staff passing on Pennsylvania Avenue near the Treasury. Photograph by Mathew Brady, May 1865

heretofore, the war will be prosecuted for the object of practically restoring the constitutional relation between the United States and each of the States, and the people thereof, in which States that relation is or may be suspended or disturbed."

The complex process of emancipation emerges clearly in the *Timeline*. In dozens of entries, various actors have their moments, and readers will come away with an appreciation of the roles played by Lincoln, the Congress, abolitionists, generals such as Benjamin F. Butler and David Hunter, African American "contrabands" who sought refuge with advancing Union armies, and black men who donned blue uniforms. Throughout the war, illustrated newspapers kept readers abreast of progress toward emancipation with woodcuts depicting contrabands, African American military units in various theaters, and, in early 1865, the historic vote in the House of Representatives supporting the Thirteenth Amendment.

The *Timeline* establishes a critical moment on May 24, 1861, when "at Fort Monroe, Union general Benjamin Butler refuses to return three runaway slaves to their master, a Confederate colonel, calling the slaves 'contraband of war.' The designation takes hold throughout the North; hundreds of thousands of 'contrabands' will enter Union lines during the war — not without stirring controversy." The accompanying illustration, an 1861 lithograph titled *The [Fort] Monroe Doctrine* and intended as a humorous comment on Butler's action, deploys cruel racial stereotypes common in wartime cartoons dealing with African Americans.

Although military affairs dominated news throughout the war, the *Timeline* reminds us that political unrest also made headlines. In the Confederacy, women took to Richmond's streets in April 1863 to protest food shortages, and farmers bitterly opposed an impressment act that took part of their harvests. As in all American wars, questions relating to civil liberties ignited fierce debates — most notably when both Jefferson Davis and Abraham Lincoln suspended the writ of habeas corpus and the two national legislatures passed conscription acts.

Democrats accused the Lincoln administration of trampling the Constitution and deplored Republican support for emancipation. Sometimes their anger exploded in violence. On March 6, 1863, records the *Timeline*, a "mob of white men rampages through the African American section of Detroit, destroying thirty-two houses, killing several black people, and leaving more than two hundred homeless." New York City experiences a greater eruption of mob activity from July 13 to 17, 1863, which fuses anger with conscription and emancipation among working-class men and women: "The draft is temporarily suspended in New York City as the government sends more troops and the human cost of the violence becomes clear: hundreds have been injured; at least 105 people — including eleven African Americans, eight soldiers, two police officers, and dozens of rioters — have been killed."

On a more positive note, the Republican Party passed landmark legislation made possible by the departure from Congress of Democratic members from seceded states. A burst of legislative energy in 1862, just more than a year into the war, produced the Homestead Act, the Pacific Railroad Act, and the Land-Grant College Act. The last of these, typically called the Morrill Act after its sponsor, Representative Justin Smith Morrill of Vermont, ranks, as the *Timeline* notes, among "the most important pieces of educational legislation in United States history" and transferred "public lands — mostly in the West — to all states loyal to the Union. Colleges devoted to 'agriculture and the mechanic arts' are to be built with money accumulated from selling these lands." Many great state universities serve as continuing reminders of Morrill's expansive vision.

Equally engaging and informative, the *Timeline* will prove a boon to readers inspired by the sesquicentennial to learn more about the Civil War. Its skillful blending of facts, quotations, and illustrations recaptures the welter of information participants had to digest. Ranging across the entire military landscape, entries monitor activity along the Mississippi River, in the far reaches of the Trans-Mississippi theater, on the blood-soaked killing grounds of Virginia and Tennessee, and wherever Confederate commerce raiders and blockade runners clashed with Union naval vessels.

The kaleidoscopic coverage usefully identifies profound ties between the home front and the battle front. For example, a single week in May 1863 yields news about Joseph Hooker's humiliating defeat at Chancellorsville, the arrest in Ohio of Peace Democrat Clement Vallandigham for expressing "disloyal sentiments" that compromised the Union military effort, and a Confederate congressional resolution declaring that white officers in African American regiments could be subject to death sentences for "inciting servile insurrection." One perusal cannot do justice to the *Timeline,* which places readers in the happy position of revisiting its pages. Few exercises could be more beneficial for anyone hoping to take in the enormity of our defining national crisis.

PREFACE

On July 4, 1860, Americans at home and abroad sang, marched, recited the Declaration of Independence, and raised glasses to toast the eighty-fourth birthday of the United States of America — an unprecedented, if greatly flawed, democratic republic established by people determined to forge a future untainted by the tyrannies of the past. Yet only a few months after these grand celebrations, Southern states — whose economies rested heavily upon the backs of four million people held in slavery — began seceding from the Union. By February 1861, the American experiment in representative democracy trembled on the verge of failure.

Two weeks after the artillery barrages in Charleston Harbor ignited the Civil War, the Library of Congress celebrated its sixty-first birthday. Then located in the U.S. Capitol, the Library held seventy thousand volumes and a small collection of maps that members of Congress consulted as they addressed the increasingly complex issues confronting the troubled nation. Southern legislators who had withdrawn from Congress and returned to their states still had some 276 volumes charged out to them that historic April; and Commander in Chief Lincoln would soon be borrowing books from the Library's collections as he schooled himself in military strategy during the first years of the war. In May 1861, President Lincoln appointed a political supporter, Indiana physician John G. Stephenson, as the fifth Librarian of Congress. This proved to be beneficial for many of the soldiers who garrisoned the nation's capital, for, in addition to heading the small Library staff, Stephenson volunteered his medical services in some of Washington's hospitals and makeshift infirmaries. In 1863, he served as a volunteer aide-de-camp during the battles of Chancellorsville and Gettysburg.

Stephenson and the assistant librarian, Ainsworth Rand Spofford, who became the sixth Librarian of Congress in 1864, also began acquiring material pertaining to the Civil War, a process that continues to the present day. Among the more than 145 million items that the Library now holds for Congress, the nation, and the world are well over a thousand discrete manuscript collections, including the papers of Abraham Lincoln, "Angel of the Battlefield" Clara Barton, abolitionist and former slave Frederick Douglass, and Confederate general Jubal A. Early, as well as letters and diaries of many less well-known soldiers and civilians on both sides.

Our Civil War collections also include military maps created by both Confederate and Union topographical engineers; photographs by Mathew Brady, George Barnard, Timothy O'Sullivan, and others; original drawings made by Alfred R. Waud and other Union special artist-correspondents and by soldier-artists such as William McIlvaine, James Fuller Queen, and Charles Wellington Reed; sheet music written and sung during the war; envelopes decorated with Union and Confederate political messages; law books and other administrative publications of the Confederate and United States; color and black-and-white lithographs depicting battles, leaders, and patriotic wartime themes; political cartoons, newspapers, and broadsides; dime novels, poetry, and memoirs published during the war; and thousands upon thousands of postwar memoirs and histories, including contemplations of the war and its reverberations published during the fiftieth, seventy-fifth, and one hundredth anniversaries of our nation's most rending conflict.

Published as the sesquicentennial commemoration of the war begins, *The Library of Congress Illustrated Timeline of the Civil War* includes more than 350 illustrations as well as a rich compendium of facts and quotations drawn from this unparalleled wealth of material. Starting with the journeys that presidents-elect Lincoln and Davis began on February 11, 1861, departing their homes to travel to their inaugurations, and concluding with a brief survey of postwar changes and challenges, this absorbing outline of four of the most difficult years in American history reflects the complexity, anguish, stubborn determination, and valor that characterized both sides of this bitter, fratricidal war. More than a history, the *Illustrated Timeline* is also an invitation to delve more deeply into Civil War history by visiting the Library — online at www.loc.gov, in person, and via the Library's other print and electronic publications. To begin your investigation, see "Civil War Collections in the Library of Congress," on page 244 of this book.

Emerging from the war terribly wounded but still very much intact, with slavery finally and forever outlawed within its borders, the United States has gone on to celebrate 146 birthdays since 1865. Each year of the country's existence brings stunning accomplishments and formidable challenges; each challenge underlines the importance of moving into the future armed with the best possible understanding of the past. In the Library of Congress, so often and aptly called the "Nation's Memory," history is alive and accessible in media from books to movies, from manuscripts to "tweets." I hope you will accept this invitation to explore our collections. You will be amazed, moved, stimulated, and enlightened by what you will find.

James H. Billington
The Librarian of Congress

The Grand Review of the Army. General Henry W. Slocum (Army of Georgia) and staff passing on Pennsylvania Avenue near the Treasury. Photograph by Mathew Brady, May 1865

INTRODUCTION

GARY W. GALLAGHER

The Library of Congress Illustrated Timeline of the Civil War draws readers into a turbulent world of violence and uncertainty. One hundred and fifty years have passed since Confederate artillery at Charleston shelled the United States garrison holding Fort Sumter. The incident shocked many people but struck others as a predictable outgrowth of sectional tensions that had been building for decades. Though bound by a common language, religion, and shared history, the white North and South had grown increasingly polarized about the expansion of slavery into Federal territories and other issues related to what white Southerners referred to as the "peculiar institution."

Between the 1840s and the end of the 1850s, major Protestant denominations split along sectional lines, the Second Party System of Whigs and Democrats fractured, and a significant percentage of Northerners and white Southerners came to believe that fundamental differences divided them and that they should expect the worst from fellow citizens across the Ohio River or Mason and Dixon's Line.

The election of Abraham Lincoln, a Republican pledged to barring slavery from the territories, ignited passions that sent the seven states of the Deep South out of the Union within three months. Four Upper South states followed in the wake of Fort Sumter. The war that soon pitted residents of the incipient Confederate nation against the loyal population of the United States far surpassed in fury, duration, and consequences anything imagined by even the most prescient observers in April 1861. More than a million citizen-soldiers became casualties — 620,000 of them dead from wounds or disease; millions of civilians directly experienced economic, political, and social disruption; and, perhaps most strikingly within a mid-nineteenth-century context, four million enslaved African Americans emerged from the war as free men, women, and children.

Different groups of participants subsequently developed contending memories of the war. Most white Northerners chose to highlight salvation of the Union, which preserved the work of the Founding generation and safeguarded democracy in a Western world that still clung to aristocracy and monarchy. Black and white abolitionists, almost all African Americans, and a few others looked first to emancipation as a grand outcome of the war, while former Rebels embraced a Lost Cause vision that celebrated gritty determination in the face of long odds and denied the centrality of slavery to the establishment of the Confederacy. Some people from both sides eventually adopted a tone of reconciliation, finding what they deemed *American* characteristics of gallantry and perseverance among white soldiers in both Union and Confederate armies. Echoes of the war and its conflicting memories remind modern Americans that hotly contested issues of the mid-nineteenth century can still provoke passionate debates regarding race and citizenship, the relative power of central and local government, and the fate of civil liberties amid the pressures of waging war.

Fashioned from a breathtaking array of written and pictorial material in the unequaled and constantly growing collections of the Library of Congress, this timeline charts the ebb and flow of events between February 1861 and May 1865. Scholars and other researchers have mined these rich veins of evidence for many decades, and it is no exaggeration to say that much of what we know about the conflict has emerged from the manuscripts, rare books, broadsides, lithographs, photographs, newspapers, government documents, maps, and other items preserved and made available by the Library's superb staff. The quotations and illustrations that accompany this detailed chronological record, all selected from the Library's holdings — including many items newly acquired or never before published — shed new light on this crucial period. Photographs, eyewitness sketches by artists in the field, and passages from wartime letters and diaries communicate a sense of immediacy, while postwar interpretations are implicit in artistic prints produced by Louis Prang & Company and other firms.

The contrast between wartime and postwar evidence reminds us that history and historical memory can diverge sharply. For example, Kurz & Allison's *Battle of Wilson's Creek — Aug. 10, 1861 — Union (Gen. Lyon) . . . Conf. (Gen. McCulloch)*, an 1893 lithograph (see page 33), depicts in the heroic style embraced by postwar reconciliationists the moment of Brigadier General Nathaniel Lyon's mortal wounding. In fact, Lyon received his wound in the midst of a battle he had badly mismanaged — "a folly," one Union officer said, "which the gallant death of Gen. Lyon does not atone for." In contrast, English-born sketch artist Alfred R. Waud's wartime drawing of five Union soldiers enduring punishment as a pair of utterly unmoved guards looks on conveys the brutality of army discipline (see page 36). Waud's starkly descriptive text similarly betrays no hint of compassion: "Drunken soldiers tied up for fighting and other unruly conduct."

The *Timeline* demonstrates why chronology is central to understanding historical events. It helps readers appreciate how battles, political decisions, and social currents intersected and shaped one another in the conflict's overarching narrative. Too often we approach the past from the end of the story, falling prey, in the case of the Civil War, to what might be called the Appomattox syndrome. Robert E. Lee's surrender to Ulysses S. Grant confirmed the United States' triumph over the Confederacy and guaranteed that slavery would die.

For most Americans, no other outcomes seem possible. The United States possessed far more men and material wealth than did the Confederate States and, with its greater urban development, industrial might, and large immigrant population, looked much like the modern American nation. Few can imagine how victory might have gone to a Confederacy predicated on slavery and dependent on a largely agricultural economy. Oddly, Appomattox often stands more as beginning than conclusion, the place to commence a search for factors that explain how Grant and Lee came to that sleepy Virginia village for their seemingly inevitable meeting on April 9, 1865.

Reading forward in the *Timeline* undermines any notion of preordained Union victory. The book details how soldiers and civilians reacted to news from increasingly bloody battlefields, coped with escalating intrusions from central governments that levied new taxes and conscripted citizens, confronted sweeping social adjustments, and engaged in heated political debates. Morale rose and fell, sometimes in violent swings, and the final result remained uncertain until deep into the conflict.

Perceptive leaders on both sides knew that in wars between democratic republics the key to victory lay with civilians, something evident in statements such as Lee's to Confederate secretary of war John C. Breckinridge in early 1865: "Everything in my opinion has depended and still depends upon the disposition and feelings of the people." Union morale dipped to critical low points several times, with the summer of 1864 marking an especially precarious moment. Lincoln despaired of victory that dark August, doubting Republican chances in the election of 1864. Major General William Tecumseh Sherman's capture of Atlanta in early September and Major General Philip H. Sheridan's smashing victories in the Shenandoah Valley in September and October transformed sentiment in the loyal states, paving the way for Republican success in November. Republican triumph in turn guaranteed that emancipation, which as late as the middle of 1864 remained far from certain, would be a non-negotiable element of any peace settlement.

A close perusal of the *Timeline* for the first half of 1862 underscores the contingent nature of events. Entries between early February and mid-June point toward imminent Union victory. In the western theater, United States land and naval forces repeatedly vanquish Rebel opponents and take control of vast stretches of Confederate territory. Grant's victories at Fort Henry, Fort Donelson, and Shiloh oblige Confederates to abandon middle Tennessee, including the crucial city of Nashville, by the middle of April. New Orleans and Memphis fall in April and June, respectively, thereby removing the Mississippi River as a vital artery of Confederate commerce (though Union control of the entire river will wait until the fall of Confederate strongholds at Vicksburg and Port Hudson in July 1863). By the end of May, a United States army seizes Corinth, Mississippi, an important railroad junction. Progress in the eastern theater nearly matches that in the West, as Major General George B. McClellan advances with his Army of the Potomac to within a few miles of Richmond by June 1.

Shortly thereafter, *Harper's Weekly* prophesied that the "great drama of the age draws slowly to a close. Twelve months

ago the rebels held all of Virginia, all of Tennessee, half of Kentucky." But Union forces had closed the Mississippi, taken all of Kentucky and most of Tennessee, "and our troops are thundering at the gate of Richmond." Had McClellan captured Richmond that summer, a likely scenario with General Joseph E. Johnston in charge of the defending army, it is difficult to envision continued Confederate resistance. The war would have ended with McClellan, who opposed forced emancipation, as the preeminent Union military idol and slavery largely intact.

The *Timeline*'s entry for June 1, 1862, explains why McClellan did not take Richmond and why, over the next three months, the strategic landscape changed dramatically. "As the Battle of Fair Oaks (Seven Pines) concludes with an ineffective assault by Confederates under James Longstreet," reads the text, "Jefferson Davis 'temporarily' relieves Robert E. Lee of his duties as chief military adviser to the Confederate president and places him in command of the troops protecting Richmond — a force now officially known as the Army of Northern Virginia." The next few entries set up Lee's offensive in the Seven Days battles, which unfold between June 25 and July 1 and closes with McClellan's retreat to Harrison's Landing, on the James River below Richmond. The *Timeline* neatly summarizes the impact of the Seven Days: "Union civilians seek someone to blame for the campaign's failure: Republicans tend to blame McClellan; many Democrats zero in on Secretary of War Stanton. In the Confederacy, citizens and soldiers breathe a sigh of relief. 'Lee has turned the tide,' Confederate war department clerk John Jones writes in his diary. Lee and his Army of Northern Virginia will henceforth remain central to Southern hopes."

Those hopes rose over the next nine weeks, as Lee won the second battle of Bull Run in late August and, during the first week of September, crossed the Potomac onto United States soil. Even before news of Lee's invasion reached London, British politicians concluded the Union was in peril. On September 8, the *Timeline* relates, Prime Minister Palmerston observed that another major defeat would render the Federal cause "manifestly hopeless" — a statement that attested to the primacy of the eastern theater in European calculations as well as the degree to which Union fortunes had declined since the end of May. Lee's retreat from the battlefield at Antietam on September 18 ended his string of victories begun at the Seven Days, but the Army of Northern Virginia stayed close to the Potomac frontier. Confederate morale remained high because of Lee's overall strategic success, which, ironically, furthered the cause of emancipation by extending the war.

As casualties mounted over succeeding months, loyal white citizens, most of whom cared little about enslaved African Americans, increasingly accepted the need to strike at slavery as a means to undermine the Confederacy. Lincoln correctly gauged Northern attitudes, and his preliminary proclamation, issued on September 22 in the wake of Lee's withdrawal from Maryland, presented emancipation as a military measure designed to help win the war. The first printed edition of that document, reproduced in the *Timeline*, deployed uninspiring language to reassure the loyal public that "hereafter, as heretofore, the war will be prosecuted for the object of practically restoring the constitutional relation between the United States and each of the States, and the people thereof, in which States that relation is or may be suspended or disturbed."

The complex process of emancipation emerges clearly in the *Timeline*. In dozens of entries, various actors have their moments, and readers will come away with an appreciation of the roles played by Lincoln, the Congress, abolitionists, generals such as Benjamin F. Butler and David Hunter, African American "contrabands" who sought refuge with advancing Union armies, and black men who donned blue uniforms. Throughout the war, illustrated newspapers kept readers abreast of progress toward emancipation with woodcuts depicting contrabands, African American military units in various theaters, and, in early 1865, the historic vote in the House of Representatives supporting the Thirteenth Amendment.

The *Timeline* establishes a critical moment on May 24, 1861, when "at Fort Monroe, Union general Benjamin Butler refuses to return three runaway slaves to their master, a Confederate colonel, calling the slaves 'contraband of war.' The designation takes hold throughout the North; hundreds of thousands of 'contrabands' will enter Union lines during the war — not without stirring controversy." The accompanying illustration, an 1861 lithograph titled *The [Fort] Monroe Doctrine* and intended as a humorous comment on Butler's action, deploys cruel racial stereotypes common in wartime cartoons dealing with African Americans.

Although military affairs dominated news throughout the war, the *Timeline* reminds us that political unrest also made headlines. In the Confederacy, women took to Richmond's streets in April 1863 to protest food shortages, and farmers bitterly opposed an impressment act that took part of their harvests. As in all American wars, questions relating to civil liberties ignited fierce debates — most notably when both Jefferson Davis and Abraham Lincoln suspended the writ of habeas corpus and the two national legislatures passed conscription acts.

Democrats accused the Lincoln administration of trampling the Constitution and deplored Republican support for emancipation. Sometimes their anger exploded in violence. On March 6, 1863, records the *Timeline,* a "mob of white men rampages through the African American section of Detroit, destroying thirty-two houses, killing several black people, and leaving more than two hundred homeless." New York City experiences a greater eruption of mob activity from July 13 to 17, 1863, which fuses anger with conscription and emancipation among working-class men and women: "The draft is temporarily suspended in New York City as the government sends more troops and the human cost of the violence becomes clear: hundreds have been injured; at least 105 people — including eleven African Americans, eight soldiers, two police officers, and dozens of rioters — have been killed."

On a more positive note, the Republican Party passed landmark legislation made possible by the departure from Congress of Democratic members from seceded states. A burst of legislative energy in 1862, just more than a year into the war, produced the Homestead Act, the Pacific Railroad Act, and the Land-Grant College Act. The last of these, typically called the Morrill Act after its sponsor, Representative Justin Smith Morrill of Vermont, ranks, as the *Timeline* notes, among "the most important pieces of educational legislation in United States history" and transferred "public lands — mostly in the West — to all states loyal to the Union. Colleges devoted to 'agriculture and the mechanic arts' are to be built with money accumulated from selling these lands." Many great state universities serve as continuing reminders of Morrill's expansive vision.

Equally engaging and informative, the *Timeline* will prove a boon to readers inspired by the sesquicentennial to learn more about the Civil War. Its skillful blending of facts, quotations, and illustrations recaptures the welter of information participants had to digest. Ranging across the entire military landscape, entries monitor activity along the Mississippi River, in the far reaches of the Trans-Mississippi theater, on the blood-soaked killing grounds of Virginia and Tennessee, and wherever Confederate commerce raiders and blockade runners clashed with Union naval vessels.

The kaleidoscopic coverage usefully identifies profound ties between the home front and the battle front. For example, a single week in May 1863 yields news about Joseph Hooker's humiliating defeat at Chancellorsville, the arrest in Ohio of Peace Democrat Clement Vallandigham for expressing "disloyal sentiments" that compromised the Union military effort, and a Confederate congressional resolution declaring that white officers in African American regiments could be subject to death sentences for "inciting servile insurrection." One perusal cannot do justice to the *Timeline,* which places readers in the happy position of revisiting its pages. Few exercises could be more beneficial for anyone hoping to take in the enormity of our defining national crisis.

THE LIBRARY OF CONGRESS
ILLUSTRATED TIMELINE OF THE
CIVIL WAR

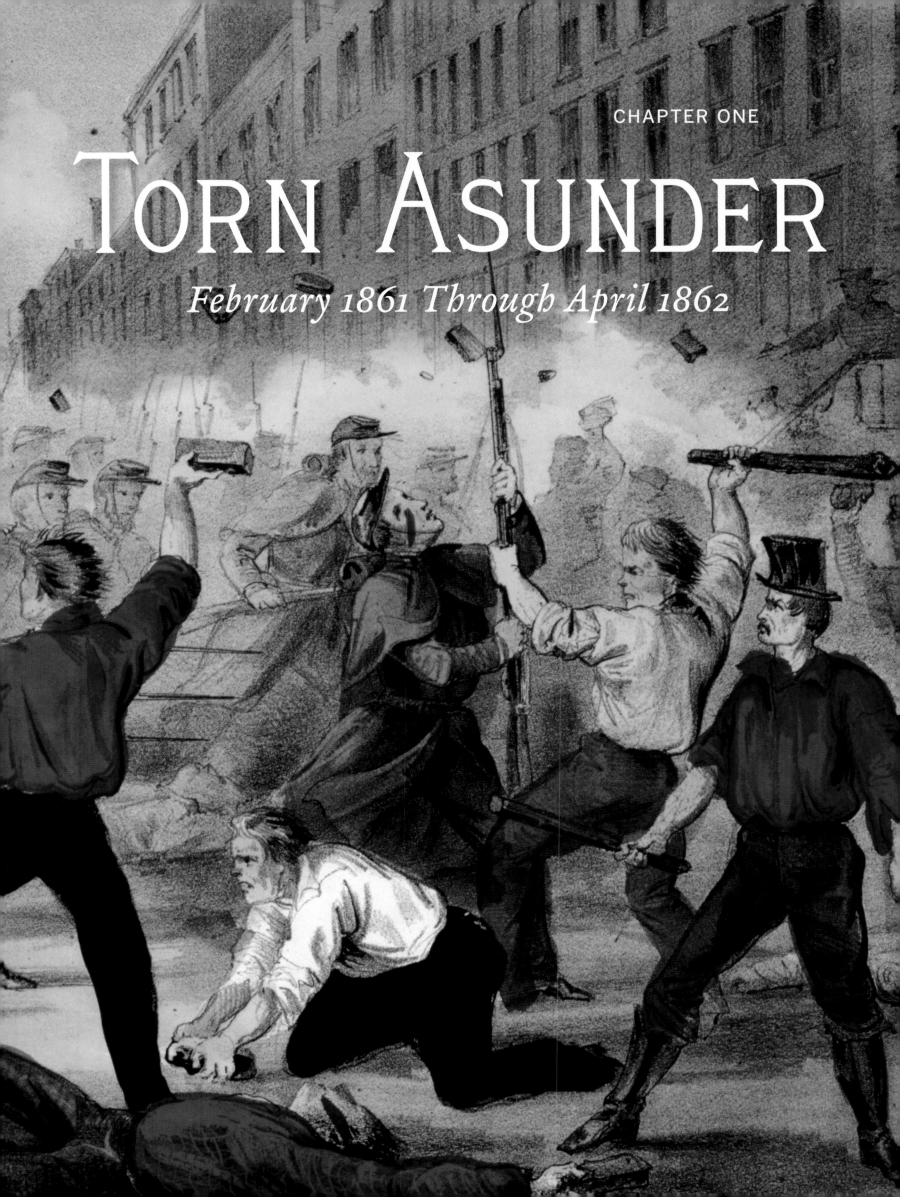

TORN ASUNDER

February 1861 Through April 1862

BY JANUARY 1861, the young United States of America was beginning to tear apart. After the November 1860 election of Abraham Lincoln, whose Republican Party opposed the spread of slavery beyond the states where it already existed, Southern states economically dependent on what Southerners termed the "peculiar institution" of slavery were afraid that the balance of power in the Union would soon tip irrevocably in favor of the industrial, free-labor North. To avoid suffering the consequences of such a shift in political influence, they began carrying through on a threat Southern "fire-eaters" — ardent secessionists — had been making periodically since the 1830s. With South Carolina leading the way, by February 1 Mississippi, Florida, Alabama, Georgia, Louisiana, and Texas had declared their ties to the United States null and void.

PRECEDING OVERLEAF: *The Lexington of 1861.* Detail (see page 17).

LEFT: *Inauguration of Mr. Lincoln, March 4, 1861.* There were several photographers present at this seminal event, some quite close to the platform (where Lincoln stands under the wood canopy), but the only surviving photographs are those taken from a distance. This picture by an unknown photographer shows some of the scaffolding being used to replace the Capitol dome and a portion of the closely packed crowd — which includes reporters, and perhaps Southern agents, who will convey the new president's words to the leaders and people of the Confederacy.

Published in 1862 by Bacon and Company of London, England, this *Military Map of America* uses different colors for the slaveholding states (pink and yellow) and free states and territories (light blue), delineating the central difference between North and South that led to the Civil War.

To ardent secessionists, the time had come to form a confederacy of slaveholding states neither dependent on the North nor aggravated by it and true to its own interpretation of the intent of the Founding Fathers — who had, after all, included provisions supporting slavery in the Constitution. To dedicated Unionists, secession was unthinkable, the death knell of the great American experiment in representative democracy.

On February 11, two men — Jefferson Davis and Abraham Lincoln — embarked on journeys that marked the deepening fault line dividing the Northern and Southern regions of the United States.

A West Point graduate and a former U.S. secretary of war and senator from Mississippi, Davis left Brierfield, his plantation just south of Vicksburg, for a five-day steamboat and railroad journey to the Confederate capital, Montgomery, Alabama. Although he had expected the delegates from six Southern states meeting there to name him to a major post in the new government, Davis was far from jubilant when a messenger from Vicksburg had arrived two days earlier with the notification telegram.[3] He was all too aware of the challenges confronting the Confederacy that he would be heading.

Throughout the South, transportation, education, and communications systems, as well as business and industry, were all far less developed than in the North; economically, the South leaned heavily on "King Cotton" and the slave labor that planted and harvested that prize crop and performed much other manual and domestic labor. Though heavily dependent on waterborne commerce, the South had no navy; most American shipbuilders were located in the North, thus most experienced merchant seamen were based there.[4] "We are without machinery, without means, and threatened by a powerful opposition," Davis will write to his wife, Varina, on February 20.[5] The Confederate States of America would need the strength and resources of as many of the remaining eight Southern and border slave states as possible if it was to succeed as a separate political entity.

The Confederate president-designate was forced by the comparatively haphazard structure of Southern railroads to follow a circuitous route to Montgomery: north and east through parts of northern Alabama and Tennessee; south to Atlanta, Georgia; then west into south-central Alabama and his final destination. Along the way, he was buoyed by what the *Charleston (SC) Mercury* termed "continuous ovations . . . military demonstrations, salutes of cannon, &c." Davis made more than two dozen speeches during the five-day trip, culminating in an address to the jubilant crowd that greeted him on his arrival in Montgomery on February 16. There, the *Mercury* reported, Davis declared that the new Confederacy's "only hope was in a determined maintenance of our position, and to make all who oppose us smell Southern powder and

Abraham Lincoln (1809–1865), photograph, May 16, 1861, by the Brady National Photographic Art Gallery, Washington, DC; and Jefferson Davis (1808–1889), photograph by Julian Vannerson in *McClees' Gallery of Photographic Portraits of the Senators, Representatives & Delegates* *of the Thirty-Fifth Congress* (1859). Both men were born in what was to become the crucially important border state of Kentucky and then traveled very different paths to become the political leaders of the warring American regions.

feel Southern steel. . . . Our separation from the old Union is complete. NO COMPROMISE; NO RECONSTRUCTION CAN BE NOW ENTERTAINED." These sentiments were received, the paper noted, with "tremendous applause."[6]

Preparing to leave Springfield, Illinois, on a cold, damp February 11, Abraham Lincoln hoped, as did many other Northerners, that Unionist sentiment, even in the seceded states, remained sufficiently strong to allow peaceful closure of the regional rift. To Lincoln, the Union was permanent and indissoluble, and it was now his principal job to lead the way to its preservation. "The Chief Magistrate derives all his authority from the people," he will say in the inaugural address that he was still crafting as he began his journey to Washington, "and they have conferred none upon him to fix terms for the separation of the States." The final address will be both a firm declaration of principles and an attempt to reassure those Southerners who feared "that by the accession of a Republican Administration, their property, and their peace, and personal security, are to be endangered." It will also single out the one issue that lay at the heart of the nation's political ferment: "One section of our country believes slavery is *right,* and ought to be extended, while the other believes it is *wrong,* and ought not to be extended. This is the only substantial dispute."[7]

Lincoln delivered the first of many speeches he was to give on his slow progress to Washington from the rear platform of his special train before it even left Springfield: a moving, ad hoc farewell address to the people of that city, his neighbors for a quarter of a century, to whose kindness, he declared, "I owe every thing. . . . I now leave, not knowing when, or whether ever, I may return, with a task before me greater than that which rested upon [George] Washington." Sad and pensive as his journey began, the president-elect quickly regained his spirits as he greeted the celebratory crowds that met his train at each of its many scheduled stops. On February 13, in Columbus, Ohio, he learned that feared secessionist attempts to disrupt the meeting of the electoral college in Washington had not materialized, and the electors, unmolested, had confirmed his election. As the train moved on through Pennsylvania, New York, and New Jersey, he attempted to calm rather than emphasize the regional tensions that had raised the specter of war. "*There is no crisis* excepting such a one as may be gotten up at any time by designing politicians," he told the people of Pittsburgh on February 15. "My advice, then, under such circumstances, is to keep cool. If the great American people will only keep their temper, on both sides of the line, the troubles will come to an end."[8]

ALEX. H. STEPHENS,
VICE PRESIDENT.

W.M. L. YANCEY,
LEADER OF THE SECESSION PARTY.

JEFF. DAVIS,
FIRST PRESIDENT.

HOWELL COBB,
PRESIDENT OF THE SENATE.

THE STARTING POINT OF THE GREAT WAR BETWEEN THE STATES.
INAUGURATION OF JEFFERSON DAVIS

As President of the Confederate States of America, at Montgomery, Alabama, February 18, 1861. Painted by James Massalon from a Photograph taken on the spot, and owned by Col. Wm. C. Howell, of Prattville, Autauga County, Alabama. Size of Painting 5 feet 2 inches x 6 feet 2 inches—copyrighted. Then Chromoed from said Painting by Strobridge
& Co., of Cincinnati, Ohio. Any infringement upon the Copyright of this Chromo will be prosecuted to the fullest extent of the law.
Entered according to Act of Congress, in the year 1878, by Wm. C. Howell and James Massalon, in the office of the Librarian of Congress, at Washington, D. C.

The Starting Point of the Great War Between the States. Inauguration of Jefferson Davis. Color lithograph by Strobridge & Co., 1878, from a painting by James Massalon, based on a photograph of the event. While Lincoln believed there was still hope for reconstructing the Union, Davis addressed this assemblage as the first president of what secessionists foresaw as a permanent Confederation: "Obstacles may retard, they cannot long prevent the progress of a movement sanctified, by its justice," Davis said, "and sustained by a virtuous people."

February 1861
Through
April 1862

FEBRUARY

1 2 3 **4** 5 6 7 **8** 9 10 11 12 13 14 15 16 17 **18** 19 20 **21** 22 23 24 25 26 27 28

FEBRUARY 1861

FEBRUARY 4, 1861: Representatives of six of the seven states that have seceded to date (delegates from recently seceded Texas are not yet present) meet in Montgomery, Alabama, and begin deliberations that will shortly culminate in the creation of the Confederate States of America. *At the same time,* the Peace Convention, suggested in January by Governor John Letcher of Virginia, begins at the Willard Hotel in Washington. Although delegates from twenty-one states take part in the conference, its outcome is doomed from the start. None of the seceded states are represented; several Northern states elect not to participate; and the overall purpose of the conference soon gets lost amid the machinations of radicals and endless waves of empty rhetoric.[9] *In the Arizona Territory,* inexperienced U.S. Army second lieutenant George N. Bascom lures Chiricahua Apache chief Cochise and several members of his family to his camp, then attempts to hold them all hostage. Cochise, falsely accused of raiding a ranch and kidnapping the rancher's stepson, manages to escape; others in his party are not as fortunate. Over the next several days, ignorance, mistrust, and miscalculations escalate into the bloody opening chapter of a brutal years-long conflict.[10]

FEBRUARY 8, 1861: In Montgomery, the convention of seceding states unanimously adopts the Provisional Constitution of the Confederate States, which is largely based on the U.S. Constitution — with several significant differences.[11]

FEBRUARY 18, 1861: "Dixie" becomes the unofficial Confederate States anthem when it is played at a ceremony marking Jefferson Davis's inauguration as provisional president of the Confederate States of America. Davis does not include any mention of slavery in his inaugural address. Instead he emphasizes the right of each sovereign state to determine its own course: "Through many years of controversy with our late associates, the Northern States, we have vainly endeavored to secure tranquillity, and to obtain respect for the rights to which we were entitled. As a necessity, not a choice, we have resorted to the remedy of separation; and henceforth our energies must be directed to the conduct of our own affairs." Georgian Alexander H. Stephens, who had initially opposed disunion, is chosen provisional vice president this same day.[12]

FEBRUARY 21, 1861: The Provisional Confederate Congress (the delegates to the Montgomery convention) passes legislation creating the Navy Department, to be headed by Stephen R. Mallory, former U.S. senator from Florida and onetime chairman of the Senate Naval Committee.[13] However, the legislature resists Georgian Thomas R. R. Cobb's suggestion that it pass an export tax on cotton, creating an artificial shortage that would pressure the European Powers — particularly Britain, whose textile mills heavily depend on Southern cotton — to recognize the Confederate States as an independent nation. Most of Cobb's colleagues believe there is no need for such pressure. "The firm and universal conviction here," Cobb

FEBRUARY

1   2   3   4   5   6   7   8   9   10   11   12   13   14   15   16   17   18   19   20   21   **22**   23   24   25   26   **27   28**

writes his wife, "is, that Great Britain, France, and Russia will acknowledge us at once in the family of nations."[14] *In Washington, DC,* the Senate rejects President Buchanan's nomination of Jeremiah Sullivan Black of Pennsylvania to become an associate justice of the U.S. Supreme Court. It will fall to Lincoln to make a new nomination — the first of five appointments he will make to the Supreme Court.[15]

FEBRUARY 22, 1861: One day after Lincoln is advised by private detective Allan Pinkerton that a plot exists to kidnap or assassinate him as he travels through Baltimore, Maryland (a slaveholding state with deep sympathies for the South), Fred Seward, son of the incoming secretary of state, brings the president-elect a similar warning from U.S. Army General in Chief Winfield Scott. Though he was unwilling, based solely on Pinkerton's report, to take special precautions traveling through Baltimore, this second warning from a respected and unrelated source leads Lincoln to agree, reluctantly, to change his travel arrangements. He leaves for Washington tonight, rather than the following afternoon as originally scheduled, and he agrees to wear a less conspicuous felt hat instead of his usual tall stovepipe. Passing through Baltimore without incident, he will arrive in Washington early on the morning of February 23 — and begin immediately to rue the cautious last portion of his journey, which quickly becomes grist for unfriendly political cartoonists.[16]

FEBRUARY 27, 1861: South Carolina governor Francis W. Pickens writes President Davis: "We feel that our honor and safety require that Fort Sumter should be in our possession at the very earliest moment." The seceded states have been taking over Federal facilities, including arsenals and forts, within their borders; but two forts that remain in Federal hands are emerging as particular bones of contention: Fort Pickens, at Pensacola, Florida; and Fort Sumter, in the Charleston, South Carolina, harbor. Tensions are particularly high in Charleston, where the secession movement started. On January 9, cannon fire from Charleston batteries forced the steamship *Star of the West* to turn back without delivering the reinforcements and supplies it was attempting to bring to the fort's Union garrison. At that time, the garrison commander, Major Robert Anderson, did not allow his men to open fire on the batteries that drove the vessel away, thus preserving a tenuous peace. But the fort now has Confederate guns trained on it from three directions, and its garrison cannot endure this state of siege too long without some assistance.[17]

FEBRUARY 28, 1861: As each of the seceded states begins forming military regiments, the Confederate Congress passes legislation creating the Provisional Army of the Confederate States (PACS), a force equivalent to the Volunteer Army that will be organized in the North. One week later, on March 6, Congress will pass legislation creating the seceded states'

TORN ASUNDER

"regular" army, the Army of the Confederate States of America (ACSA), which President Jefferson Davis — a former U.S. secretary of war — envisions as an echo of the small standing army maintained by the United States. Because the Confederacy will be at war almost from the start and many troops will have to be raised quickly, virtually all new Confederate soldiers will be mustered into the Provisional Army.[18]

MARCH 1861

MARCH 1, 1861: President Jefferson Davis appoints Brigadier General P. G. T. (Pierre Gustave Toutant) Beauregard to the command of Confederate forces in Charleston, South Carolina, and informs Governor Francis W. Pickens that he and Beauregard have discussed the measures that would be necessary to expel the Federal garrison from Fort Sumter. Beauregard will find the city already preparing for conflict, and he will set to work immediately improving upon the measures already taken. On March 22, he will report that his preparations are almost complete — and that the troops in Fort Sumter are nearly out of fuel and provisions.[19]

MARCH 4, 1861: As Jefferson Davis holds his first cabinet meeting in Montgomery, Abraham Lincoln is inaugurated in Washington; in the crowded capital city, extraordinary security precautions are taken to guarantee his safety. Though Davis, his cabinet, and the Provisional Confederate Congress now claim the loyalty of the seven seceded states, in his inaugural address, Lincoln seeks to keep avenues open to reconstruct the divided nation. He reminds the assembled audience, including reporters who will transmit his words to the South, that he was elected on a platform that included a pledge to maintain inviolate the rights of the states, "especially the right of each State to order and control its own domestic institutions." Yet the Federal government must enforce its own authority and laws. "All the power at my disposal will be used to reclaim the public property and places which have fallen; to hold, occupy, and possess these, and all other property and places belonging to the government, and to collect the duties on imports; but beyond what may be necessary for these, there will be no invasion of any State. . . . In *your* hands, my dissatisfied fellow countrymen, and not in *mine,* is the momentous issue of civil war. The government will not assail *you,* unless you *first* assail *it.*" He concludes the address with an eloquent appeal: "We are not enemies, but friends. We must not be enemies. Though passion may have strained, it must not break, our bonds of affection. The mystic chords of memory, stretching from every battle-field, and patriot grave, to every living heart and hearthstone, all over this broad land, will yet swell

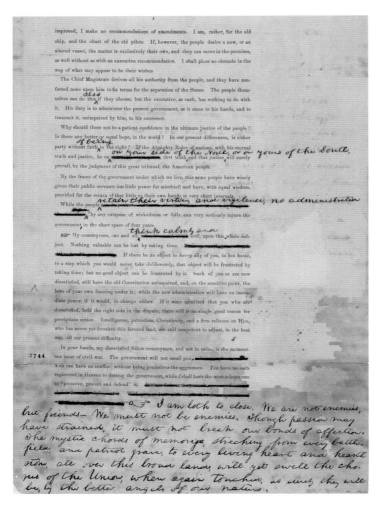

ABOVE: *The Cabinet at Washington.* Wood engraving published in *Harper's Weekly,* July 1861, showing, left to right: Postmaster General Montgomery Blair, Secretary of the Interior Caleb B. Smith, Secretary of the Treasury Salmon P. Chase, President Lincoln, Secretary of State William H. Seward, Secretary of War Simon Cameron, Attorney General Edward Bates, and Secretary of the Navy Gideon Welles.

LEFT: Final page of Abraham Lincoln's First Inaugural Address, with handwritten emendations, 1861. Lincoln began work on the address in Illinois and continued to hone it, accepting suggestions from a few confidants, including his Illinois friend Orville H. Browning and the venerable politician Francis Preston Blair. William H. Seward's suggestions were, perhaps, the most influential. Lincoln transformed Seward's draft of a final conciliatory paragraph from his secretary of state's pedestrian prose into the speech's final, poetic, and powerful conclusion, shown, in Lincoln's hand, on this page.

the chorus of the Union, when again touched, as surely they will be, by the better angels of our nature."[20]

MARCH 6, 1861: As the Provisional Confederate Congress authorizes an army of one hundred thousand volunteers for twelve months, the people of New Orleans turn out to salute former U.S. general David E. Twiggs, who has surrendered nineteen Texas army posts to Confederate authorities.[21] *From Maryland,* Henry Winter Davis writes President Lincoln, urging him to nominate his cousin, Judge David Davis of Illinois — a longtime colleague of Lincoln's who had been his campaign manager at the 1860 Republican Convention — to fill the vacancy on the U.S. Supreme Court. This is one of *many* names put forward, for the Supreme Court and for myriad other positions that the new Republican administration has to fill. In this era of political patronage, Lincoln must spend much of his time considering pleas from would-be officeholders, even as the rift between North and South is widening.

MARCH 7, 1861: Gideon Welles joins the Lincoln cabinet as secretary of the navy. A former Connecticut state legislator and newspaper publisher and editor, Welles served President Polk as chief of the naval Bureau of Provisions and Clothing. He will immediately embark on vastly expanding the navy, including the construction of ironclad ships.[22]

MARCH 9, 1861: Lincoln holds his first formal cabinet meeting. Three of the men in the room, Secretary of State William H. Seward, Secretary of the Treasury Salmon P. Chase, and Attorney General Edward Bates, were top contenders for the presidential nomination at the 1860 Republican convention. As a whole, the cabinet — which also includes Secretary of War Simon Cameron, Gideon Welles (see March 7, 1861), Secretary of the Interior Caleb B. Smith, and Postmaster General Montgomery Blair — reflects Lincoln's attempt to fill each post with well-suited people, include men of various views, and, especially in Cameron's case, pay political debts he acquired during the presidential campaign.[23]

MARCH 12, 1861: The *New York Times* reports the comments of T. S. Gourdin of Florida, editor of the *Southern Confederacy:* "We must abandon the old idea of our forefathers that 'all men were born free and equal' and teach the doctrine of the diversity of the races, and of the supremacy of the Anglo-Saxon race over all others. We must take the ground never dreamed of by the men of '76, that African Slavery is right in itself, and therefore should be preserved."[24]

MARCH 14, 1861: The *Washington Evening Star* prints a roster of Jefferson Davis's initial cabinet choices that, though tongue-in-cheek, nevertheless reflects one aspect of what will emerge as the new Confederate president's governing style — a reluctance to delegate: "For Secretary of State, Hon. Jeff.

The Cabinet of the Confederate States at Montgomery, from photographs by Whitehurst, of Washington, and Hinton, of Montgomery, Alabama. Wood engraving published in *Harper's Weekly,* June 1, 1861. The Davis cabinet, which was to undergo more changes than Lincoln's, initially included (seated, left to right) Attorney General Judah P. Benjamin, Secretary of the Navy Stephen R. Mallory, Secretary of the Treasury Christopher G. Memminger (standing), Vice President Alexander H. Stephens, Secretary of War Leroy P. Walker (standing), President Davis, Postmaster General John H. Reagan, and Secretary of State Robert A. Toombs.

William Howard Russell (1820–1907). Roger Fenton (1819–1869) took this photograph of Russell in 1855, during the Crimean War, when Russell emerged as one of the first modern war correspondents (his reports inspired celebrated nurse Florence Nightingale's groundbreaking hospital work at the front). His dispatches from the United States in 1861–62 gave Britons telling glimpses of events and people on both sides of the Civil War.

MARCH

1 2 3 4 5 6 7 8 9 10 11 12 13 14 15 16 17 18 19 20 21 22 23 24 25 26 27 **28 29** 30 31

Davis of Miss.; War and Navy, Jeff. Davis of Miss.; Interior, ex-Senator Davis, of Miss.; Treasury, Col. Davis of Miss., Attorney General, Mr. Davis of Miss." In fact, the cabinet now comprises Robert A. Toombs of Georgia, secretary of state; Christopher G. Memminger of South Carolina, secretary of the treasury; Leroy P. Walker of Alabama, secretary of war; Stephen R. Mallory of Florida, secretary of the navy; John H. Reagan of Texas, postmaster general; and Judah P. Benjamin of Louisiana, attorney general.[25]

MARCH 28, 1861: Famed British newspaper correspondent William H. Russell, currently in Washington, notes in his journal that the city is giving a "cold shoulder . . . to Mr. Lincoln, and all kinds of stories and jokes are circulated at his expense." In the evening Russell attends a White House dinner, where he meets politicians and cabinet members, is more favorably impressed by Mary Todd Lincoln than "the Secessionist ladies at Washington" have led him to expect — and discovers that the president himself is adept at the art of good-humored storytelling. He also discovers that members of Lincoln's cabinet "seemed to think that England is bound by her anti-slavery antecedents to discourage to the utmost any attempts of the South to establish its independence on a basis of slavery" — an assumption they'll have reason to doubt in the stormy months ahead, and one directly counter to expectations of foreign recognition that prevail in the Confederate capital.[26]

MARCH 29, 1861: After much consultation with advisers, whose opinions are divided, President Lincoln determines that the United States shall not abandon Forts Sumter and Pickens. He orders preparations made for a relief expedition to Sumter. Yet Martin J. Crawford, John Forsyth, and A. B. Roman, three Confederate commissioners Davis has sent to Washington to attempt negotiations, have, without Lincoln's knowledge, been given the impression, via an intermediary's discussions with Secretary of State Seward, that Sumter's garrison will be withdrawn. *This same day,* Seward presents Lincoln with a plan to reinforce Fort Pickens. Lincoln directs that the plan be carried out, and Seward complies — with such secrecy that Secretary of the Navy Welles is not even made aware of it. Preparations for the Seward-backed Pickens expedition will ultimately conflict with those for the relief of Fort Sumter.[27]

FORT PICKENS.

PENSACOLA HARBOR FLORIDA

New York, Published by Currier & Ives, 152 Nassau St.

FORT M'RAE.

APRIL 1861

APRIL 1, 1861: Secretary of State Seward sends Lincoln a paper titled "Some Thoughts for the President's Consideration." It is a document that reflects Seward's initially low estimation of Lincoln's abilities and his belief that, as a more experienced politician, he, rather than Lincoln, is the most appropriate person to steer the country's course — and that Lincoln will allow him to do so. "We are at the end of a month's Administration, and yet without a policy either domestic or foreign," Seward begins, ignoring the policies that Lincoln stated in his inaugural address. The secretary then advocates abandoning Fort Sumter (as he has led the Confederate commissioners to believe will happen) and concentrating on the relief of Fort Pickens. Other recommendations include deflecting attention from domestic problems by provoking a crisis, or even a war, with the European Powers and designating Seward as the chief designer and prosecutor of administration policy. Lincoln will answer Seward in person, refuting each point and making it clear that, in the case of designing and pursuing a vigorous administration policy, "*I* must do it." This marks a turning point in Seward's relationship with Lincoln. The secretary of state will soon grow to respect the president's abilities and become one of Lincoln's closest and most trusted advisers.[28]

APRIL 8, 1861: A U.S. State Department clerk, Robert S. Chew, delivers a message from President Lincoln to South Carolina governor Francis W. Pickens and Confederate general P. G. T. Beauregard: "An attempt will be made to supply Fort-Sumpter [*sic*] with provisions only; and that, if such attempt be not resisted no effort to throw in men, arms, or amunition [*sic*], will be made, without further notice, or in case of an attack upon the Fort." This notice does nothing to quell the secessionists' growing impatience at having a Federal garrison in Charleston Harbor.[29] *Outside Cincinnati,* Associate Justice John McClean dies of pneumonia. There are now two vacancies on the U.S. Supreme Court.[30]

APRIL 11, 1861: "The North is swollen with pride and drunk with insolence," the "fire-eating" *Charleston Mercury* editorializes today. "The North needs proof of the earnestness of our intentions and our manhood. Experience shall be their teacher. Let them learn."[31]

APRIL 12–13, 1861: "If Anderson does not accept terms — at four — the orders are — he shall be fired upon," Charlestonian Mary Boykin Chesnut writes in her diary on April 12. "I count four — St. Michael chimes. I begin to hope. At half-past four, the heavy booming of a cannon." Guns from the fort answer the volleys from Charleston, and the Civil War begins. As will often be the case in this fratricidal war, the two men commanding the opposing Union and Confederate forces are not strangers to each other. Both Major Robert Anderson, commander of the garrison in Fort Sumter, and Brigadier

ABOVE: Major Robert Anderson (left, 1805–1871), USA. Engraving published in the *Illustrated London News,* May 1, 1861. Brigadier General Pierre Gustave Toutant (P. G. T.) Beauregard (1818–1893), CSA. Wood engraving published in *Harper's Weekly,* April 27, 1861.

OPPOSITE: *Fort Pickens, Pensacola Harbor, Florida.* Hand-colored lithograph by Currier & Ives, between 1860 and 1870. One of the two most significant bones of contention as the seceded states took over Federal facilities early in 1861, Fort Pickens fell under Confederate siege after Florida's secession on January 10. Reinforced after Fort Sumter fell, Pickens remained in Union hands throughout the war.

RIGHT: *The Housetops in Charleston during the Bombardment of Sumter.* Wood engraving published in *Harper's Weekly,* May 4, 1861.

APRIL

1 2 3 4 5 6 7 8 9 10 11 12 13 14 **15** 16 **17** **18** 19 20 21 22 23 24 25 26 27 28 29 30

General P. G. T. Beauregard, commander of Confederate forces in Charleston, had served on General Winfield Scott's staff during the Mexican War (1846–48); both are West Point graduates (Anderson, class of 1825; Beauregard, class of 1838), and at one time Anderson was Beauregard's much-respected artillery instructor. After months of siege and many hours of bombardment, Anderson, whose ties to the South run deep, surrenders the fort with more sorrow than anger. "Our Southern brethren . . . have attacked their father's house and their loyal brothers," he will later write. "They must be punished and brought back, but this necessity breaks my heart."[32]

APRIL 15, 1861: President Lincoln issues a proclamation calling for a special session of Congress to convene on July 4 (giving congressmen ample time to travel from all parts of the nation). The document also calls "forth, the militia of the several States of the Union, to the aggregate number of seventy-five thousand . . . to cause the laws to be duly executed." These volunteers are to serve for ninety days — not enough time to provide the men more than the most basic training. By this time, the Confederacy has already enrolled sixty thousand men in its armed forces, while the Regular (professional) U.S. Army comprises only some sixteen thousand men. Slightly increased in strength, the U.S. Regular Army will remain a separate service throughout the war. The overwhelming majority of Union soldiers will serve in the Volunteer Army (raised for this emergency), to which Regular Army units will be assigned as needed.[33]

APRIL 17, 1861: While Missouri and Tennessee refuse to fill their quotas of Union militia, and Maryland secessionists hold a meeting in Baltimore, the Virginia State Convention votes 88–55 in favor of secession, a decision that will be confirmed by popular referendum on May 23. Among the facilities that will be taken over by the government of this crucial upper-South state are the U.S. armory at Harpers Ferry and Gosport Navy Yard, near Norfolk, Virginia, the largest shipbuilding and repair facility in the South (see April 20, 1861).[34] *In the Confederate Capital at Montgomery,* Jefferson Davis, whose armed forces include only the barest rudiments of a navy, invites applications for letters of marque, which permit privately owned armed vessels to act "in the service of the Confederate States on the high seas, against the United States of America, its ships and vessels, and those of its citizens . . ." The Lincoln administration, which does not regard the Confederate States as a separate political entity, will see this as an instigation of the criminal act of piracy, which, under United States law, is a capital offense.[35]

APRIL 18, 1861: Five companies of Pennsylvanians become the first forces to reach Washington, DC, to assist in the capital's defense. Within their ranks is sixty-five-year-old Nicholas Biddle, one of the few African American men who have been allowed to join all-white units, in Biddle's case as the orderly to Captain James Wren. The previous day, as Biddle marched through Baltimore, Maryland, his presence in the ranks had

"NICK BIDDLE,"
Of Pottsville, Pa. the first man wounded in the Great
American Rebellion, "Baltimore, April 18, 1861."
Published by W. R. Mortimer, Pottsville, Schuylkill Co., Pa.

"Everything is in an uproar here and the war feeling is on the increase."

—WILLIAM DEAN HOWELLS,
APRIL 21, 1861

LEFT: Nicholas Biddle (ca. 1796–1876). Photograph by W. R. Mortimer, between 1861 and 1865. Born a slave, Biddle escaped to freedom via the Underground Railroad, eventually settling in Pottsville, Pennsylvania. He was among the first men wounded in the Union cause.

OPPOSITE: *The Lexington of 1861.* Hand-colored lithograph by Currier & Ives, ca. 1861. The deadly melee between Union troops and Confederate sympathizers on the streets of Baltimore, Maryland, took place on the anniversary of the first engagements of the American Revolution at Lexington and Concord, Massachusetts, April 19, 1775.

particularly incensed a crowd of whites who were sympathetic to the Confederacy and already angry at having Union soldiers in their streets. Shouting insults at Biddle, some also threw stones and other missiles, wounding Biddle and several of his comrades. Thus one of the first people to shed blood for the Union is a black man.[36] *As the Pennsylvanians arrive in the capital city,* the U.S. Army's legendary general in chief, Winfield Scott, meets with Colonel Robert E. Lee (whom Scott had once called "the very best soldier that I ever saw in the field"). He offers Lee command of the main Union army; Lee declines. Two days later, he will write to Scott, tendering his resignation:

> It would have been presented at once, but for the struggle it has cost me to separate myself from a service to which I have devoted all the best years of my life & all the ability I possessed. . . . I shall carry with me to the grave the most grateful recollections of your kind consideration. . . . Save in the defense of my native State, I never desire again to draw my sword.[37]

This same day, civilian railroad executive George Brinton McClellan, a West Point graduate who had served as a junior officer under Winfield Scott and Robert E. Lee during the Mexican War of 1846–48 — and who was considered an intellectual light of the prewar U.S. Army — writes to his friend Fitz John Porter. Though McClellan is a conservative Democrat with no love for abolitionists, he proclaims himself four-

square for the Union: "I throw to one side now all questions as to . . . political parties etc — the Govt is in danger, our flag insulted & we must stand by it."[38] *At Sewell's Point, near Norfolk, Virginia,* Union gunboats clash with Confederate batteries as Union forces attempt to seize control of the vital waterways leading to the interior of Virginia. At the same time, the Confederacy is seeking to block access to Washington, DC, via Chesapeake Bay and the Potomac River.[39]

APRIL 19, 1861: In Baltimore, rioters attack the Sixth Massachusetts as the regiment makes its way through the streets of this crucial railroad hub. Some soldiers open fire; four soldiers and twelve civilians are killed, and many people are wounded. Tension increases as other Marylanders tear down railroad bridges and telegraph lines leading to Washington. With Virginia poised to join the Confederacy, these pro-secessionist rumblings in Maryland make many Northerners fearful that Washington might soon be surrounded and cut off from the rest of the Union. Many remember the *Richmond (VA) Examiner*'s editorial challenge, published in its December 25, 1860, edition: "Can there not be found men bold and brave enough in Maryland to unite with Virginians in seizing the Capital in Washington?"[40] *Also on this day,* by proclamation, Lincoln initiates a Union naval blockade of Confederate ports in South Carolina, Alabama, Florida, Georgia, Louisiana, Mississippi, and Texas, made necessary by "an insurrection against the Government of the United States." Among the actions that

THE LEXINGTON OF 1861.

he cites as justification for the blockade is the Confederacy's threat "to grant pretended letters of marque to authorize the bearers thereof to commit assaults on the lives, vessels, and property of good citizens of the country lawfully engaged in [seagoing] commerce."[41] (See April 17, 1861.)

APRIL 20, 1861: In anticipation of Confederate attack, the Union prematurely abandons the Gosport Navy Yard in Virginia after destroying part of the facility and scuttling a number of vessels. Parts of four vessels will be salvaged by the Confederates, including the remnants of the steam frigate USS *Merrimack,* destined to be rebuilt as an ironclad and rechristened CSS *Virginia. Farther to the north,* at Annapolis, Maryland, home of the U.S. Naval Academy, the revered warship USS *Constitution* is moved away from shore as a precaution against Confederate capture. On April 24, *Constitution,* under tow and with midshipmen on board, will depart for Newport, Rhode Island, via New York. Given the secessionist sympathies of many in Maryland, Newport will remain the Naval Academy's home until August 1865.[42]

APRIL 21, 1861: USS *Saratoga* captures a vessel with the romantic name *Nightingale,* which is carrying a cargo of 961 slaves. Though the domestic slave trade still thrives, international trade in slaves has been against U.S. law since 1808. But Africans have been brought into the Deep South illegally since well before the outbreak of the Civil War.[43] *In Maryland,* state

authorities sever the telegraph lines that carry messages north from Washington. For a full week, telegrams from the capital will reach only Baltimore.[44] *Also today,* Illinois senator Lyman Trumbull, one of many Northern citizens whose apprehension over the vulnerability of Washington, DC, increased when a Baltimore mob attacked Union regiments (see April 18 and 19, 1861), writes President Lincoln, urging him to "take possession of Baltimore at once." A few days later, Lincoln will receive a warning that the pending meeting of the Maryland legislature in Annapolis will probably result in a vote to "arm the people of that State against the United States." Some advisers suggest that he direct the army to arrest the state's legislators before that can occur — an action Lincoln deems improper, unless the Maryland lawmakers actually act against the Federal government.[45] Meanwhile, patriotic fervor is spreading among the people of both regions. In the North, William Dean Howells, author of Lincoln's presidential campaign biography, writes to his wife from Columbus, Ohio: "Everything is in an uproar here and the war feeling is on the increase, if possible. The volunteers [for military service] seemed to be in very good spirits and to look on campaigning as something of a frolic."[46]

APRIL 23, 1861: Courted by the governors of Pennsylvania (where he was born), Ohio (where he now works), and New York (where he attended West Point), George B. McClellan today accepts Ohio governor William Dennison's offer to place McClellan in charge of the forces Ohio is raising for the

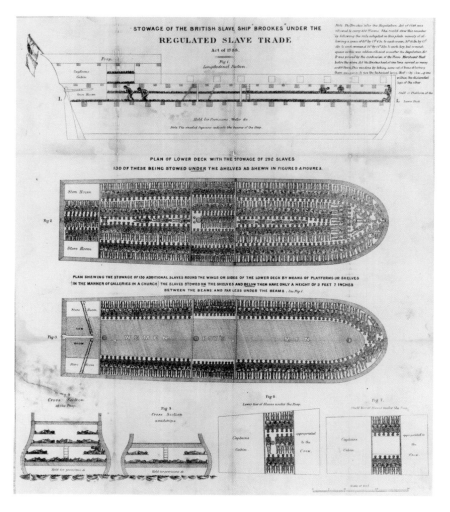

ABOVE: *Great Meeting of the Ladies of New York at the Cooper Institute, on Monday, April 29, 1861, to organize a society to be called "Women's Central Association of Relief," to make clothes and lint bandages, and to furnish nurses for the soldiers of the Northern Army.* Reproduction of a wood engraving, 1861.

LEFT: *Stowage of the British Slave Ship "Brookes" Under the Regulated Slave Trade Act of 1788.* Etching published as a broadside ca. 1788. Since 1808, participation in the international slave trade had been illegal in the United States. Yet smugglers continued to bring Africans into the South, each ship interdicted by U.S. authorities providing a bitter reminder of the inhumanity inherent in this brutal commerce in human lives.

APRIL

1 2 3 4 5 6 7 8 9 10 11 12 13 14 15 16 17 18 19 20 21 22 23 **24** **25** 26 **27** 28 29 30

war effort, with the rank of major general of volunteers. As McClellan starts immediately to work, thousands more Ohio men are volunteering than are required under the state's quota of thirteen regiments (about ten thousand men); all are eager to participate in what most believe will be the short-term dispatch of the rebellious Southerners.[47]

APRIL 24, 1861: Lincoln replies to a letter from former Maryland senator Reverdy Johnson, who reported "excitement and alarm . . . of my own State and of Virginia" because it is feared "that it is your purpose to use the military force you are assembling in this District" to invade those two states. "I have no objection to declare a thousand times that I have no purpose to *invade* Virginia or any other State," Lincoln writes, "but I do not mean to let them invade us without striking back."[48]

APRIL 25, 1861: At the train station in Galena, Illinois, West Point graduate and Mexican War veteran Ulysses S. Grant, retired from the army for over six years and, until today, employed in his brother's store in Galena, bids farewell to his wife, Julia. He departs for Camp Yates, near Springfield, with the Illinois militia company he has helped form.[49]

APRIL 27, 1861: President Lincoln extends the naval blockade to include the ports in Virginia and North Carolina, thus committing the navy to a blockade of more than 3,500 miles of Confederate coastline — though, at this time, the U.S. fleet

includes only ninety ships. (Plans are in motion to augment this force.) At the urging of Secretary of State Seward, among others, Lincoln also sends the following written instruction to General in Chief Scott:

> You are engaged in repressing an insurrection against the laws of the United States. If at any point on or in the vicinity of the military line, which is now used between the City of Philadelphia and the City of Washington . . . you find resistance which renders it necessary to suspend the writ of Habeas Corpus for the public safety, you, personally or through the officer in command at the point where the resistance occurs, are authorized to suspend that writ.

Habeas corpus, the right to "have the body" of an arrested person brought before a court, which would determine the reasonableness of his arrest, is a fundamental tenet of English law and American democracy that the U.S. Constitution specifically states (Article 1, Section 9) "shall not be suspended unless when in cases of rebellion or invasion the public safety may require it." The writ has been suspended only twice before in U.S. history: by General Andrew Jackson in New Orleans during the War of 1812 and by the Rhode Island legislature in 1842 during what became known as Dorr's Rebellion. Both Lincoln and Jefferson Davis will suspend, or seek to suspend, habeas corpus at times during the Civil War — and each instance will provoke storms of criticism and controversy.[50]

Elizabeth Blackwell (1821–1910). The first American woman to receive an MD (Geneva Medical College, New York, 1849), Blackwell helped select suitable candidates to be trained as nurses throughout the war, doing all she could to support the Union in what she deemed its struggle for "freedom and justice."

General Winfield Scott (1786–1866), USA. Engraving published in the *Illustrated London News,* March 16, 1861. Known as "Old Fuss and Feathers," Scott had fought in every U.S. conflict since the War of 1812 and, by 1861, was a near legend to most Americans and many abroad.

APRIL–MAY

29 30 **1** 2 **3** 4 5 6 7 8 9 10 11 12 13 14 15 16 17 18 19 20 21 22 23 24 25 26 27 28 29

APRIL 29, 1861: Under the principal leadership of Elizabeth Blackwell, America's first female medical doctor, three thousand women and several prominent men meet at the Cooper Institute in New York City and form the Women's Central Association of Relief to coordinate the efforts of many small Northern war-relief groups. Although this organization will suffer a rebuff when it attempts to establish a connection with the U.S. Army, it will be the nucleus of the United States Sanitary Commission, or USSC (see June 13, 1861).[51] *Also this day,* free African American men organize their own drill company in Boston, since a Federal law prohibits black men from serving in state militias and there are no blacks in the U.S. Army. Other black drill companies will be organized in the North — but their efforts are unwelcome. "This is a white man's war," they will be told.[52] *In Montgomery,* President Davis issues a message to the Provisional Confederate Congress, reiterating the South's right to secede and declaring Lincoln's April 15 proclamation (calling for seventy-five thousand volunteers) a declaration of war. When Davis asks for authority to prosecute the war, Congress responds by granting the president power to use all land and naval forces and to raise volunteers.[53]

MAY 1861

MAY 1, 1861: Having tendered his resignation on April 26, John Archibald Campbell of Alabama (who had urged Secretary of State Seward to meet with the three Confederate peace commissioners; see March 29 and April 1, 1861) leaves the U.S. Supreme Court, which now has three vacancies.[54] *On duty overseas,* U.S. Navy lieutenant George Hamilton Perkins writes home: "This news about our country is so absorbing we cannot think or talk of anything else. . . . No doubt many officers of our squadron will resign; but, as a Northern man, I, for one, hope that all the North will pull together and go in and win."[55]

MAY 3, 1861: President Lincoln issues a proclamation calling for 42,034 volunteers to serve in the infantry and cavalry "for the period of three years, unless sooner discharged" and 18,000 volunteers to serve in the navy for not less than one year or more than three. The proclamation also expands the Regular Army by 22,714 men — both measures reflecting the possibility that the war might not be as short as everyone hopes. The training of three-year volunteers in the same units as men who answered the initial call for three-month enlistments will present an administrative challenge to Volunteer Army organizers.[56] *On this same day,* U.S. General in Chief Winfield Scott proposes an envelopment strategy for fighting the Confederacy that would include a powerful movement down the Mississippi River as well as the blockade of Southern seaports.

THE EIGHTH MASSACHUSETTS REGIMENT IN THE ROTUNDA OF THE CAPITOL, WASHINGTON.—[See Page 331.]

The Eighth Massachusetts Regiment in the Rotunda of the Capitol, Washington. Wood engraving published in *Harper's Weekly*, May 25, 1861. For a limited time, the Capitol served as an impromptu barracks, and the behavior of new and undisciplined soldiers did nothing to soothe the nerves of architect Thomas U. Walter.

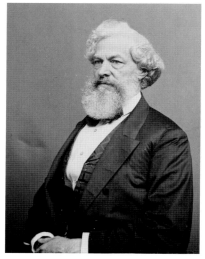

Thomas Ustick Walter (1804–1887). Photograph between 1855 and 1865. Appointed architect of the Capitol extension by President Millard Fillmore in 1851, Walter added the north (Senate) and south (House) wings to the building and replaced the existing copper-covered wooden dome with one made of cast iron—continuing to work despite wartime distractions.

MAY

1 2 3 **4** 5 **6** 7 **8 9** 10 11 12 13 14 15 16 17 18 19 20 21 22 23 24 25 26 27 28 29 30 31

Though immediately subject to ridicule by those confident of quick victory (see June 29, 1861), Scott's plan will become an essential aspect of the overall strategy ultimately adopted by the Union. Scott has also spoken favorably to Lincoln of the qualities of George B. McClellan, and today McClellan is placed in command of the entire military Department of the Ohio (initially comprising the states of Ohio, Indiana, and Illinois; later expanded). McClellan is proving to be a tireless and adept organizer and trainer of military forces, and he is generally well regarded by his men. Yet he is also displaying flashes of a troublesome arrogance toward, and impatience with, both superiors and subordinates who criticize his plans or do not immediately acquiesce to his demands.[57]

MAY 4, 1861: As news of the American conflict spreads through Europe, the *London Morning Post* joins critics of the American experiment in democracy, now so obviously on the verge of failure. "Equal citizenship, popular supremacy, vote by ballot and universal suffrage may do well for a while," the paper sniffs editorially, "but they invariably fail in the day of trial."[58]

MAY 6, 1861: Arkansas secedes from the Union by a 69–1 vote of the state legislature. The Tennessee legislature approves holding a public referendum on secession, an action that is tantamount to secession. (See June 8, 1861.)[59]

MAY 8, 1861: From Washington, architect Thomas U. Walter, in charge of an ongoing project to replace the dome on the U.S. Capitol, writes to his wife of the distractions he faces now that Washington is filling with troops, some of whom are billeted in the Capitol: "The smell is awful. The building is like one grand water closet. Every hole and corner is defiled." There is also the somewhat happier distraction of "about 100 drummers all the time drumming, having a head drummer to teach them; they have been going over the same *toodle-de-toodle-de toodle-de too* for the last 2 hours." By the time Congress convenes in July, the troops will have moved out of the building, and the "water-closet" odors will have been replaced by the scent of bread for the troops that is baking in twenty ovens located in the Capitol's basement. (This sweet-smelling enterprise will come to an end due to growing complaints about bread-delivery wagons cluttering Capitol driveways — and after smoke damage is detected in some books in the Library of Congress, located in rooms directly above the ovens.)[60]

MAY 9, 1861: In the troubled border state of Missouri, St. Louis civilians sympathetic to the Confederacy riot as U.S. brigadier general Nathaniel Lyon and his troops march captured pro-Southern militia through the city. Twenty-eight civilians and two soldiers are killed. Many Missourians who had not as yet taken sides tumble into the secessionist camp.[61]

England and America. The December 16th, 1856 visit to the Arctic ship
Resolute of her majesty Queen Victoria, to whom this engraving is by
special permission respectfully dedicated by her obedient servants,
P. & D. Colnaghi & Co [publishers]. Color lithograph by G. Zobel after a
painting by W. Simpson, 1859. Britain, whose powerful naval and commercial interests were intertwined with those of the United States, was,
throughout the war, a central focus of diplomatic efforts by both the
Confederacy (which craved British recognition as a sovereign nation) and
the Union (which sought to prevent such recognition and to keep Britain
from intervening in the U.S. domestic conflict).

The Hon. Beriah Magoffin of Ky.
(1815–1885). Photograph between
1865 and 1880. A Democrat,
Magoffin alienated almost everyone
with his losing battle to maintain
Kentucky's neutrality. Threatened
with assassination, he resigned
as governor in August 1862 and
returned to the practice of law.

MAY

1 2 3 4 5 6 7 8 9 10 11 12 **13** **14** 15 16 17 18 19 **20** 21 22 23 24 25 26 27 28 29 30 31

Also this day, Jefferson Davis signs a bill authorizing the enlistment of up to four hundred thousand additional volunteers for
three years, or the duration of the war. The response will be
overwhelming. The next day, Davis will sign legislation allowing the Confederacy to procure six warships, weapons, and
stores from sellers overseas.[62]

MAY 13, 1861: Criminal lawyer and Massachusetts politician
Benjamin F. Butler, among the first major generals of volunteers appointed by President Lincoln, arrives in Baltimore
with his regiment and institutes martial law. After establishing
a bastion on Federal Hill, Butler's troops begin arresting
suspected Confederate supporters in the city. *On the same
day,* Britain, via an official proclamation by Queen Victoria,
declares its intention to remain neutral in the festering civil
conflict between the United States and "the states styling
themselves the Confederate States of America" and to accord
to both sides the rights of belligerents. Although this is far
short of recognition of the Confederate States as a sovereign
nation, it is recognition of the South's separate status, which
the United States had wished to avoid. France will soon issue a
similar declaration.[63]

MAY 14, 1861: Already a major general of volunteers, today
George B. McClellan is appointed a major general in the
Regular Army, currently the highest rank attainable. Though

many Regular Army officers are senior to him in age and
length of service, he now outranks all but General in Chief
Winfield Scott.[64]

MAY 20, 1861: As Virginians prepare for the May 23 referendum on the question of whether or not to confirm their state
convention's vote for secession, the Provisional Congress of the
Confederacy votes to move the capital of rebellious states from
Montgomery, Alabama, to Richmond, Virginia.[65] *In the western
theater of operations,* with Confederate forces positioned across
his state's southern border in Tennessee and Union troops
under McClellan massing in Ohio to the north, Kentucky
governor Beriah Magoffin issues a proclamation of neutrality
for his deeply divided border state, forbidding "any movement
upon Kentucky soil, or occupation of any port or place therein
for any purpose whatever, until authorized by invitation
or permission of the legislative and executive authorities."
Though understandable under the circumstances, the proclamation will inspire some harsh editorial comment. The *New
York Times* will accuse Magoffin of acting "as if Kentucky were
an independent kingdom, of which he is at the head," condemn
the governor's refusal to "furnish his quota of regiments called
for by the President," and declare (inaccurately) that "it is only
because loyalty in Kentucky is too strong for him, that he . . . is
not now in the ranks of the enemy."[66] *Also this day,* North
Carolina secedes from the Union.[67]

DEATH OF COL. ELLSWORTH,
after hauling down the rebel flag, at the taking of Alexandria, V.ª Mar 24ᵗʰ 1861.

THE (FOR T) **MONROE DOCTRINE.**

ABOVE: *The [Fort] Monroe Doctrine.* Lithograph, 1861. Almost as soon as General Benjamin Butler declared escaped slaves to be contraband of war, thus not to be returned to their Southern masters, an unknown cartoonist drew this crude caricature—part of a wave of publicity that made "contrabands" the popular designation for people who had successfully fled from Confederate slavery.

LEFT: *Death of Col. Ellsworth After Hauling down the Rebel Flag, at the Taking of Alexandria, Va., May 24, 1861.* Hand-colored lithograph by Currier & Ives, 1861. Private Brownell, at left, is shown avenging Ellsworth's death by killing James Jackson.

MAY 24, 1861: During an overnight movement of U.S. troops across the Potomac River to secure positions on the Virginia side, dashing young Union colonel Elmer Ellsworth, a friend and former law clerk of Abraham Lincoln, is shot dead by James Jackson while removing a secessionist flag from Marshall House, Jackson's Alexandria, Virginia, hotel. (One of Ellsworth's men, Private Francis E. Brownell, immediately kills Jackson.) A popular figure whose military-drill team, the U.S. Zouave Cadets, was renowned before the war, and whose newly raised regiment, the New York Fire Zouaves, is becoming equally celebrated, Ellsworth is the first well-known casualty of the Civil War, and his death spreads grief throughout the North.[68] *Farther south in Virginia,* at Fort Monroe, Union general Benjamin Butler refuses to return three runaway slaves to their master, a Confederate colonel, calling the slaves "contraband of war." The designation takes hold throughout the North; hundreds of thousands of "contrabands" will enter Union lines during the war — not without stirring controversy. "What shall we do with the slaves that may fall into our hands by the fortunes of the war, who to the South are chattels — to the North human beings?" the *New York Times* asks a week after Butler's declaration. "We may have a hundred thousand slaves on our hands before the questions raised are solved."[69] *In Illinois,* Ulysses S. Grant, involved in organizing the Illinois state militia (see April 25, 1861), writes U.S. Army adjutant general Lorenzo Thomas: "I have the honor, very respectfully, to tender my services, until the close of the war . . . I would say, in view of my present age and length of service, I feel myself competent to command a regiment, if the President, in his judgment, should see fit to intrust [*sic*] one to me." He will receive no reply — nor will his subsequent attempts to see Department of the Ohio commander George B. McClellan yield any better results.[70]

MAY 25, 1861: At 2:00 AM, Union troops arrest John Merryman at his home outside Baltimore, Maryland. A farmer, Confederate sympathizer, and lieutenant in the Maryland State Militia, he is known to have obstructed passage of Union troops through Baltimore by burning bridges and sabotaging railroads. The troops confine him in Fort McHenry — without lodging any formal charges.[71] *A New Orleans* paper, the *Bee,* reports that seven Union vessels have thus far been brought into port there as war "prizes." Captured by the armed Confederate privateer steamships *Calhoun, Music,* and *Ivy,* the prizes are worth an estimated $170,000. "This great success will give vast encouragement to many capitalists who have not yet embarked in privateering [through buying stock in privateer vessels], to do so," the paper confidently predicts. "As . . . the North has no war vessels to spare for the protection of its ships, every sea on the globe is a fruitful field for captures, and at the end of the war the South will have a splendid commercial marine of prizes within her own ports."[72]

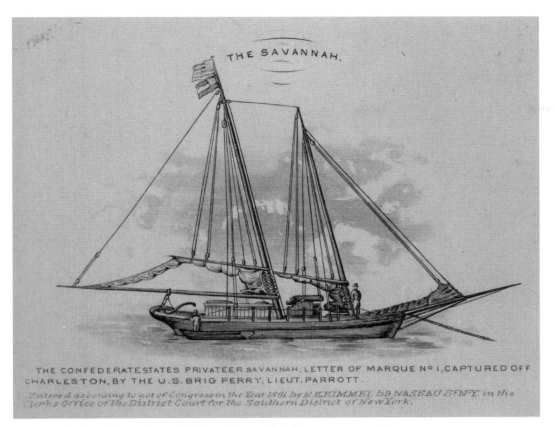

THE SAVANNAH.

THE CONFEDERATE STATES PRIVATEER SAVANNAH, LETTER OF MARQUE Nº 1, CAPTURED OFF CHARLESTON, BY THE U.S. BRIG PERRY, LIEUT. PARROTT.

Entered according to act of Congress in the Year 1861 by E.K.KIMMEL 59 NASSAU ST.N-Y in the Clerks Office of the District Court for the Southern District of New York.

The Confederate States Privateer Savannah, Letter of Marque No. 1, Captured off Charleston by the U.S. Brig Perry, Lieut. Parrott. Engraving by E. K. Kimmel, 1861. Initial Confederate enthusiasm for privateering was matched by Union determination not to tolerate what it regarded as acts of piracy.

LEFT: Chief Justice Roger B. Taney (1777–1864). Etching by Max Rosenthal, 1899.

RIGHT: Major General George C. Cadwalader (1806–1879) USA. Photographic reproduction of a painting, n.d. A native of Pennsylvania, Cadwalader was U.S. military commander in Maryland when he was summoned to Judge Taney's Baltimore courtroom regarding the case of John Merryman.

MAY
1 2 3 4 5 6 7 8 9 10 11 12 13 14 15 16 17 18 19 20 21 22 23 24 25 **26** **27** 28 29 30 31

MAY 26, 1861: Spurred by reports that Confederate troops have been burning bridges used by the Union's vital Baltimore & Ohio Railroad line as it slices through the area, Major General George B. McClellan orders troops into western Virginia, a region with few slaveholders and much greater Unionist sympathy than characterizes the rest of that Confederate state. In this early stage of the war, it is Union policy to safeguard Southern civilians and their property during military operations. But in his proclamation to the people of western Virginia, issued from his headquarters in Cincinnati, McClellan will include a pledge that will place him in a permanently unfavorable light with many Northern abolitionists: not only will Union troops not "interfere" with slaves held in the area, McClellan declares, "but we will on the contrary with an iron hand, crush any attempt at insurrection on their part."[73] *During Sunday service at the Galesburg, Illinois, Brick Congregational Church,* Dr. Edward Beecher (brother of Harriet Beecher Stowe and Henry Ward Beecher) reads a letter from Dr. Benjamin Woodward, a young physician with Illinois volunteers stationed at Cairo, at the southern tip of the state. A rending description of the pitiful hospital conditions, lack of supplies and medical personnel, and many resulting deaths from disease in the Cairo camps, the letter turns Sunday service into a symposium on what might be done to help the men in uniform without offending military or political policies. The people decide to send medical supplies, along with a representative strong enough to demand remedial action. They choose Mary Ann Bickerdyke, a widow with two children, knowledge of herbal medicines — and powerful determination. "It was pretty well established in Galesburg," a biographer will later write, "that when Mary Ann Bickerdyke took sides, her side won."[74]

MAY 27, 1861: Having issued a writ of habeas corpus for John Merryman's release (see May 25, 1861), Roger Taney, chief justice of the United States, acting as a Federal circuit court judge, convenes a hearing in Baltimore. He expects to see before him both Merryman and the Union's military district commander, General George Cadwalader. He sees only an officer bearing Cadwalader's respectful refusal to comply, the general's request that he be given time to communicate with the president, and Cadwalader's assertion that Merryman is guilty of "acts of treason." In 1849, Justice Taney had sustained Rhode Island's suspension of habeas corpus during Dorr's Rebellion (see April 27, 1861), declaring that the state had the right to "use its military power to put down an armed insurrection, too strong to be controlled by the civil authority." Yet, in a written opinion on the Merryman arrest, Taney (whose sympathies lie with the South and who is well acquainted with Merryman's father) argues that the president's suspension of the writ is unconstitutional and that such power belongs to Congress (which is not in session). Lincoln, who does not immediately respond to Taney's opinion, claims that the president has the power to suspend habeas corpus in certain cases.

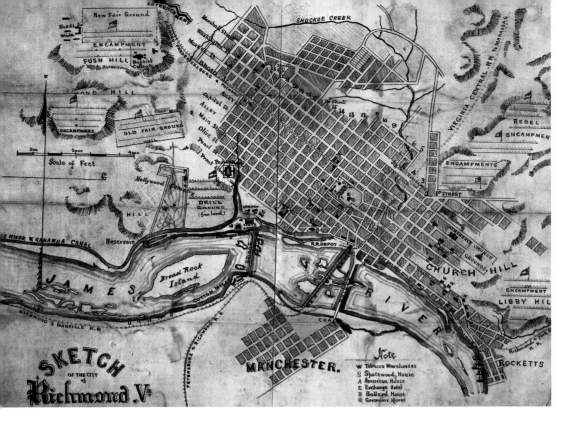

Sketch of the City of Richmond, Va. Drawing by R. K. Sneden, Topographical Headquarters, Third Corps, U.S. Army, December 1861. Located less than one hundred miles from Washington, DC, Richmond became the Confederate capital in May 1861. A few months after this drawing was made, the city became the target of the first major campaign by the Union Army of the Potomac.

Page from the manuscript diary of Washington Navy Yard worker Michael Shiner, showing the entry for June 1, 1861.

MAY–JUNE

| **30** | 31 | **1** | 2 | **3** | 4 | 5 | 6 | 7 | 8 | 9 | 10 | 11 | 12 | 13 | 14 | 15 | 16 | 17 | 18 | 19 | 20 | 21 | 22 | 23 | 24 | 25 | 26 | 27 | 28 | 29 |

Merryman will eventually be released and will never be tried for treason.[75]

MAY 30, 1861: In Richmond, the *Daily Enquirer* publishes a lengthy report on President Davis's trip from Montgomery to the new Confederate capital, where he arrived on May 29: "No matter where the [railroad] cars stopped, even though it was only for wood or for water, throngs of men, women and children would gather around the cars, asking in loud shouts, '*Where is President Davis?*' '*Jeff Davis!*' '*the old hero!*'. . . In Atlanta, Augusta, Wilmington and Goldsborough, the crowds assembled were very large, and the enthusiasm unbounded. . . . The whole soul of the South is in this war; and the confidence manifested in our President, in the many scenes which transpired on this trip, shows that the mantle of [George] Washington falls gracefully upon his shoulders."[76]

JUNE 1861

JUNE 1, 1861: People enjoying a concert on the White House grounds are alarmed by the sounds of cannon fire from across the Potomac. Assuming there is a battle in progress, they scatter into the high points of nearby buildings to see what they can of the encounter — only to discover that Union forces in and around recently occupied Alexandria, Virginia, are simply testing their guns. *Across town,* a laborer notes in his diary: "Justice Clark was sent Down to the Washington navy yard For to administer the oath of allegiance to the mechanics and the Labouring Class of working men With out DistincSion of Colour for them to Stand by the Stars and Stripes and defend for the union . . . and I believe at that time I Michael Shiner was the first Colered man that taken the oath in Washington DC and that oath Still Remains in my heart and when I taken that oath I Taken It in the presence of God without predudice [*sic*] or enmity to any man And I intend to Sustain That oath with The assistance of the Almighty God until I die."[77]

JUNE 3, 1861: In mountainous western Virginia, Union forces surprise Confederates near the town of Philippi. This relatively minor clash, with its concluding Confederate retreat ("Out they swarmed," one Ohio soldier will report, "like bees from a molested hive"), catches the fancy of Northern politicians and newspapers, which dub the victory the "Philippi races."[78] *In St. Louis,* U.S. Army veteran William Tecumseh Sherman, director of the city's Fifth Street Railway, is

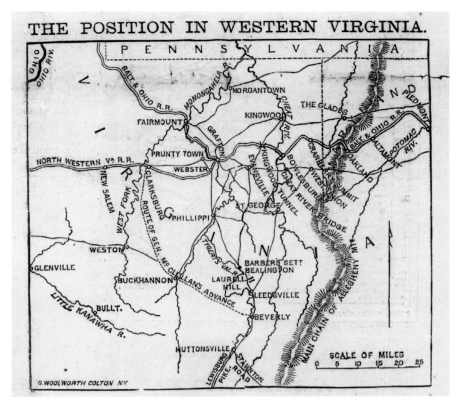

THE POSITION IN WESTERN VIRGINIA.

One of a group of war maps published by the *New-York Daily Tribune*, July 30, 1861, *The Position in Western Virginia* delineates "The Route of Gen. McClellan's Advance," with the town of Phillippi [*sic*] just left of the center.

Eng.d by A.H.Ritchie

Mrs. Mary A. Bickerdyke (1817–1901). Engraving from *Woman's Work in the Civil War: A Record of Heroism, Patriotism and Patience* by L. P. Brockett and Mary C. Vaughan, 1867. "There is but one 'Mother' Bickerdyke," the authors write. "No woman connected with the philanthropic work of the army has encountered more obstacles in the accomplishment of her purposes, and none ever carried them through more triumphantly."

JUNE

1 2 3 4 5 6 7 **8 9 10 11** 12 13 14 15 16 17 18 19 20 21 22 23 24 25 26 27 28 29 30

summoned to Washington to reenter the military as colonel of a new U.S. Army regiment (he will shortly be reassigned to command a brigade of volunteers). A well-connected West Point graduate (his brother John is a U.S. senator from Ohio), Sherman is extremely familiar with the South: his previous army service included stints in Florida and Charleston, South Carolina; and he was the first superintendent of the Louisiana State Seminary of Learning and Military Academy (which will become Louisiana State University). Though he has little quarrel with slavery, he is an adamant Unionist — and he is deeply concerned that Northern politicians, including President Lincoln, do not comprehend the magnitude of the challenge they are facing.[79]

JUNE 8, 1861: Tennessee voters approve secession, 104,913–47,238, ratifying legislative action taken in May. Yet this general count does not reflect sentiment in the eastern part of the state, where the vote is 2–1 *against* leaving the Union.[80]

JUNE 9, 1861: Dispatched by her church to assist Illinois volunteers in the Union army (see May 26, 1861), Mary Ann Bickerdyke arrives in Cairo, at the southern tip of the state, with $100 in relief supplies. She is met by the doctor who requested help and discovers that conditions in the army camp's hospital tents are even worse than he had described. She sets quickly to work, organizing baths for the patients, sweeping and scouring filth from their tents, and providing

clean bedding for as many men as she can. At the end of the day, she informs the doctor that she intends to stay and help out for a while.[81]

JUNE 10, 1861: Humanitarian and reformer Dorothea Lynde Dix is appointed superintendent of women nurses for the U.S. Army, her mandate "to select and assign women nurses to general or permanent military hospitals, they not to be employed in such hospitals without her sanction and approval, except in cases of urgent need." She will, over the next four years, work to organize hospitals, care for the sick and wounded, and establish the army's first professional nursing corps — though her personality and problematical administrative techniques will earn her the name "Dragon Dix."[82] *Eight miles from the Union bastion of Fort Monroe,* opposite Norfolk, Virginia, twelve hundred Confederates defeat some forty-four hundred Union soldiers dispatched by Major General Benjamin Butler to destroy an artillery emplacement the Rebels have placed near Bethel Church (Big Bethel). Confusion in the Union ranks, which causes two Federal units to open fire on each other, warns the Confederates and contributes to this small but stinging Northern defeat.[83]

JUNE 11, 1861: Delegates representing the pro-Union element in Virginia meet at Wheeling, in the western part of the state. They will organize a Unionist "Restored" state government, headquartered at Wheeling, under Governor

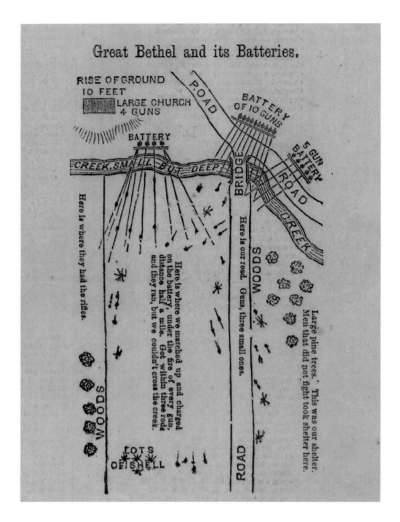

Great Bethel and its Batteries.

RISE OF GROUND 10 FEET
LARGE CHURCH 4 GUNS
P. ROAD
BATTERY OF 10 GUNS
BATTERY
5 GUN BATTERY
CREEK. SMALL BUT DEEP
BRIDGE
ROAD
CREEK
WOODS
Here is where they had the rifles.
Here is where we marched up and charged on the battery, under the fire of every gun, distance half a mile. Got within three rods and they ran, but we couldn't cross the creek.
Here is our road. Guns, three small ones.
Large pine trees. This was our shelter. Men that did not fight took shelter here.
WOODS
WOODS
LOTS OF SHELL
ROAD

Dorothea Lynde Dix (1802–1887). As superintendent of women nurses for the Union, Dix was dubbed a "Dragon," as she enforced standards of dress, deportment, and training for her female volunteers.

LEFT: *Great Bethel and Its Batteries.* Published by the *New-York Daily Tribune,* July 30, 1861, this map includes some eccentric personal notations by its unnamed creator.

Francis H. Peirpoint (later spelled Pierpont). In *The Declaration of the People of Virginia,* the delegates will condemn the state's unlawful secession and traitorous activities and "imperatively demand the reorganization of the government of the Commonwealth."[84]

JUNE 13, 1861: Somewhat reluctantly, President Lincoln signs an executive order creating the United States Sanitary Commission, a civilian organization established to assist the army in providing care for sick and wounded soldiers and to assist soldiers' dependents. Although the president initially fears that the new organization, a novelty in the United States, might become "a fifth wheel to the [war effort] coach," he will soon come to appreciate its value. USSC will grow to be the largest and most effective of many such organizations that operate during the war, and a power in national politics, with some seven thousand local aid societies and several regional branch offices by 1863, all coordinated through a central office in Washington, DC.[85]

JUNE 16, 1861: At the request of Illinois governor Richard Yates, who has become aware of a discipline problem and bizarrely incompetent leadership in one Illinois volunteer regiment, Ulysses S. Grant accepts command of the Twenty-first Illinois Volunteers, with the rank of colonel.[86]

JUNE 17, 1861: In Washington, Professor Thaddeus S. C. Lowe demonstrates the possible wartime use of aerial observation when he ascends in a balloon that is connected to the War Department by a telegraph wire, over which he communicates with President Lincoln.[87] *About fifteen miles away,* near Vienna, Virginia, men of Confederate colonel Maxcy Gregg's First South Carolina Volunteers send troops of the First Ohio Volunteer Infantry tumbling off a train by the simple expedient of firing on it with artillery — after which the Rebels happily abscond with the train. Though it will be, in retrospect, a minor embarrassment, Lincoln will refer to the episode a month later as "the disaster at Vienna."[88]

JUNE 20, 1861: In Cincinnati, Ohio, General George B. McClellan finds himself enmeshed in a political storm after he seemed to recognize Kentucky's neutrality during a meeting with Kentucky home guard commander Simon Bolivar Buckner, whom he had known at West Point. With a keen appreciation of the power of battlefield victory to dispel political clouds, McClellan today embarks on a well-publicized journey to take personal command of the Union forces operating in western Virginia. It is a morale-boosting trip for the man credited with success at the "Philippi races" (see June 3, 1861) — though he had been far from that battlefield. In a letter to his wife, Ellen, he will describe the journey as a "continuous ovation. Gray-headed old men & women; mothers holding up their children to take my hand, girls, boys, all sorts, cheering and crying,

THE HERCULES OF THE UNION,
SLAYING THE GREAT DRAGON OF SECESSION.

*"The South must be made
to feel* full *respect for the
power and* honor *of the North."*

—NEW YORK TIMES,
JUNE 26, 1861

The Hercules of the Union, Slaying the Great Dragon of Secession. Lithograph by Currier & Ives, 1861. A tribute to the Union's general in chief, and perhaps a play upon his much-maligned "Anaconda" strategy, this cartoon shows Winfield Scott wielding "Liberty and Union" as a weapon to slay a hydra with seven very prominent Confederate heads.

JUNE

1 2 3 4 5 6 7 8 9 10 11 12 13 14 15 16 17 18 19 20 21 22 23 24 25 **26** 27 28 **29** **30**

God bless you!" Meanwhile, in the wake of the Philippi defeat, Robert E. Lee, commander of the provisional army and navy of Virginia, has sent reinforcements into western Virginia.[89]

JUNE 26, 1861: Impatient with what they perceive as lack of sufficient military action against the Confederacy, a few Northern papers begin to trumpet what Horace Greeley's *New York Tribune* terms "The Nation's War Cry." In blaring headlines, the *Tribune* urges the Lincoln administration "Forward to Richmond! Forward to Richmond! The Rebel Congress must not be allowed to meet there on the 20th of July! BY THAT DATE THE PLACE MUST BE HELD BY THE NATIONAL ARMY!" The *Chicago Tribune* adds to this public hue-and-cry criticism of General in Chief Scott as slow and overcautious. Yet the clamor for offensive action is not universal. The *New York Times* will report approvingly that Scott plans to amass an intimidating number of troops in northern Virginia and the border states, so that "the presence of our forces will encourage the loyal citizens [of the South] to rise in sufficient numbers to prevent any further outrages." "The South must be made to feel *full* respect for the power and *honor* of the North," the *Times* declares. "She must be humbled, but not debased by a forfeiture of self-respect, if we wish to retain our motto — *E pluribus unum* — and claim for the whole United States the respect of the world."[90]

JUNE 29, 1861: At a special meeting of the Lincoln administration cabinet that includes leading Union generals — among

them Irvin McDowell, commander of the Union force protecting Washington — U.S. Army general in chief Winfield Scott reiterates the military strategy that he proposed in a memo the previous month (see May 3, 1861). Combining the naval blockade of seaports on the Atlantic and Gulf coasts with moves to establish U.S. military control of the Mississippi River, this strategy, Scott says, would "envelop the insurgent states and bring them to terms with less bloodshed than by any other plan." Some Northern papers are already ridiculing this approach as Scott's "Anaconda Plan," after the snake that kills, slowly, by constriction. Yet the only alternative, Scott believes, is to launch a full-scale army invasion of the South, which he had earlier estimated would take "two or three years . . . with 300,000 disciplined men, estimating a third for garrisons, and the loss of yet a greater number by skirmishes, sieges, battles and Southern fevers. The destruction of life and property on the other side would be frightful, however perfect the moral discipline of the invaders." Despite this argument, Lincoln, enmeshed in immediate pressures, insists on a move against the Confederate troops camped at Manassas, Virginia, within the next few weeks. Scott reluctantly agrees.[91]

JUNE 30, 1861: Confederate navy captain Raphael Semmes engages in a duel of wits and sailing skill with the commander of the Union blockader, USS *Brooklyn,* as he attempts to take his ship, CSS *Sumter,* into open water below New Orleans. *Brooklyn,* Semmes will report in memoirs published three years

RUNNING THE BLOCKADE.

(The Sumter and the Brooklyn.)

later, "was [*Sumter*'s] superior in speed, and moreover, carried guns of heavier caliber and longer range." Yet Semmes, his ship, and his crew win their race. "[T]he crew of the Sumter gave three hearty cheers, as her baffled pursuer put up her helm, and . . . turned sullenly back to her station at the mouth of the river." Proceeding into the Gulf of Mexico, Semmes embarks on his soon-to-be legendary career as a commerce raider.[92]

JULY 1861

JULY 4, 1861: The U.S. Congress, which had adjourned in March and normally would not reconvene until December, opens a special session that lasts thirty-four days. In his lengthy message to Congress, read on July 5, Lincoln summarizes the events that have occurred since he took office. To those, including Chief Justice Taney, who have criticized his suspension of the writ of habeas corpus (see April 27, 1861), which, he notes, was done "very sparingly" (i.e., between Philadelphia and Washington, DC), he poses a question: "[W]ould not the official oath be broken, if the government should be overthrown, when it was believed that disregarding the single law [habeas corpus], would tend to preserve it?" Turning to necessary military preparations, he asks for $400 million and four

hundred thousand men as a means for "making this contest a short, and a decisive, one."[93]

JULY 5, 1861: Approaching Rich Mountain, in western Virginia, where he plans to engage Confederate forces, George B. McClellan writes his wife: "I shall feel my way & be very cautious, for I recognize the fact that everything requires success in my first operations." He has already spent much time preparing for his first combat command, reporting to General in Chief Scott's adjutant that he would not move "until I know that everything is ready" and that he intends to gain victory "by manoeuvring rather than by fighting; I will not throw these men of mine into the teeth of artillery & intrenchments, if it is possible to avoid it."[94] *At Carthage, Missouri,* motley secessionist troops under Missouri governor Claiborne Jackson — a fiery proslavery Democrat who was deposed when he took his followers to the town of Neosho and formed a Confederate state "government" — meet German American troops under Union brigadier general Franz Sigel and force the Federals to retreat.[95]

JULY 9, 1861: The U.S. House of Representatives approves a resolution proffered by Congressman John F. Potter (R-WI) creating an investigative committee, which Potter will head, that will "ascertain the number of persons . . . now employed in the several Departments of the Government, who are known to entertain sentiments of hostility to the Government." Three weeks later, Potter will declare his astonishment "at the

ABOVE: Congressman John F. Potter (1817–1899). Photograph by Julian Vannerson in *McClees' Gallery of Photographic Portraits of the Senators, Representatives & Delegates of the Thirty-Fifth Congress*, 1859.

OPPOSITE: *Running the Blockade. (The Sumter and the Brooklyn.)* Color lithograph frontispiece from *The Cruise of the Alabama and the Sumter* by Raphael Semmes, CSN, 1864.

Incident in the Blockade. Pencil, Chinese white, and black ink wash drawing on olive paper by Alfred R. Waud (1828–1891). The source of often harrowing naval encounters, the Northern blockade of Southern ports also led at times to international tensions. Writing to U.S. ambassador to Britain Charles Francis Adams May 21, 1861, Secretary of State Seward instructed him to inform the British that "the blockade is now and it will continue to be so maintained, and therefore we expect it to be respected by Great Britain."

JULY

1 2 3 4 5 6 7 8 9 **10** **11** 12 13 14 15 16 17 18 19 20 21 22 23 24 25 26 27 28 29 30 31

number of well-authenticated cases of disloyalty to the Government." Yet the committee's definition of "well-authenticated" includes behind-closed-doors, often unsubstantiated testimony from informants whose names are kept secret. Accused persons are not told of the charges against them and cannot defend themselves before the committee. Despite spirited opposition to its methods by a few members of Congress, the Potter Committee's secret proceedings will continue. On January 28, 1862, it will report that, to that date, it has considered "about five hundred and fifty charges of disloyalty."[96]

JULY 10, 1861: *Quaker City,* a private vessel chartered to the U.S. Navy for blockade duty and under the command of a naval officer, Commander Overton Carr, stops the Virginia-owned vessel *Amy Warwick* off Cape Henry, at the mouth of Chesapeake Bay. The vessel and its cargo of 5,100 bags of coffee are sent to Boston, where legal proceedings will begin that will result in *Amy Warwick*'s being declared a prize of war. After that determination is made, the value of the ship's cargo, less an amount due to a British claimant, is divided between the U.S. government, for deposit in the Navy Pension Fund, and the crew of *Quaker City* — "a bounty," Attorney General Bates will explain to Lincoln, "designed to stimulate the zeal and courage of our naval men." Several U.S. district courts will hear similar prize cases as the U.S. blockade of Confederate ports continues — including the court in Key West, Florida, which will remain in Federal hands throughout the war, with William Marvin (to July 1863),

then Thomas Jefferson Boynton, the only sitting U.S. Federal judges south of the nation's capital, presiding.[97]

JULY 11, 1861: The U.S. Congress formally expels the senators from Arkansas, North Carolina, Texas, and Virginia, and one senator from Tennessee — all of whom have already withdrawn. Andrew Johnson of Tennessee, a loyal Unionist, is the only Southern senator who keeps his seat.[98] *As this legislative ceremony takes place,* J. D. B. DeBow, in New Orleans, celebrates the Southern rebellion in the July edition of his popular *Review:* "We have been Yankee imitators and worshippers until now . . . and never learned to walk alone," he states, before proudly declaring that this unhappy situation is at an end: "We of the South are about to inaugurate a new civilization. We shall have new and original thought; negro slavery will be its great controlling and distinctive element."[99] *In western Virginia,* action begins at Rich Mountain as George B. McClellan sends William Rosecrans and eighteen hundred men up the mountainside to attack John Pegram's defending Confederates from the rear, after which McClellan plans to attack from the front. The subsequent action suffers from delays and confusion. Though Rosecrans finally overruns the Confederate position, the overcautious McClellan, uncertain because his plan has gone partially awry, fails to attack. In follow-up action, the retreating Pegram and some six hundred of his men surrender. On July 13, Robert S. Garnett will become the first general killed in the Civil War when McClellan's forces defeat

J. D. B. (James Dunwoody Brownson) De Bow (1820–1867). Engraving by W. G. Jackman, n.d.

RIGHT: *Plan of the Battle of Rich Mountain.* Manuscript map drawn by Lieutenant Orlando M. Poe, U.S. Army Topographical Engineers, ca. July 11, 1861.

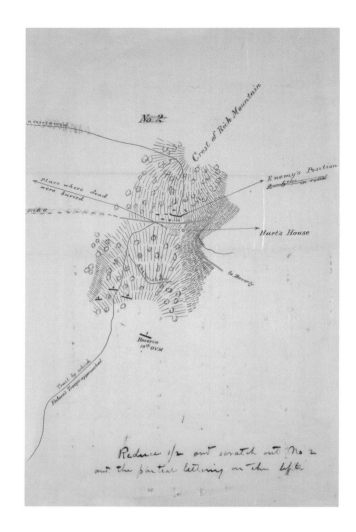

Garnett's Confederate troops at Corrick's Ford. McClellan claims a sweeping victory, telegraphing Washington, "Our success is complete & secession is killed in this country."[100]

JULY 13, 1861: In New York City, Charles A. Dana, managing editor of Horace Greeley's *New York Tribune,* publishes a scathing reply to Major General Benjamin Butler's recent order restricting the activities of reporters because, the general complained, the newsmen were revealing his plans to the enemy. "Whose fault is this?" Dana bellows editorially. "Is the Major General such an old lady that he cannot hold his tongue? . . . to suppose that paid men, sent expressly to obtain information, will not use it when obtained, is to exhibit a fatuity unworthy of a major general." In fact, Butler's complaint is not unique to him, and Confederates *are* garnering information from Northern newspapers.[101]

JULY 16, 1861: Under pressure to strike a telling offensive blow, General Irvin McDowell begins moving more than thirty thousand Union troops toward Manassas, Virginia, some twenty-five miles from Washington, DC. The objective: to smash P. G. T. Beauregard's twenty-thousand-man Confederate force — soon to be augmented by troops under Joseph E. Johnston, who evades a Federal force sent to stop him from leaving the lower Shenandoah Valley. McDowell's progress is very slow. Most of his troops are inexperienced, ill-trained volunteers, in many cases led by equally inexperienced volunteer officers; some are at or near the end of three-month enlistments

and resent the army's determination that they must remain in the ranks until August. Discipline, not tight to begin with, deteriorates along the way. Troops amble along, leave the line of march, pilfer food and drink from farms — and are suspiciously close when one or two house fires erupt as the column passes. In one of his daily dispatches to Washington, McDowell will write, "I am distressed to have to report excesses by our troops." As the Union force nears Manassas, William T. Sherman also notes his concern over the largely amateur army's discipline in a letter to his wife: "With my regulars I would have no doubts, but these volunteers are subject to stampedes."[102]

JULY 21, 1861: McDowell's Federal troops engage thirty thousand Confederates under Beauregard and Johnston at the first battle of Bull Run (First Manassas), where the "Rebel yell" makes its unnerving debut — and General Barnard Bee provides Thomas Jonathan Jackson with his soon-to-be-celebrated nickname by describing Jackson standing like a "stone wall" under fire. Early in the encounter, the Federals seem poised to achieve a great victory. "The Yankees in such a superiority of numbers . . . poured forth such a destructive fire into our ranks that our men were becoming confused and began to fall back," Lieutenant Richard Lewis, of the Fourth South Carolina Volunteers, later reported. "The gallant and noble General Barnard Bee dismounted his horse to rally the men, telling them as Carolinians they should never disgrace or dishonor their banner but die under its folds, and all of them rallied again,

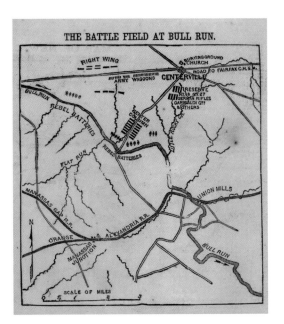

The Battle Field at Bull Run, reproduced in *Tribune War Maps*, published by the *New-York Daily Tribune* on July 30, 1861.

THE CIVIL WAR IN AMERICA : THE STAMPEDE FROM BULL RUN.—FROM A SKETCH BY OUR SPECIAL ARTIST.—SEE NEXT PAGE.

The Civil War in America: The Stampede from Bull Run. Engraving based on a drawing by Frank Vizetelly, published in the *Illustrated London News,* August 17, 1861. "Retreat is a weak term to use," Vizetelly wrote in the description accompanying his drawing, "when speaking of this disgraceful rout."

JULY

1   2   3   4   5   6   7   8   9   10   11   12   13   14   15   16   17   18   19   20   21   **22   23**   24   25   26   27   28   29   30   31

and, with a shout and yell that might have been heard for miles, they charged and repulsed the enemy, and drove them back from their position." The day turns against the Union, as confusion becomes an uncertain retreat that deteriorates into what English artist-correspondent Frank Vizetelly describes as a "disgraceful rout. . . . The terror-stricken soldiers threw away their arms and accoutrements, herding along like a panic stricken flock of sheep, with no order whatever in their flight." Troops become tangled up with panicked congressmen and civilians who had followed them from Washington to witness their triumph. "Today will be known as *Black Monday,*" Northerner George Templeton Strong notes in his diary. "Only one great fact stands out unmistakably, total defeat and national disaster on the largest scale." This evening Jefferson Davis, who arrived at the battlefield while combat was still raging, promotes Beauregard to full general, and sends a dispatch to Richmond: "Our forces have won a glorious victory. . . . Too high praise cannot be bestowed whether for the skill of the principal officers or for the Gallantry of all the Troops." Casualties on both sides (killed, wounded, and missing) number some forty-seven hundred. General Bee is among the Confederate dead.[103]

JULY 22, 1861: In the early morning hours, as survivors from Bull Run are still limping into the Union capital, a telegram summons General George B. McClellan to Washington.[104] *Later this day, at the Capitol,* Congress, concerned over ineffective leadership by militia officers hastily appointed by state politicians in the rush to develop a volunteer army, authorizes the creation of military boards to examine officers and remove those found to be unqualified. *In other legislative action,* the U.S. House of Representatives overwhelmingly passes the Crittenden Resolution (named for Representative John Crittenden of Kentucky), which stresses the need to preserve the Union and to maintain noninterference with slavery where it exists. Senator Andrew Johnson of Tennessee introduces a similarly worded resolution that will pass the Senate three days later. Today and tomorrow, President Lincoln signs two bills authorizing enlistments of a total of one million three-year volunteers.[105] *Also in Washington,* U.S. Patent Office clerk Clara Barton hears stories from Bull Run survivors of inadequate supplies and poor facilities for treating the wounded. After she publicizes these conditions and asks for donations, provisions come pouring in. The resourceful former schoolteacher will soon establish an agency that will see to their distribution.[106]

JULY 23, 1861: Horace Greeley's *New York Tribune,* which had so eagerly urged Union forces "On to Richmond!," is now equally eager to fix blame for the North's Bull Run defeat — an event that ran so terribly counter to the widespread conviction that the Union's just cause, defended by soldiers displaying manly vigor and courage (whether or not they had received adequate military training), should have resulted in a quick and decisive victory. In an editorial written by the intensely

Major General George B. McClellan (1826–1885), USA, and his wife, Mary Ellen Marcy McClellan, called Ellen or Nelly (1830–1915). Photograph between 1860 and 1865. After their 1860 marriage, McClellan, who had pursued Marcy for more than five years, wrote ecstatically to his mother, "I believe I am the happiest man that ever lived & am sure that I have the dearest wife in all the world."

James Moore Wayne (1790–1867), associate justice of the U.S. Supreme Court, 1835–1867. Daguerreotype, ca. 1850. Born in Georgia, educated at Princeton, and a lover of good food and spirits, Wayne had no objection to slavery (he was himself a slaveholder) but was devoted to the Union.

OPPOSITE: *Battle of Wilson's Creek — Aug. 10, 1861 — Union (Gen. Lyon) . . . Conf. (Gen. McCulloch).* Color lithograph, 1893, published by Kurz & Allison. In this chaotic clash, poorly armed and loosely organized Confederates outnumbered the Union force two to one, a fact that did not discourage General Nathaniel Lyon — whose battle plan left much to be desired. "The truth is," a surviving Union officer, Colonel John M. Palmer, later wrote his wife, "that the Creek was a folly which the gallant death of Gen. Lyon does not atone for."

25 26 27 28 29 30 31 1 2 **3** **4** **5** 6 7 8 9 10 11 12 13 14 15 16 17 18 19 20 21 22 23 24

Unionist Charles A. Dana, the *Tribune* thunders: "A decimated and indignant people will demand the immediate retirement of the present Cabinet from the higher places of power." There are those, however, who understand that, whatever the faults of Lincoln's cabinet, the North faces a greater problem. "The South is not composed of cowards or fools," future Union general Thomas Kilby Smith writes from his home in Ohio, "and the North will find before they get through that they are not so easily conquered as they had supposed."[107] *In Washington,* on this day when Lincoln also visits troop encampments to boost faltering morale, George B. McClellan calls at the White House and speaks with the president (who informs him he will command McDowell's army and the defenses of Washington), then goes on to attend a swirl of conferences and inspections. At night, the general writes an ebullient letter to his wife: "Presdt, Cabinet, Genl Scott & all deferring to me — by some strange operation of magic I seem to have become *the* power of the land. I almost think that were I to win some small success now I could become Dictator or anything else that might please me — but nothing of that kind would please me — *therefore* I *won't* be Dictator. Admirable self denial!"[108]

JULY 25, 1861: Famed explorer and 1856 Republican presidential candidate John C. Frémont, now a general, arrives in St. Louis to take command of Union forces in Missouri, beginning what will become a stormy and controversial early chapter of the war in the West.[109]

AUGUST 1861

AUGUST 3, 1861: Congress passes legislation directing the U.S. Department of the Navy to construct three prototype ironclad vessels.[110]

AUGUST 4, 1861: The *New York Herald* doffs its editorial cap to Supreme Court associate justice James M. Wayne, a native of Georgia who has remained loyal to the Union, characterizing Wayne's loyalty as "a living rebuke to the small souled political tricksters whose mad ambition have [*sic*] brought us to the horrors of civil war." Few Georgians feel the same way, however. In a few months a Savannah grand jury, having declared the justice an "alien enemy," will confiscate all Wayne's property, including slaves, and transfer it to his son, Henry, a former U.S. Army officer who is now adjutant and inspector general of Georgia. Wayne's situation is far from unique in a judicial system that is shaken by the war.[111]

AUGUST 5, 1861: As war-related expenses explode (Treasury Secretary Salmon P. Chase has calculated that the government will need $320 million for the war in the next fiscal year), the U.S. Congress levies the first Federal income tax in United States history, establishing rates of 3 percent for people earning between $600 and $10,000 and 5 percent on incomes exceeding $10,000. Equally pressed for funds, the Confederate Congress enacts a property tax this month, at a rate of one-half of 1 percent of the assessed value of property. Collection,

BATTLE OF WILSON'S CREEK.

which remains the responsibility of each seceded state, will be problematical, however, and a relatively small amount of revenue will enter Confederate coffers as the result of this tax (a higher percentage of the total collected will be derived from the value of slaves than from land).[112]

AUGUST 6, 1861: The U.S. Congress approves legislation declaring that "all the acts, proclamations and orders of the President . . . [after March 4, 1861, the day of Lincoln's inauguration] respecting the army and navy of the United States, and calling out or relating to the militia or volunteers from the States, are hereby approved and in all respects legalized and made valid . . . as if they had been issued and done under the previous express authority and direction of the Congress of the United States." The First Confiscation Bill, also passed by Congress and signed (with some hesitation) by the president this day, states, among other provisions, that contrabands who had been employed *directly* by Confederate armed forces are no longer slaves, but otherwise leaves their status uncertain. The president also signs legislation increasing pay for ordinary soldiers and, in this time of great anxiety over Confederate agents and sympathizers in the government, a bill establishing a new, more elaborate oath of office for Federal employees — and stipulating that any Federal employee who refuses to take the oath "shall be immediately dismissed."[113]

AUGUST 8, 1861: Fraught with anxiety, George B. McClellan reports to General in Chief Scott that "at least 100,000" Confederate troops under P. G. T. Beauregard are preparing to attack Washington, and insists that all possible reinforcements immediately be dispatched to the capital. It is the first of many times that McClellan will hugely overestimate enemy forces, and the fact that Scott disagrees with his assessment ("I have not the slightest apprehension for the safety of the government here," the old general writes) only incenses McClellan. "I do not know whether he is a *dotard* or a *traitor*," he writes to his wife about Scott. "I am leaving nothing undone to increase our force — but that confounded old Genl always comes in the way — he is a perfect imbecile." But the "imbecile" is correct. Now, and for months to come, the Confederate army facing McClellan's troops will number fewer than forty-five thousand.[114]

AUGUST 10, 1861: Antisecessionists in Missouri are dealt a stinging blow at the battle of Wilson's Creek when fifty-four hundred Federal troops facing ten thousand Confederates under Brigadier General Ben McCulloch and Major General Sterling Price withdraw after their commander, Union general Nathaniel Lyon, is killed. Coming less than a month after the Union debacle at First Bull Run (see July 21, 1861), this Federal defeat is a double blow for the North: a huge section of Missouri is now under secessionist sway; and Lyon, whose battle to keep Missouri in the Union has made him a hero, is deeply

CAMP OF THE MASSACHUSETTS SECOND COMPᵞ, LIGHT ARTILLERY

AT STEWARTS PLACE, BALTIMORE, Mᴰ.

mourned. Again, people search for someone to blame, some this time turning to Secretary of War Simon Cameron. Northerners know, the *Chicago Tribune* declares, "that he is mainly, if not wholly, responsible . . . and they check the accusation by citing his culpable neglect to send the reinforcements that the gallant Lyon begged."[115] *Near Fort Monroe, Virginia,* well-known aeronaut John La Montain ascends in a balloon tethered to the Union ship *Fanny* at Hampton Roads and delineates the location of Confederate tents and batteries at Sewell's Point in one of the earliest sketches to be made from an aerial platform.[116]

AUGUST 13, 1861: "The 13th New York have refused duty," William T. Sherman wires McClellan from his camp near Washington. "They simply refuse to form ranks, to go on details or obey any orders whatsoever. Appeals to them are treated with ridicule." Disgruntled over grievances, including a dispute over whether they had enlisted for three months (as they believe) or three years (as the U.S. Army assures them they have), a few volunteer Union regiments stage a mutiny — which department commander McClellan, his Regular Army officers, and an armed and unsmiling Regular Army detachment quickly end with tough measures. More than sixty soldiers will be imprisoned in the Dry Tortugas, off the Florida Keys, and the Seventy-ninth New York will suffer the humiliation of being deprived of its regimental colors until it proves it is worthy again to carry them.[117]

AUGUST 16, 1861: Lincoln issues the Proclamation Forbidding Intercourse with Rebel States, which, with some exceptions, bars commercial relations between the Union and the Confederacy.[118]

AUGUST 17, 1861: As part of the retraining and reorganizing of the North's eastern theater forces, the military departments of northeastern Virginia, Washington, and the Shenandoah are merged to form the Department of the Potomac — and the Union's soon-to-be powerful Army of the Potomac is born; General McClellan will be named its commander on August 20. *At a meeting in Willard's Hotel in Washington* with General Robert Anderson (former Union commander at Fort Sumter) and politicians from Kentucky and Tennessee, newly promoted brigadier general of volunteers William T. Sherman agrees to become Anderson's second in command in the Department of the Cumberland, to be headquartered in Louisville in the still supposedly "neutral" state of Kentucky.[119]

AUGUST 28–29, 1861: A Union amphibious expedition under Major General Benjamin Butler and Flag Officer Silas Stringham attacks and secures Forts Clark and Hatteras, which guard Hatteras Inlet, North Carolina, an important haven for Confederate blockade runners. The Federals lose one man, secure some 670 Confederate prisoners — and now have their first base of operations on the Carolina coast.[120]

> *"I think to lose Kentucky*
>
> *is nearly the same*
>
> *as to lose the whole game."*
>
> —ABRAHAM LINCOLN,
> AUGUST 30, 1861

OPPOSITE: *Camp of the Massachusetts Second Compy, Light Artillery at Stewarts [sic] Place, Baltimore, Md.* Color lithograph published by Sachse & Co., November 1861. After the Army of the Potomac was created in August 1861, defenses in the Washington area were significantly strengthened.

RIGHT: *John Charles Frémont.* Lithograph by J. C. Buttre, February 1859. A famed explorer and a man with political ambitions, Frémont was the first presidential candidate of the new Republican Party in 1856.

AUGUST–SEPTEMBER

30 31 **1** 2 **3** 4 5 6 7 8 **9** 10 11 12 13 14 15 16 17 18 19 20 21 22 23 24 25 26 27 28 29

AUGUST 30, 1861: In Missouri, the Union's department commander, Major General John C. Frémont, assuming the administrative powers of the state, confiscates the property of *all* Missourians who favor the Confederacy and declares their slaves free. Such a firmly aggressive stance is heartily approved by Northerners eager to press the war effort. But Frémont's action offends border-state Unionists and threatens Lincoln's delicate maneuvering to keep the vital border state of Kentucky in the Union. ("I think to lose Kentucky is nearly the same as to lose the whole game," Lincoln will write to his friend Senator Orville Browning. "Kentucky gone, we can not hold Missouri, nor, as I think, Maryland. These all against us, and the job on our hands is too large for us.") On September 11, calling Frémont's emancipation measure *"purely political, and not within the range of military* law, or necessity," Lincoln will order the general to modify it to conform with the First Confiscation Bill (see August 6, 1861). In certain circles, the president's order will not be popular. Radical Republican senator Benjamin F. Wade will write to a colleague, "I have no doubt that by it, he has done more injury to the cause of the Union . . . than McDowell did by retreating from Bull Run." His confidence in Frémont eroding, Lincoln will relieve the general of command on November 2 — causing Frémont's supporters to further question the president's judgment.[121]

SEPTEMBER 1861

SEPTEMBER 1, 1861: The first school for contrabands established in the South is started by Mary Chase, a freedwoman of Alexandria, Virginia.[122]

SEPTEMBER 3, 1861: Confederate forces under General (and Episcopal bishop) Leonidas Polk enter Kentucky from Tennessee and occupy the city of Columbus, an act that ends this border state's "neutrality." Three days later, to block Southern troops from taking the city, Ulysses S. Grant will occupy Paducah; and on September 9, Confederates under Simon Bolivar Buckner will move into Bowling Green. As Union Department of the Cumberland commander Robert Anderson settles into his Louisville headquarters, his second in command, William T. Sherman, will make a circuit of nearby Union states, securing troops to help preserve this crucial border state for the Union. Political assistance will come in the form of a resolution that passes the Kentucky legislature just over a week after Polk brings his troops into the state, calling on the governor to order Confederate forces out. Yet both Union and Confederate troops remain in the area. There is now one continuous front dividing South from North, extending from the Atlantic Ocean to Kansas and the Frontier.[123]

SEPTEMBER 9, 1861: President Lincoln responds to a demand from Kentucky governor Beriah Magoffin (see May 20, 1861) that Federal troops be withdrawn from his state: "I

SEPTEMBER

1 2 3 4 5 6 7 8 9 10 **11** 12 13 14 **15** **16** **17** 18 19 20 21 22 23 24 25 26 27 28 29 30

most cordially sympathize with your Excellency in the wish to preserve the peace of my own native state, Kentucky; but it is with regret I search, and cannot find, in your not very short letter, any declaration or intimation that you entertain any desire for the preservation of the Union. Your obedient servant, A. Lincoln."[124]

SEPTEMBER 11, 1861: Transferred from Paducah to Cairo, Illinois, and now a brigadier general of volunteers, Ulysses S. Grant confronts a still-too-familiar problem; today the *Chicago Tribune* reports on the general's remedial action, General Order Number 5: "It is with regret the General commanding sees and learns that the closest intimacy exists between many of the officers and soldiers of his command; that they visit together the lowest drinking and dancing saloons; quarrel, curse, drink and carouse on the lowest level of equality. . . . Discipline cannot be maintained when the officers do not command respect, and such conduct cannot insure it. In this military district discipline shall be maintained, even if it is at the expense of the commission of all officers who stand in the way of attaining that end."[125] *In western Virginia,* Confederate area commander Robert E. Lee opens the five-day Cheat Mountain campaign. Waged in increasingly foul weather, plagued by low troop morale and difficulties among Confederate commanders, and hampered by a complex battle plan that calls for close cooperation among five Southern units, the campaign fails. Other Confederate operations in

western Virginia prove equally fruitless, something that incites acidic editorial commentary in newspapers throughout the South — and results in a new, uncomplimentary nickname for the commanding general: "Grannie" Lee. "I am sorry," Lee will comment sarcastically in a letter to his wife, "that the movement of our armies cannot keep pace with the expectations of the editors of the papers."[126]

SEPTEMBER 15, 1861: President Lincoln issues a statement concerning the ongoing arrests (September 13–16) of a number of public officials in Maryland, including Baltimore mayor George W. Brown and secessionist members of the state legislature: "The public safety renders it necessary that the grounds of these arrests should at present be withheld, but at the proper time they will be made public. Of one thing the people of Maryland may rest assured: that no arrest has been made, or will be made, not based on substantial and unmistakable complicity with those in armed rebellion against the Government of the United States." Those taken into custody will be released, a few at a time, on parole or after taking an oath. By November 27, 1862, all will have been freed.[127]

SEPTEMBER 16–17, 1861: Union forces occupy Ship Island, between New Orleans and Mobile, where the United States will develop a base for the Gulf Blockading Squadron as well as for the campaign against New Orleans.[128]

SEPTEMBER 22, 1861: At Fort Lyon, in New Mexico Territory, a horse race between militia troops and Navajo men erupts into violence after the Navajo accuse the army of cheating and the army opens fire, killing many Navajo. The United States is now engaged in hostilities with both the Apache (see February 4, 1861) and the Navajo, two conflicts that will merge and become known as the Apache and Navajo War.[129] *From Washington,* where he has gone to begin work as Assistant Librarian of Congress, Ainsworth Rand Spofford sends one last dispatch as a correspondent for the *Cincinnati Commercial:* "At the top of the finished portion of the Capitol dome [which is being replaced], there is a fine opportunity . . . for viewing the encampments of our army and the locality of the advanced lines of the enemy. The dome is visited daily by thousands of people, including nearly all the newly arrived soldiers . . ." He also notes one of the problems the rapidly expanding Volunteer Army is facing: "There is a scarcity of surgeons in the army, and some are graciously volunteering . . . to attend the numerous cases of illness. . . . Dr. [and recently appointed Librarian of Congress] J. G. Stephenson . . . has generously devoted a large share of his time to these sufferers, a temporary hospital for whom has been established in the Patent Office."[130]

SEPTEMBER 26, 1861: From a camp in Kentucky, where he has been sent to protect the route of the Louisville & Nashville Railroad from both Confederate troops and Kentucky secessionists, an overworked and harassed William T. Sherman writes to his wife: "I have no doubt that the railroad and tele-

graph will be cut off behind us . . . the people of Kentucky will not rally in my judgment but turn on us who came to save them from the Despot of the South."[131]

OCTOBER 1861

OCTOBER 1, 1861: During a strategy conference at Centreville, Virginia, President Davis and Generals Johnston and Beauregard decide that, despite public pressure for action against the North, the Confederate army does not have sufficient strength and logistical support to make such a move and thus will have to await whatever offensives the Union army will undertake in the spring.[132]

OCTOBER 7, 1861: As some people in the Union grow restless at the time George McClellan is taking to organize and train the Army of the Potomac, Horace Greeley publishes an editorial castigating other newspapers "which evince impatience at Gen. McClellan's inactivity," for only a commanding general can know when his army is ready for battle. Greeley's opinion of McClellan will change for the worse — something that's already occurring among Republican members of Congress, who are beginning to wonder if the general's affiliation with

⊶ Reporting the War ⊷

The Press, the Field, the Sketchbook. Wood engraving by Thomas Nast (1840–1902), published in *Harper's Weekly,* April 30, 1864.

A literate and news-hungry nation, the divided United States of 1861–1865 supported hundreds of newspapers, from the powerful, widely read *New York Tribune* and *Richmond Examiner* to papers with more limited reach, such as the *Chattanooga Rebel* and William "Parson" Brownlow's *Knoxville Whig* (which, after exile in the North, the passionately Unionist Brownlow reopened in 1863 as the *Knoxville Whig and Rebel Ventilator*). A seventeen-year-old communications system, the telegraph, made it possible for news reports to travel on wings—when correspondents could gain access to what they dubbed "the lightning." The fifteen thousand miles of telegraph wire that the Union operated by the end of the war, and the thousand miles controlled by the Confederacy, were often reserved for military and political use first; reports that included information deemed useful to the enemy were sometimes censored or simply not allowed to go out; and lines were not always available close to the battlefront.

As the war lengthened, war reports increasingly crowded non-news articles off the front pages, and new press associations were formed to improve the circulation of news

dispatches. The Southern Associated Press, whose high fees and poor service had been irritating many Confederate newsmen since 1861, was joined by the Press Association of the Confederate States of America in March 1863. In the Union, similar dissatisfaction with the service provided by the fourteen-year-old New York Associated Press to papers farther west led to the incorporation of the Western Associated Press in late 1862.

Competition was fierce, and there was no shortage of reporters, many of them temporary and amateur. Franc B. Wilkie, retained by the *New York Times,* reported from Cairo, Illinois, in December 1861, "Every other civilian one met was a correspondent, or claimed to be. . . . Each regiment had its special representative from the home paper, and quite often each company had a 'war correspondent' in its mess." Yet professional newsmen, both domestic and foreign, provided most of the war news that circulated throughout the country and beyond. Prominent members of the North's so-called Bohemian Brigade of reporters included Henry Villard, Whitelaw Reid, and Charles Carleton Coffin. Peter W. Alexander, Felix Gregory de Fontaine, and poet and essayist Henry Timrod were notable among the more than one hundred volunteer and paid Confederate correspondents.

Whether produced by professionals or amateurs, however, news reports were often far from objective and sometimes wildly inaccurate. Major misrepresentations could be the source of much political trouble and resentment in the ranks; inaccuracies of a minor nature often stimulated resigned bemusement. "The march to-day . . . lay through a miserable looking country," Union lieutenant colonel Alfred B. McCalmont wrote to his brother in November 1862. "We could hear the drivers whipping and swearing and sometimes see a wagon stuck fast in the mud. On the way a boy met us with the 'Philadelphia Inquirer,' and there was a great deal of laughing over one of the headings of army news which pithily stated . . . in large capitals, that the army's advance was not impeded by the rain."

Photographers also covered the conflict (see "Photographing the War," page 100), but the era's cumbersome cameras were not yet able to capture "action" shots. Thus, a hardy band of special artist-correspondents traveled—and sometimes served—with the Union armies, making sketches and finished drawings that brought to life battlefield action, camp life, and, as the armies advanced, vignettes of Southern life under Union occupation. Wearing sturdy clothes and wide-brimmed hats to shade their eyes, and carrying large portfolios containing the paper, pencil crayons, charcoal, ink, pens, brushes, and watercolors necessary to their jobs, the artists became experts at finding good vantage points in the midst of chaos. Alfred Waud (the most prolific and among the most daring of the band), his brother William, Edwin Forbes, Theodore Davis, Arthur Lumley, Henry Lovie, and Winslow Homer were among the best and best known of these dedicated artist-newsmen based in America; Frank Vizetelly was the most prominent artist working for an overseas publication, the *Illustrated London News.*

Copied by engravers onto printing blocks (sometimes with mistakes or editorial changes), black-and-white versions of the special-artists' sketches appeared regularly in the North's three illustrated papers, *Harper's Weekly, Frank Leslie's Illustrated News,* and, until 1864, the *New York Illustrated News.* (Richmond publishers Ayers and Wade established the *Southern Illustrated News* in September 1862, but constant shortages of everything from paper and presses to sketch artists and cartoonists forced the journal to close just over two years later.)

Political cartoonists—including the North's Frank Bellew, Henry Stephens, John McLenan, and Thomas Nast; Southern sympathizer Adalbert Volck; and famed London illustrator John Tenniel, who also favored the Confederacy—skewered or celebrated, as they saw fit, political and military figures and events. Their work was widely circulated not only in illustrated journals but also through the shops of Currier & Ives, Louis Prang, and other popular lithographers in the North. The supply of popular-art lithographs in the South was more limited, primarily because of shortages, but some were available through such publishers as Ayers and Wade and Hoyer and Ludwig (both based in Richmond), Blanton Duncan (Columbia, South Carolina), and Pessou and Simon (New Orleans). In addition to cartoons, these shops sold color and black-and-white battlefield maps, depictions of military clashes (heroic scenes that were sometimes wildly inaccurate), and portraits of prominent wartime figures.

Throughout the conflict, men and women in both the North and the South "reported" their understanding of and feelings about the war via the literary and theatrical arts. Wartime compositions ranged from Julia Ward Howe's American classic "Battle Hymn of the Republic" to much less lasting and celebrated works. Among the latter was a poetic broadside (single-sheet publication) that reflected a turning point in the North's war effort, and in American history. Titled "The New Version of The Colored Volunteer," it read, in part: "when they gave us arms, and all a soldier's right . . . how we made the Rebels stare, / For they could not stand the charge of the colored Volunteer."[133]

THE NEWSPAPERS IN CAMP.

Untitled cartoon. Pencil drawing on brown paper by Alfred R. Waud, ca. 1861. Northern eagerness to have Union armies march "Onward to Richmond" is reflected in this atypical Waud cartoon drawing, in which Lincoln, Stanton, and an unidentified general regard the imperious McClellan hopefully as he stands beside a protective Uncle Sam.

the Democratic Party is dulling his enthusiasm for war. On October 8, Senator Benjamin Wade will bemoan the quiescence of McClellan's increasingly strong army, which remains behind its entrenchments "occasionally sending forth a *bulletin* announcing that 'the *Capital* is safe.'"[134]

OCTOBER 8, 1861: Fatigued and unwell, Department of the Cumberland commander Robert Anderson summons William T. Sherman to Louisville and informs him that he is the new department commander. In addition to Kentucky secessionists and Confederate forces present in the state, Sherman now must deal with manpower shortages, lack of quartermasters and funds for supplies, and myriad administrative duties. Unbeknownst to Sherman, Confederate commanders in the area are facing similar difficulties and sending complaints about lack of supplies and ill-trained volunteers to Richmond. Under these circumstances, both sides move with caution in Kentucky.[135] *In Washington*, British correspondent William Russell attempts to see General McClellan and is told by an aide that the general was tired and has gone to bed and that the general had "sent the same message to the President, who came inquiring after him ten minutes ago. This poor President!" Russell writes in his diary. "Surrounded by such scenes, and trying with all his might to understand strategy, naval warfare . . . and all the technical details of the art of slaying. He runs from one house to another, armed with plans, papers, reports, recommendations, sometimes good-humoured, never angry, occasionally

dejected, and always a little fussy. . . . But for all that, there have been many more courtly Presidents who, in a similar crisis, would have displayed less capacity, honesty, and plain dealing than Abraham Lincoln."[136]

OCTOBER 16, 1861: After a meeting in Louisville, during which he is surprised by Sherman's grim assessment of conditions in the Department of the Cumberland, Secretary of War Cameron wires Lincoln, "Matters are in a much worse condition than I expected to find them." He also requests supplies and reinforcements. Cameron and his entourage, which includes newspaper reporters, are struck by Sherman's tense demeanor — and their speculations blossom into rumors, which will live long after the war, that at this time the general is "touched in the head." Assessments contradicting the rumors are not as widely circulated. On October 25, the *Cincinnati Daily Commercial* will publish a report from its Louisville correspondent, who finds Sherman "a very superior man . . . clear headed and strong headed — loving his profession, his fame and his men."[137]

OCTOBER 21, 1861: Under orders from Major General McClellan to make a "slight demonstration" against Leesburg, Virginia, to lure Confederates out of that city, Brigadier General Charles Pomeroy Stone sends several companies of the Fifteenth Massachusetts across the Potomac from their camp in Maryland. They do not get very far before encounter-

Colonel Edward D. Baker (1811–1861), USA. Photographic print on a carte de visite mount by the firm of E. & H. T. Anthony, ca. 1861. Senator from the new state of Oregon, Baker was a nationally known politician who had become so close to Abraham Lincoln when both men lived in Illinois that the Lincolns named their second son after him.

The Civil War in America—Retreat of the Federalists after the Fight at Ball's Bluff, Upper Potomac, Virginia.
Engraving based on a drawing by Frank Vizetelly, published in the *Illustrated London News*, November 23, 1861. "The whole affair appears to have been ill-planned," the *News* editorialized, "and adds another to the grievous blunders committed by the Federal commanders."

ing Confederates, who force them back to the edge of the river at the steep ridge known as Ball's Bluff. Though reinforced by troops under Colonel Edward Baker — U.S. senator from Oregon and an old friend of President Lincoln's — the Union force, under heavy fire from well-placed Confederates, is pushed back over the steep bank and into the river, where many are forced to swim for their lives, few boats being there to support them. More than 700 Federal troops are captured or missing, 158 are wounded, and 49, including Colonel Baker, are killed. As the public learns of this humiliating defeat, three months to the day after the Union's drubbing at Bull Run, shock waves reverberate throughout the North. "The massacre at Ball's Bluff," U.S. State Department translator Count Adam Gurowski writes in his diary, "is the work of either treason, or of stupidity, or of cowardice, or most probably of all three united."[138]

OCTOBER 25, 1861: As relations between Generals Scott and McClellan continue to deteriorate (see August 8, 1861) and their disagreements become public knowledge, Republican senators Benjamin Wade, Zachary Chandler, and Lyman Trumbull meet with McClellan at the home of Postmaster General Montgomery Blair, pressing the general to put his army in motion. McClellan blames General Scott for the delay — so successfully that he is able to inform his wife this evening in a letter that the senators will "make a desperate effort tomorrow to have General Scott retired at once." McClellan is aware that

the infirm seventy-six-year-old general in chief has already tendered his resignation; the president and his cabinet had decided to accept it on October 18. However, the disaster at Ball's Bluff has delayed Scott's departure. McClellan states to his wife, "Until that is accomplished I can effect but little good — he is ever in my way."[139]

NOVEMBER 1861

NOVEMBER 1, 1861: A White House messenger brings General George B. McClellan the presidential order he has been eagerly anticipating: "I have designated you to command the whole Army," Lincoln writes. "You will, therefore, assume this enlarged duty at once, conferring with me so far as necessary." General Scott's retirement is official, and McClellan is now general in chief of United States armies.[140]

NOVEMBER 5, 1861: Jefferson Davis appoints General Robert E. Lee commander of the Confederate Department of South Carolina, Georgia, and East Florida, removing Lee from the storms of criticism that continue over the Southern army's failures in western Virginia.[141]

LEFT: Commander, later Captain Percival Drayton (1812–1865), USN. Photograph between 1855 and 1865.

RIGHT: Brigadier General Thomas F. Drayton (1808–1891), CSA. Photograph between 1861 and 1865.

Slaves of the Rebel Genl. Thomas F. Drayton, Hilton Head, S.C.
Photograph by Henry P. Moore (1833–1911), May 1862. Left behind by Drayton after his defeat at Port Royal, these contrabands participated in agricultural and educational programs; some of the men may have joined the Union army when that was finally allowed.

NOVEMBER

1 2 3 4 5 **6 7 8** 9 10 11 12 13 14 15 16 17 18 19 20 21 22 23 24 25 26 27 28 29 30

NOVEMBER 6, 1861: Voters in the Confederacy elect Jefferson Davis president (thereby changing his status from provisional president to president) and also elect members of the first "regular" (not provisional) Congress.[142]

NOVEMBER 7, 1861: U.S. Navy flag officer Samuel Du Pont and Brigadier General Thomas W. Sherman lead a huge combined land-and-sea force into Port Royal Sound, South Carolina, beginning operations to secure the Hilton Head–Port Royal area, between Savannah, Georgia, and Charleston, South Carolina. This daring operation, deep in Southern territory, includes a particularly bitter reminder of the fratricidal nature of this growing war: Among the vessels bombarding the forts protecting the sound is USS *Pocahontas,* captained by Commander Percival Drayton, a South Carolina native who remains loyal to the Union. The Confederates his ship fires upon are under the command of his older brother, General Thomas Drayton — who is soon forced to order a retreat. Remaining in Union hands for the rest of the war, the Port Royal area will become an important base for refueling and supplying blockaders. Home to some ten thousand contrabands abandoned by their Confederate owners (including General Drayton), the islands will also become a testing ground for educational and agricultural programs to assist freed slaves and, in time, a recruiting ground for black regiments.[143] *In the western theater of operations,* Brigadier General Ulysses S. Grant, en route to raid and reconnoiter the

key Confederate stronghold of Columbus, Kentucky, alters his plans when he discovers that a Rebel force has crossed the Mississippi River into Missouri. A clash at Belmont (Grant's thirty-one hundred facing an estimated five thousand Confederates under Gideon Pillow) doesn't go well for the Federals, who are repulsed, with some five hundred killed, wounded, and captured. Yet with little Union action anywhere, this engagement (though criticized by some as unnecessary and barren of results) at least gives Northerners a sense that movement is occurring. It also gives Grant valuable operational and combat experience after his years in civilian life.[144]

NOVEMBER 8, 1861: General in Chief McClellan agrees to William T. Sherman's request that he be relieved from command of the Department of the Cumberland. Don Carlos Buell will replace him.[145] *On the high seas,* a major international incident begins when USS *Jacinto* violates traditional U.S. regard for the rights of neutral vessels and stops the British ship HMS *Trent,* forcing *Trent*'s reluctant captain to relinquish two important passengers who boarded the ship in Cuba. *Jacinto*'s captain, Charles Wilkes, had not consulted any higher authorities before removing John Slidell and James M. Mason, Confederate envoys to Great Britain and France, respectively, who are en route to their overseas posts. Though his action will be popular with newspapers and the public in the North, it presents the United States government with a serious problem. The outraged British will soon begin sending additional

> *"You will keep constantly before the public view in Great Britain, the tyranny of the Lincoln Government, its utter disregard of the personal rights of its citizens, and its other notorious violations of law."*
>
> —Robert M. T. Hunter
> to Henry Hotze,
> November 11, 1861

Abraham Lincoln with his secretaries, John Nicolay (left, 1832–1901) and John Hay (1838–1905). Lincoln appointed Nicolay U.S. consul to Paris early in 1865. After the war, Hay became U.S. ambassador to Britain and secretary of state. He also collaborated with Nicolay on a ten-volume biography of Lincoln (1890).

NOVEMBER

1 2 3 4 5 6 7 8 9 10 **11** 12 **13** 14 15 16 17 18 19 **20** 21 22 23 24 25 26 27 **28** 29 30

troops and naval vessels to their Canadian garrisons, obviously preparing for war if the envoys are not released — and the French will declare their support for the British position. The Lincoln administration, struggling to meet the challenges of war at home, suddenly faces the prospect of a second war abroad.[146] (See also December 26, 1861.)

NOVEMBER 11, 1861: The ongoing campaign to gain recognition for the Confederacy as an independent nation is reflected in a letter Confederate secretary of state Robert M. T. Hunter sends to Henry Hotze, who will become the Confederacy's propagandist and agent in London. "You will keep constantly before the public view in Great Britain, the tyranny of the Lincoln Government, its utter disregard of the personal rights of its citizens, and its other notorious violations of law."[147]

NOVEMBER 13, 1861: Having begun to consult with his new general in chief almost daily, President Lincoln arrives this evening at McClellan's headquarters, accompanied by his secretary John Hay and Secretary of State Seward. Told that McClellan is out, the president decides to wait for him. An hour later, the general returns and, despite being informed the president is waiting, goes directly to bed. Hay rages at this "insolence of epaulettes," but the president refuses to become angry. He will, however, begin to summon McClellan to the White House when he wishes to see him, something the general will find both inconvenient and irritating. "I found 'the original gorilla' about as intelligent as ever," he will write to his wife after a White House meeting on November 17. "What a specimen to be at the head of our affairs!"[148]

NOVEMBER 20, 1861: General Henry W. Halleck, who replaced John C. Frémont as commander of the Department of the Missouri on November 9, issues General Order No. 3, which forbids fugitive slaves from entering Union lines in the area under his command. Many Republicans in Congress, already angered by Lincoln's reversal of Frémont's unauthorized emancipation proclamation, are incensed by the order.[149] (See August 30, 1861.)

NOVEMBER 28, 1861: The Confederate Congress admits Missouri as the twelfth Confederate State, the Southern-leaning legislators of the state having adopted a "secession ordinance" November 3 at Neosho, Missouri, while retreating from Union forces. Missouri will, in fact, remain in the Union, its Confederate state officials serving as a "government in exile" outside their state for most of the war. Nevertheless, the Confederacy will add a star to its flag to represent the state.[150]

Frederick Douglass (1818–1895). Photograph by J. W. Hurn, date unknown. The eloquent abolitionist pressed Lincoln to allow black men to serve in the U.S. Army, recruited black soldiers (including two of his own sons) once that was allowed, and defended their rights in the face of discrimination in the service.

Contrabands Escaping. Pencil drawing by Edwin Forbes (1839–1895), May 29, 1864.

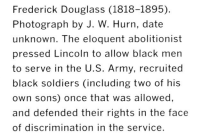

DECEMBER 1861

DECEMBER 1, 1861: U.S. Secretary of War Simon Cameron includes in his departmental annual report a paragraph on what is to be done with "those slaves who were abandoned by their owners on the advance of our troops into southern territory" — officially advocating emancipation and employment of such contrabands in the military. Still deeply concerned over maintaining the loyalty of the border states, and knowing that a majority in the North do not favor abolition, much less the arming of freed slaves (legal restrictions still prevent free black men in the North from serving in the Union army), Lincoln orders copies of the report already in circulation to be confiscated and tells Cameron to delete the incendiary passage. This inspires another round of protests from Radical Republicans and antislavery citizens at large. The greatly shortened final version of the paragraph relies on Congress, in its "wisdom and patriotism," to decide the matter after the war. For many Americans, waiting is not an option. "We wage war against slaveholding rebels, and yet protect and augment the motive which has moved the slaveholders to rebellion," author, publisher, activist, and former slave Frederick Douglass thundered in the August 1861 issue of *Douglass Monthly*. "Fire will not burn it out of us — water cannot wash it out of us, that this war with the slaveholders can never be brought to a desirable termination until slavery, the guilty cause of all our national troubles, has been totally and forever abolished."[151]

DECEMBER 3, 1861: In the first of his annual messages to Congress, President Lincoln recommends that "steps be taken" to colonize the slaves who had come into Union lines, along with any free blacks who wish to emigrate. Struggling to end the war and reconstruct the sundered nation in which a majority of whites, in both North and South, fear the consequences of emancipation, the president has turned to a solution first embraced in 1817, when the American Colonization Society (ACS) was established to raise funds for sending free blacks to Africa. In 1821, the ACS purchased land and founded Liberia on Africa's west coast; in 1847, the colony became the independent Republic of Liberia. During the first three years of war, the Lincoln administration will also seek other overseas areas for settling freed blacks, including Haiti. In response to today's presidential request, Congress will appropriate six hundred thousand dollars throughout 1862 to help finance the voluntary emigration of free black people. Yet colonization has no appeal for the overwhelming majority of African Americans. The *Anglo-African* paper will call Lincoln's message "a speech to stir the hearts of all Confederates," while lawyer and orator John Rock will condemn colonization in a January 23, 1862, speech: "Does any one pretend to deny that this is our country? Or that much of the wealth and prosperity found here is the result of the labor of our hands? Or that our blood and bones have not crimsoned and whitened every battlefield from Maine to Louisiana? It is true, a great many simple-minded people have been induced to go to Liberia and

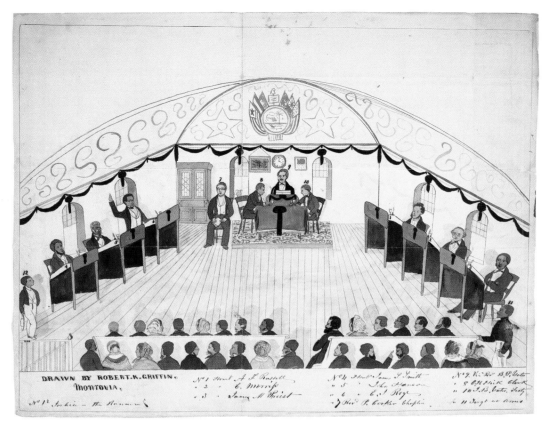

A meeting of the Liberian Senate, Monrovia, Liberia. Watercolor and graphite drawing by Robert K. Griffin (b. ca. 1836), ca. 1856.

John Rock, Colored Counselor. Wood engraving based on a photograph by Richards published in *Harper's Weekly*, February 25, 1865. Born of free parents in New Jersey, Rock (1825–1867) became a successful teacher, dentist, medical doctor, and lawyer; in February 1865 he became the first African American admitted to practice before the U.S. Supreme Court (see page 218).

DECEMBER

1 2 3 4 5 6 7 **8** **9** **10** 11 12 13 **14** 15 16 17 18 19 20 21 22 23 24 25 **26** 27 28 29 30 31

to Hayti, but, be assured, the more intelligent portion of the colored people will remain here . . . where we have withstood almost everything."[152]

DECEMBER 8, 1861: In the mid-Atlantic, Captain Raphael Semmes and the crew of CSS *Sumter* capture the Union whaling ship *Ebenezer Dodge.* "Forty-three prisoners were now on board," Semmes will later write, "cooped up with the crew in the narrow berth deck, when the weather forbade their appearance on deck, and the little *Sumter* was beginning to feel herself overcrowded."[153]

DECEMBER 9, 1861: Shortly after the Thirty-seventh Congress convenes in Washington and in the wake of the stinging military failures at Bull Run and Ball's Bluff, the U.S. Congress creates the seven-member (three senators, four representatives) Joint Committee on the Conduct of the War to investigate all aspects of the ongoing conflict. Chaired by the Radical Republican senator Benjamin F. Wade of Ohio, the committee initially includes Democratic senator Andrew Johnson of Tennessee and Representative Moses Fowler Odell, Democrat of New York. Attended by stenographer William Blair Lord, the committee will grow increasingly powerful — and controversial — as it conducts its business, both in secret sessions in the Capitol and out in the field, where members will observe the military situation and interview witnesses.[154]

DECEMBER 10, 1861: Kentucky becomes the thirteenth state claimed by the Confederacy when the Confederate Congress admits its "provisional government." Although the Confederate flag will henceforth bear thirteen stars, Kentucky, like Missouri (see November 28, 1861), will remain in the Union.[155]

DECEMBER 14, 1861: Brigadier General Henry Hopkins Sibley assumes command of the District of Arizona in the Confederate Trans-Mississippi Department. Heading thirty-seven hundred troops (a force designated the Army of New Mexico), Hopkins has been engaged since November in a campaign to sweep the Federals from what is today New Mexico and Arizona and to open the door to California for the Confederates.[156]

DECEMBER 26, 1861: After discussions in Washington and written consultation with the U.S. ambassador to Britain, Charles Francis Adams, Secretary of State Seward dispatches a note to the British that extricates the U.S. government from the tense situation created by the arrest of Confederate commissioners to Britain and France Mason and Slidell (see November 8, 1861). While stating that the United States has done nothing illegal, and without conveying a U.S. apology, Seward agrees to release the Confederates. He also administers a refined diplomatic dig by noting that the American government has based this "adjustment of the present case, upon principles confessedly American." Britain's failure to recognize that the rights of neutral vessels should be respected has long been a

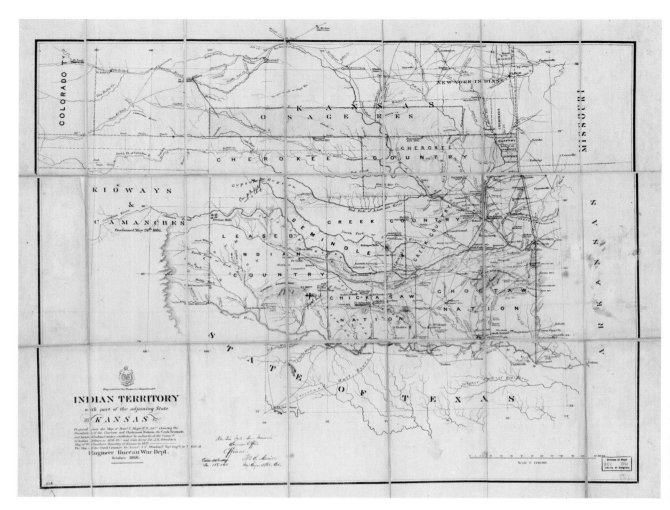

Indian Territory
with Part of the
Adjoining State of
Kansas. Engineer
Bureau, (U.S.)
War Department,
1866.

bone of contention between the two nations. *In Missouri,* U.S. authorities declare martial law in St. Louis and in and about all railroads operating in the state.[157] *In the Indian Territory* (directly south of Kansas), Confederates have exacerbated long-existing tensions between factions in the Creek Nation, having signed a treaty of alliance with the Lower Creeks to which Upper Creeks, who are either neutral or loyal to the Union, objected. Clashes between the two Indian factions, which began in November, culminate today in a battle at Chustenahlah, when white Confederates and their Lower Creek, Choctaw, Cherokee, and Chickasaw allies catch up with Opothleyahola and his hungry and exhausted band of Upper Creeks, who are retreating toward Kansas. Many Upper Creeks are either killed or captured. Others will find a degree of safety — though not much in the way of adequate food and shelter — in Kansas.[158]

DECEMBER 31, 1861: At 7:30 PM members of the Joint Committee on the Conduct of the War meet with Lincoln and his cabinet at the White House. In what becomes a stormy session, the impatient congressmen "were very earnest," Treasury Secretary Chase will later write, "in urging vigorous prosecution of the war, and in recommending the appointment of Major-General McDowell to command the Army of the Potomac" as a replacement for McClellan.[159]

1862

JANUARY 1862

JANUARY 9, 1862: Flag Officer David G. Farragut is ordered to command the Union's West Gulf Blockading Squadron, which has been given a critical mission: the capture of New Orleans, the largest city in the Confederacy.[160]

JANUARY 10, 1862: Still distressed over the continuing inaction of McClellan's Army of the Potomac, President Lincoln writes a three-sentence note to Secretary of War Cameron on a letter he has just received from a commanding general in the West: "The within is a copy of a letter just received from General Halleck. It is exceedingly discouraging. As everywhere else, nothing can be done." Lincoln is planning to do something about Cameron, however. For some time, he has been receiving complaints of mismanagement and corruption in War Department operations, and his own estimation of Cameron's effectiveness is such that he has met with Secretary of State Seward to discuss candidates for a replacement secretary of war.[161]

JANUARY 13, 1862: In a letter to Brigadier General Don Carlos Buell, Lincoln reveals the effectiveness of his study of military matters, and his overall strategy for winning the war: "[M]y general idea of this war [is] that we have the *greater* num-

Reception of the Officers of the Army by Secretary of War Stanton. Monday PM, at the War Dept. Washington D.C. Pencil and black ink drawing on tan paper by Arthur Lumley (1837–1912), January 20, 1862. The new secretary of war is shaking hands with General Daniel E. Sickles as General in Chief McClellan stands between them.

Manuscript draft of page one of President Lincoln's two-page General War Order No. 1, January 27, 1862, by which the president tried, unsuccessfully, to spur General in Chief McClellan to take some definite (preferably multifront) action against Confederate forces.

bers, and the enemy has the *greater* facility of concentrating forces upon points of collision; that we must fail, unless we can find some way of making *our* advantage an over-match for *his;* and that this can only be done by menacing him with superior forces at *different* points, at the *same* time; so that we can safely attack, one, or both, if he makes no change; and if he *weakens* one to *strengthen* the other, forbear to attack the strengthened one, but seize, and hold the weakened one, gaining so much."[162]

JANUARY 15, 1862: Simon Cameron is gently removed from the cabinet, leaving to become U.S. envoy to Russia, and the U.S. Senate confirms Edwin M. Stanton as the new secretary of war. A formidable lawyer whose initial impressions of Lincoln were far from favorable, he will prove to be exceptionally energetic and efficient in the challenging post.[163]

JANUARY 16, 1862: The balance of naval power on the western rivers tilts further to the Union with the commissioning of seven ironclad river gunboats, including *Carondelet, St. Louis,* and *Cincinnati,* all of which will prove essential in forthcoming combined (army and navy) operations.[164]

JANUARY 19, 1862: Nine days after both Union and Confederate forces claim victory in an engagement at Middle Creek in eastern Kentucky, Confederate brigadier general Felix Zollicoffer is killed and Union troops under Brigadier General George H. Thomas push a Confederate force under Major General George B. Crittenden back across the Cumberland River at the battle of Mill Springs (Logan's Cross Road), one of the two principal Civil War battles in that border state. Eastern Kentucky will remain under Union control until Confederate major general Braxton Bragg launches an offensive in the summer.[165]

JANUARY 27, 1862: Impatient with the inactivity of Union armies, and under increasing pressure from the press and Radical Republican members of Congress, President Lincoln takes the unprecedented step of issuing General War Order No. 1, which "Ordered that the 22d of February 1862, be the day for a general movement of the Land and Naval forces of the United States against the insurgent forces." General McClellan does not approve of the order. Four days later he will meet with the president at the White House and offer to deliver comprehensive objections in writing. The resulting twenty-two-page paper includes a rationale for a movement toward Urbanna at the mouth of Virginia's Rappahannock River, aimed at flanking Joe Johnston's army and isolating Confederate batteries plaguing Union traffic on the lower Potomac River. Despite the president's continuing efforts to put McClellan's army on the offensive, there will be no forward movement in February.[166]

JANUARY 31, 1862: With passage of the Railways and Telegraph Act, the U.S. Congress authorizes the president to take over any railroad "when in his judgment the public safety may

LEFT: *Capture of Fort Henry by U.S. Gun Boats.* Color lithograph by Strobridge & Co., n.d.

OPPOSITE: *The Burnside Expedition Landing at Roanoke Island — Feb. 7th 1862.* Color lithograph by Sachse & Co., n.d. "Burnside threw out a large force which landed & walked over a Swamp — which our engineers had pronounced *impassable!*," horror-stricken Southern diarist Catherine Edmondston wrote on February 10. "When will our rulers begin to think that we have a deadly & determined foe to conquer."

require it." Though the measure is rarely used in the Northern territory proper, it will be the basis of major U.S. government railroad activity in the occupied South. *Also today,* President Lincoln issues Special War Order No. 1, specifically aimed at forcing McClellan to launch the Army of the Potomac on offensive operations in Virginia.[167]

FEBRUARY 1862

FEBRUARY 3, 1862: The Union government decides to treat captured Confederate privateer (nonmilitary raider) crews as prisoners of war rather than pirates — thus averting eye-for-an-eye executions of Union prisoners of war. Confederate privateers will gradually be displaced, however, by commerce raiders, such as Raphael Semmes, who are military personnel.[168] *Also today,* Maintaining his international diplomatic correspondence (which thus far has included missives to such far-flung heads of state as the queens of England and Spain, the Tycoon of Japan, and the viceroy of Egypt), President Lincoln writes to the King of Siam, thanking him for his letters and gifts that will be deposited in "the archives of the Government" — and politely noting that one gift, "a stock from which a supply of elephants might be raised on our own soil," would, regrettably,

not be as useful as his majesty hoped: "Our political jurisdiction does not reach a latitude so low as to favor the multiplication of the elephant, and steam on land, as well as on water, has been our best and most efficient agent of transportation in internal commerce."[169]

FEBRUARY 6, 1862: Brigadier General Ulysses S. Grant and Flag Officer Andrew H. Foote launch what is intended to be a combined army-navy operation against Fort Henry, Tennessee, a bastion on the Tennessee River near the middle of the Confederate western defensive line. The operation does not go exactly as planned. The fort, poorly placed on low ground overlooked by hills, is so weakly defended (some of its cannons are submerged due to recent flooding and its garrison numbers less than thirty-five hundred) that its commander, Brigadier General Lloyd Tilghman, orders all but about one hundred artillerymen to withdraw to Fort Donelson, some ten miles away. A smashing riverine attack by Foote's men overcomes the artillerymen's defense (though not without some damage to Foote's vessels), and Tilghman surrenders the fort before Grant and his troops arrive. Loss of the fort, which opens the Tennessee River to Union gunboats and shipping as far as Muscle Shoals, Alabama, will impel the Confederate military department commander, General Albert Sidney Johnston, to withdraw with half his troops from Bowling Green, Kentucky, to Nashville, Tennessee. He will dispatch the other half of his force to Fort Donelson, which will be Grant's next objective.[170]

THE BURNSIDE EXPEDITION LANDING AT ROANOKE ISLAND.
FEB. 7TH 1862.

Brigadier General Daniel C. McCallum (1815–1878), USA. Photograph by the Brady National Photographic Art Gallery, between 1860 and 1865.

FEBRUARY

1 2 3 4 5 6 **7** 8 9 10 **11** **12** 13 14 **15** 16 17 18 19 20 21 22 23 24 25 26 27 28

FEBRUARY 7, 1862: Confederate flag officer William F. Lynch sends an official report to his superiors from the waters off Roanoke Island, North Carolina: "Sir: I have the honor to report that the enemy, at 10 A.M. to-day, with twenty-two heavy steamers and one tug, made an attack upon this squadron and the battery at Pork Point." Lynch faces, and is soon defeated by, elements of a Union naval flotilla of nearly one hundred ships, commanded by Flag Officer Louis M. Goldsborough, part of an amphibious operation that lands seventy-five hundred infantry under Major General Ambrose Burnside on this inadequately defended Confederate outpost. Although three thousand Southerners under Colonel H. M. Shaw do what they can to resist, they are forced to surrender on February 8 — a loss that inspires distress and recriminations throughout the Confederacy. With Roanoke Island secure, the Union is able to tighten its blockade of Southern ports.[171]

FEBRUARY 11, 1862: U.S. Secretary of War Edwin Stanton establishes the United States Military Railroads (see also April 22, 1862), and President Lincoln issues an executive order effectively appointing engineer Daniel McCallum, former official of the New York & Erie Railroad, superintendent. McCallum is charged with ensuring the "safe and speedy transport" of men and supplies, a task that will become more challenging as the war — and the military railroad system — expand. (Beginning with seven miles of Virginia railway, McCallum will ultimately control 2,105 miles of track

extending as far south as the Division of the Mississippi.) *In the Confederate States,* control of railroads will not be as centralized or efficient. States jealously guard their own railroad systems, so the Southern network will include many different gauges; and most rail lines will remain unconnected, forcing military and civilian suppliers to transport goods by wagon between them.[172]

FEBRUARY 12, 1862: Ulysses S. Grant and fifteen thousand Union troops arrive outside Fort Donelson, Tennessee, on the Cumberland River, where Grant positions his forces as he waits for Flag Officer Andrew Foote's naval flotilla. It will arrive two days later — and be forced to withdraw after receiving a drubbing from Confederate guns well placed on high ground above the river. Unlike the contest for Fort Henry (see February 6, 1862), the battle for Donelson will be an army affair.

FEBRUARY 15, 1862: Despite the repulse of the Union naval assault, Fort Donelson's commanding officer, prewar U.S. cabinet member John B. Floyd, convinced that the fort cannot be defended, orders elements of his Confederate force to break through Union lines so that the garrison might withdraw toward Nashville. Men in Confederate gray and Union blue grapple in the cold, snowy day until finally Grant's troops push the Confederates back to the fort. Floyd then determines that someone must surrender Donelson — but leaves that odious task to Brigadier General Simon B. Buckner as Floyd himself

CAPTURE OF GENERAL S.B.BUCKNER AND HIS ARMY, FEBRUARY 16TH 1862.   COPYRIGHTED 1887 BY KURZ & ALLISON, ART PUBLISHERS, 76 & 78 WABASH AVE, CHICAGO, U.S.A.

BATTLE OF FORT DONELSON.

FEBRUARY

1 2 3 4 5 6 7 8 9 10 11 12 13 14 15 **16** 17 **18** 19 **20** 21 22 23 24 25 26 27 28

along with his second in command, Gideon Pillow, and some twenty-five hundred men escape by boat under cover of a wind-and-sleet-laced night. (Disgusted with Floyd's action, Colonel Nathan Bedford Forrest of the Third Tennessee Cavalry — who will prove to be one of the South's most effective cavalry officers — also leads his troopers out.) *As they leave,* and amid the random firing of Union and Confederate soldiers, the U.S. Sanitary Commission hospital ship *City of Memphis* quietly arrives, shades covering its portholes to block any light that might give its position away to enemy gunners. Among its passengers is Mary Ann Bickerdyke (see May 26 and June 9, 1861), who will help care for the wounded once stretcher-bearers are able to bring them to safety.[173]

FEBRUARY 16, 1862: General Grant replies to General Buckner's request for terms of surrender: "No terms except an unconditional and immediate surrender can be accepted. I propose to move immediately upon your works." The Confederate commander — who had been at West Point with Grant, served with him in the Mexican War, and later loaned Grant money to see him through a tight time — unhappily yields to what he deems in his reply Grant's "ungenerous and unchivalrous terms." *After the surrender,* stretcher-bearers search for wounded who have survived the bitter-cold night. One man they save will be the son of respected legal scholar and passionate Unionist Francis Lieber. When Lieber visits Tennessee to comfort his son, he will meet General Henry

W. Halleck — an encounter that will ultimately result in an important step in the governance of wartime military forces (see April 24, 1863). In the meantime, news of the Donelson victory, and Grant's ultimatum, sweeps through the North — and "Unconditional Surrender" Grant, who has opened the way for further operations deep into Confederate territory, enters the limelight.[174]

FEBRUARY 18, 1862: As the permanent Confederate Congress convenes in Richmond, Virginia, Union commanders Ambrose Burnside and Louis Goldsborough, recent victors at Roanoke Island (see February 7, 1862), issue a proclamation to the people of North Carolina: "The mission of our joint expedition is not to invade any of your rights, but to assert the authority of the United States, and to close with you the desolating war brought upon your State by comparatively a few bad men in your midst. . . . They impose upon your credulity by telling you of wicked and even diabolical intentions on our part . . . all of which, we assure you, is . . . utterly and willfully false. . . . Those men are your worst enemies. They, in truth, have drawn you into your present condition."[175]

FEBRUARY 20, 1862: At the White House, elation over Grant's Tennessee victories is erased by terrible grief when eleven-year-old Willie Lincoln, the apple of his father's eye, dies at 5:00 PM of typhoid fever, from which he has been suffering for two agonizing weeks. The president bursts

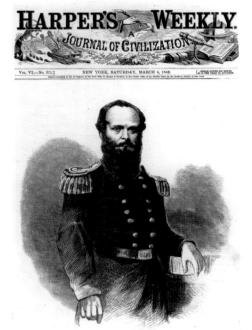

HARPER'S WEEKLY.
JOURNAL OF CIVILIZATION

LEFT: *Major-General Ulysses S. Grant, USA, the Hero of Fort Donelson.* Wood engraving published in *Harper's Weekly*, March 8, 1862. This issue of *Harper's* introduced Grant, wearing the longer beard he sported early in the war, to a wide Northern public eager to see some progress in the Union's war effort.

RIGHT: Willie Lincoln (standing at center) with his brother Tad (right) and their cousin Lockwood Todd. Photograph by the Brady National Photographic Art Gallery, ca. 1861.

Brady   New York.

OPPOSITE: *Battle of Fort Donelson—Capture of General S. B. Buckner and His Army, February 16th 1862.* Color lithograph by Kurz & Allison, 1887. Grant's first major victory of the war, the Union capture of Donelson opened the way for Union progress into the South.

FEBRUARY

1 2 3 4 5 6 7 8 9 10 11 12 13 14 15 16 17 18 19 20 **21** **22** **23** 24 25 26 27 28

into tears as he tells his secretary John Nicolay, "my boy is gone — he is actually gone!" He will twice order that Willie's body be exhumed so that he can look on the boy's face again. Suffering convulsions of anguish, Mary Lincoln will take to her bed for three weeks and later seek solace through spiritualism and séances — something many other people will do as Civil War casualties mount. Eight-year-old Tad Lincoln, also critically ill, will be equally inconsolable once he recovers, repeatedly crying that he will never be able to talk to Willie again.[176]

FEBRUARY 21, 1862: Continuing a military campaign in the Arizona and New Mexico territories intended to open the door to California for the Confederates, troops under Southern general Henry Hopkins Sibley defeat a Union detachment at Valverde, New Mexico. Among the Union troops killed is Captain George N. Bascom, who, as a young lieutenant a year earlier, created the incident that sparked the ongoing war between the United States and the Apache Nation. (See February 4, 1861.)[177]

FEBRUARY 22, 1862: "At the darkest hour of our struggle the Provisional gives place to the Permanent Government," Jefferson Davis declares at his inauguration as permanent president of the Confederate States (see November 6, 1861). Accusing the North of promoting a revolution against states' rights and slavery, thus perverting the goals of the Founding

Fathers, and oppressing the South with "the tyranny of an unbridled majority," he celebrates the spirit of the Southern citizenry — and acknowledges a downturn in Confederate fortunes. "After a series of successes and victories, which covered our arms with glory, we have recently met with serious disasters. But in the heart of a people resolved to be free these disasters tend but to stimulate to increased resistance." The following day, Robert E. Lee will write to his son, expressing concern over Confederate resolve. "The victories of the enemy increase & Consequently the necessity of increased energy & activity on our part. Our men do not seem to realize this, & the same supineness & Carelessness of their duties Continue. If it will have the effect of arousing them & imparting an earnestness & boldness to their work, it will be beneficial to us. If not we shall be overrun [*sic*] for a time, & must make up our minds to great suffering. All must be sacrificed to the country."[178]

FEBRUARY 23, 1862: In an exchange being echoed in many families North and South, seventeen-year-old student James Billingslea Mitchell writes to his father from the University of Alabama at Tuscaloosa: "Dear Father. I have [reflected on your letter] & come to the conclusion that if I do not participate in this war it will be a source of the deepest regret & disappointment through life. Like a bird of evil omen it will follow me & mar all my undertakings. You said that you would not except in case of the direst necessity consent to have my course

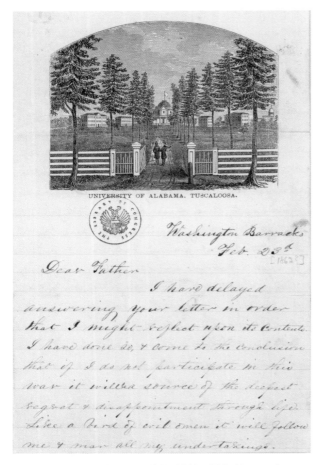

James Billingslea Mitchell (1844–1891), CSA. Manuscript letter to his father, February 23, 1862.

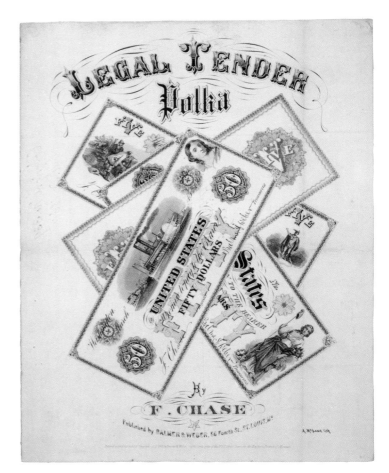

Legal Tender Polka. Color lithograph music cover. Music by F. Chase; lithograph by A. McClean, 1863.

interrupted. . . . What direr necessity can there be than the present, unless it be the very burnings of our own homes. . . . It is true hundreds of my age have fallen victims to disease and death while yet upon the threshold of the service. But why should not I die as well as they? Shall I sit ignobly here and suffer them to fight my battles & endure all for me? Never."[179]

FEBRUARY 25, 1862: After taking possession of Bowling Green, Kentucky, on February 16, Union general Don Carlos Buell and his troops occupy Nashville, the first Confederate state capital and important industrial center to fall to the Union.[180] *In Washington,* as the Union struggles with the problems of financing the war (difficulties so acute that, for a period, the government had to suspend payments to soldiers and contractors), Abraham Lincoln signs the Legal Tender Act, creating the first successful government-sponsored national paper money system in U.S. history. The notes, popularly called "greenbacks," are unsecured by specie (gold or silver), something that creates anxiety among the many people who question the legislation. Treasury Secretary Chase is among those discomfited, but he is also the person who best knows the scope of the Union's economic problem. "*Immediate action is of great importance,*" he has said. "*The Treasury is nearly empty.*" A significant extension of Federal authority, and meant as a temporary wartime measure, the bill authorizes the government to issue $150 million in greenbacks. This will prove insufficient. More than $400 million will be put in circulation by the war's

end.[181] *In New York,* USS *Monitor* is commissioned. Looking to some like "a cheesebox on a raft," the ironclad has radically new features: a revolving turret housing two eleven-inch Dahlgren smoothbore cannon and forced draft ventilation that allows the crew to live in an artificial, "submarine" environment. *Monitor* is also uniquely ironclad — not simply converted from a preexisting vessel, as was CSS *Virginia.*[182]

FEBRUARY 27, 1862: The Confederate Congress authorizes the president to suspend the writ of habeas corpus in areas that "in his judgment, be in such danger of attack by the enemy as to require the declaration of martial law for their effective defense." Davis immediately suspends the writ in Norfolk and Portsmouth, Virginia, and he suspends it in Richmond on March 1 — cities that are in danger not only of attack from without but also of collapse within due to rising crime and violence among their wartime populations, which have ballooned with refugees, war workers, black marketeers, and others, making a volatile mix.[183]

BATTLE OF PEA RIDGE, ARK.

ABOVE: Captain Franklin Buchanan (1800–1874), CSN. Photograph between 1860 and 1870. A career naval officer, Buchanan was the first superintendent of the U.S. Naval Academy before resigning his U.S. commission to join the Confederate service.

LEFT: *Battle of Pea Ridge, Ark.* Color lithograph by Kurz & Allison, n.d. This Confederate defeat helped keep the troubled border state of Missouri securely in Union hands.

MARCH 1862

MARCH 6, 1862: In a message to Congress, Lincoln calls for cooperation with any state that will gradually abolish slavery and proposes offering compensation to slaveholders. He notes that the cost of the war would quickly "purchase, at a fair valuation, all the slaves in any named state." Adopted by Congress on April 10, the resolution is not accepted even by the border states, which are its principal focus. *Also today,* USS *Monitor* sails from New York for Hampton Roads, Virginia.[184]

MARCH 7-8, 1862: Cherokee allied with the South are among the Confederate troops who fight in the two-day battle of Pea Ridge (Elkhorn Tavern), Arkansas. In this action, the culmination of a Union campaign by General Samuel R. Curtis to drive Major General Sterling Price's Confederates out of Missouri, Price's men, joined by a force under Brigadier General Ben McCulloch and Major General Earl Van Dorn, find that Curtis has anticipated their planned attack against the pursuing Federals. The Confederates are roundly defeated.[185]

MARCH 8, 1862: As preparations begin for a massive Union push up the Virginia peninsula to take the Confederate capital city of Richmond via the Virginia peninsula (the Peninsula Campaign, March–August 1862), President Lincoln relieves McClellan of his duties as general in chief, leaving him in command of the Army of the Potomac only. This is ostensibly so that the general can concentrate his full attention on the

forthcoming campaign. The president (who has proven to be a singularly adept student of military strategy) and Secretary of War Stanton now assume the duties of general in chief themselves. *In the same military directive,* Lincoln creates the Mountain Department in western Virginia and places John C. Frémont in command — a move that pleases Radical Republicans who disagreed with the president's removal of Frémont from command in Missouri the previous fall (see August 30, 1861).[186] *At Hampton Roads, Virginia,* the U.S. Navy suffers the worst day in its eighty-six-year history when the ironclad CSS *Virginia* (formerly USS *Merrimack*), captained by Confederate flag officer Franklin Buchanan, attacks the wooden ships of the Federal blockading fleet. Sweeping through Union fire, severely damaging the frigate USS *Congress* on the way, *Virginia* smashes into the side of the large sloop of war USS *Cumberland,* tearing a hole that causes the vessel to sink, its crew continuing to fire at their attacker until the last minute — and managing to blow the muzzles off two of *Virginia*'s guns. Yet the Confederate vessel is still formidable, dispatching shore batteries along the James River and destroying a transport ship before turning on USS *Congress,* which had run aground, raking the Union frigate with fire. After an hour-long battle, *Congress,* severely damaged and with heavy casualties, is forced to surrender. As the Confederates set it ablaze, Buchanan is wounded; command of *Virginia* passes to Commander Catesby ap Roger Jones — who immediately sets the vessel's sights on *Minnesota,* also aground and already taking fire from

BATTLE BETWEEN THE MONITOR AND MERRIMAC.

Battle Between the Monitor and Merrimac—Fought March 9th 1862 at Hampton Roads, near Norfolk, Va.
Color lithograph published by Kurz & Allison, 1889.

Admiral John L. Worden (1818–1897), USN. A lieutenant at the time of *Monitor*'s battle with CSS *Virginia*, Worden was promoted to admiral in 1872 while serving as superintendent of the U.S. Naval Academy.

MARCH

1 2 3 4 5 6 7 8 **9** 10 11 12 **13** **14** 15 16 **17** 18 19 20 21 22 23 24 25 26 27 28 29 30 31

Confederate gunboats. *Virginia* adds to the damage they are doing, but as night falls, the Southern ironclad withdraws. The consternation that reigns among Union naval forces at the destructive power of the South's armored vessel is tempered later in the evening when, under cover of darkness, the Union ironclad USS *Monitor* arrives on the scene. The stage is set for the first clash in history between ironclad vessels.[187]

MARCH 9, 1862: In April 1861, Lieutenant John L. Worden became the first Federal officer taken prisoner by the Confederates while he was on a mission to Pensacola, Florida. Today he carves a deeper niche for himself in history when he commands USS *Monitor* in its historic encounter with CSS *Virginia*, a clash that presages a new era in naval history. For two hours, the two ironclads battle each other, each taking hits and delivering blows — though neither is significantly damaged. Finally, they stop fighting, neither vessel able to claim a victory this day. But the cumulative victory of two days of fighting clearly belongs to *Virginia*, and the damage it did to the Union's wooden vessels will be celebrated throughout the Confederacy. "Our single iron clad vessel — the Virginia has . . . sunk the Cumberland, burned the Congress, crippled the Minnesota, repulsed the Roanoke & the St Lawrence, and drove all the other vessels under the shelter of the guns of Fortress Monroe," Catherine Edmondston exults in her diary on March 10. "This is glorious news & will cheer the heart of the nation now cast down with the reverses in Tennessee."[188]

MARCH 13, 1862: A new U.S. article of war forbids army officers, under penalty of court-martial, to return fugitive slaves to their masters.[189]

MARCH 14, 1862: Union troops under Ambrose Burnside, having secured Roanoke Island, North Carolina (see February 7, 1862), move to the mainland and attack Confederate defenses protecting the city of New Bern, an important railroad depot strategically located at the confluence of the Trent and Neuse rivers. Among the Federal soldiers wounded before the defenses are successfully penetrated is a sergeant of the Fifth Rhode Island Infantry — who is promptly dragged to safety by his wife, Kady Brownell. One of an estimated four hundred to six hundred women who will have campaigned with Civil War armies by the end of the war, Brownell has become so much a part of the Fifth Rhode Island's camp life that the men have dubbed her a "daughter of the regiment." She rescues several other wounded men during this day's fighting before returning home with her injured husband. New Bern will remain in Union hands for the rest of the war, a bitter loss to the Confederacy.[190]

MARCH 17, 1862: A convoy of army transports and navy warships begins the monumental task of moving Major General George B. McClellan's 105,000-man Army of the Potomac, and its equipment, to the York and James rivers for the start of the Peninsula Campaign of 1862.[191] *At about this same time,* Jefferson

TORN ASUNDER

ABOVE: Kady Brownell (1842–1915), "daughter of the regiment," USA. Child of a Scottish soldier, Brownell accompanied her husband, Robert, into service in the Union Army.

RIGHT: General Thomas Jonathan "Stonewall" Jackson (center, 1824–1863), CSA, and staff — including talented mapmaker Jedediah Hotchkiss (to the left and slightly above Jackson's picture). Photograph by Vannerson & Jones, from original negatives, ca. 1861–1863.

MARCH

1 2 3 4 5 6 7 8 9 10 11 12 13 14 15 16 17 **18** 19 20 21 22 **23** 24 25 **26** 27 28 29 30 31

Davis appoints Robert E. Lee as his principal military adviser, placing him in charge of "military operations in the armies of the Confederacy." McClellan, who served with Lee during the Mexican War, assumes this means that Lee will take command of the forces defending Richmond (a premature assumption; Joseph Johnston retains that field command). McClellan will write Lincoln in April that Lee "is *too* cautious & weak under grave responsibility . . . & is likely to be timid & irresolute in action" — a character sketch that some restive Republicans have been drawing of McClellan himself.[192]

MARCH 18, 1862: Judah P. Benjamin, former Confederate States attorney general whose short stint as secretary of war ended ingloriously after Roanoke Island fell to the Union, now becomes secretary of state, the cabinet post in which he will serve until May 10, 1865.[193]

MARCH 23, 1862: As the Army of the Potomac moves into position for its campaign against Richmond, Confederate general Stonewall Jackson puts into motion a plan suggested by Robert E. Lee — a campaign in the Shenandoah Valley intended to draw Union strength away from McClellan's campaign. Today, Jackson suffers a tactical defeat at the first battle of Kernstown. But the encounter does prove to be a successful diversion, as alarmed Union officials in Washington send troops slated to join McClellan's force to deal with Jackson instead. Meanwhile, Jackson must cope with a problem that

has been plaguing Civil War field commanders on both sides: the lack of accurate maps.[194]

MARCH 26, 1862: "Soon after we reached camp Gen. [Stonewall] Jackson sent me a message that he wished to see me," Confederate topographical engineer Jedediah Hotchkiss writes in his journal. "I promptly reported, when he said, . . . 'I want you to make me a map of the Valley, from Harper's [*sic*] Ferry to Lexington, showing all the points of offence and defence [*sic*] in those places. . . .' bidding goodbye to my battalion [I] rode back to Mt. Jackson to secure my outfit so I could get to work on the 'big job' entrusted to me." One of the most accomplished mapmakers in the Confederacy, Hotchkiss had been born in the North, but was a schoolteacher in Staunton, Virginia, when the war began. He will prove to be a singularly valuable asset, as Jackson turns his Shenandoah Valley Campaign into a hallmark in military history. After engaging in a clever ruse (marching half his command *out* of the valley, then rushing them back via railroad), Jackson will defeat Union forces at the battle of McDowell (May 8), at Front Royal (May 23), in the first battle of Winchester (May 25 — a defeat that will cause near panic in some parts of the North), at Cross Keys (June 8), and at Port Republic (June 9). His men will march so often and so far throughout the campaign that they will become known as "Jackson's Foot Cavalry." And Jackson himself will emerge from the Shenandoah Valley — eluding converging Union forces sent to defeat him — the foremost hero of the Confederacy.[195]

MARCH–APRIL

30 31 1 2 3 4 5 6 7 8 9 10 11 12 13 14 15 16 17 18 19 20 21 22 23 24 25 26 27 28 29

MARCH 30, 1862: Vincent Colyer, an agent of the Brooklyn YMCA, is appointed superintendent of the poor for the Union Department of North Carolina. He will shortly report: "Upwards of fifty [black] volunteers of the best and most courageous, were kept constantly employed on the perilous but important duty of spies, scouts, and guides. . . . They frequently went from thirty to three hundred miles within the enemy's lines . . . bringing us back important and reliable information."[196]

MARCH 31, 1862: As pressure for battlefield manpower intensifies, some Union and Confederate men face a dilemma: either personally or as members of a religious group, they are opposed, as a matter of conscience, to bearing arms. Today, Sydney S. Baxter of the Confederate War Department reports, "I have examined a number of persons . . . who were arrested at Petersburg. . . . As all these persons are members in good standing in these [Dunker and Mennonite] churches and bear good characters as citizens and Christians, I cannot doubt the sincerity of their declaration that they left home to avoid the draft of the militia and under the belief . . . they would be placed in a situation in which they would be compelled to violate their consciences. . . . I recommend all the persons in the annexed list be discharged on taking the oath of allegiance and agreeing to submit to the laws of Virginia and the Confederate States in all things except taking arms in war."[197]

APRIL 1862

APRIL 3, 1862: With the campaign beginning against Richmond, and in a surge of optimism after Grant's victories in the west and the tactical victory over Jackson at Kernstown (see March 23, 1862), U.S. Secretary of War Edwin Stanton, believing that current manpower will be enough to bring the war to a successful conclusion, orders all U.S. recruiting offices closed. They will not remain closed for very long.[198]

APRIL 4, 1862: The Union armored gunboat *Carondelet*, at night and in a terrific thunderstorm, fights its way past the batteries on Confederate-held Island No. 10, at the heart of a U-shaped dip in the Mississippi River near New Madrid, Missouri. As soon as the war started, Southerners had commenced fortifying the island and nearby river bluffs in order to interrupt Union river traffic. *Carondelet*'s passage of Island No. 10 is the first step toward cutting off and reducing this island stronghold. (See also April 7, 1862.)[199]

APRIL 5, 1862: The Army of the Potomac launches the Peninsula Campaign by initiating a siege of Yorktown, Virginia, at the tip of the Virginia Peninsula. McClellan has chosen to besiege rather than attack the town because he considers it too strong a Confederate position to carry with a single frontal assault, estimating at one point that he is facing a force of "not less than 100,000 men." In fact, Major General John B. Magruder is holding the Confederate defensive line

with only seventeen thousand troops — keeping them in motion to give the impression that his force is much more substantial and dotting his line with "Quaker guns" (logs painted black to resemble cannon), which add to the illusion of strength. "I have made my arrangements to fight with my small force," he reports, "but without the slightest hope of success."[200] (See also May 3, 1862.) *In the western theater,* a Confederate army is on the march from the important railroad hub of Corinth, Mississippi. Led by Albert Sidney Johnston and P. G. T. Beauregard (who proposed this offensive), the Southern force includes many raw recruits wholly unaccustomed to military discipline and marching in bad weather through rugged terrain. Progress, and stealth, suffer accordingly — so much so that Beauregard urges Johnston to turn back. But the ranking general presses on. His objective: Ulysses S. Grant's forty-thousand-man army now camped, and awaiting reinforcements, just across the state border, on the Tennessee River. Neither Grant nor his leading division commander, William T. Sherman, is expecting a major Confederate offensive, believing that the Rebels are still recovering from their recent defeats at Forts Henry and Donelson (see February 6, 12, 15, 16, 1862). Perhaps for that reason, Grant has not adequately fortified his position, concentrating instead on training the many green troops in his army.[201]

APRIL 6, 1862: At dawn, Union patrols probing the area in front of Grant's main encampment at Shiloh Church near Pittsburg Landing, Tennessee, run into the leading elements of Johnston's army and manage to bring a last-minute warning to Union lines. Hot on their heels, the vanguard of forty thousand Southern troops slams into the Northern position, beginning the battle of Shiloh. Sherman's division and that of John A. McClernand take the brunt of the initial assault, but Union forces are hard hit all along their line; some untried Federal units break and run to the rear. Having rushed to the field from his headquarters upriver as soon as the firing started, Grant rallies his troops as he moves from division to division — particularly noting, as the day progresses, the exemplary behavior of an officer who, not long before, some members of the press had labeled "touched in the head" (see October 16, 1861). ("I never deemed it important to stay long with Sherman," Grant will later report. "[B]y his constant presence . . . [he] inspired a confidence in [his untried] officers and men that enabled them to render services on that bloody battle-field worthy of the best of veterans.") Meanwhile, at a sunken road in deep woods, Benjamin Prentiss, leading remnants of his division and elements of others, buys valuable time for the Union, holding firm against repeated assaults in fighting so ferocious that the Confederates dub the area the "Hornet's Nest" before they overwhelm and capture Prentiss and other survivors. By the end of the day, the Southerners have pushed Union lines more than two miles back toward the river — but they have lost their commander. Albert Sidney Johnston bled to death on the field after a bullet severed an

Lt. Smith
Capt. Lent
Capt. S.C. Eaton
1st N.Y. Engrs
Col. W.B. Barton and wife
48th N.Y.
Capt. Elfwing
and his dog.
Capt. Hurst
Lieut. Nichols
Capt. A. Elmendorf

Fort Pulaski, Mouth of Savannah River, and Tybee Island, Ga.
Photographer and date unknown. The strategically placed fort fell
to the Union on April 10, 1862, after a fierce artillery battle.

APRIL

1 2 3 4 5 6 **7** 8 9 **10** 11 12 13 14 15 **16** 17 18 19 20 21 22 23 24 25 26 27 28 29 30

artery, the highest-ranking officer to be killed in the Civil
War. Later, under cover of lightning-streaked darkness, a
thunderstorm adding to the misery of the torn and exhausted
armies, Grant's reserve moves into the Union line, which is also
augmented by the awaited reinforcements led by Don Carlos
Buell — a total of twenty-five thousand fresh troops. Confederates, now led by Beauregard, are not reinforced — and suffer
more casualties as Union gunboats shell their position through
a long and sleepless night.

APRIL 7, 1862: Regrouped, reinforced, and now outnumber-
ing the Confederates, Union troops at Shiloh attack and
gradually, through hours of brutal combat, regain all their lost
ground and force Beauregard to order a retreat to Corinth.
"Our condition is horrible," Southern general Braxton Bragg
will write the next day. "Troops utterly disorganized and
demoralized. Road almost impassable. No provisions and no
forage." They leave behind them a field littered with dead and
wounded and a Union force shaken by the most terrible battle
yet seen on the American continent: more than fifty-four
hundred men have been killed; more than sixteen thousand
are wounded or missing. A precursor to the huge Civil War
battles to come, Shiloh is regarded as a Union victory. It is so
dearly bought and such a near thing, however, that the recently
lionized Grant becomes a magnet for criticism. As he weathers
the storm, he also takes away from the battle a sobering lesson,
which he will later describe in his memoirs. "Up to the battle

of Shiloh I, as well as thousands of other citizens, believed that
the rebellion against the Government would collapse suddenly
and soon, if a decisive victory could be gained over any of its
armies. [After Shiloh], I gave up all idea of saving the Union
except by complete conquest." *As Shiloh concludes,* the Confederate bastion on Island Number 10 in the Mississippi River falls
to Union troops commanded by Major General John Pope,
who becomes a new Northern hero.[202]

APRIL 10, 1862: Near Savannah, Georgia, Federal troops
who had established a base on Tybee Island commence firing
on Fort Pulaski at the mouth of the Savannah River, a bastion whose defenses had been improved some three months
earlier with the help of slave labor. Employing rifled cannon
(more accurate and powerful than smoothbore weapons), the
Union artillerymen cut a breach in the fort's formidable walls
within five hours. On April 11, after shells penetrate the fort's
magazine, the Confederate commander, Colonel Charles H.
Olmstead, will surrender. Without this defensive fortification
guarding the city from ocean attack, Savannah is no longer an
effective port for Confederate blockade runners.[203]

APRIL 16, 1862: As bad news continues to come in from
the West, and with the Union army less than ten miles from
Richmond, the Confederate Congress initiates the first general
military draft in American history. This first of three Confederate conscription acts provides that white men between ages

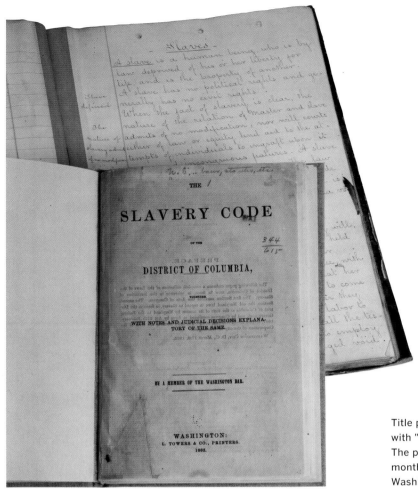

"Our condition is horrible. . . .

Troops utterly disorganized

and demoralized. Road almost

impassable. No provisions

and no forage."

—GENERAL BRAXTON BRAGG,
APRIL 8, 1862

Title page, *The Slavery Code of the District of Columbia*, 1862, pictured with "Slavery Code of the District of Columbia" manuscript, 1860. The printed Slavery Code was published on March 17, 1862, just one month before President Lincoln signed the law that ended slavery in Washington, DC.

APRIL

1 2 3 4 5 6 7 8 9 10 11 12 13 14 15 16 17 **18** 19 20 **21** 22 23 24 25 26 27 28 29 30

eighteen and thirty-five might be drafted for three-year terms or until the end of the war, should that come sooner — and it extends to three years the terms of men already in service who had enlisted for shorter periods. Because the Confederacy is short of arms, the law includes a passage encouraging conscripts and volunteers to bring their own weapons. It also includes two provisions that will prove to be increasingly troublesome: that conscription applies only to men "who are not legally exempted from military service," and that "persons not liable for duty may be received as substitutes for those who are, under such regulations as may be prescribed by the Secretary of War."[204] *In Washington,* it is a momentous day. More than ten years before, when he was a representative from Illinois in the Thirtieth Congress, Lincoln had proposed introducing a bill to end slavery in the District of Columbia but could find little support. Today, as president, he signs the sort of bill he had envisioned. The only example of compensated emancipation in the United States, this law provides for a payment of up to $300 to loyal Unionist masters for each slave, for whom they can prove a claim, who is freed by this act — and also authorizes $100,000 for colonization of freedmen. (The Federal government must continue to enforce fugitive slave laws, which are still in force, however; thus, runaways from loyal slave states who are apprehended in Washington must still be returned to their owners.) Abolitionists throughout the North are elated by the law, despite its flaws. "If we rejoice and give thanks to the Almighty for this great boon," the *Anglo-African*

journal declares, "we rejoice less as black men than as part and parcel of the American people. . . . We can point to our Capital and say to all nations, 'IT IS FREE!' Americans abroad can now hold up their heads when interrogated as to what the Federal Government is fighting for, and answer, 'There, look at our Capital and see what we have fought for.'"[205]

APRIL 18, 1862: Pursuing the Union goal of securing control of the Mississippi River, and thus splitting the Confederacy, David Farragut's fleet begins five days of mortar bombardment of heavily armed Fort Jackson (seventy-four guns), on the west bank of the Mississippi, and Fort St. Philip (fifty-two guns), on the east bank, below New Orleans.[206]

APRIL 21, 1862: The Confederate government legitimizes many of the guerrilla organizations already fighting throughout the Confederacy by passing the Partisan Ranger Act, a relatively short and nonspecific piece of legislation that states, in essence:

> [T]he President . . . is hereby authorized to commission such officers as he may deem proper with authority to form bands of partisan rangers, in companies, battalions or regiments. . . . [They] shall be entitled to the same pay, rations, and quarters . . . and be subject to the same regulations as other soldiers.

LEFT: Brigadier General Herman Haupt (1817–1905), USA. Photograph between 1860 and 1865 by the Brady National Photographic Art Gallery. A graduate of West Point (1835), Haupt left the service only a few months after graduation and established a reputation as an engineering and railroad authority before he was called back to the colors in 1862.

RIGHT: This map, published in the *New York Herald*, April 26, 1862, shows the forts and other defenses standing between Admiral Farragut's naval squadron and the South's largest city, a prime target in the Union's quest to control the entire Mississippi River.

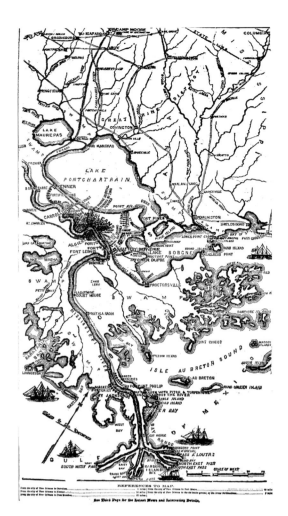

APRIL

1 2 3 4 5 6 7 8 9 10 11 12 13 14 15 16 17 18 19 20 21 **22** 23 **24** 25 26 27 28 29 30

A range of partisan leaders, from former cavalry scout John Singleton Mosby to Missouri "bushwacker" William Clarke Quantrill, will officially enroll their men in the Confederate armed forces under this act. Yet most Union officers, bitterly frustrated by guerrillas and the Southern civilians who support them, will refuse to recognize any partisans as anything other than outlaws, directing their men to "Pursue, strike, and destroy the reptiles."[207]

APRIL 22, 1862: Secretary of War Stanton summons civil engineer, author, and inventor Herman Haupt to Washington, where the secretary will appoint Haupt chief of construction and transportation of U.S. military railroads (see also February 11, 1862). Haupt will fulfill the role with admirable efficiency, establishing repair crews that become so adept at rebuilding lines damaged by Confederates that it will be said that "the Yankees can build bridges quicker than the Rebs can burn them down."[208]

APRIL 24, 1862: U.S. flag officer David G. Farragut leads his fleet through the gunfire from Forts Jackson and St. Philip below New Orleans in a hair-raising, artillery-punctuated predawn advance that is later described by Bradley Osbon, an officer and newspaper correspondent on Farragut's flagship, USS *Hartford:* "We were struck now on all sides. A shell entered our starboard beam, cut our cable, wrecked our armory and exploded at the main hatch, killing one man instantly and wounding several more. Another entered the muzzle of a gun, breaking the lip and killing the sponger who was in the act of 'ramming home.' A third entered the boatswain's room, destroying everything in its path and, exploding, killed a colored servant who was passing powder." All but three vessels of Farragut's fleet make it past the forts — stunning news to the people of New Orleans, where alarm bells ring and the Confederate garrison commander, Major General Mansfield Lovell, declares martial law.[209]

GOING ASHORE AT NEW ORLEANS.

Going Ashore at New Orleans. Engraving published in *Letters of George Hamilton Perkins, USN,* 1886. Then a twenty-five-year-old lieutenant, Perkins accompanied Captain Theodorus Bailey through this irate crowd to secure the official surrender of the city.

APRIL

1 2 3 4 5 6 7 8 9 10 11 12 13 14 15 16 17 18 19 20 21 22 23 24 **25** 26 27 28 29 30

APRIL 25, 1862: Admiral Farragut's fleet arrives at New Orleans. "Ah me! I see them now as they come slowly round Slaughterhouse Point into full view," young citizen George Washington Cable will later write, "silent, grim, and terrible; black with men, heavy with deadly portent; the long-banished Stars and Stripes flying against the frowning sky." As there are fewer than three thousand Confederate troops in the city, far too few to defend it, General Lovell marches them out and declares New Orleans an open city. Laced with smoke from burning stores of cotton and tobacco and the unfinished warship CSS *Mississippi,* which the Southerners burned so it would not fall into Northern hands, it is also an angry city: "The crowds on the levee howled and screamed with rage," Cable will remember. "The swarming decks answered never a word; but one old tar on the Hartford, standing with lanyard in

hand beside a great pivot-gun, so plain to view that you could see him smile, silently patted its big black breach and blandly grinned." After the mayor declines the honor of surrendering the city, Farragut's second in command, Captain Theodorus Bailey, and Lieutenant George H. Perkins walk through a hostile crowd and lower the Louisiana state flag from over city hall, replacing it with the Stars and Stripes — an act that Cable will describe as "one of the bravest deeds I ever saw done." News that the Confederacy's largest and most cosmopolitan city has fallen to the Union stuns the people of the South. "No event was considered more unlikely during the whole progress of this war," *Memphis Appeal* correspondent John R. Thompson will write on May 8, "than that New Orleans would fall into the hands of the enemy."[210]

CHAPTER TWO

Toward a New Birth of Freedom

May 1862 Through April 1863

"*I approve of the [emancipation] proclamation, but I don't think it is going to scare the South into submission. I think it will result in the total overthrow of slavery, but next winter will witness scenes so bloody that the horrors of the French Revolution will be peace in comparison to it. If the South will have it so, the blood be on her own head. Seward was right — the "irrepressible conflict" will continue till freedom or slavery rules the nation.*"

PRIVATE OLIVER WILLCOX NORTON,
EIGHTY-THIRD PENNSYLVANIA VOLUNTEERS,
LETTER TO HIS FATHER, SEPTEMBER 29, 1862[1]

"*We of the South remain calm and full of* faith, *knowing that victory must be ours, & that the falsehoods of the Yankee Generals cannot long be concealed. Oh! When is it to end, when are they going to be convinced that they cannot overcome those who have justice & God upon their side.*"

MRS. CORA IVES, LETTER TO HER MOTHER,
SEPTEMBER 11, 1862[2]

"It is nearly a hundred years since our people first declared to the nations of the world that all men are born free; and still we have not made our declaration good," Louisiana-based Union general John Wolcott Phelps wrote, in the spring of 1862. Confronting a growing population of "contraband" men, women, and children under Federal protection in the Union-occupied portion of the state, Phelps revealed his own abolitionist bent in a long letter to military authorities in New Orleans. "It is clear that the public good requires slavery to be abolished," he declared, although that assertion was still far

PRECEDING OVERLEAF: *General Kearney's [sic] Gallant Charge, at the Battle of Chantilly, Va., 1st of September 1862,* detail (see page 90).

LEFT: Dead in front of the Dunker Church, Antietam, MD. Photograph by Alexander Gardner, 1862.

Lieutenant Oliver Willcox Norton (1839–1920), USA. As a private with the Eighty-third Pennsylvania Volunteers, Norton was the first bugler to play the version of "Taps" that Americans know today. In November 1863, after going through a battery of tests, the eloquent young soldier became an officer in the Eighth United States Colored Troops.

Unidentified African American Union Soldier at Benton Barracks, Saint Louis, Missouri. Hand-colored quarter-plate tintype by photographer Enoch Long (1823–1898). Finally allowed to join the U.S. Army (see August 25 and September 22, 1862, and January 1, 1863), African American soldiers fought discrimination from many of their white comrades-in-arms even as they faced particular dangers in action against Confederate forces. More than 186,000 black men eventually served with Union forces.

from acceptable to many in the North and most in the South. And he asked a question troubling even to those who favored emancipation: "in what manner is it to be done?" Free black men in the North continued to pose another vexing, and related, question: when would they be allowed to serve in the Union army?

That same spring, the powerful Union Army of the Potomac was finally on the offensive, having been transported to the Virginia Peninsula, where its ultimate target was the Confederate capital at Richmond. Northern morale and expectations were high: with Federal armies so lately triumphant in the West (at Forts Henry and Donelson, New Orleans, and, despite fearful losses and postbattle recriminations, at Shiloh), a similar outcome on the Peninsula seemed certain. This would surely mean a swift and successful end to the war — and Army of the Potomac troops were determined to play their proper part in securing that overall victory. "[T]here seems to be a determination on the part of this army, that, if it depends on us, the honor of restoring the Union shall not rest wholly on the army of the west," Bugler Oliver Willcox Norton, of the Eighty-third Pennsylvania

Volunteers, wrote in his diary, on May 1, 1862. "That portion of the army has done nobly. They have had the hardest fighting to do, but, if I do not mistake the character of the men I see in the army here, they only wait the opportunity to do as well."

Norton and the other 115,000 men of the Army of the Potomac pushed forward, hampered not only by Confederate forces but also temperamental weather, inferior roads, unhappy geographical surprises not indicated on the army's unsatisfactory maps, and General George B. McClellan's overcautious leadership. As this massive armed force moved slowly up the Peninsula, clouds of apprehension descended on Richmond. The Confederate Congress adjourned and members fled the city; stores of gold and important papers were packed for shipment farther south should the worst occur; refugees fleeing before the Union army surged into the city even as Richmond citizens crowded into train stations and onto wharves trying to get away. Yet few Southerners, whether in Richmond or awaiting news of its fate, were seriously contemplating defeat or surrender. From North Carolina, fervent Confederate Catherine Edmondston surveyed recent

Toward a New Birth of Freedom

Campaign in Virginia. Game with military figures housed in a wooden box, circa 1890. Although some of the uniforms on the pieces are less than accurate, this game clearly commemorates the four years of near cease-less battlefield clashes and strategic maneuvering that occurred in Virginia. The first major Union campaign in the state, George B. McClellan's Peninsula Campaign, took place in spring 1862 and brought Robert E. Lee to the forefront of the Confederacy's military efforts.

Southern defeats and current threats with an air of grim determination: "Now indeed begins the war of Endurance," she wrote in her diary, on May 2, 1862, "a war in which we women must show the men that we are their equals — nay their superiors! . . . Endurance! Patience! Cheerfulness! Faith! — these be my Captains under whose banners I enlist! God grant that under them my country men may all be united into a glorious band . . ."³

ABOVE AND RIGHT: Details from one envelope printed during the Civil War include a potent Confederate declaration borrowed from the American Revolution, "Don't Tread on Us," and the motto "*Sic Semper Tyrannis*" (Thus always to tyrants), which John Wilkes Booth will shout one terrible night near the end of the war (see April 14, 1865).

The War in America: Confederate Sharpshooters Firing on a Federal Supply Train on the Tennessee River. Cover illustration from the *Illustrated London News*, December 5, 1863. Based on a drawing by British special artist-correspondent Frank Vizetelly (see July 21, 1861), this engraving, whether featuring Regular Army sharpshooters or guerrillas, demonstrates tactics that did not sit well with Union targets.

May 1862 Through April 1863

MAY

1 **2** 3 4 **5** 6 7 8 9 10 11 12 13 14 15 16 17 18 19 20 21 22 23 24 25 26 27 28 29 30 31

MAY 1862

MAY 2, 1862: With Union forces engaged in cutting Confederate east-west communications through the northern part of Alabama, Colonel John Beatty, of the Third Ohio Volunteer Infantry, reacts strongly after guerrillas wound several of his soldiers as their train passes through the village of Painted Rock. "I had the train stopped and, taking a file of soldiers, returned to the village," he writes in his diary.

> Calling the citizens together, I said to them that this bushwhacking must cease. The federal troops had tolerated it already too long. Hereafter every time the telegraph wire was cut we could burn a house; every time a train was fired upon we should hang a man; and we would continue to do this until every house was burned and every man hanged between Decatur and Bridgeport. If they wanted to fight they should enter the army, meet us like honorable men, and not, assassinlike, fire at us from the woods and run. We proposed to hold the citizens responsible for these cowardly assaults, and if they did not drive these bushwhackers from amongst them, we should make them more uncomfortable than they would be in hell.[4]

MAY 3, 1862: "The fight for Yorktown . . . must be one of artillery, in which we cannot win," Confederate general Joseph Johnston wrote to Robert E. Lee on April 29. Indeed, George McClellan, still convinced (erroneously) that his army is vastly outnumbered, has had troops working furiously to prepare emplacements for powerful cannons that will help even the odds and smash the city's defenses when the final Union assault begins on May 5. The work proceeds mostly at night under Confederate fire; Union engineer Gilbert Thompson will later remember "a thousand [men] strung along like a train of busy ants in the night, shoveling away, with now and then a shell bursting near." This night, however, Confederate shells rain down in a heavy bombardment that sends Union troops to ground all along the line until it finally ceases, replaced by an ominous quiet. The reason will become clear to the Federals in the morning: under cover of cannon fire, Johnston's Confederates have withdrawn from the city. They have left in their wake a countryside sown with "torpedoes" (land mines) devised by General Gabriel J. Rains, behavior that McClellan condemns as "murderous and barbarous conduct." Their successful retreat has also left Northerners with mixed feelings. Though Yorktown is now in Union hands, it is not the victory the Federals had hoped for. Johnston's army is still intact and moving back to protect Richmond.[5]

MAY 5, 1862: Two Union divisions pursuing Johnston's army on the Virginia Peninsula clash with entrenched Confederates, beginning the battle of Williamsburg, an intense back-and-forth encounter during which each side suffers some two thousand casualties. Sergeant Felix Brannigan, of the Seventy-

Kearney [sic] at Battle of Williamsburg. Black ink wash drawing by Alfred Waud, ca. May 4–5, 1862. A one-armed veteran of the Mexican War who had been awarded the Cross of the Legion of Honor for his service with the French cavalry in Italy, Union brigadier general Philip Kearny (1814–1862) was cited for bravery in the Williamsburg battle after leading his men, double-quick, through seas of mud to reinforce Joseph Hooker's endangered line. "At their head was General Kearny flourishing a sword in his only arm," one of Hooker's men later recalled of the timely reinforcement. "Never was our eyes more gladdened than at this sight."

OPPOSITE: *Destruction of the Rebel Monster "Merrimac" off Craney Island, May 11th, 1862.* Hand-colored lithograph by Currier & Ives, ca. 1862.

MAY

1 2 3 4 5 **6** 7 **8** **9** 10 11 12 13 14 15 16 17 18 19 20 21 22 23 24 25 26 27 28 29 30 31

fourth New York Volunteers, will later recall that, at one point in the battle, "We were so close to the rebels that some of our wounded had their faces scorched with the firing. . . . The air perfectly whistled, shrieked, and hummed with the leaden storm." The sounds of battle are clearly audible at Yorktown, yet General McClellan chooses to continue monitoring the loading of troop transports there — even after he receives messages from the front requesting his presence. He is greeted by lusty cheers from the men in the ranks when he does arrive, after most of the shooting is over and Johnston's army has resumed its withdrawal. *South of the Texas border,* another battle rages. Taking advantage of American preoccupation with the Civil War, in January France, Britain, and Spain tested the Monroe Doctrine by landing troops in troubled Mexico, which had declared a two-year moratorium on the payment of foreign debt. Now France alone maintains a military presence, and French troops are pushing toward Mexico City. Today they attack the fortified city of Puebla and are dealt a humiliating defeat by Mexican forces under General Ignacio Seguín Zaragoza, an event that will be commemorated henceforth by the Mexican national holiday Cinco de Mayo. As the French reinforce their army (they will take Puebla one year later), Mexican president Benito Juárez will start to send secret agents into the United States to purchase weapons — a difficult assignment, since the Union has initiated an embargo on the export of arms.[6]

MAY 6, 1862: President Lincoln, Secretary of War Edwin M. Stanton, and Secretary of the Treasury Salmon P. Chase arrive at Fort Monroe, at the tip of the Virginia Peninsula. Informed that General McClellan is too busy to see his commander in chief, Lincoln acquaints himself as closely as possible with the status of the general's campaign. Consulting a map, he notes that the Confederate withdrawal from Yorktown has made the port of Norfolk vulnerable to Union forces — something the Confederate area commander, Major General Benjamin Huger, has also divined. After a Unionist tugboat captain brings Federal authorities the news that Huger has begun withdrawing his troops, Lincoln will join in a scouting foray to Hampton Roads to help choose a suitable landing site for Federal troops moving to take the Southern port city.[7]

MAY 8, 1862: At the battle of McDowell, Virginia, Stonewall Jackson wins the first victory of his Shenandoah Valley Campaign (see March 26, 1862), repulsing an attack by Union troops commanded by General Robert Schenck. Subsequent success in battles at Front Royal (May 23) and Winchester (May 25) will allow Jackson to march to the Potomac River, causing consternation among Federal authorities and residents of Washington, who will fear for the safety of the capital city.[8]

MAY 9, 1862: Major General David Hunter, in command of the Union's Department of the South (including South Carolina, Georgia, and Florida, in all of which Union forces have

TOWARD A NEW BIRTH OF FREEDOM

established footholds), issues General Orders No. 11. Noting that he had placed the department under martial law (April 25) and that "[s]lavery and martial law in a free country are altogether incompatible," Hunter proclaims that "the persons in these three States . . . heretofore held as slaves, are therefore declared forever free." Like a similar action by John C. Frémont in Missouri (see August 30, 1861), this takes President Lincoln by surprise — and it places him squarely on the horns of a dilemma.[9]

MAY 10, 1862: With Treasury Secretary Chase accompanying Major General John E. Wool as an informal co-commander, Union troops land near Norfolk and march on the town while, aboard an accompanying vessel, President Lincoln does everything he can to make certain the troops have adequate backup. *On the Mississippi River,* as Union mortar boat No. 16, protected by the gunboat USS *Cincinnati,* fires on the Confederate bastion of Fort Pillow, Tennessee, eight boats of the Confederate River Defense Fleet, commanded by Captain James Montgomery, attack the two Union vessels, beginning the battle of Plum Run (Plum Point) Bend, Tennessee. Caught off-guard and some distance away, the rest of the Union flotilla raises steam, four powerful ironclads soon joining the fight. Although the Southern fleet manages to sink two ironclads (they will later be raised and repaired), the Confederates suffer heavy damage to four of their boats and withdraw, thus ending one of the rare fleet actions of the Civil War. *In Florida,* Union forces occupy Pensacola, which will become a vital base for the U.S. Navy's blockade of other ports along the Gulf of Mexico.[10]

MAY 11, 1862: With his ship's home base of Norfolk now in Union hands, before sunrise, Flag Officer Josiah Tatnall, in command of CSS *Virginia* (formerly USS *Merrimack*) and fearful that his risky plan to take the ironclad upriver will be unsuccessful, runs the vessel aground and sets it afire. The resulting explosion, when the flames reach its magazine, ends the career of this much-feared linchpin of the Confederacy's eastern seaboard navy.[11]

MAY 12–13, 1862: In the Charleston, South Carolina, harbor, Robert Smalls, a slave working as an assistant pilot on the Confederate side-wheel steamer *Planter,* bids good night to the ship's white officers as they leave the vessel in his hands to be battened down for the night. Instead, Smalls takes on some passengers: his wife and children and those of his brother, John, another member of the *Planter*'s all-black crew. In the wee hours of the morning, Smalls quietly gives orders to cast off, and *Planter* begins a short but harrowing voyage, running past the fortifications in Charleston harbor to reach the Union blockaders patrolling just beyond. Any of the fortifications, or the blockaders, could open fire, sinking the vessel and killing all aboard, for Smalls, his crew, and their passengers have vowed not to be recaptured by Confederates. A familiar sight in the harbor, *Planter* sails unchallenged under the Southern

Bluebeard of New Orleans. Reproduction of a drawing on a *carte de visite*, 1862. Among the first generals of volunteers appointed by President Lincoln, Major General Benjamin Franklin Butler (1818–1893), USA, also proved to be among the most problematical. As commander of occupied New Orleans, he issued the infamous "Woman's Order," which offended the South and dismayed Confederate sympathizers overseas (note John Bull, aghast, in the background).

LEFT: *Heroes in Ebony—The Captors of the Rebel Steamer Planter, Robert Small [sic, top], W. Morrison, A. Gradine and John Small [sic].* Wood engraving published in *Frank Leslie's Illustrated Newspaper*, June 2, 1862.

guns, saucily whistling the usual salutes, then raises a white flag, which is recognized by the Federal blockaders. "When they discovered that we would not fire on them," an eyewitness aboard USS *Onward* will later report, "there was a rush of contrabands out on her deck, some dancing, some singing, whistling, jumping. . . . [O]ne of the Colored men stepped forward, and taking off his hat, shouted, 'Good morning, sir! I've brought you some of the old United States guns, sir!'" Smalls and his crew will receive a reward for transferring this Confederate "prize" to the Union; and Smalls and *Planter,* which he will eventually captain, will provide valuable service to the Union for the rest of the war.[12]

MAY 15, 1862: After much rude behavior toward Federal troops by devotedly Confederate New Orleans women culminates in a woman dumping the contents of a chamber pot out a window and onto Admiral David Farragut's head, the Union area commander, Major General Benjamin Butler, issues General Order No. 28:

> As the officers and soldiers of the United States have been subject to repeated insults from the women (calling themselves ladies) of New Orleans in return for the most scrupulous non-interference and courtesy on our part, it is ordered that hereafter when any female shall by word, gesture, or movement insult or show contempt for any officer or soldier of the United States she shall

be regarded as a woman of the town [prostitute] plying her avocation.

Outrage sweeps through the South and erupts as far away as Britain, where the prime minister, Lord Palmerston, declares the edict "infamous." Yet overt rudeness toward Federal troops in New Orleans does ebb perceptibly, although many people, in the city and elsewhere, will henceforth refer to the Union commander by a less than polite new nickname, "Beast" Butler. *In Washington,* Lincoln approves the creation of the Department of Agriculture "to acquire and diffuse among the people . . . useful information on subjects connected with agriculture." *On the Virginia Peninsula,* five Union warships, including the ironclad *Monitor,* move up the James River, under orders to "push on to Richmond if possible, without any unnecessary delay, and shell the place into surrender." The small fleet is able to get within eight miles of the capital, but must turn back after a harrowing four-hour artillery duel with Confederates stationed at strategically placed Fort Darling, which overlooks the river at Drewry's Bluff.[13]

MAY 19, 1862: "[N]either General Hunter, nor any other commander, or person, has been authorized by the Government of the United States, to make proclamations declaring the slaves of any State free," President Lincoln states in the Proclamation Revoking General Hunter's Order of Military Emancipation (see May 9, 1862). Decisions regarding emancipation "I reserve

ABOVE: *Lt. Custer Wading in the Chickahominy River.* Pencil drawing by Alfred R. Waud, May 1862. By wading across the uncertain waters of the Chickahominy to determine a safe ford for Union forces, then reconnoitering the enemy's position on the other side, recent West Point graduate George Armstrong Custer impressed General George B. McClellan to such an extent that McClellan named Custer one of his aides—the first step in Custer's rise through the ranks to become one of the youngest Union wartime generals.

LEFT: *The Chickahominy—Alexanders Bridge.* Watercolor drawing by William McIlvaine (1813–1867), 1862. A more volatile body of water than Union forces initially appreciated, the Chickahominy was prone to flooding that could overwhelm the low-lying bridges across it.

to myself," the president notes. He goes on to remind the nation (and especially the border states) of the possibility of gradual, compensated emancipation (see March 6, 1862) and pleads with the people of the border states to reconsider that proposal. His plea will go unanswered.[14]

MAY 20, 1862: Congress passes and President Lincoln signs the Homestead Act, granting 160 acres of land to any adult citizen or intended citizen (man or woman) who stays on the land five years and makes certain improvements. Alternatively, a settler might purchase land for $1.25 an acre after only six months' residence. A policy opposed before the war by Southern politicians fearful that homesteaders would bring antislavery sentiment with them into the territories, the act will make it possible for some twenty-five thousand settlers to stake claims to more than three million acres before the war ends.[15] *On the Virginia Peninsula,* General McClellan divides his army, sending two corps across the Chickahominy River to the south bank, closest to Richmond, while retaining three corps north of the river. Neither McClellan nor his officers fully appreciate, at first, the temperament and treacheries of the Chickahominy. Surrounded by swamps and spongy ground that make hard going for cavalry and artillery, lined by thick woods that disguise terrain the infantry will have to cross, the river is prone to widespread flooding after soaking rains; its level has been known to rise enough to threaten the bridges that span the river. And it will soon begin to rain.[16]

MAY 24, 1862: "We approach the stronghold of the enemy," Colonel Thomas Kilby Smith, of the Fifty-fourth Ohio Volunteer Infantry, states in a letter home. "For every commanding ridge or hill there is a fight." Union forces are slowly pursuing P. G. T. Beauregard's Confederate army to the railroad center of Corinth, Mississippi, in the aftermath of the battle of Shiloh (see April 6–7, 1862); and as they press after the enemy, Smith writes,

> It is a terrible war. . . . unholy, unnatural fratricide. As well might he who has buried his knife in his brother's heart rush forth and exultingly brandish the dripping blade as evidence of good deed done, as he, the executioner of the law (for we are nothing else than executioners sent forth by Government to see the law enforced), offer his trophies, the wrung heart of the widow and fatherless, the ruined plantation . . . the destruction of the fond hopes of the living, the ruined patrimony of the unborn. . . . In sadness and sorrow we draw the sword.

In Corinth, Rufus W. Cater, of the Nineteenth Louisiana Volunteers, writes to his cousin Fanny: "The battle of Corinth has not yet been fought. . . . If we have anything like fair play you may rest assured we will send back the obnoxious hirelings of Lincolndom howling to the shelter of their ironclad boats." In fact, there will be no battle. On the night of May 29–30, under orders from General Beauregard,

RIGHT: Rufus W. Cater (ca. 1840–1863), CSA.

BELOW: Colonel Thomas Kilby Smith (1820–1887), USA.

ABOVE: *Professor Lowe's Balloon Eagle in a Storm.* Wood engraving, undated. For the first two years of the war, Professor Thaddeus S. C. Lowe (1832–1913) was the principal driving force behind the U.S. Army's new Balloon Corps, which provided intelligence on troop movements and geographical information required for making good maps. Balloons and balloonists were particularly vulnerable to the unexpected whims of nature, such as the furious thunderstorm that struck the contending armies on the Virginia Peninsula May 30, 1862.

OPPOSITE: *The Civil War in America: Destruction of the Confederate Flotilla off Memphis.* Engraving, based on a drawing by Frank Vizetelly, from the *Illustrated London News,* July 19, 1862. "Memphis . . . the proud city that would never surrender to the Northern vandal is now garrisoned by Federal soldiers," Vizetelly wrote in his accompanying dispatch. "Commodore Davis, who commands the national flotilla, need scarcely have wasted words in writing his despatch. 'I came, I saw, I conquered,' would have expressed everything."

MAY

1 2 3 4 5 6 7 8 9 10 11 12 13 14 15 16 17 18 19 20 21 22 23 24 25 26 **27** 28 29 30 **31**

Confederate troops will evacuate the disease-ridden city, which Union troops will enter on May 31.[17]

MAY 27, 1862: At Confederate headquarters on the Virginia Peninsula, General Joseph Johnston receives what later proves to be inaccurate intelligence that forty-one thousand reinforcements are on their way from Fredericksburg to join McClellan's army, and he decides that he must strike now against that portion of the Army of the Potomac that is encamped south of the Chickahominy. Johnston formulates a plan of attack that will require close coordination among three columns that will be separated by swamps and forests; but he will fail to provide his generals with explicit written orders. Meanwhile, the effects of a drenching rain May 26–27 will be compounded by a furious and lethal thunderstorm the evening of May 30; lightning strikes kill men in both the opposing armies. The Chickahominy rises, threatening the bridges that are the only avenues by which Union forces north of the river can cross over and support their comrades on the other side.[18]

MAY 31, 1862: From first to last, confusion plays havoc with the execution of General Johnston's battle plan during what will become known as the battle of Fair Oaks (Seven Pines), Virginia. It begins hours late, when one Confederate column, under D. H. Hill, pushes across swampy ground and into a storm of Union fire. "[M]y horse's head was blown off, and falling so suddenly as to catch my foot and leg under the horse,"

Lieutenant Colonel Bryan Grimes, of the Fourth Carolina, will later report. "The regiment seeing me fall, supposed I was killed or wounded, and began to falter and waver, when I, still penned to the earth by the weight of my horse, waved my sword and shouted forward! forward! Whereupon some of my men came to my assistance. . . . [S]eeing the flag upon the ground, the flag-bearer and all the color-guard being killed or wounded, I grasped it and called upon them to charge! Which they did, and together with others captured the fortifications." Forced to fall back several times during this day of disjointed attacks and seesaw action, Union troops are reinforced in late afternoon, when the venerable and pugnacious General Edwin Sumner brings men across the swollen Chickahominy via the one bridge that is still viable. As Sumner's troops repel an attack by Confederates under Brigadier General William H. C. Whiting, their fire hits General Johnston, who is watching Whiting's progress from a knoll well within the Northerners' range. Seriously wounded, Johnston will be taken back to Richmond for medical care. Major General Gustavus W. Smith assumes interim command of the Confederate troops on the Peninsula.[19]

JUNE 1862

JUNE 1, 1862: As the battle of Fair Oaks (Seven Pines) concludes with an ineffective assault by Confederates under James Longstreet, Jefferson Davis "temporarily" relieves Robert E. Lee of his duties as chief military adviser to the Confederate president and places him in command of the troops protecting Richmond — a force now officially known as the Army of Northern Virginia. Among Lee's first priorities: improving the system for moving food and other needed supplies to the field (while urging greater attention to the care and preservation of these limited materials) and the overall well-being of his troops — some of whom have been reduced to trapping and eating rats. Faced with the need to improve fortifications, Lee, like Johnston before him, encounters a problem: "Our people are opposed to work," he will write Davis on June 5. "Our troops, officers, Community & press, All ridicule & resist it." Yet his men buckle down to their duties when he establishes work details, and they rapidly improve the defensive environment. Lee also appoints Albert H. Campbell head of the Commission of Engineers and Draughtsmen and orders him to prepare accurate detailed maps of the area, something that both Confederate and Union forces sadly lack.[20]

JUNE 6, 1862: "The guns of the enemy!" Union naval inventor Charles Ellet shouts to the crewmen of his two vessels, *Queen of the West* and *Monarch,* as he hears the rumble of naval artillery from downstream on the Mississippi River. "Round out and follow me! Now is our chance!" His two rams — ships with iron-reinforced prows — quickly join in the battle already raging in the waters just off Memphis, Tennessee, between Commodore Charles Davis's Union flotilla of five ironclads and two rams versus Confederate captain James E. Montgomery's determined but inferior makeshift squadron of eight vessels. Thousands of people watch from shore as the battle continues for nearly two hours. Many of the spectators weep as the Union boats emerge triumphant, having either captured or knocked out of commission seven of the Confederate vessels. (The Federals suffer only one fatality from this encounter; Charles Ellet will die from his wounds two weeks later.) Now under Union control, Memphis will rapidly become a refuge for runaway slaves and a humming center of commerce, both legal and illegal. An estimated $20 million in black-market goods will flow through the city and into Confederate hands over the next two years.[21]

JUNE 8–9, 1862: Stonewall Jackson's legendary Shenandoah Valley Campaign, which kept Union troops occupied that might have otherwise reinforced McClellan's army on the Peninsula, comes to a close with Confederate victories at Cross Keys and Port Republic. Within a week, an exchange of letters between Jackson and Robert E. Lee will result in a decision to bring Jackson and his "foot cavalry" back to join the forces protecting Richmond. "To be efficacious the movement must be secret," Lee will write to Jackson on June 16. "Let me know the force you can bring and be careful to guard from friends

ABOVE: *The Burial of Latane.* Engraving by Campbell A. Gilchrist after a painting by William Dickinson Washington (1833–1870), undated. Shortly after Captain William Latane's death during Stuart's ride around McClellan's forces on the Virginia Peninsula, the *Southern Literary Messenger* published a poem by John Reuben Thompson (1823–1873) that included the lines "The aged matron and the faithful slave / Approached with reverent feet the hero's lowly grave." Inspired by the poem, the painting became an icon of the "Lost Cause" after the war.

LEFT: *Gen. J. E. B. Stuart's Raid Around McClellan, June 1862.* Reproduction of a painting by Henry Alexander Ogden (1856–1936), ca. 1900. Dubbed "the eyes of the army" by Robert E. Lee because of the invaluable intelligence he provided to Confederate commanders, James Ewell Brown (Jeb) Stuart (1833–1864) was adept at "seizing the moment"—as he did during his famous ride around the Army of the Potomac on the Virginia Peninsula.

JUNE

1 2 3 4 5 6 7 8 9 10 11 **12 13 14 15 16 17** 18 **19** 20 21 22 23 24 **25** 26 27 28 29 30

---

and foes your purpose and your intention of personally leaving the Valley. The country is full of spies and our plans are immediately carried to the enemy."[22]

JUNE 12–16, 1862: On the Virginia Peninsula, Brigadier General James Ewell Brown (Jeb) Stuart exceeds Robert E. Lee's orders to scout the Union's left flank and instead leads twelve hundred Confederate cavalrymen on a reconnaissance completely around Union lines, "routing the enemy in a series of skirmishes, taking a number of prisoners, and destroying and capturing stores to a large amount," as General Lee will write in a congratulatory order several days later. "Having most successfully accomplished its object, the expedition recrossed the Chickahominy almost in the presence of the enemy with the same coolness and address that marked every step of its progress, and with the loss of but one man, the lamented Captain [William] Latane." With this deed, Stuart and his men secure a place in the history books; and circumstances surrounding the burial of Captain Latane will inspire a poem and a painting that will live long in Southern mythology.[23]

JUNE 17, 1862: Suffering from a persistent throat ailment, General P. G. T. Beauregard relinquishes his command of the Confederacy's Western Department to his subordinate, the energetic but quarrelsome General Braxton Bragg. Beauregard deems this action temporary; but President Davis, who has become critical of Beauregard's performance as department

commander (particularly his retreat from the battlefield at Shiloh and his evacuation of Corinth, Mississippi), will make the change permanent. In September Beauregard will return to Charleston, where he led Confederate troops as the war began, as commander of the Department of South Carolina and Georgia. *In Washington,* the U.S. Congress passes the Land Grant College Act, also called the First Morrill Act, after its sponsor, Congressman Justin Smith Morrill of Vermont. One of the most important pieces of educational legislation in United States history, the bill transfers public lands — mostly in the West — to all states loyal to the Union. Colleges devoted to "agriculture and the mechanic arts" are to be built with money accumulated from selling these lands.[24]

JUNE 19, 1862: President Lincoln signs into law a measure prohibiting slavery in the territories of the United States. There is no question of compensation to those people in the territories who might currently be slaveholders, for Republicans believe that slavery has never been valid outside the established states in which it already existed. More conservative members of Congress are not comfortable with what they view as another emancipationist measure; the vote on the bill was strictly along party lines — Republicans yea, Democrats and border state representatives nay.[25]

JUNE 25, 1862: The first wartime Union League is established in Pekin, Illinois, providing a template for many other

Rebels Leaving Mechanicsville. Union Batteries Shelling the Village. Pencil and Chinese white drawing by Alfred R. Waud, May 24, 1862. Driven from Mechanicsville by Union troops under Brigadier General William F. ("Baldy") Smith on May 24, 1862, Lee's Confederates were unsuccessful in an attempt to retake the village on June 26.

JUNE

1 2 3 4 5 6 7 8 9 10 11 12 13 14 15 16 17 18 19 20 21 22 23 24 25 **26 27** 28 29 30

such leagues that will form in the North over the next year. Complete with publication boards, the Leagues will seek to bolster Northern morale and faith in the Union cause and counteract the activities of Copperheads, or Peace Democrats, and the subversive plans (real and rumored) of clandestine organizations, such as the Knights of the Golden Circle, that are sympathetic to the Confederacy.[26] *On the Virginia Peninsula,* one day before Robert E. Lee plans to embark on an offensive, a Union reconnaissance-in-force dispatched from the main body of the Army of the Potomac south of the Chickahominy River sparks a lively engagement at Oak Grove, a premature opening encounter in what will become known as the Seven Days Campaign. The following day, Lee will attack Brigadier General Fitz John Porter's Union Fifth Corps north of the river at Mechanicsville. Even though Federal troops manage to repulse that attack (which suffers from sluggish action by Stonewall Jackson), Major General George McClellan will order Porter's troops to pull back to Gaines' Mill.[27]

JUNE 26, 1862: President Lincoln consolidates several Union forces, creating a new force, the Army of Virginia, and placing it under the command of Major General John Pope. He directs this new force to "operate in such manner as, while protecting western Virginia and the national Capitol from danger or insult, it shall in the speediest manner attack and overcome the rebel forces under [Stonewall] Jackson and [Richard] Ewell, threaten the enemy in the direction of Charlottesville, and

render the most effective aid to relieve General McClellan and capture Richmond."[28]

JUNE 27, 1862: Amazed by the retreat of Union forces north of the Chickahominy (see June 25, 1862), Lee strikes again. Leading some fifty-seven thousand men, he hits Union general Fitz John Porter's reinforced thirty-five-thousand-man Fifth Corps at the battle of Gaines' Mill (First Cold Harbor) — while McClellan and seventy thousand troops remain south of the river, tied down, McClellan believes, by a far superior force (in fact, he faces some twenty-five thousand Confederates). After nine hours of vicious fighting observed by Jefferson Davis and other prominent Confederate figures from behind Rebel lines, the Confederates are victorious at Gaines' Mill. This costly Union defeat and his own supposed predicament completely unnerve McClellan. "I have lost this battle because my force was too small," he will write to Secretary of War Stanton on June 28. "The government must not and cannot hold me responsible for the result. . . . this Government has not sustained this army." As Lee pursues him, through engagements at Savage's Station (June 29) and Glendale (Frayser's Farm, June 30), McClellan will determine to end his campaign to take Richmond. In the meantime, both sides pay heavily in blood: all told, some thirty-six thousand soldiers (twenty thousand Confederate, sixteen thousand Union) will be killed, wounded, or declared missing during the Seven Days Campaign. Writing to his wife on June 29, regimental surgeon

5th U.S. Cavalry Charge at Gaines' Mill, 27th June 1862. Reproduction of a painting by William B. T. Trego (1859–1909), published in *The Army and Navy of the United States from the Period of the Revolution to the Present Day,* by William Walton, 1899, Vol. 1.

Spencer Glasgow Welch, of the Thirteenth South Carolina Volunteers, will tell of huge numbers of wounded. "Not only are the houses full, but even the yards are covered with them. There are so many that most of them are much neglected. The people of Richmond are hauling them away as fast as possible." Many of the Union injured will be taken to Washington by boats with "every deck, every berth and every square inch of room covered with wounded men," as U.S. Sanitary Commission nurse Katharine Wormeley writes to her mother in June, "even the stairs and gangways and guards filled." Eighteen new hospitals will be established in the capital city during and in the aftermath of the Seven Days Campaign, some of them in such makeshift quarters as Caspari's Hotel on Capitol Hill, the synagogue on Eighth Street, and a former Republican Party campaign headquarters.[29]

JULY 1862

JULY 1, 1862: At the battle of Malvern Hill, Virginia, which ends the Seven Days Campaign, Robert E. Lee makes his final attempt to deal George B. McClellan's Army of the Potomac a lethal blow — but the Confederate attacks, launched against well-placed Union lines, are neither well planned nor well coordinated. Rebel troops march over open fields under lacerating and unrelenting fire from Union army artillery and Flag Officer Louis M. Goldsborough's river-based gunboats. "It was not war," General D. H. Hill will later declare, recalling the scene as shells tore into his Confederate troops, "it was murder." McClellan rejects suggestions from some of his officers that he take advantage of this bloody victory and renew the drive toward Richmond. He continues his retreat to Harrison's Landing, where navy gunboats can protect the Union camps and communications. The Peninsula Campaign, upon which McClellan embarked with both undermining caution and overweening confidence, has failed. As President Lincoln's dissatisfaction with McClellan's generalship increases, Union civilians seek someone to blame for the campaign's failure: Republicans tend to blame McClellan; many Democrats zero in on Secretary of War Stanton. In the Confederacy, citizens and soldiers breathe a sigh of relief. "Lee has turned the tide," Confederate war department clerk John Jones writes in his diary. Lee and his Army of Northern Virginia will henceforth remain central to Southern hopes — including the hope that the European Powers will recognize the Confederate States

Private Edwin Francis Jemison (d. 1862), CSA, a soldier in the Second Louisiana Infantry, was one of 869 Confederate soldiers and 314 Federals killed at the Battle of Malvern Hill.

Mount Pleasant Hospitals, Washington, DC. Color lithograph by Charles Magnus, 1862. Hospitals were relatively scarce when the Civil War started; as the war dragged on and tens of thousands of men fell ill or became battle-field casualties, both sides established many permanent and makeshift hospital facilities. Military barracks were converted into the Mount Pleasant Hospitals in March 1862.

JULY

1 **2 3** 4 5 6 7 8 9 10 11 12 13 14 15 16 17 18 19 20 21 22 23 24 25 26 27 28 29 30 31

as an independent nation, an event that now seems tantalizingly close: the Confederacy's recent battlefield successes have impressed European governments, and the war-related dearth of Southern cotton is now causing significant layoffs among British textile workers, giving Britain added reason to intercede in the American conflict. *In Washington,* President Lincoln signs the Pacific Railroad Act, granting land and loans to corporations organized to build a railroad and telegraph line from Omaha, Nebraska, to Sacramento, California. (The first rails will be laid eastward from Sacramento in 1863.) An infinitely more painful piece of legislation, the U.S. Internal Revenue Act of 1862, also becomes law today. Establishing taxes on just about everything, from luxuries to a wide variety of professions and occupations — including, as Representative James G. Blaine notes, "bankers and pawn brokers, lawyers and horse-dealers, physicians and confectioners, commercial brokers and peddlers" — the bill will eventually raise monies that cover almost a quarter of wartime expenditures. Most of the taxes will not live long past the war; but the Bureau of Internal Revenue, also established under the act, will become a permanent fixture in American lives.[30]

JULY 2, 1862: "The question often occurred to me," author Nathaniel Hawthorne will write of a visit to Washington in July 1862, "what proportion of all these people . . . were true at heart to the Union, and what part were tainted with treasonable sympathies and wishes." It is a question that has troubled

many others since the beginning of the war (see July 9, 1861). Thus, on this day when he issues a call for three hundred thousand new volunteers, President Lincoln also signs into law the Ironclad Test Oath, by which elected or appointed government officials must swear that they have never "borne arms against the United States" and will "support and defend the Constitution." The president has already approved less stringent loyalty oaths for shipmasters headed to foreign ports, Federal government employees, and military personnel. In addition, Union military commanders require Southerners in occupied territory, or suspected Confederate sympathizers in the border states, to take loyalty oaths. With his eye on cooperation and future reconstruction, Lincoln will later order that these oaths require only a promise of future loyalty. In 1867, the Supreme Court will declare the Ironclad Oath unconstitutional.[31]

JULY 3, 1862: As Union forces are increasingly plagued by Confederate guerrillas and other irregulars, General Ulysses S. Grant, in command of the District of West Tennessee, issues the following order:

The system of guerrilla warfare now being prosecuted by some troops organized under the authority of the so-called Southern Confederacy, and others without such authority, being so pernicious to the welfare of the community where it is carried on, and it being within the power of

A Jerilla [sic] / A Deserter. Pencil drawing by Alfred R. Waud, between 1860 and 1865. Plagued by guerrillas who harassed army columns, attacked civilians sympathetic to the Union, and often behaved viciously toward African Americans attempting to aid the Union army, Department of West Tennessee commander Ulysses S. Grant issued stern guidelines for coping with such irregular warfare.

"I shall do nothing in malice.

What I deal with is too vast

for malicious dealing."

—ABRAHAM LINCOLN,
JULY 28, 1862

the communities to suppress this system, it is ordered that wherever loss is sustained by the Government, collections shall be made by seizure of a sufficient amount of personal property from persons in the immediate neighborhood sympathizing with the rebellion to remunerate the government for all loss and expense of collection.

Persons acting as guerrillas without organization and without uniform to distinguish them from private citizens are not entitled to treatment as prisoners of war when caught, and will not receive such treatment.[32]

JULY 4, 1862: The people of Boston open a Discharged Soldiers' Home for honorably discharged Union soldiers who are suffering due to wounds or illness stemming from their army service and who need help finding jobs or reestablishing their community ties. One year later, the home's first annual report will note that it is a "model only, on a scale far too small, and one which will soon be found, as indeed it already is, inadequate to the proper care of the disabled Soldiers who are likely to be thrown upon the community for support" (see also March 3, 1865). *At Himrods Corners, New York,* Frederick Douglass delivers a Fourth of July speech in which he criticizes Lincoln's conservative approach to emancipation — and lambastes General McClellan: "I feel quite sure that this country will yet come to the conclusion that Geo. B. McClellan is either a cold blooded Traitor, or that he is an unmitigated military Impostor."[33]

JULY 8, 1862: When President Lincoln visits the Union encampments at Harrison's Landing, Virginia, to personally observe the state of the Army of the Potomac after its defeat on the Peninsula, General McClellan hands the president a long, unsolicited letter, in which he expresses his views on the conduct of the war. "It should not be at all a war upon population, but against armed forces and political organizations. Neither confiscation of property, political executions of persons, territorial organization of States, or forcible abolition of slavery should be contemplated for a minute. . . ." The president does not answer the letter. But it is clear that the Union's experience thus far in the war has caused him to contemplate more forceful policies. On July 28, he will answer at length a letter protesting Union policies in occupied Louisiana. "What would you do in my position? Would you drop the war where it is? Or, would you prosecute it in future, with elder-stalk squirts, charged with rose water? Would you deal lighter blows rather than heavier ones? Would you give up the contest, leaving any available means unapplied. . . . I shall do *all* I can to save the government, which is my sworn duty as well as my personal inclination. I shall do nothing in malice. What I deal with is too vast for malicious dealing."[34]

JULY 11, 1862: "McClellan is an imbecile if not a traitor," Radical Republican senator Zachariah Chandler writes to his wife. "He has virtually lost the army of the Potomac." A powerful member of the Joint Committee on the Conduct

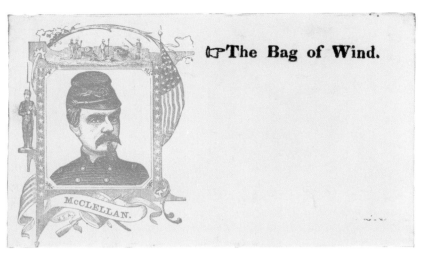

☞ The Bag of Wind.

McCLELLAN.

Although well thought of by many of his Army of the Potomac soldiers, Major General George B. McClellan was a source of increasing aggravation to some of his subordinate officers, most Radical Republicans, and other Northern civilians eager for fewer excuses and more victories. McClellan's detractors might have snapped up copies of this illustrated envelope to both enclose and advertise their criticism of the general.

Major General Henry W. Halleck (1815–1872), USA. Dubbed "Old Brains" because of his intelligence and prewar intellectual pursuits, Halleck proved to be an undistinguished battlefield commander and a disappointing general in chief.

JULY

1 2 3 4 5 6 7 8 9 10 11 12 **13 14 15** 16 17 18 19 20 21 22 23 24 25 26 27 28 29 30 31

of the War, Chandler has won approval to use heretofore restricted testimony taken by that committee in open congressional debate. Tomorrow, he will criticize McClellan on the Senate floor. *On the other end of Pennsylvania Avenue,* President Lincoln appoints Major General Henry W. Halleck "to command the whole land forces of the United States as General-in-Chief," a post that has been vacant since the president relieved McClellan of that responsibility months before. Learning of the appointment, McClellan will write to his wife and others that he regards the appointment of "a man whom I know by experience to be my inferior" to be a "slap in the face." Halleck, meanwhile, telegraphs the president that he will travel to the capital as soon as he has had a conference with the general who will succeed him in command of the Department of the Mississippi, Ulysses S. Grant.[35]

JULY 13, 1862: On the same day that President Lincoln receives a "manifesto" from border state congressmen rejecting his proposed policy of financial compensation for slaveholders whose slaves are emancipated, Secretary of State William Seward and Secretary of the Navy Gideon Welles accompany the chief executive on a carriage ride to Oak Hill Cemetery, where they are to attend interment services for Secretary of War Edwin Stanton's infant son. During the ride, Lincoln informs the two cabinet members, as Welles will later record in his journal, that "in case the rebels did not cease to persist in their war," he intends to issue an Emancipation Proclamation,

having reached the conclusion, after much contemplation, "that it was a military necessity absolutely essential for the salvation of the Union, that we must free the slaves or be ourselves subdued." *In Murfreesboro, Tennessee,* Brigadier General Nathan Bedford Forrest and his Confederate cavalry stage a spectacularly successful raid, capturing Brigadier General Thomas L. Crittenden's entire 1,040-man Federal garrison, its weapons, and $1 million in supplies. Forrest will continue his disruption of Union forces in middle Tennessee through the end of the month. *To the north, in Kentucky,* Confederate colonel John Hunt Morgan and his men are in the midst of a three-week cavalry raid through the state, raising fears of pro-Confederate uprisings there and creating consternation in neighboring Ohio.[36]

JULY 14, 1862: Lincoln signs the General Pension Law, establishing the Federal pension system for men who become disabled "from causes which can be directly traced to injuries received or disease contracted while in the military service." Retroactive to March 1, 1861, the act also provides pension benefits to widows and families of military personnel killed in the war.[37]

JULY 15, 1862: The recently commissioned Confederate ironclad ram CSS *Arkansas,* captained by Lieutenant Isaac Newton Brown, battles its way down the Yazoo River, where three Union vessels are conducting a reconnaissance. Disabling

PLAN OF HOMOGRAPH.

To be made with a Sword, Tiller, Stick, Stretcher, and a Handkerchief, or Flag.

Nos.	Figure.	Position.
1st Repeater and Affirmative.		Sword in each hand extended perpendicular over the head.
2d Repeater and Negative.		Sword in each hand extended horizontally.
3d Repeater.		Hat off, left arm extended.
Preparatory.		Handkerchief or Flag spread.
Answering.		Sword waved over the head with right arm.
Numeral.		Sword in right hand extended horizontally, left arm held perpendicular over the head.
Interrogatory.		Sword in each hand waved over the head.
At the end of each complete signal.		Hands against the hips, elbows extended.

Major General Thomas C. Hindman (1828–1868), CSA. A veteran of the Mexican War, Hindman played a leading role in the Arkansas secession movement. As commander of the Trans-Mississippi Department (May–July 1862), his policies, including strict enforcement of conscription, provoked protest among local civilian authorities.

LEFT: *Plan of Homograph. To Be Made with a Sword, Tiller, Stick, Stretcher, and a Handkerchief, or Flag.* Chart in *Code of Flotilla and Boat Squadron Signals for the United States Navy,* 1861. Throughout the war, manual signaling was an essential means of communication between individual naval vessels and between ships and installations ashore. The sudden appearance of an enemy vessel, such as CSS *Arkansas* in pursuit of two Union vessels, often sent signalers scrambling.

OPPOSITE: *Parole Camp, Annapolis, Md.* Color lithograph by Sachse & Co., May 1864. Based on the French *parole d'honneur,* the Civil War system of paroling prisoners sometimes involved sending captives to a special camp run by their own army until formal prisoner exchange was completed. Discipline could be lax. "The guard that do duty over us are raw Pennsylvania Militia and seem disposed to grant us . . . the largest degree of liberty," Union soldier Warren H. Freeman wrote to his father after his capture by Confederates at Gettysburg and subsequent parole. "Consequently some of the men have gone home, others work for the farmers in the neighborhood at haying, etc."

USS *Carondelet, Arkansas* sustains heavy damage as it pursues USS *Tyler* and *Queen of the West* out of the Yazoo and into the Mississippi River — where Brown runs into a thirty-vessel Union fleet anchored above Vicksburg, blockading the city. Initially unprepared for battle, the Union ships soon begin firing, repeatedly hitting *Arkansas* as the Confederate vessel moves past them (scoring hits on several Union ships). With ten of his crewmen dead and sixteen wounded, Brown finally gets the battered *Arkansas* to relative safety at a wharf protected by Vicksburg's guns, where it is met by wildly cheering soldiers and civilians from the city. Yet the duel is not over. After nightfall, Admiral David Farragut, enraged that *Arkansas* got past his fleet, leads several ships in a run past Vicksburg, targeting the ironclad (while other vessels, under Charles Henry Davis, give them covering fire). But this, and a follow-up attempt on July 22, are unsuccessful; although it sustains additional damage, the Confederate ironclad remains afloat. "I need not say to you," Secretary of the Navy Gideon Welles wires the two Union commanders, "that the escape [of the *Arkansas*] and its attending circumstances have been the cause of serious mortification to the Department and the country." *In Cincinnati,* five days of growing racial tensions explode into a riot as a mob of perhaps a thousand white men rages through the black section of the city, unrestrained by police (many of whom have rushed to Lexington, Kentucky, to defend that city against a possible Confederate raid; see July 13, 1862). Black citizens stay under cover as the rampaging whites take control

of the streets; it will take a full day for authorities to reestablish calm. "The difficulty . . . grew out of a difference between white and colored hands upon steamboats," the Cincinnati *Daily Enquirer* will report on July 18, "the latter working for smaller wages than the former, and therefore being preferred by the employers."[38]

JULY 17, 1862: After acrimonious debate, the U.S. Congress passes the Second Confiscation Act. Among its provisions are freedom for the slaves of all those who support the Rebellion when those slaves come within Union control, and an authorization for the president to "employ as many persons of African descent as he may deem necessary and proper for the suppression of this rebellion." Congress also authorizes the president to provide for colonization "in some tropical country beyond the limits of the United States, of such persons of the African race, made free by the provisions of this act, as may be willing to emigrate." Later in the war, this act will serve to inspire a growing conflict between Congress and the president over which more properly should have authority over slavery and reconstruction measures. *Congress also approves* "An Act to amend the Act calling for the militia to execute the Laws of the Union" (Militia Act), which states, in part: "the President . . . is hereby authorized to receive into the service of the United States, for the purpose of constructing intrenchments, or performing camp service or any other labor, or any military or naval service for which they may be found competent, persons

of African descent."[39] *West of the Mississippi River,* Confederate Trans-Mississippi Department commander Major General Thomas C. Hindman issues an order that will be the catalyst for many brutal encounters between regular and irregular forces in Arkansas after Union forces take Little Rock in 1863. The order states, in part:

> For the more effectual annoyance of the enemy upon our rivers and in our mountains and woods all citizens of this district who are not subject to conscription are called upon to organize themselves into independent companies of mounted men or infantry . . . arming and equipping themselves, and to serve in that part of the district to which they belong. . . . Their duty will be to cut off federal pickets, scouts, foraging parties, and trains, and to kill pilots and others on gunboats and transports, attacking them day and night, and using the greatest vigor in their movements.[40]

JULY 20, 1862: Major General William T. Sherman arrives to take command at Memphis, Tennessee, and surprises its citizens with his generous policies toward this former Confederate city. Sherman will fast become perturbed, however, over the brisk commerce in cotton and other goods eagerly sought by the Union that sends funds flowing into Confederate coffers, and by the smuggling of salt and other materials from Memphis into Confederate-held territory. "I have no hesitation in saying that the possessing of the Mississippi River by us is an enormous advantage to our enemy," he will write in August, "for by it and the commercial spirit of our people . . . the enemy, get directly or indirectly all the means necessary to carry on the war." Contrabands seeking refuge, guerrilla activity, and increasingly strained relations with the Memphis press will be other vexing problems Sherman will face as commander at Memphis.[41]

JULY 22, 1862: Union general John Dix and Confederate general D. H. Hill agree on an exchange cartel for prisoners of war — now, after more than one year of warfare, numbering in the thousands and presenting both governments with problems of proper housing and care. The cartel provides for the parole and exchange of prisoners and bases the rate of exchange on a prisoner's rank. A parole, to be put in effect within ten days after capture, permits a prisoner to return to his own lines, provided that he does not take up arms until he is officially exchanged. Most prisoners will be returned with relative speed to their own side under this system, which will remain effective until late spring of 1863, when fundamental disagreements between the two sides, most particularly regarding the treatment of black Union soldiers, will cause it to break down. *In Washington,* Lincoln reads his draft of the preliminary Emancipation Proclamation to his cabinet (see also July 13, 1862). As the president has anticipated, reaction is mixed: Secretary of War Stanton and Attorney General

LEFT: *A Short History of Braxton Bragg.* Booklet in a series designed to be included in cigarette packs, 1888. A West Point graduate and veteran of the Seminole and Mexican wars, Bragg (1817–1876), CSA, had a difficult personality that alienated many of his subordinate officers. A friend of President Davis's, he was placed in command of the Army of Tennessee in June 1862.

RIGHT: Belle Boyd (1843–1900). Boyd's final undercover adventure, sailing for England in 1864 to deliver letters from President Davis, ended in her capture, imprisonment, and release. She later married her captor.

OPPOSITE: *Destruction of the Rebel Ram "Arkansas": By the United States Gunboat "Essex," on the Mississippi River, near Baton Rouge, August 4th [sic], 1862.* Hand-colored lithograph by Currier & Ives, ca. 1862. Although *Essex* and other Union vessels were bearing down on CSS *Arkansas*, this print exaggerates their role in the Confederate ship's demise.

JULY

1 2 3 4 5 6 7 8 9 10 11 12 13 14 15 16 17 18 19 20 21 22 **23** 24 **25** 26 27 28 **29** 30 31

Bates firmly endorse immediate release of this hallmark decree (Bates insisting that the freed slaves be transported out of the country). Secretary of the Treasury Chase, heretofore a firm advocate of emancipation, counsels a less radical move; and Postmaster General Blair firmly opposes the proclamation, fearing its effect on the fall elections and on Unionists in the border states. Yet the president has already told his advisers that he is determined to take this step. He does, however, listen to an argument put forth by Secretary of State Seward. At this time, when Union forces have suffered reverses and there is bubbling political unrest in the North, the secretary of state advises Lincoln not to issue the proclamation until it can be backed up by a substantial military victory, lest it be viewed "as the last measure of an exhausted government, a cry for help." Lincoln agrees to wait.[42]

JULY 23, 1862: In the first phase of a planned invasion of Kentucky, Confederate general Braxton Bragg begins the largest Confederate railroad movement of the war, sending thirty thousand men via a roundabout rail route of 776 miles from Mississippi to Chattanooga, Tennessee.[43]

JULY 25, 1862: The Union's new general in chief, Henry W. Halleck (see July 11, 1862), arrives at Harrison's Landing, Virginia, to discuss with General McClellan the future of the Army of the Potomac. After observing the strategic situation, Halleck will write to his wife that McClellan "does

not understand strategy and should never plan a campaign." Accepting McClellan's estimate that Lee has two hundred thousand men (in fact, the Confederate general has substantially fewer than a hundred thousand), Halleck is concerned that Lee will be able to concentrate on and destroy, in turn, McClellan's scattered forces and John Pope's newly formed Army of Virginia. In fact, Lee does have something of that nature in mind: Stonewall Jackson and his men are now heading in Pope's direction.[44]

JULY 29, 1862: Eighteen-year-old Belle Boyd is captured by Union forces near Warrenton, Virginia. Accused of being a spy and courier for the Confederates, she will be sent to the Old Capitol Prison in Washington — the same facility that recently housed Mrs. Rose O'Neal Greenhow, a celebrated Washington hostess whose many connections in the city had allowed her to warn Confederate forces in July 1861 of the Union's impending attack at First Bull Run. (On June 2, 1862, after signing a pledge that she would not go north of the Potomac River, Greenhow was released from prison and sent south.) During Stonewall Jackson's recent Shenandoah Campaign, Boyd provided similar useful information to Confederate troops, gleaned from artful eavesdropping on Union officers. Federal authorities lack sufficient evidence to hold her, however, and on August 28 she will be released. By now, both sides have learned to fully appreciate the value of accurate intelligence; both are engaged in spying and espionage. Enemies caught in the act are generally impris-

oned — but some are executed, including the Union's Timothy Webster, hanged in Richmond, Virginia, on April 29, 1862, and the Confederacy's Sam Davis, executed in Giles County, Tennessee, on November 27, 1863.[45]

JULY 30, 1862: In honor of his decisive victory at New Orleans, David Farragut becomes the first U.S. flag officer to be commissioned rear admiral.[46]

AUGUST 1862

AUGUST 1, 1862: *The Liberator* publishes prominent African American John Rock's observations on President Lincoln's policies regarding emancipation: "I have never doubted but that the President was on the side of freedom and humanity, but I confess I do not understand how it is, that when the national life has been assailed, he has not availed himself of all the powers given him; and, more especially, why he has not broken every yoke, and let the oppressed go free. . . . We all know that emancipation, if early proclaimed, would not only have saved many precious lives, but the nation itself. Why then delay, when delays are dangerous, and may prove fatal?"[47]

AUGUST 6, 1862: Suffering from severe engine trouble, the celebrated ironclad CSS *Arkansas* (see July 15, 1862) is heavily damaged in a battle with four Union vessels during a Confederate attempt to wrest the Louisiana state capital of Baton Rouge from the Union forces that have occupied the city since May 9. Before abandoning ship, its crew sets *Arkansas* ablaze — bringing to a fiery end the twenty-three-day career of the Rebel warship, the last of its kind on the Mississippi River.[48]

AUGUST 9, 1862: Having thwarted McClellan's attempt to take Richmond, Robert E. Lee now aims to recover lost territory and supplies and more effectively secure the area north of the Confederate capital, with its vital railroads to the Shenandoah Valley. The first Union contingent in his sights is Major General John Pope's Army of Virginia. Today, twenty-four thousand Confederates under Stonewall Jackson encounter elements of Pope's army — some nine thousand Federals led by Nathaniel Banks — at the battle of Cedar Mountain. "At first, we sustained a fire from the rebels only in the woods, which was not very severe, but soon the enemy made their appearance in an oblique line and commenced a cross fire which was perfectly fearful," Lieutenant Charles F. Morse of the Second Massachusetts Infantry will later record in his diary. "Our poor men were dropping on every side, yet not one of them flinched but kept steadily at his work. . . . I never was more surprised in my life than when I heard the order to

1 2 3 4 5 6 7 8 9 **10** 11 12 13 **14** 15 16 17 18 19 20 21 22 23 24 25 26 27 28 29 30 31

retreat." The battle, which continues well into the night, is a Confederate victory. But before Jackson withdraws to embark on a singular mission (see August 25, 1862), on August 10 both sides hastily bury their dead and tend to the wounded. "A house with quite a large yard had been taken for hospital use," Morse will write, "the scene in and about it was very painful. Soldiers lying in all directions, with every variety of wounds." Among those tending the wounded is Clara Barton, who nurses both Union wounded and Confederate prisoners.[49]

AUGUST 10, 1862: Riding from around Fredericksburg in the middle of Texas, and heading for Mexico, more than sixty Unionist Texans, recent immigrants from Germany, are overtaken by ninety-five Confederate soldiers at the Nueces River. In the pitched battle that follows, two soldiers and about thirty Unionists are killed. Many other real and suspected Unionists in the Fredericksburg, Texas, area will be arrested, hanged, or killed by other means in the following weeks before relative calm returns to the region. "Nowhere else in the Confederacy," historian William C. Davis will later write, "did the military put so many disloyal citizens to death."[50]

AUGUST 14, 1862: Two weeks after he first received the order from General in Chief Halleck (and as Lee's army closes in on Pope's Army of Virginia), General McClellan begins withdrawing his troops from Harrison's Landing, moving to

the embarkation points from which they will travel by boat to northern Virginia, where they will be in a position to assist Pope and protect the Union capital; but the transport of so many men will take time. *In the western theater,* the Confederate Heartland Campaign begins as General Edmund Kirby Smith leads ten thousand troops out of Knoxville, Tennessee, into Kentucky. *In Washington,* a deputation of black leaders headed by Edward M. Thomas, president of the Anglo-African Institute for the Encouragement of Industry and Art, visits the White House at the invitation of the president and hears a lengthy presidential discourse advocating colonization of African Americans outside the continental United States (see also December 3, 1861). "Your race are suffering, in my judgment, the greatest wrong inflicted on any people," the president says. "But even when you cease to be slaves, you are yet far removed from being placed on any equality with the white race. . . . It is better for us both, therefore, to be separated." Lincoln asks the men to recruit from twenty-five to one hundred families for a nascent colonization project in Central America, pledging government support. He does note that "one of the principal difficulties in the way of colonization is that the free colored man cannot see that his comfort would be advanced by it" — and the overwhelmingly negative reaction to his remarks at this meeting proves the truth of his assessment. "Pray tell us, is our right to a home in this country less than your own, Mr. Lincoln?" A. P. Smith, of Saddle River, New Jersey, will ask in a published reply to

Description on the back of sketch —

Soldier's dummies and quakers, left in the works at Harrison's landing

AUGUST

1 2 3 4 5 6 7 8 9 10 11 12 13 14 15 16 17 18 **19** 20 **21** **22** 23 24 25 26 27 28 29 30 31

the president. "Are you an American? So are we. Are you a patriot? So are we. Would you spurn all absurd, meddlesome, impudent propositions for your colonization in a foreign country? So do we."[51]

AUGUST 19, 1862: Horace Greeley, the influential editor of the *New York Tribune*, publishes a long open letter he has written and titled "The Prayer of the Twenty Millions," calling on Lincoln to enforce the recently passed Confiscation Act and no longer tolerate the behavior of Union officers who display what Greeley terms a "mistaken deference to Rebel slavery."

> You, Mr. President, elected as a Republican, knowing well what an abomination Slavery is, and how emphatically it is the core and essence of this atrocious Rebellion, seem never to . . . give a direction to your Military subordinates, which does not appear to have been conceived in the interest of Slavery rather than of Freedom. . . . there is not one disinterested, determined, intelligent champion of the Union cause who does not feel that attempts to put down the Rebellion and at the same time uphold its inciting cause are preposterous and futile . . . and that every hour of deference to Slavery is an hour of added and deepened peril to the Union.[52]

AUGUST 21, 1862: Responding to rumors that the Union is enlisting black soldiers in the Northern-occupied portions of Louisiana and South Carolina, Confederate army headquarters issues a general order that such "crimes and outrages" require "retaliation" in the form of "execution as a felon" of any officer of black troops who is captured.[53]

AUGUST 22, 1862: "I have just read yours of the 19th addressed to myself through the New-York Tribune," Lincoln writes to Horace Greeley, referring to the editor's pro-emancipation editorial, "The Prayer of the Twenty Millions" (see August 19, 1862).

> If there be perceptible in it an impatient and dictatorial tone, I waive it in deference to an old friend, whose heart I have always supposed to be right. As to the policy I "seem to be pursuing" as you say, I have not meant to leave any one in doubt. I would save the Union. I would save it the shortest way under the Constitution. . . . If I could save the Union without freeing *any* slave I would do it, and if I could save it by freeing *all* the slaves I would do it; and if I could save it by freeing some and leaving others alone I would also do that. . . . I have here stated my purpose according to my view of *official* duty; and I intend no modification of my oft-expressed *personal* wish that all men every where could be free.

Horace Greeley (1811–1872). Print by Armstrong & Co., 1872. One of the North's most influential editors, Greeley spoke out against monopolies, for labor unions, in support of experiments in "constructive democracy"—and against slavery.

This hand-colored 1864 print published in New York by George Whiting portrays Abraham Lincoln as determined protector of the Constitution, loyal citizens, and the Union they are defending. The legend under the art reads: "The people of these United States are the rightful masters of both Congresses and Courts, not to over-throw the Constitution, but to over-throw the men who pervert that Constitution."

AUGUST

1 2 3 4 5 6 7 8 9 10 11 12 13 14 15 16 17 18 19 20 21 22 23 **24** **25** 26 27 **28** 29 30 31

Lincoln's letter prepares the public to accept the Emancipation Proclamation, which he has still not issued.[54]

AUGUST 24, 1862: Having relinquished command of the battered CSS *Sumter,* in which he and his crew had captured or sunk some eighteen Union vessels, Confederate commerce raider Raphael Semmes takes command of a new vessel, CSS *Alabama,* which is commissioned as a cruiser in the Confederate navy today near the Azores in the Atlantic.[55]

AUGUST 25, 1862: A month after passage of the Second Confiscation Act and the Militia Act of 1862 (see July 17, 1862), which include provisions on which this action is based, the U.S. War Department authorizes Brigadier General Rufus Saxton, military governor of the South Carolina Sea Islands, to raise five regiments of black troops on the islands, with white men as officers. An important provision of this order is the specification that these troops are to receive "the same pay and rations as are allowed by law to volunteers in the service." It is with this understanding that other black regiments will be recruited until the summer of 1863. *In Virginia,* Stonewall Jackson's "foot cavalry" begin a spectacular march from below the Rappahannock River that by August 27 will bring them to the Army of Virginia's main supply depot at Manassas Junction. There, the Confederate soldiers, suffering from a dearth of their own supplies, will eat and drink, stuff everything they can carry into their knapsacks, and burn the rest. Jackson will

then withdraw from Manassas and establish lines along the Warrenton Turnpike, near the First Bull Run battlefield.[56]

AUGUST 28, 1862: General Braxton Bragg leads the thirty-thousand-man Army of Mississippi north from Chattanooga, Tennessee, and into Kentucky on a course parallel to that of Edmund Kirby Smith's smaller force (see August 14, 1862). Union general Don Carlos Buell, whose Army of the Ohio is being constantly harassed by Confederate cavalry, will only belatedly react to this Rebel incursion and leave Tennessee, following the Confederates into Kentucky. *In Virginia,* after a confused pursuit of Stonewall Jackson and his troops, a division of Union troops commanded by Rufus King approaches Jackson's concealed position, and the Confederate general decides to engage them, precipitating the battle of Groveton (Brawner's Farm), an hours-long musket-fire duel that ravages the lines of both sides. As night falls and the firing stops, Union Army of Virginia commander John Pope, believing that Jackson is retreating, determines to concentrate his forces on the elusive Confederate commander and his troops. As this occurs, another Confederate force under James Longstreet is approaching Pope's army from the west while, from his headquarters in Alexandria, Virginia, McClellan determines he cannot send troops to reinforce Pope, despite orders to the contrary from Halleck. "Pope is in a bad way," McClellan writes to his wife, "& I have not yet the force at hand to relieve him."[57]

Toward a New Birth of Freedom

Major General John Pope (1822–1892), USA. Steel engraving from *The Southern Rebellion, Being a History of the United States from the Commencement of President Buchanan's Administration to the Inauguration of General Ulysses S. Grant as President Grant*, 1870.

Circular panoramic view of the Second Bull Run battlefield by French artist Theodore Poilpot. Illustration in *A Comprehensive Sketch of the Battle of Manassas, or Second Battle of Bull Run*, 1886.

AUGUST 29–30, 1862: Just over one year after the war's first major battle, the Federal defeat at First Bull Run, the Union suffers another humiliating loss at Second Bull Run, as Robert E. Lee continues his successful campaign against John Pope's Army of Virginia. Throughout the two-day battle, Pope makes a series of misjudgments that will bring his Civil War battlefield service to an inglorious end. Beginning with the erroneous conviction that he has trapped Stonewall Jackson, and continuing with his failure to believe General Fitz John Porter's report that thirty thousand Confederates under James Longstreet have arrived on the battlefield, Pope ends the first day of the battle by mistaking Confederate moves to consolidate their lines as evidence that the Rebels are retreating; his report to Washington that his troops have won the battle proves spectacularly inaccurate. (Meanwhile, General McClellan continues to resist sending Pope reinforcements, now informing General in Chief Halleck that 120,000 Rebels are advancing to attack Washington.) August 30 finds Lee's army still in line of battle and full of fight. A day of ferocious Rebel-yell-punctuated combat will conclude with Pope's army in full retreat, saved from complete disaster only by stubborn rear-guard action. As the Federals pause and regroup near Centreville (while Stonewall Jackson and his tired troops slog through rain and mud to occupy a position at nearby Chantilly and prepare to strike Pope again), Pope promises "as desperate a fight as I can force our men to stand up to" in a dispatch to Halleck. He also asks the general in chief an unsettling question: "I should like to know whether you feel secure about Washington should this army be destroyed."[58]

AUGUST 30, 1862: Edmund Kirby Smith's Confederate force defeats a sixty-five-hundred-man Union garrison at Richmond, Kentucky. After the surviving Federal troops withdraw toward Louisville, Smith continues on to Lexington and the state capital of Frankfort. [59]

SEPTEMBER 1862

SEPTEMBER 1, 1862: In a driving rainstorm, Stonewall Jackson initiates a fierce firefight with Pope's Army of Virginia at the battle of Chantilly, an encounter that becomes a soggy stalemate in which two popular Union generals, Isaac Stevens and Phil Kearny, are killed. Shortly after the battle, Pope is ordered to fall back toward Washington. While the Federals retreat, Secretary of War Edwin Stanton calls for volunteer nurses to aid the wounded strewn along their way. Many of the male volunteers behave abysmally; but the women, led by Clara Barton, perform admirably — even as, once again, a Confederate army threatens Washington.[60]

General Kearney's [sic] Gallant Charge, at the Battle of Chantilly, Va., 1st of September 1862. Color lithograph by Augustus Tholey, 1867. Called "the bravest man I ever saw, and a perfect soldier" by former Union general in chief Winfield Scott, General Philip Kearny added to the esprit de corps of his men by having them wear a distinctive red "Kearny patch." "You are marked men," he said; "you must be ever in the front." Riding up to investigate a rumored gap in Federal lines, Kearny was killed at the battle of Chantilly.

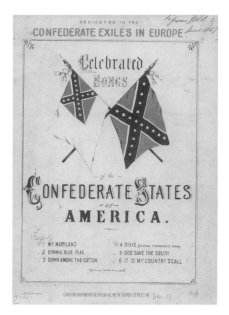

Celebrated Songs of the Confederate States of America. Sheet music cover published in London, ca. 1862. As shown, No. 1 in this series of Southern favorites is "My Maryland." Yet despite the many Confederate sympathizers within its borders, Maryland remained with the Union.

SEPTEMBER

1 **2** 3 4 **5** 6 **7** **8** 9 10 11 12 13 14 15 16 17 18 19 20 21 22 23 24 25 26 27 28 29 30

SEPTEMBER 2, 1862: Over the vigorous objections of Secretary of War Stanton and Secretary of the Treasury Chase, Lincoln reluctantly gives George McClellan command of the Union forces in Virginia and surrounding Washington — including Pope's Army of Virginia. (Pope will soon be transferred to the West.) In an amazingly short time, McClellan will reorganize and revitalize the troops under his command. Although the general has displayed minimal aggression in the field, "he excels in making others ready to fight," Lincoln will observe to his secretary, John Hay.[61]

SEPTEMBER 5, 1862: Calculating that it will take time to restore the strength and morale of Union forces surrounding Washington and determined to maintain the initiative despite the fatigue of his army, Robert E. Lee writes to President Davis: "This army is about entering Maryland, with a view of affording the people of that State an opportunity of liberating themselves. Whatever success may attend that effort, I hope at any rate to annoy and harass the enemy." His Army of Northern Virginia soon begins to cross the Potomac River.

SEPTEMBER 7, 1862: Robert E. Lee issues a proclamation to the people of Maryland in which he outlines "wrongs and outrages" they have suffered at Union hands. To rescue them from this intolerable situation, "our army has come among you, and is prepared to assist you with the power of its arms in regaining the rights of which you have been despoiled."

This is a prospect that holds little appeal, however, for the overwhelmingly Unionist population of western Maryland, where Lee's troops are encamped. *To the northeast,* the *New York Times* asks a question that is reverberating throughout the Union shocked by a series of battlefield losses: "Of *what use* are all these terrible sacrifices? Shall we have nothing but defeat to show for all our valor?"[62]

SEPTEMBER 8, 1862: After leading elements of the Army of the Potomac out of Washington on September 5, George McClellan has established headquarters in Rockville, Maryland, from which he writes General in Chief Halleck that he does not yet have adequate intelligence about the disposition of Lee's forces to determine a course of action. "As soon as I find out where to strike," he declares, "I will be after them without an hour's delay." *Twenty-five miles away,* Robert E. Lee writes to President Davis: "The present posture of affairs, in my opinion, places it in the power of the Government of the Confederate States to propose with propriety to that of the United States the recognition of our independence.... The proposal of peace would enable the people of the United States to determine at their coming elections whether they will support those who favor a prolongation of the war, or those who wish to bring it to a termination." The Union's fast-approaching fall elections are also a subject of concern (for Republicans and War Democrats) and hope (for Peace Democrats), while both the elections and the military outcome of Lee's Maryland raid are

General Robert E. Lee. Engraving by John C. McRae, after a photograph by Mathew Brady, ca. 1867. A former commandant of West Point who held the complete confidence of President Davis, Lee (1807–1870) never hesitated to seize the initiative. His first foray into Northern territory ended near Sharpsburg, Maryland, in the bloodiest one-day battle of the war.

Operatives Reading the Latest News from America — A Scene in Camp-field Free Library, Manchester. Engraving in the *Illustrated London News,* November 29, 1862. While most British aristocrats favored recognition of the Confederacy, many working-class Britons were sympathetic to the Union. In January 1863, after President Lincoln issued the final Emancipation Proclamation, the people of Manchester sent the president a letter stating, in part: "Since we have discerned . . . that the victory of the free north, in the war which has so sorely distressed us as well as afflicted you, will strike off the fetters of the slave, you have attracted our warm and earnest sympathy."

SEPTEMBER

1   2   3   4   5   6   7   8   9   **10**   11   **12**   **13**   **14**   **15**   16   17   18   19   20   21   22   23   24   25   26   27   28   29   30

of interest to the European powers, still trying to determine whether to recognize the Confederacy or otherwise intercede in the American war. "If the Federals sustain a great defeat," Prime Minister Palmerston will write, as British deliberations continue, "[their] Cause will be manifestly hopeless . . . and the iron should be struck while it is hot. If, on the other hand, they should have the best of it, we may wait . . . and see what may follow."[63]

SEPTEMBER 10, 1862: Marching out of Frederick, Maryland, the Army of Northern Virginia splits into four columns as specified in Robert E. Lee's Special Orders No. 191, issued the previous day. Three of the columns are to cooperate in a pincer movement aimed at protecting the Army of Northern Virginia's supply lines by taking the Federal garrison at Martinsburg, in western Virginia, and the larger garrison protecting the Union army arsenal at Harpers Ferry (with its large and tempting stores of clothing and munitions). Lee remains in Maryland with the balance of his troops.[64]

SEPTEMBER 12, 1862: Advance units of the Army of the Potomac enter Frederick, Maryland, recently vacated by Lee's Confederates, and receive a tumultuous, morale-boosting welcome. McClellan and other Union leaders, meanwhile, remain perplexed about Lee's whereabouts, his intentions, and the size of his force, which McClellan sets at 120,000. The Rebel commander has significantly less than half that number.[65]

SEPTEMBER 13, 1862: In a field where he has stopped to rest, Corporal Barton W. Mitchell, of the Twenty-seventh Indiana Infantry, finds a copy of Lee's Special Orders No. 191 wrapped around three cigars. Quickly realizing the importance of his find, he sends it on its way to headquarters, where McClellan exults, "Here is a paper with which if I cannot whip 'Bobbie Lee,' I will be willing to go home," and he wires President Lincoln, "I have the plans of the rebels, and will catch them in their own trap." But instead of acting quickly to take advantage of this windfall, McClellan proceeds with caution, giving Lee (who soon learns that McClellan has captured his plan) time to effectively react. He sends troops to cover the passes through South Mountain that he correctly anticipates the Federal columns will use when they move against him.[66]

SEPTEMBER 14, 1862: Confederates and Federals battle each other in a series of fierce engagements at South Mountain that leave Confederate forces battered and give McClellan the impression that he has won, as he telegraphs Washington, "a glorious victory." For a time, Lee agrees with his Union counterpart. He determines to retreat to Virginia.[67]

SEPTEMBER 15, 1862: "God bless you, and all with you," President Lincoln wires McClellan. "Destroy the rebel army, if possible." Lee also receives an important communication today. Stonewall Jackson reports that Harpers Ferry has surrendered, freeing troops to rejoin Lee's main force. The

Burning of Mr. Muma's [sic] Houses and Barns at the Fight of the 17th Sept. Pencil and Chinese white drawing by Alfred R. Waud, September 17, 1862. The Mumma family of Sharpsburg, which had donated land for the construction of the Dunker Church — a landmark of the battle of Antietam — removed themselves from harm's way before the fighting began. Returning to find their home in ashes, they rebuilt it the following year.

1 2 3 4 5 6 7 8 9 10 11 12 13 14 15 **16 17 18** 19 20 21 22 23 24 25 26 27 28 29 30

Confederate commander rescinds his decision to retreat and decides to stand where his main force is now located, outside the town of Sharpsburg, near a tributary of the Potomac River called Antietam Creek.[68]

SEPTEMBER 16, 1862: Rather than seizing the moment to smash the portion of Lee's army now facing him at Antietam, General McClellan spends this day developing a battle plan — based on the assumption that the Army of Northern Virginia, in its entirety, is three times larger than it actually is. By the time McClellan is ready, all but one division of the Harpers Ferry contingent has rejoined Lee at Antietam, though the Confederates are still significantly outnumbered (thirty-six thousand, without the division still at Harpers Ferry, versus some seventy-five thousand Federals).[69]

SEPTEMBER 17, 1862: Scattered gunfire at dawn turns into roaring waves of artillery and musket fire, the shouts of men battling at close quarters, and the screams of the dying as the battle of Antietam (Sharpsburg) becomes the costliest single-day clash of the American Civil War. Union general Joseph Hooker lives up to his nickname, "Fighting Joe," as he leads his corps against Stonewall Jackson's men through woods and across a cornfield that is quickly reduced to bloody husks covered with the dead and dying. "Never have I seen men fall as fast and thick," South Carolina soldier Stephen Welch, of John Bell Hood's Confederate division, will later write to his parents.

"In about one hour's time our whole division was almost annihilated." Burnside's Bridge, the West Woods, and Bloody Lane are among other pivotal sites of this lacerating battle, as McClellan persists in committing only a portion of his greater force, and then only in piecemeal attacks, allowing Lee to shift his Confederates to reinforce areas under greatest threat. One major threat occurs in the late afternoon, when Ambrose Burnside's Union corps seems set to cut off the Rebels' only line of retreat. At a key moment, A. P. Hill arrives with his division from Harpers Ferry. Though weary from their rapid seventeen-mile march, Hill's men smash into Burnside's flank, which disintegrates; and McClellan fails to send Burnside reinforcements. Thus Lee's avenue of retreat remains open. By the end of the day, although the badly battered Confederates have been forced back from their original positions, they still maintain a continuous line, and Lee is not yet prepared to retreat.[70]

SEPTEMBER 18, 1862: The rising sun reveals a tableau of the horrors of war all across the Antietam battlefield as both sides brace for the anticipated renewal of fighting. With untouched reserves and new reinforcements, McClellan does contemplate attacking Lee; but, as the morning wears on and he considers what he believes to be the odds, he decides against it. While he reaches this decision, burial details and medical workers go about their somber duties despite sporadic gunfire. Clara Barton, who arrived at the blood-soaked cornfield while the battle was raging the previous day, continues providing such

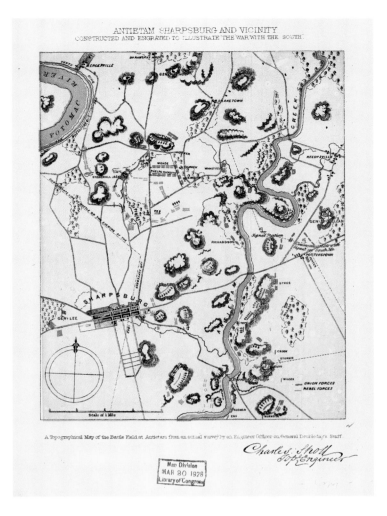

Clara Barton (1821–1912). Photographic print on a *carte de visite*, ca. 1865. Though called the Angel of the Battlefield, Barton spent much of her time behind the lines procuring desperately needed provisions. A tireless fund-raiser for that purpose, she also established a parcel post service for soldiers.

Antietam Sharpsburg and Vicinity. Color map by Charles Sholl, 1864, published in *The War with the South*, 1862–1867.

SEPTEMBER

1 2 3 4 5 6 7 8 9 10 11 12 13 14 15 16 17 18 19 20 **21** **22** 23 24 25 26 27 28 29 30

valuable aid to the wounded that one of the Union surgeons, Dr. James Dunn, will dub her the Angel of the Battlefield. Antietam is the first full-scale test of a system of care recently developed by Army of the Potomac medical director Dr. Jonathan Letterman. In his diary, Union soldier John W. Jaques salutes the men of "the new . . . Ambulance Corps. . . . they could be seen with the green [identification badges] on their arm, faithfully tending to their duties." They were not the only soldiers daring to move between the hostile forces: "Many from either side met in the space between the lines," James Steptoe Johnston, of the Eleventh Mississippi Volunteers, will write to his sweetheart, Mary Green, "and while the dead and wounded were being cared for, chatted as pleasantly as though they have never done each other harm." Lee has concluded, meanwhile, that McClellan will make no move against his army, and the reports he has been receiving from his officers about the condition of men and equipment lead him to order his army to withdraw. The Confederates quietly recross the Potomac during the night, a fact that Union scouts will discover the next morning. "Our victory was complete," McClellan will crow, in a telegram to Halleck. "The enemy is driven back into Virginia."[71]

SEPTEMBER 21, 1862: "I suppose the battle of 'An-Tee-Tam' must be set down as the greatest ever fought on this continent," Union sergeant Warren H. Freeman writes to his father. "Our loss in killed and wounded will exceed 10,000 men. That

of the rebels will never be known, but it exceeds ours by thousands." (Final casualty estimates for the battle will be more than twenty-three thousand killed, wounded, and missing for both sides.) "We have been in the advance and on picket duty since the battle began till yesterday," Freeman continues. "The rebels are in full view on the opposite bank of the Potomac." Yet, despite some grumbling from within his own ranks, and pressure from Washington, McClellan makes no move to pursue Lee's army.[72]

SEPTEMBER 22, 1862: "I think the time has come now," President Lincoln tells his cabinet. Though far from a sweeping triumph, the Union victory at Antietam has placed the administration in a position of sufficient strength to issue the preliminary Emancipation Proclamation that Lincoln has had in his desk drawer for three months (see July 13, 22, 1862). Released this day, the proclamation states that unless the Confederate States end their rebellion and return to the Union before the end of the year, on January 1, 1863, "all persons held as slaves, within any state, or designated part of a state, the people whereof shall then be in rebellion against the United States shall be then, thenceforward, and forever free." Reactions are intense: waves of jubilation animate some in the Union, heated protests erupt among others, particularly Democrats and citizens of the border states; near-universal condemnation roars out of the Confederacy. As news travels slowly to Europe, first of Lee's retreat from Antietam, then

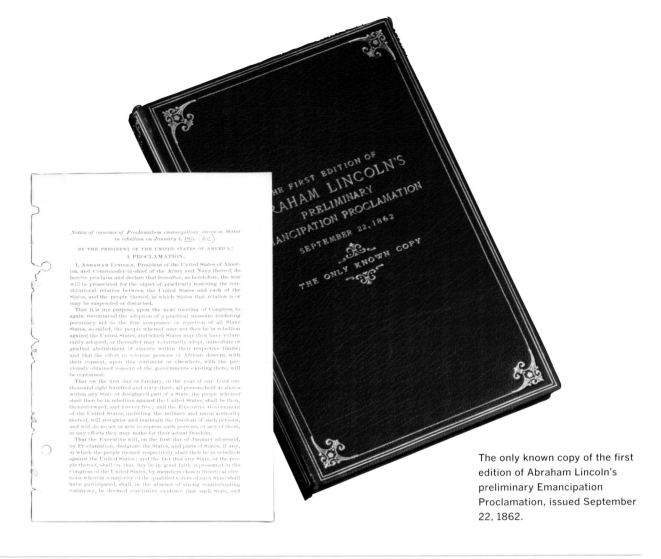

The only known copy of the first edition of Abraham Lincoln's preliminary Emancipation Proclamation, issued September 22, 1862.

of the preliminary Emancipation Proclamation, the pro-Confederate but antislavery leaders in England will back away from their determination to intercede in the war. "I am convinced," Lord Palmerston will write in October, "that we must continue merely to be lookers-on till the war shall have taken a more decided turn." Yet this day does mark a decided political turn — for the Union. The way is now open, should the South still be in rebellion at the first of the year, to broadening U.S. war aims from simple reconstruction of the Union to achieving reconstruction *without slavery*.[73]

SEPTEMBER 24, 1862: In the wake of violent resistance to militia drafts under the recently passed U.S. Militia Act (see July 17, 1862), President Lincoln issues a proclamation subjecting to martial law "all persons discouraging volunteer enlistments, resisting militia drafts, or guilty of any disloyal practice affording aid and comfort to the rebels" and suspending the writ of habeas corpus in cases of persons under military arrest. As in the Confederacy, persons deemed to be engaged in disloyal activities have been incarcerated without the writ's protections since early in the war; but Democrats seize upon today's action, and the release of the preliminary Emancipation Proclamation, as political issues that will strengthen their chances of making gains in the approaching state and congressional elections. *Also in Washington,* the U.S. Secretary of War creates the office of provost marshal general. In 1863, the Provost Marshal General's Bureau of the War Department

will help enroll eligible men under the first effective national conscription act (see March 3, 1863).[74]

SEPTEMBER 27, 1862: In the Confederate States, the Second Conscription Act goes into effect, expanding the military draft to white males ages eighteen to forty-five. The act also allows pacifist members of Dunkard, Mennonite, Nazarene, and Quaker religious communities to avoid military service that conflicts with their beliefs by providing a substitute or paying a $500 exemption tax. *In Union-occupied New Orleans,* the First Regiment of the Louisiana Native Guards, U.S. Army, comprising free black Louisianans and ex-slaves, becomes the first black unit to be *officially* mustered into United States military service. (The Second and Third Louisiana Native Guards will be mustered in during October and November.) Organized under Major General Benjamin F. Butler, these regiments include some seventy-five black officers — a step that will be reversed after Butler is succeeded by Nathaniel Banks in December. Declaring that "the appointment of colored officers is detrimental to the service," Banks will methodically drive black officers in his jurisdiction out of the service, using charges of incompetence (an ineffective tactic; most charges will prove to be unfounded) and a steady campaign of slights and humiliations. During the war, only thirty-two other black officers will be commissioned in the Union army: thirteen of them chaplains and at least eight physicians (who will be required to meet far more stringent requirements than those generally demanded of white army doctors).[75]

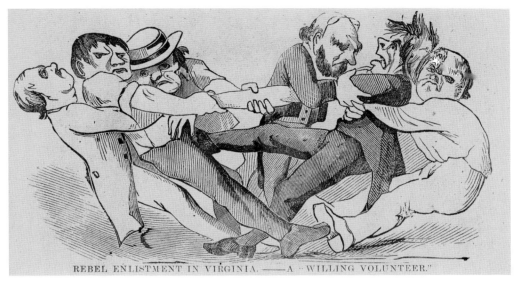

Rebel Enlistment in Virginia—a "Willing Volunteer." Cartoon, ca. 1862. Although patriotism ran high in both warring regions, conscription was far from popular.

The cover of *Frank Leslie's Illustrated Newspaper,* March 7, 1863, saluted the first black regiment officially mustered into the U.S. Army with this illustration, *Pickets of the First Louisiana "Native Guard" Guarding the New Orleans, Opelousas and Great Western Railroad.*

OCTOBER

1   2   **3**   **4**   5   6   **7**   8   9   10   11   12   13   14   15   16   17   18   19   20   21   22   23   24   25   26   27   28   29   30   31

OCTOBER 1862

OCTOBER 1, 1862: President Lincoln overrides the objections of some of his cabinet and travels by train to Army of the Potomac headquarters at Antietam, where, for three days, he views the battlefield, reviews the troops, and converses with General McClellan and his officers. Noting that the army seems well rested, battle-ready, and eager for action, the president presses McClellan to pursue Lee's Confederates.[76]

OCTOBER 3–4, 1862: Twenty-two thousand Confederates under Sterling Price and Earl Van Dorn attack Corinth, Mississippi, which has been occupied by Union forces for more than four months (see May 24, 1862). In addition to General William Rosecrans's twenty-three thousand Federals, the Rebels meet with a series of almost biblical challenges — including heat, water shortages, and three earthquake tremors — as they try to regain Corinth as a base for operations into Tennessee. Though they make some headway, at one point pushing the Federals back to their interior line, they are forced to withdraw on the second day of this intense clash that causes some five thousand Union and Confederate casualties. *As the Southerners withdraw,* President Lincoln concludes an impromptu address at a Maryland railroad station on his way back to Washington from Antietam with a poignant wish for the future: "May our children and our children's children to a thousand generations, continue to enjoy the benefits conferred upon us by a united country."[77]

OCTOBER 7, 1862: Though his first reaction to the preliminary Emancipation Proclamation was to call it "infamous," and he briefly considered opposing the proclamation publicly, today General George McClellan issues a general order reminding his officers — many of whom are equally disgruntled by the president's action — that the military is subordinate to civilian authority. He adds, apparently with the fast-approaching midterm elections in mind, "The remedy for political errors, if any are committed, is to be found only in the action of the people at the polls." *In Washington,* General in Chief Halleck fumes, in a letter to his wife, that McClellan "has lain still twenty days since the battle of Antietam. I cannot persuade him to advance an inch." Even the president's recently concluded visit to Antietam (see October 1, 1862) and a follow-up presidential order directing McClellan to "cross the Potomac and give battle to the enemy or drive him south" have not inspired McClellan to pursue Lee's army. The continuous barrage of complaints and excuses that the Army of the Potomac commander sends in response to the chief executive's subsequent exhortations to action will result, on October 24, in an uncharacteristically testy Lincoln telegram: "I have just read your dispatch about sore-tongued and fatigued horses. Will you pardon me for asking what the horses of your army have done since the battle of Antietam that fatigues anything?"[78]

Army of the Potomac intelligence agent Allan Pinkerton (standing, left) and Major General John A. McClernand (right) pose with President Lincoln during his visit to Antietam. Photograph by Alexander Gardner, October 3, 1862.

ABOVE: Illustration on a Civil War–era envelope. Concern over maintaining proper control of the slave population as war increasingly disrupted Southern life resulted in the October 1862 draft exemption for overseers of twenty or more slaves.

LEFT: Major General Don Carlos Buell (1818–1898), USA. An 1841 graduate of West Point, Buell helped George B. McClellan organize the Army of the Potomac in 1861. His timely arrival at the Shiloh battlefield in April 1862 proved the high point of his Civil War service—which reached its nadir when he failed to pursue Braxton Bragg's Confederates as they withdrew from Kentucky that October.

OCTOBER

1 2 3 4 5 6 7 **8** 9 **10** **11** **12** **13** **14** 15 16 17 18 19 20 21 22 23 24 25 26 27 28 29 30 31

OCTOBER 8, 1862: The Confederate Heartland Campaign (see August 14, 28, and 30) comes to an unsuccessful conclusion at the battle of Perryville (Chaplin Hills), Kentucky, a disjointed clash in which only portions of each force are engaged. Deemed at least a partial Union victory, this battle, the largest fought in Kentucky, precipitates what many in the South will consider a premature Confederate withdrawal to Tennessee. Though Braxton Bragg is subject to a barrage of criticism for the disappointing outcome of this operation, President Davis will leave him in command of the Confederacy's Western Department. Union general Don Carlos Buell will not be as fortunate: his overcautious and quickly abandoned pursuit of Bragg's army after Perryville will cause public outrage in the North. He will be replaced by General William S. Rosecrans on October 24.[79]

OCTOBER 10–12, 1862: Jeb Stuart leads his Confederate cavalry on a raid into Pennsylvania, during which he and his men secure valuable information, dozens of prisoners, and twelve hundred fresh horses. For the second time (see June 12–16, 1862), Stuart embarrasses the Union by riding completely around McClellan's army, despite the Federal cavalry's furious attempts to catch him. "Humiliating" and "disgraceful" are two words Secretary of the Navy Gideon Welles uses in his diary to describe the incident, and he adds, "The country groans."[80]

OCTOBER 11, 1862: The Confederate government expands draft exemptions for various occupations. Among those added are owners or overseers of twenty or more slaves, a provision that creates considerable resentment among poorer white families and raises objections by some Confederate senators, who call it legislation "in favour of slave labour against white labour." *On the high seas,* the Confederate commerce raider CSS *Alabama,* captained by Raphael Semmes, sinks the Union ship *Manchester,* loaded with grain.[81]

OCTOBER 13, 1862: "You remember my speaking to you of what I called your over-cautiousness," President Lincoln writes at the beginning of a long, carefully reasoned letter urging McClellan to move. "Are you not over-cautious when you assume that you can not do what the enemy is constantly doing? Should you not claim to be at least his equal in prowess, and act upon the claim?" *In Illinois,* the *Chicago Tribune* editorializes: "What malign influence palsies our army and wastes these glorious days for fighting? If it is McClellan, does not the President see that he is a traitor?"[82]

OCTOBER 14, 1862: Congressional elections in four Northern states result in gains for the Democratic Party, which generally favors a negotiated settlement with the Confederacy (the Peace Democrats more so than the War Democrats) and opposes emancipation. Other elections this fall will see Democratic gains in some state legislatures and two governors'

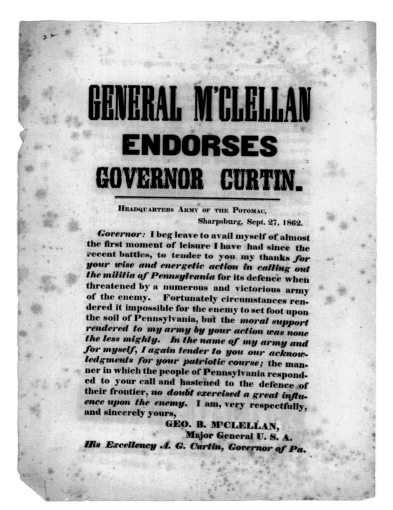

Benjamin Wade (1800–1878), senator from Ohio, Thirty-fifth Congress. Photograph, ca. 1859, by Julian Vannerson. One of George B. McClellan's severest Radical Republican critics, Wade once told the general that the Army of the Potomac could "whip the whole Confederacy if they were given the chance; if I [Wade] were commander."

General M'Clellan Endorses Governor Curtin. Broadside published in Sharpsburg, Md., 1862. Although he was a dedicated Democrat, McClellan on this occasion saluted the Republican governor of Pennsylvania for calling out the militia to aid in defending against Lee's first incursion into Northern territory.

OCTOBER

1 2 3 4 5 6 7 8 9 10 11 12 13 14 15 16 17 18 19 **20** 21 22 23 24 25 **26** 27 28 **29** 30 31

mansions. Although these gains are far from sweeping (due in large measure to the victory at Antietam and Lee's retreat from Northern soil), most Democrats are greatly heartened and most Republicans greatly concerned that the election results indicate waning support for Republican war aims, including the principal goal of reuniting the divided Union.[83]

OCTOBER 20, 1862: "Mr. Brady has done something to bring home to us the terrible reality and earnestness of war," the *New York Times* states, describing an exhibition of images taken on the Antietam battlefield by Alexander Gardner and James Gibson, two of Mathew Brady's photographers. On display at Brady's New York studio, *The Dead of Antietam* unveils, via images that evoke "a terrible fascination," the rending human costs of this fratricidal conflict.[84]

OCTOBER 26, 1862: The Army of the Potomac finally begins to cross the Potomac River in pursuit of Lee's Army of Northern Virginia. But its slow progress (the crossing itself takes more than six days) does little to temper President Lincoln's frustrations, especially since McClellan's deliberate pace allows Lee to deploy his troops between the Army of the Potomac and Richmond. Yet the president's concern with McClellan's generalship pales beside that of Radical Republicans in Congress, who have been increasingly critical of the general's "soft war" policies and lack of aggressiveness. McClellan, meanwhile, has long maintained close ties with leaders of the

Democratic Party, including influential newspaper editors, keeping them informed of his own complaints and accusations against his civilian superiors in Washington — partisan political activity wholly inappropriate for the commander of the Union's largest army.[85]

OCTOBER 29, 1862: Some two and a half months before it will be officially mustered into the Union army on January 13, 1863, the First Kansas Volunteer Colored Infantry becomes the first black regiment to undergo a "baptism of fire" when some of its soldiers engage a unit of Confederate guerrillas at Island Mound, Missouri.[86]

General McClellan Accompanied by General Burnside Taking Leave of the Army of the Potomac. Pencil, Chinese white, and wash drawing by Alfred R. Waud, November 10, 1862. "In parting from you I cannot express the love and gratitude I bear to you," McClellan said in his farewell address. "The glory you have achieved, our mutual perils and fatigues, the graves of our comrades fallen in battle and by disease . . . unite us still by an indissoluble tie."

NOVEMBER

1 2 3 4 **5** 6 7 8 9 **10** 11 12 13 **14** 15 16 17 18 19 20 21 22 23 24 25 26 27 28 29 30

NOVEMBER 1862

NOVEMBER 5, 1862: With the fall elections concluded, and the Army of the Potomac still making glacial progress in pursuit of Lee (while McClellan fails to keep his superiors in Washington fully apprised of his movements and strategy), Lincoln makes a change. He sends Halleck an order "that Major General McClellan be relieved from the command of the Army of the Potomac; and that Major General Burnside take the command of that Army." Two days later, in the midst of an early snow, General Catharinus P. Buckingham, dispatched from Washington by Secretary of War Stanton, arrives at Army of the Potomac headquarters in Virginia. He persuades a reluctant Burnside to accept his new command, in part by letting him know that, should he refuse, the command will go to Joseph Hooker, of whom Burnside has a less than stellar opinion. Both men proceed to McClellan's tent, where Buckingham personally delivers the order. "I am sure that not a muscle quivered nor was the slightest expression of feeling visible on my face," McClellan will write to his wife. "They shall not have that triumph." On November 10, McClellan will conduct a final, emotional review of "his" army. Many soldiers weep; some officers urge McClellan to resist the change in command. But the general quiets those protests and leaves for Washington aboard a special train on November 11.[87]

NOVEMBER 10, 1862: "Your dispatch giving the names of three hundred Indians condemned to death, is received," President Lincoln writes to Major General John Pope, now on duty in Minnesota. "Please forward, as soon as possible, the full and complete records of these convictions." The president is dealing with the aftermath of a Sioux uprising that occurred from mid-August through September in which several hundred white Minnesotans were killed. Restricted to a narrow strip of land in south-central Minnesota and forbidden to hunt, the Indians had also been deprived of promised government food and supplies by unscrupulous whites (including trader Andrew Myrick, who reportedly said hungry Indians "should eat grass or their own dung"). After the fighting stopped, a military tribunal sentenced 303 Sioux to die by hanging and expected quick authorization for the executions from the commander in chief. But Lincoln will ask two lawyers to review the trial records and determine which of the condemned men actually led the uprising. The day after Christmas, 38 of the Sioux will be executed.[88]

NOVEMBER 14, 1862: General in Chief Halleck notifies General Burnside that the president has approved Burnside's plan to cross the Rappahannock River at Fredericksburg, Virginia, midway between Washington and Richmond, in order to surprise Lee and turn the Army of Northern Virginia's flank. Lincoln's caveat is that the plan "will succeed if you move rapidly; otherwise not." Secrecy will also be essential, lest Lee

Photographing the War

"Decidedly one of the institutions of our army is the traveling portrait gallery," a correspondent reported, via *Moore's Rural New-Yorker*, in October 1862. "A camp is hardly pitched before one of the omnipresent artists in collodion and amber-bead varnish drives up his two-horse wagon, pitches his canvas gallery, and unpacks his chemicals. Our army here (Fredericksburg) is now so large that quite a company of these gentlemen have gathered about us. . . . Their tents are thronged from morning to night."

Smith Cook, J. D. Edwards, A. J. Lytle, James M. Osborn (with his business partner, F. W. Durbec), and Julian Vannerson have survived to enrich the visual archive.

Documenting the war, and the people who fought it, photographers faced a number of challenges, particularly the problems involved in transporting cameras, tripods, lenses, chemicals, glass plates, distilled water, measuring cups, developing trays, portable darkrooms, and other assorted gear, weighing between 100 and 150 pounds. The odd conveyances

An unidentified soldier in the Confederate uniform of Company E, "Lynchburg Rifles," Eleventh Virginia Infantry. Photograph by Charles R. Rees, ca. 1861.

This unidentified girl in mourning dress is holding a framed photograph of a cavalryman, presumably her father, a casualty of the war.

Developed in the 1830s by Frenchmen Joseph-Nicéphore Niépce and Louis-Jacques Mandé Daguerre, and almost simultaneously by England's William Henry Fox Talbot, the young art of photography grew in popularity during the 1850s with the introduction of stereoscopic images (photographs that became three-dimensional when viewed through a handheld stereoscope) and *cartes de visite* (visiting cards featuring paper prints of individual portrait photographs). By 1860 it had advanced enough to become a vivid means of documenting the Civil War.

Between 1860 and 1865, Civil War photographers took an estimated one million photographs. The vast majority of these images were taken by Northern cameramen. A lack of supplies and operating capital made Southern photographers — who were much less numerous than those based in the North in the prewar years — extremely scarce after the early years of the conflict. Yet photographs taken by Southerners George

photographers generally used to carry their gear were soon dubbed *what-is-it? wagons* by the soldiers. Once these peculiar wagons halted, and the photographers set up to shoot, they had to take the time, and make certain their bulky cameras were stable enough, to ensure that they got a proper exposure for each shot. The required exposure time and the need for stability are what made "action photography" all but impossible. (Capturing battlefield action was the province of special artist-correspondents; see "Reporting the War," page 38.)

The most prominent name associated with Civil War photography is Mathew Brady (1823?–1896), an early and ardent student of photography who opened his own daguerreotype studio in New York City in 1844 and a second studio, run by brilliant Scottish photographer Alexander Gardner, in Washington, DC, in 1858. From then until 1863, when Gardner opened his own studio, the two men worked together to make an indelible mark on American history.

Gardner almost certainly helped Brady organize a corps of photographers to document the war soon after the firing started. Photographers were assigned to cover various Union armies and areas of operation, with Brady securing permits and ample cooperation from Federal authorities while paying all expenses himself. Prominent wartime figures also sat for portraits in Brady's studios. The toll the war was taking on President Lincoln is vividly evident in a series of Brady studio portraits made from 1860 to 1865. Photographs of battlefield leaders who, as one reporter wrote, "are as brilliant but as distant from us as planets" placed civilians "upon whispering terms with the Generals who are now to the nation as gods."

James Gibson and Timothy H. O'Sullivan (both affiliated with Brady during the first half of the war), Gardner, and Brady himself, along with independent photographer George N. Barnard, all made stunning contributions to the visual record of this bitter conflict. Other cameramen, who descended on army camps to take portrait photographs purely for profit, added their own haunting gallery of faces, many of them of people now unknown to us, to the perpetually moving photographic history of the American Civil War.[89]

Alexander Gardner's Photographic Gallery, Seventh and D streets, NW, Washington, DC, ca. 1863.

The wagons and camera of Sam A. Cooley, U.S. photographer, Department of the South, between 1861 and 1865.

Brady, the Photographer, Returned from Bull Run, Photograph, July 22, 1861.

The Court Martial of Major General Fitz-John Porter. Pencil drawing by Alfred R. Waud, December 1862. A still controversial legal proceeding with heavy political overtones, the court-martial resulted in a presidential order issued January 21, 1863, that Porter be "cashiered and dismissed from the service . . . and forever disqualified from holding any office of trust or profit under the Government of the United States."

Major General Fitz John Porter (1822–1901), USA, between 1860 and 1870.

divine Burnside's intentions and fortify the heights around the town. Burnside will run into trouble from the very beginning: Organizational snafus will delay by almost two weeks the arrival of pontoon bridges needed to cross the river; and, soon after the plan is approved, the Northern press will start publicly debating its merits.[90]

NOVEMBER 17, 1862: Having learned of Lincoln's "astonishing step" of relieving McClellan and appointing Burnside, North Carolina's Catherine Edmondston etches an acid character sketch of the Union's new Army of the Potomac commander in her diary:

> Burnside is the valiant gentleman who came here to NC to subdue us last winter [see February 7, 1862] & who . . . issued a proclamation to assure us he was "a Christian," but his after acts . . . showed that he was either a hypcrite [sic] or a backslider. Witness the ravages & thefts of his command through the whole Eastern part of our State — "the most Christian Gen Burnside," we salute you! & hope that our Gen Lee will give you a reception worthy your [sic] merits and distinguished Christianity.[91]

In Washington, the War Department charges General Fitz John Porter with disobeying orders during the Second Bull Run Campaign. A confidant of George B. McClellan (sharing

McClellan's dim view of John Pope, under whom Porter served at Bull Run) and an outspoken critic of the Lincoln administration's war policies, Porter was relieved of command of the Army of the Potomac's Fifth Corps by the same order that relieved McClellan (see November 5, 1862). His court-martial will reflect the corrosive political currents affecting the North's war effort: held as the Union recoils from a devastating military defeat (see December 13, 1862), it will be tainted by personal prejudice, political bias, and false testimony. Convicted and cashiered from the army in January, Porter will fight to have his conviction reversed, and he will be exonerated — in 1879.[92]

NOVEMBER 21, 1862: President Davis appoints Virginian James Alexander Seddon secretary of war, the fifth man thus far to serve in the post under a president who tends to operate as his own war secretary. Seddon will serve the longest, remaining in office until early 1865, perhaps because he will choose to operate principally as an administrator and Davis partisan.[93]

NOVEMBER 27, 1862: "I have just had a long conference with Gen. Burnside," President Lincoln writes General Halleck, from a ship off Aquia Creek, Virginia. "He believes that Gen. Lees whole army, or nearly the whole of it is in front of him, at and near Fredericksburg. Gen. B. says . . . that he thinks he can cross the river in face of the enemy and drive him away, but

The First Snow Storm. Gen Pleasanton Advancing from Orleans to Waterloo via Warrington [sic], 6th Nov. Pencil and Chinese white drawing by Arthur Lumley, November 6, 1862. This early Virginia snowstorm heralded the onset of winter, "and winter in Virginia," as Army of the Potomac soldier Oliver Willcox Norton wrote, on December 6, 1862, "is just as fatal to a campaign as frost is to cucumbers, or arsenic to rats." Yet this winter, Virginia would see one more terrible battle.

DECEMBER

1 **2** 3 4 5 6 **7** 8 9 10 **11** 12 13 14 15 16 17 18 19 20 21 22 23 24 25 26 27 28 29 30 31

that, to use his own expression, it is somewhat risky." *Across the Rappahannock River,* General Lee writes President Davis: "The reports of the scouts received today state that the whole force of the enemy is concentrated between Fredericksburg and Aquia Creek. . . . Their object may be to make a winter campaign, under the belief that our troops will not be sufficiently guarded against the cold for operations in the field. Our army at present is in good health, and I think capable of making a strong resistance."[94]

DECEMBER 1862

DECEMBER 2, 1862: In some areas of the Confederacy, shortages and enemy armies are not the most immediate home front worries. Civilians are also plagued by bands of marauders, some of them legally organized under the Partisan Ranger Act (see April 21, 1862), some of them not. "We look to you for protection," a "Minister of the Gospel" writes to Georgia governor Joseph Brown today, from "so called Partizan [sic] rangers who have formed them selves into companies." These lawless bands are stealing food, thus "robbing little children who will have to suffer after bread. We must have help or our county is ruined."[95]

DECEMBER 7, 1862: At Prairie Grove, Arkansas, on this bitter cold day, a Confederate bid to regain control of northwest Arkansas and southwest Missouri fails when Rebels under Major General Thomas C. Hindman (including Missouri "bushwackers" led by William C. Quantrill) are defeated in an encounter with Federals under Major General James G. Blunt and Major General Francis J. Herron. After the battle, Union troops will find many unwounded Confederates frozen to death on the battlefield.[96]

DECEMBER 11, 1862: At about 2:00 AM, Union engineers, covered by infantry and artillery, begin laying pontoon bridges across the Rappahannock River. When the fifteen hundred Confederate infantrymen occupying Fredericksburg have enough light to take aim, their fire initiates a daylong struggle during which Union detachments cross the river by boat, Federal artillery smashes buildings and sets raging fires, and infantrymen engage in bitter house-to-house fighting. Late in the day, Robert E. Lee wires Adjutant and Inspector General Samuel Cooper: "Enemy . . . succeeded in driving back our sharpshooters and occupying Fredericksburg. . . . We hold the hills around the city." The following day, as loss of the element of surprise and questions over Burnside's battle plan raise doubts among some Union officers, the bulk of the Army of the Potomac will cross the completed pontoon bridges and occupy the town, where many soldiers will descend into anarchy: "we stole or destroyed everything in the City," Private

night. the Sacking of Fredericksburg — & Bivouac of Union troops.

LEFT: *Night. The Sacking of Fredericksburg — & Bivouac of Union Troops.* Pencil drawing by Arthur Lumley, December 12, 1862.

OPPOSITE: *Uebergang über den Rappahannock* [Crossing the Rappahannock]. This rare German color lithograph depicting the first stages of the battle of Fredericksburg reflects European interest in the war — often stemming from personal connections. An estimated 1.3 million Germans lived in the United States (North and South) during the Civil War; between 180,000 and 216,000 served in the Union army, and an estimated 18,000 wore Confederate gray. Among the all-German units serving the North were Illinois's Hecker Jaeger Regiment, Blenker's Division, under the command of Louis (Ludwig) Blenker, and the Thirty-second Indiana Infantry.

DECEMBER

1 2 3 4 5 6 7 8 9 10 11 **12 13** 14 15 16 17 18 19 20 21 22 23 24 25 26 27 28 29 30 31

Roland E. Bowen, of the Fifteenth Massachusetts, will write to his mother, "great was the ransacking thereof."[97]

DECEMBER 12, 1862: General William T. Sherman makes feverish preparations to sail with thirty-two thousand men down the Mississippi River to a position just above Vicksburg, where they will attack that Confederate bastion from the north, while Grant and his troops divert Confederate attention by approaching from the east. Shipping requirements alone will cause some delays as the expedition begins. Confederate "torpedoes" (mines) will further slow the expedition as Sherman's troops and their naval escort under Commander David Dixon Porter reach their destination (see December 29, 1862).[98]

DECEMBER 13, 1862: The Union suffers one of its worst defeats of the Civil War when Major General Ambrose Burnside sends the Army of the Potomac — in formation and over open ground — against General Robert E. Lee's smaller Army of Northern Virginia, well positioned in the hills beyond Fredericksburg, Virginia. "When within some three hundred yards of the rebel works, the men burst into a cheer and charged," Union soldier Josiah Marshall Favill will write in his diary, after surviving the battle.

> Immediately the hill in front was hid from view by a continuous sheet of flame. . . . The rebel infantry poured in a murderous fire while their guns from every available

point fired shot and shell and canister. The losses were so tremendous, that before we knew it our momentum was gone, and the charge a failure. . . . I wondered while I lay there how it all came about that these thousands of men in broad daylight were trying their best to kill each other. Just then there was no romance, no glorious pomp, nothing but disgust for the genius who planned so frightful a slaughter.

London *Times* reporter Francis Charles Lawley witnesses the wholesale bloodletting from Confederate lines and will report on its stunning cost: "There, in every attitude of death, lying so close to each other that you might step from body to body, lay acres of the Federal dead. . . . [within the town] layers of corpses stretched in the balconies of houses as though taking a *siesta*. . . . [M]ore appalling to look at [were] . . . piles of arms and legs, amputated as soon as their owners had been carried off the field." In all, eighteen thousand men of both sides are killed, wounded, or missing this bloody day; two-thirds of the casualties are Union. Waves of shock, dismay, and anger will ripple through the North as the extent of the disaster becomes known. Democratic newspapers will blame the administration, Manton Marble's *New York World* editorializing: "Again have you, Abraham Lincoln, by the hands of Henry Halleck and Edwin M. Stanton sent to death thousands upon thousands of our brothers and friends." Some will demand that McClellan be reinstated.[99]

Uebergang über den Rappahannock.

Am 13. Dezember hatte bei Fredericksburg am Rappahannock eine blutige Schlacht stattgefunden. Der Erfolg blieb unentschieden, doch haben die Südlinger das Schlachtfeld behauptet. Der Verlust auf beiden Seiten war ungeheuer und soll auf Seiten der Unionisten 10,000 Mann betragen haben, während im Ganzen sich etwa 40,000 Mann am Kampfe betheiligt haben mögen.

ABOVE: *Rebel Pickets Dead in Fredericksburg.* Pencil drawing by either Alfred R. Waud or Arthur Lumley, December 1862. Written on the back of this drawing is the following inscription: "Six Rebel Pickets—lay dead in front of this city, and up to Sunday were not buried—they wore the U.S. over-coat over the secesch.—they were killed when the Union forces were building the Pontoon bridge—a good many lay scattered around with dead horses."

DECEMBER

1 2 3 4 5 6 7 8 9 10 11 12 13 14 15 16 17 **18** 19 20 **21** 22 23 24 25 26 27 28 29 30 31

DECEMBER 18, 1862: "[T]he country is gone unless something is done at once," Senator Zachariah Chandler writes to his wife. "We must have men in command of our armies who are anxious to crush the rebellion." Many Republicans believe one major problem rests with conservative elements within the country's civilian leadership. This evening a delegation of nine Republican senators presents a resolution to President Lincoln calling for "a partial reconstruction of the Cabinet." Both Lincoln and Secretary of State Seward have been forewarned that Seward is the senators' particular target, his conduct, and that of the cabinet in general, having been repeatedly, if cautiously, maligned by Secretary of the Treasury Chase. During a long and difficult meeting on the evening of December 19, Lincoln will patiently and deftly defuse the cabinet crisis. Seward will remain at his post.[100]

DECEMBER 21, 1862: "It seems to me now clearly developed that the enemy has two principal objects in view," President Davis, in Vicksburg, Mississippi, writes Trans-Mississippi Department commander General T. H. Holmes, "one to get control of the Missi. River, and the other to capture the capital of the Confederate States.... [T]o prevent the enemy getting control of the Mississippi and dismembering the Confederacy, we must mainly depend upon maintaining the points already occupied by defensive works; to-wit, Vicksburg and Port Hudson." Vicksburg is the principal object of operations by Ulysses S. Grant's western theater army, but things are not

going well. On December 20, Confederate cavalry under Major General Earl Van Dorn raided Grant's secondary supply depot at Holly Springs, Mississippi, capturing the entire fifteen-hundred-man Union garrison and destroying munitions and food. Similar action by Nathan Bedford Forrest's cavalry in Tennessee and Kentucky temporarily severed Grant's communications with the North, forcing Grant to suspend his movement toward Vicksburg and withdraw to Oxford, Mississippi. These setbacks, Grant will write in his memoirs,

> caused much rejoicing among the people remaining in Oxford. They came with broad smiles . . . to ask what I was going to do now without anything for my soldiers to eat. I told them . . . that I had already sent troops and wagons to collect all the food and forage they could find for fifteen miles on each side of the road. Countenances soon changed, and so did the inquiry. The next was, "What are *we* to do?" My response was that we had endeavored to feed ourselves from our own northern resources . . . but their friends in gray had been uncivil enough to destroy what we had brought along, and it could not be expected that men, with arms in their hands, would starve in the midst of plenty. I advised them to emigrate east, or west, fifteen miles and assist in eating up what we left.[101]

Walt Whitman (1819–1892). Photographic print on a *carte de visite*; photograph by Mathew Brady, ca. 1862.

These rough pencil sketches by Alfred R. Waud are an artistic "tribute" to a common soldier activity — sometimes officially sanctioned, as with Grant's campaigns for Vicksburg, more often ad hoc. "Every mess has and carries a *grater* — the boys call them *Armstrong mills*," Confederate infantryman Douglas J. Cater wrote in June 1862; "and as the corn in the fields we pass has not been gathered these *mills* keep us supplied with meal when the commissariat fails to give us our *three dodgers* per day."

DECEMBER 1862–JANUARY 1863

29 30 **31** **1** **2** 3 4 5 6 7 8 9 10 11 12 13 14 15 16 17 18 19 20 21 22 23 24 25 26 27 28

DECEMBER 29: Unaware that Grant has been forced to suspend his advance on Vicksburg, and plagued by bad weather, the atrocious terrain along the Yazoo River, and formidable Confederate defenses, William Sherman launches his attack on the outer defenses of Vicksburg. Nothing about the battle of Chickasaw Bluffs (Chickasaw Bayou) goes well for the Union: some Federal troops become lost, others are lacerated by Confederate crossfire, heavy rain falls, and the Yazoo rises to dangerous levels. "This has been a dreadful disaster," a distraught Sherman tells his naval counterpart, David Dixon Porter, tonight. Grant's first campaign against Vicksburg thus comes to a close, but Grant and Sherman remain determined to keep pressure on the city.[102] *From Washington,* poet Walt Whitman writes to his mother:

> I landed here without a dime. The next two days I spent hunting through the hospitals, walking day and night . . . trying to get information. . . . When I found dear brother George [who had been wounded at Fredericksburg], and found that he was alive and well, O you may imagine how trifling all my little cares and difficulties seemed. . . . And now that I . . . realize the way that hundreds of thousands of good men are now living, and have had to live for a year or more, not only without any of the comforts, but with death and sickness and hard marching and hard fighting (and no success at that) for their con-

tinual experience — really nothing we call trouble seems worth talking about.

Whitman will soon devote himself to the care of wounded and sick soldiers.[103]

DECEMBER 31, 1862: While under tow off the coast of North Carolina near Cape Hatteras, USS *Monitor* founders in a storm at about 1:00 AM. Four officers and twelve men are lost; forty-seven crewmen are rescued by USS *Rhode Island.* (In 1973, the *Monitor* wreck will be located and, in 1975, the site will be designated as the nation's first marine sanctuary.)[104]

DECEMBER 31, 1862–JANUARY 2, 1863: After a combat-eve musical interlude, during which men of both sides joined in singing "Home Sweet Home," Braxton Bragg's thirty-eight-thousand-man Confederate Army of Tennessee smashes into the right of William Rosecrans's forty-seven-thousand-man Union Army of the Cumberland to begin the battle of Murfreesboro (Stones River). It becomes the most deadly battle of the war in proportion to the number of troops fighting, with more than one-third of the Confederate force killed, wounded, or missing, and 31 percent Union casualties. "The balls flew around us like hail stones," Confederate lieutenant James B. Mitchell will write to his father. "[O]ur company suffered very severely. Six men were killed outright

TOWARD A NEW BIRTH OF FREEDOM

Captain George Washington
Whitman (1829–1901), USA,
between 1860 and 1866.

Sergeant Major Edward Paul Reichhelm, of the Third Missouri Volunteers,
included this hand-drawn map of the Chickasaw Bayou Campaign in his
memoir of the Federal attempts to take Vicksburg. "There was nothing but
deep impassable swamp and water," Reichhelm wrote, "and the only possible way of reaching the bluff was the dike. But that this was impossible,
as long as the rebels had gunpowder is apparent from the above rough
sketch; in fact every inch of the dike was under their fire. . . . To carry this
position . . . we all made up our minds to die for our country's cause, for
nothing else could be the result of a charge upon that position!"

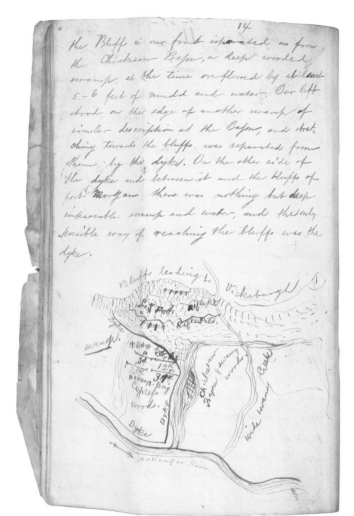

JANUARY

1 2 3 4 5 6 7 8 9 10 11 12 13 14 15 16 17 18 19 20 21 22 23 24 25 26 27 28 29 30 31

& 14 wounded. . . . Two men . . . next to me . . . were shot dead
in their tracks. One receiving a ball in his breast & the other
through his head and his brains came out. I saw it myself. . . . At
the same time a ball passed through both the coats I had on,
my overcoat & blue frock coat, but thank God I was not hurt."
On January 1 there is a lull in the fighting. "Both armies want
rest," Union brigadier general John Beatty notes in his diary,

> both have suffered terribly. Here and there little parties
> are engaged burying the dead, which lie thick around
> us. . . . A little before sundown all hell seems to break loose
> again, and for about an hour the thunder of the artillery
> and volleys of musketry are deafening; but it is simply
> the evening salutations of the combatants. The darkness
> deepens; the weather is raw and disagreeable. Fifty thou-
> sand hungry men are stretched beside their guns again on
> the field. Fortunately I have a piece of raw pork and a few
> crackers in my pocket. No food ever tasted sweeter.

Across the battlefield, young Lieutenant Mitchell welcomes
the night with two comrades: "we slept by turns . . . wrapped
in the wet blanket & sitting up by the side of a tree." The next
day, the fierce combat is renewed and Union forces eventually
push the Confederates back. Regarded as a Union victory,
this costly encounter will raise spirits in the North, which so
recently suffered the stinging defeat at Fredericksburg. "I can
never forget, whilst I remember anything," President Lincoln
will write to Rosecrans, "you gave us a hard earned victory
which, had there been a defeat instead, the nation could hardly
have lived over."[105]

1863

JANUARY 1863

JANUARY 1, 1863: Abraham Lincoln issues the Emancipation Proclamation. A stronger document than the preliminary Emancipation Proclamation (see September 22, 1862), it sanctions the enlistment of black soldiers and sailors "of suitable condition [who] will . . . garrison forts, positions, stations, and other places, and . . . man vessels of all sorts." Expanding Union war aims to include emancipation, thus changing the nature of the war, the proclamation sparks a huge celebration in Washington, as Henry M. Turner, the free black pastor of an African Methodist Episcopal church in the capital, will later report: "Great processions of colored and white men marched to and fro and passed in front of the White House and congratulated President Lincoln. . . . The President came to the window and made responsive bows, and thousands told him, if he would come out of the palace, they would hug him to death. Mr. Lincoln, however, kept at a safe distance from the multitude, who were frenzied to distraction over his proclamation. . . . It was indeed a time of times . . . nothing like it will ever be seen again in this life." *At the port city of Galveston, Texas,* Confederate forces under John B. Magruder gain an impressive victory when they successfully attack the Union garrison and naval flotilla that have controlled the city since October. Galveston will remain in Confederate hands for the rest of the war, finally surrendering on June 2, 1865.[106]

JANUARY 7, 1863: The Democrat-controlled state legislature in President Lincoln's home state of Illinois passes a resolution criticizing the president for turning the war into a mission to free the slaves and calls the Emancipation Proclamation "as unwarranted in military as in civil law" and "a gigantic usurpation." The *Valley Spirit,* in Franklin County, Pennsylvania, declares the proclamation "unwise, ill-timed, outside of the Constitution and full of mischief" and predicts that it will increase Southern resistance and "make the war still more prolonged, bloody and bitter." Lincoln can take heart from other Northern reactions, however: The *Washington Morning Chronicle* states that the proclamation "destroys the right arm of rebellion — African slavery," and the *New York Tribune* calls it "a great stride toward restoration of the union." A resolution passed by free black citizens of Harrisburg, Pennsylvania, hails "the 1st day of January, 1863, as a new era in our country's history." Yet the resolution also includes a gentle criticism, and an expression of hope: "[If] our wishes had been consulted we would have preferred that the proclamation should have been general instead of partial; but we can only say to our brethren of the 'Border States,' be of good cheer — the day of your deliverance draweth nigh."[107]

JANUARY 9, 1863: As the struggle for control of the Mississippi River continues, thirty-two thousand Federal troops under Major General John McClernand and a supporting naval squadron under Commander David Dixon Porter reach the

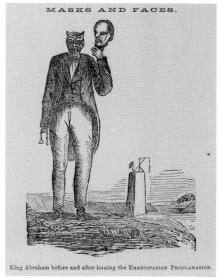

ABOVE: Celebrations of the Emancipation Proclamation were widespread, and some were particularly poignant. This wood engraving from the January 24, 1863, edition of *Frank Leslie's Illustrated Newspaper* depicts *"Emancipation Day in South Carolina"*—the Color-Sergeant of the 1st South Carolina (Colored) addressing the regiment, after having been presented with the Stars and Stripes, at Smith's plantation, Port Royal, January 1.

OPPOSITE: *Battle of Stone River, Near Murfreesborough, Tenn. Dec. 31, 62. Jan. 2–3 1863.* Color lithograph by Kurz & Allison, 1891.

JANUARY

1 2 3 4 5 6 7 8 9 10 **11** **12** 13 14 15 16 17 18 19 20 21 22 23 24 **25** 26 27 28 29 30 31

Confederate bastion of Fort Hindman, at Arkansas Post, about fifty miles from the confluence of the Arkansas and Mississippi rivers. Constructed in 1862 with the labor of some five hundred slaves, the fort, and the five-thousand-man Confederate garrison's initial stout defense, will prove formidable obstacles for McClernand's soldiers. Fierce bombardment from the naval squadron will be the decisive factor, forcing the Rebels to surrender the fort, with all its guns and supplies, on January 11. "I was at first disposed to disapprove of [the action] as an unnecessary side movement," Ulysses S. Grant will later write. "But when the result was understood I regarded it as very important. Five thousand Confederate troops left in the rear might have caused us much trouble and loss of property while navigating the Mississippi."[108]

JANUARY 11, 1863: Off Galveston, CSS *Alabama* under Raphael Semmes engages USS *Hatteras,* captained by Lieutenant H. C. Blake. This harrowing encounter, fought at times at *very* close quarters, results in *Hatteras* sinking, as Blake will later report, "with all her muskets and stores of every description, the enemy not being able . . . to obtain a single weapon." After taking the rescued Union crew to Jamaica, Semmes will sail on to continue *Alabama*'s "appointed task," as he will wryly note in his 1864 memoirs, "of annoying the enemy's commerce."[109]

JANUARY 12, 1863: In a message to the Confederate Congress, Jefferson Davis calls Lincoln's Emancipation Proclamation "the most execrable measure in the history of guilty man" and vows to turn over captured Union officers to state governments for punishment as "criminals engaged in inciting servile insurrection" — a crime punishable by death.[110]

JANUARY 25, 1863: "Well, Burnside has moved again, and got stuck in the mud," Oliver Willcox Norton, of the Eighty-third Pennsylvania Volunteers, writes to his sister. "That is the short of it. The long of it was the five days it took us to get six miles and back to camp. It beat all the Peninsula mud I ever saw, and demonstrated the falsity of Burnside's theory that if twelve horses couldn't draw a cannon twenty-four could. The more horses the worse it was." Begun with high hopes on January 20, this attempt by Ambrose Burnside to flank Lee's army by crossing the Rappahannock River above Fredericksburg, less than a month after he led the Army of the Potomac to a rending defeat at that town, will be infamous after the fact as Burnside's "Mud March." *In Washington,* Burnside meets with President Lincoln and asks him either to dismiss several officers serving under him or to accept Burnside's own resignation. Lincoln relieves Burnside of command; he already has a replacement in mind.[111]

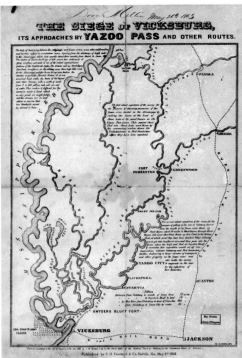

The Siege of Vicksburg, Its Approaches by Yazoo Pass and Other Routes. Lithograph by W. R. Robertson, Mobile, Alabama, 1863, after T. S. Hardee.

Why the Army of the Potomac Doesn't Move. Four pencil and Chinese white drawings by Alfred R. Waud, 1862.

JANUARY 26, 1863: "I have placed you at the head of the Army of the Potomac," Lincoln writes, in a remarkable letter to Major General Joseph Hooker. After noting Hooker's many fine qualities, including bravery, skill as a soldier, self-confidence, and tempered ambition, the president chastises his new eastern theater commander for thwarting Burnside "as much as you could, in which you did a great wrong to the country, and to a most meritorious and honorable brother officer." Further, Lincoln cautions the new commander:

> I have heard, in such way as to believe it, of your recently saying that both the Army and the Government needed a Dictator. Of course it was not *for* this, but in spite of it, that I have given you the command. Only those generals who gain successes, can set up dictators. What I now ask of you is military success, and I will risk the dictatorship. . . . And now, beware of rashness . . . but with energy, and sleepless vigilance, go forward, and give us victories.[112]

FEBRUARY 1863

FEBRUARY 2, 1863: Union troops under Lieutenant Colonel of Engineers James H. Wilson launch the Yazoo Pass expedition, an attempt to establish a water route to Vicksburg that will not bring Union boats in range of the city's guns. Wilson's men will succeed in cutting through a levee blocking the proposed route; but the Federal plan has been anticipated by Vicksburg's commanding officer, Lieutenant General John C. Pemberton, whose name has been given to a small fort that will stymie Union progress. After repeated artillery assaults and infantry probes fail to dislodge the Confederates in the fort, the expedition will end in failure on March 20.[113]

FEBRUARY 10, 1863: "It is remarked that there never were so many women and children traveling as there are now," Alabama-based Confederate nurse Kate Cumming writes in her diary. "Numbers of ladies, whose husbands are in the army, have been compelled to give up their homes for economy and protection, and seek others among their relatives. . . . We have a large floating population — the people who have been driven from their homes by the invader."[114]

FEBRUARY 13, 1863: The legislative act granting Jefferson Davis the authority to suspend the writ of habeas corpus expires. As the Confederate Congress debates an extension (which will not occur this year; see February 17, 1864), it demands an accounting of civilians currently held under

Abraham Lincoln. Letter to General Joseph Hooker, January 26, 1863.

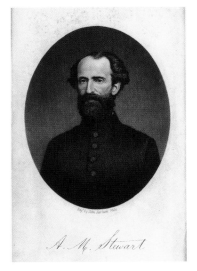

Chaplain Alexander M. Stewart (1814–1875), USA. The acutely observant Chaplain Stewart served with the Thirteenth Pennsylvania Volunteers (redesignated the 102nd after its first three-month tour of duty) and sent "almost weekly sketches" of life in the Union army to home-front newspapers.

suspicion of disloyalty by the War Department. The department responds with a list of 302 names.[115]

FEBRUARY 14, 1863: Concerned with propaganda "efforts now being made by the enemies of the Government and the advocates of a disgraceful PEACE," a group of influential New York civilians establish the Loyal Publication Society, dedicated to "the distribution of journals and documents of unquestionable and unconditional loyalty" to both civilians throughout the nation and Union troops wherever they are stationed. Headed, after the first year, by legal scholar Francis Lieber (see February 16, 1862, and April 24, 1863), the society will be cited by the *New York Times* as an organization that "deserves the support of every patriotic citizen who appreciates the importance of enlightening public sentiment as to the real objects of the war and the duties of a true loyalty."[116]

FEBRUARY 22, 1863: "It seemed as though a great battle were opening," Union chaplain A. M. Stewart will report, to a home-front newspaper, about "a heavy cannonade" that occurs on this day. It throws his camp, near Falmouth, Virginia, into an uproar over a surprise attack — until one laconic soldier, "who lay in his tent and counted the number of shots," relieves his comrades' apprehensions. "Thirty-four along the Union lines — Thirteen among the rebels [the number of states each side claimed]. 'Salute,' he shouted, 'Washington's birth-day.' Ah, yes, how stupid not to have remembered. The excitement

at once vanished, if not the veneration. Federals and Confederates both shooting at the memory of Washington! Fortunate, no doubt, that the old gentleman is dead. . . . The flames of this rebellion may yet consume all the seeming good our fathers accomplished."[117]

FEBRUARY 25, 1863: The National Currency Act (which will be renewed and renamed the National Bank Act in 1864) becomes law in the Union, providing a framework for greater investment in government bonds, by which the war is being financed, and laying the groundwork for the banking system that will prevail for more than fifty years. Establishing a Currency Bureau in the Treasury Department, headed by a comptroller of the currency, the act adds fuel to Democrats' suspicions that Republican wartime programs are attempting to "destroy the fixed institutions of the States, and to build up a central moneyed despotism."[118]

FEBRUARY 26, 1863: The Cherokee Indian National Council repeals its ordinance of secession, abolishes slavery, and proclaims itself for the Union.[119]

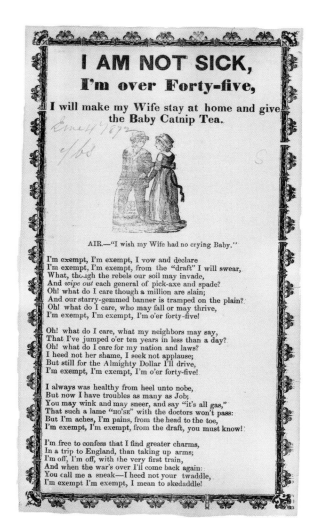

John S. Mosby (1833–1916), CSA. A captain at the time of his March 1863 raid on Fairfax Court House, the resourceful commander was a colonel by the end of the war.

"I Am Not Sick, I'm over Forty-Five," sung to the now-forgotten tune "I Wish My Wife Had No Crying Baby." This Civil War song is a waggish riff on the many dodges and excuses Northerners came up with to avoid conscription—including rapid aging: "I'm aches, I'm pains, from the head to the toe / I'm exempt, I'm exempt, from the draft, you must know!"

MARCH 1863

MARCH 3, 1863: President Lincoln signs "An Act for enrolling and calling out the National Forces, and for other purposes," the first effective Federal conscription law — but one whose administration will prove so inefficient and corrupt that the act will be divisive during the war and a model of how *not* to frame a draft law thereafter. With certain exceptions, the law deems able-bodied males between twenty and forty-five eligible for service, leaving a large loophole available to those with ready cash: a man can hire a substitute or buy his way out for three hundred dollars. *At the same time,* with the war not going well and even such fierce loyalists as *Chicago Tribune* editor Joseph Medill writing, "The Rebs can't be conquered by the present machinery," the influence of the Peace Democrats, led by Clement L. Vallandigham, of Ohio, is on the rise. In the Confederacy, organizations in favor of peace and rejoining the Union are forming, including the Peace and Constitution Society in Arkansas, the Peace Society in northern Alabama and northern Georgia, and the Heroes of America in western North Carolina and east Tennessee — although they will not be as influential as Copperheads are in the Union. *Also today,* Congress passes the Habeas Corpus Act, legitimizing Lincoln's previous suspensions of the writ (see April 27, 1861, and September 24, 1862) and allowing the president to suspend the writ, when needed, for the duration of the war.[120]

MARCH 6, 1863: A mob of white men rampages through the African-American section of Detroit, destroying thirty-two houses, killing several black people, and leaving more than two hundred homeless — one of several violent anti-black demonstrations in 1863, which are fueled by job worries and inflammatory statements made by some leaders of the Democratic Party.[121]

MARCH 8, 1863: Confederate cavalry officer John Singleton Mosby delights the South and embarrasses the North when he and twenty-nine of his officially sanctioned partisan rangers steal through Union lines and enter Fairfax Court House, Virginia, which is filled with sleepy and sleeping Union troops. Mosby's great prize is General Edwin H. Stoughton, whom the rangers find in bed, asleep. They leave town with the general, thirty-two other prisoners, fifty-eight horses, arms, and equipment — and an enhanced reputation for derring-do.[122]

MARCH 10, 1863: By a vote of five to four (with all three of the justices Lincoln has appointed to date in the majority), the U.S. Supreme Court hands down a decision favorable to the Lincoln administration in the *Prize Cases,* which involve the Union navy's seizure of four vessels (or prizes) violating the Federal blockade of the South (see July 10, 1861). At issue is whether the president exceeded his constitutional authority in ordering the blockade when Congress had not declared a state of war. The Court rules that although only Congress can

> *"I beg you to fly to arms, and smite with death the power that would bury the government and your liberty in the same hopeless grave."*
>
> —FREDERICK DOUGLASS,
> MARCH 14, 1863

General Stuart's New Aid. Wood engraving published in *Harper's Weekly*, April 4, 1863. Identified in the caption only as "a young lady residing at Fairfax Court House," this nod to the intrepid nature of a Confederate woman depicts Antonia Ford, who was arrested not long before by Federal authorities for aiding the Rebels.

MARCH
1 2 3 4 5 6 7 8 9 10 11 12 **13 14** 15 16 17 18 19 20 21 22 23 24 25 26 27 28 29 30 31

declare war, Lincoln did have the power to put down an insurrection. The rationale advanced by the Court also, by implication, supports other controversial presidential actions, such as issuance of the Emancipation Proclamation and suspension of habeas corpus.[123]

MARCH 13, 1863: In Fairfax Court House, Virginia, Union authorities arrest vivacious civilian Antonia Ford for providing such valuable information to the Confederate army that, as averred in a letter the *New York Times* will print on March 14, "[Jeb] Stuart has conferred on her the rank of major in the rebel army." Ford has, indeed, received an *honorary* commission from Lee's celebrated cavalry commander, after providing Confederate officers — partisan raider John Mosby among them — with information overheard from Union men occupying her town. Today, she embarks on another sort of adventure when Major Joseph C. Willard, her escort to Washington's Old Capitol prison, begins to fall under her charms (see March 10, 1864).[124]

MARCH 14, 1863: U.S. Navy captain David Dixon Porter embarks on another attempt to approach Vicksburg from the north (as James Wilson's Yazoo Pass expedition is failing; see February 2, 1863). Porter's Steele's Bayou expedition is to proceed through several linked bayous, blazing a route that will allow Federal troops to land behind the city. From the start it is tough going; delays caused by natural obstacles in the water are compounded by increasing Confederate resistance. Rebel troops impress slaves to throw up defenses; other slaves take refuge with troops dispatched by William Sherman to assist Porter as his operation falters. The expedition will end without achieving Porter's objectives but with vast stores of food and supplies in Union hands that would otherwise have sustained Vicksburg. *The day Porter embarks,* Admiral David Farragut leads a flotilla on a daring attempt to pass under the formidable guns the Confederates have placed on the bluffs at Port Hudson, on the Mississippi River between Vicksburg and New Orleans. Only Farragut's flagship, USS *Hartford,* and USS *Albatross* make it through the furious rain of Confederate fire; other ships are forced to fall back. USS *Mississippi,* having run aground, has to be destroyed — the explosion producing a thunderous roar and such a brilliant flash of flame and flying timbers that soldiers in a Union encampment near Baton Rouge are temporarily "stupefied."[125] *Also this day,* braced by the Emancipation Proclamation, and by U.S. War Department assurances that black and white soldiers will receive equal pay, former slave and civil rights spokesman Frederick Douglass puts the full weight of his remarkable eloquence into "Men of Color to Arms!," a statement published in the *National Anti-Slavery Standard:*

> By every consideration which binds you to your enslaved fellow-countrymen, and the peace and welfare of your country; by every aspiration which you cherish for the

·U·S·S· ALEXANDRIA·

Bayou Lafourche. La. 1864. —

·U·S·RAM· GENERAL· PRICE·

Brigadier General Fitzhugh Lee (1835–1905), CSA.

Brigadier General William W. Averell (1832–1900), USA.

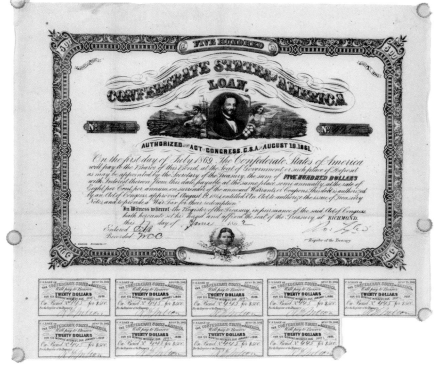

Confederate States of America bonds. The Confederate government, from the first, relied more on bond issues than unpopular taxes, issuing $15 million in bonds in 1861.

OPPOSITE: *USS Alexandria* and *US Ram General Price,* two vessels of the Union's Mississippi River Squadron depicted in watercolor by Ensign D. M. N. Stouffer, ca. 1864–65. Ironically, both these boats were originally Confederate vessels. CSS *Alexandria* was captured at Yazoo City, Mississippi, in July 1863. *General Price* was the Southern ram *General Sterling Price* (after the Confederate general) until it was sunk during the Union conquest of Memphis. Raised by the Federals, its name was shortened when it was placed in Federal service.

MARCH

1 2 3 4 5 6 7 8 9 10 11 12 13 14 15 **16** **17** **18** 19 20 21 22 23 24 25 26 27 28 29 30 31

freedom and equality of yourselves and your children; by all the ties of blood and identity which make us one with the brave black men now fighting our battles in Louisiana, in South Carolina, I beg you to fly to arms, and smite with death the power that would bury the government and your liberty in the same hopeless grave. . . . I am authorized to assure you that you will receive the same wages, the same rations, the same equipments, the same protection, the same treatment, and the same bounty, secured to white soldiers. . . . The iron gate of our prison stands half open. One gallant rush from the North will fling it wide open, while four millions of our brothers and sisters shall march out into liberty.[126]

MARCH 16, 1863: Secretary of War Edwin M. Stanton sends initial instructions to Samuel Gridley Howe, James McKaye, and Robert Dale Owen, of the newly formed American Freedmen's Inquiry Commission, which is to investigate the condition of slaves and former slaves. They will soon travel south to interview freedmen and Union officers, their work culminating in the creation of the Bureau of Refugees, Freedmen, and Abandoned Lands in 1865.[127]

MARCH 17, 1863: "You have got to stop these disgraceful cavalry 'surprises!' " Joe Hooker raged to General William Averell, after a daring penetration of Union lines by General Fitzhugh Lee's Confederate horsemen. (A taunting note that Lee, a nephew of Robert E., left Averell, his West Point classmate, rubbed salt in the wound: "If you won't go home, return my visit and bring me a sack of coffee.") Today, Averell leads twenty-one hundred Union cavalry across the Rappahannock River in pursuit of Lee. In the ensuing five-hour battle at Kelly's Ford (in which a Confederate hero of Fredericksburg, artillery major John "The Gallant" Pelham, is killed), the Union cavalry, long rated inferior to their Rebel counterparts, prove themselves equal to the Confederates. Afterwards, a jaunty Averell leaves a package with a reply to Lee's note: "Dear Fitz: Here's your coffee. Here's your visit. How do you like it?"[128]

MARCH 18, 1863: With the South racked by inflation, plagued by shortages, and strapped for funds, the Confederate Congress has authorized borrowing money through the banking house of French financier Emile Erlanger, a deal negotiated by the Confederate commissioner to France, John Slidell (see November 8, 1861). Today, Erlanger extends a loan of three million pounds — backed by Confederate bonds redeemable for Southern cotton, to be delivered within six months of the end of the war. The Erlanger loan renews, for a time, the Confederacy's ability to conduct business on the Continent.[129]

MARCH 26, 1863: The Confederate Congress passes the Impressment Act, authorizing local impressment agents to seize black freedmen and private property (including food, clothing, slaves, railroads, horses, and cattle) to supply the army and navy. Impressment had been used earlier by state government and military officials in emergency situations, but, under the new policy, property seizures will be regulated by state boards under the War Department and become a matter of course in maintaining the war effort (military units will still impress goods as needed). Fraught with inequities, impressment will prompt strong public opposition; eight state legislatures will lodge official complaints, deeming the act a violation of states' rights.[130]

APRIL 1863

APRIL 2, 1863: At a time when the food rations of the Army of Northern Virginia have been cut by 50 percent, hundreds of distraught citizens gather in the streets of crowded and inflation-ridden Richmond, Virginia — where it takes more than ten times the money to feed a family for a week today than it did just three years ago. Receiving only a platitudinous speech from Governor John Letcher when they mass in front of the Capitol, people go in search of somewhere to vent their anger, sacking stores in the business district as they storm through the city. Police and militia finally end the violence, arresting some forty-four women and twenty-nine men out of a mob of over a thousand. Amid rumors of another planned food uprising, cannons are placed in the business district, and troops slated to reinforce General Longstreet are kept in the city. Other towns across the Confederate States suffer similar disturbances as prices skyrocket and civilian food supplies dwindle.[131]

APRIL 7, 1863: A Union flotilla of nine ironclad vessels, captained by handpicked officers and led by Flag Officer Samuel Du Pont, sails into the Charleston, South Carolina, harbor. Du Pont plans to reduce Fort Sumter by smashing its weakest walls and then sail past the fort to the city, but the Charleston defenses prove formidable. "The fires of hell were turned upon the Union fleet," Du Pont's chief of staff, Christopher Rodgers, will later report. "The air seemed full of heavy shot, and as they

The Civil War in America: Attack by the Federal Ironclads on the Harbor Defenses of Charleston. Engraving published in the *Illustrated London News*, May 16, 1863. The scene depicted "demonstrated undoubtedly that the ladies of Charleston had no undue fear for the result of the attack, which, if successful, would place their homes at the mercy of an exasperated foe," artist-correspondent Frank Vizetelly declared in his written dispatch.

APRIL

1 2 3 4 5 6 7 8 9 **10** 11 12 **13** 14 **15** 16 17 18 19 20 21 22 23 24 25 26 27 28 29 30

flew they could be seen as plainly as a base-ball in one of our games." Despite their armor, the Union ships take a terrible beating; USS *Keokuk,* which Rodgers will remember being "riddled like a colander," will sink the next day. The expedition is proof positive that Charleston cannot be taken by naval forces alone.[132]

APRIL 10, 1863: Within a long state-of-the-Confederacy speech to the Southern people, President Davis addresses a subject that has caused much recent civilian unrest (see April 2, 1863):

> The very unfavorable season, the protracted droughts of last year, reduced the harvests on which we depended far below an average yield. . . . If through a confidence in early peace, which may prove delusive, our fields should be now devoted to the production of cotton and tobacco instead of grain and live stock, and other articles necessary for the subsistence of the people and the Army, the consequences may prove serious, if not disastrous. . . . Let fields be devoted exclusively to the production of corn, oats, beans, peas, potatoes, and other food for man and beast.[133]

APRIL 13, 1863: Now commanding the Department of the Ohio and concerned about the activities of Peace Democrats in his command, General Ambrose Burnside issues General Order No. 38: "The habit of declaring sympathy for the enemy

will not be allowed in this department. Persons committing such offenses will be at once arrested with a view of being tried . . . or sent beyond our lines into the lines of their friends. It must be understood that treason, expressed or implied, will not be tolerated in this department." Ohio's leading Peace Democrat, Clement L. Vallandigham, opposed to the war from its beginning and now a candidate for governor of the state, will react to the order as a bull might react to a red flag (see May 1, 7, 1863).[134]

APRIL 15, 1863: "Uncle Abe and Mrs. Abe were down, lately," Chaplain A. M. Stewart writes to his home-front readers from his army encampment, "and, what showings off were here and there!" — including the "mighty host" of the reorganized and reinvigorated Army of the Potomac passing in review before the president and General Joseph Hooker. Behind the scenes, another sort of review was going on: sometime during the Lincolns' visit (April 6–11), the president gave Hooker a memorandum on the general's planned campaign against Richmond. "My opinion is, that just now, with the enemy directly ahead of us, there is *no* eligible route for us into Richmond. . . . Hence our prime object is the enemies' army in front of us, . . . we should continually harass and menace him, so that he shall have no leisure, nor safety in sending away detachments. If he weakens himself, then pitch into him."[135]

Review by the President of the Cavalry of the Army of the Potomac. Pencil, brown wash, and Chinese white drawing by Alfred R. Waud, April 9, 1863. "You can get some idea of the number of troops reviewed when I tell you that, for nearly two hours, they were passing steadily in solid column," Captain Charles F. Morse wrote home a few days later. "In the center opposite the troops, looking sick and worn out, dressed in a plain black suit with the tallest of stove-pipe hats, was the President, seated on a fine horse with rich trimmings."

APRIL

1 2 3 4 5 6 7 8 9 10 11 12 13 14 15 **16** **17** 18 **19** 20 21 22 23 **24** 25 26 **27** 28 29 30

APRIL 16, 1863: Vicksburg citizens celebrating the impregnability of their "Gibraltar of the West" at a gala ball are alarmed by the sound of artillery as Captain David D. Porter leads a flotilla of twelve Union vessels past the city's formidable defenses. Protected by gunboats, the transport vessels in the flotilla bear the first of General Grant's army to pass Vicksburg on their way to establishing a base to its south, as Grant launches his second campaign to take the city.[136]

APRIL 17, 1863: Leading seventeen hundred Union cavalrymen, Colonel Benjamin H. Grierson embarks on a spectacular two-week, six-hundred-mile raid through Mississippi, during which the Federals tear up railroads, take captives, and divert attention and Confederate manpower from impeding Grant's operations around Vicksburg.[137]

APRIL 19, 1863: "I do not think our enemies are so confident of success as they used to be," Robert E. Lee writes to his wife. "If we can baffle them in their various designs this year & our people are true to our cause & not so devoted to themselves & their own aggrandizement. . . . next fall [after the U.S. presidential election] there will be a great change in public opinion at the North. The Republicans will be destroyed & I think the friends of peace will become so strong as that the next administration will go in on that basis. We have only therefore to resist manfully . . . [and] our success will be certain."[138]

APRIL 24, 1863: Struggling under runaway inflation, the Confederate government imposes a comprehensive tax law, including a progressive income tax, excise and license duties, and a 10 percent profits tax. A 10 percent "tax in kind" on agricultural produce is bitterly resented by farmers who are already subject to impressment of needed goods by Confederate commissary and quartermaster officers (see March 26, 1863). *In Washington,* President Lincoln issues General Order No. 100, Instructions for the Government of Armies of the United States in the Field. Generally known as the Lieber Code, after its principal author, German-American political philosopher Francis Lieber (1789–1872; see February 16, 1862, and February 14, 1863), these instructions represent the first attempt to codify the international law of war. Among its many provisions, the code includes a statement that reflects the changing nature of the war, and of U.S. armed forces: "The law of nations shows no distinction of color, and if an enemy of the United States should enslave and sell any captured persons of their Army, it would be a case for the severest retaliation, if not redress."[139]

APRIL 27, 1863: "Gen. Hooker has certainly performed wonders, during his brief command," Chaplain A. M. Stewart wrote, to his home newspaper, earlier this month. "The army, when he took it, was defeated, discouraged . . . and . . . demoralized. The contrast is now remarkable. . . . the soldiers seem universally to have the fullest confidence in Gen. Hooker,

Colonel Grierson, Sixth Illinois Cavalry.
Wood engraving published as the cover illustration of *Harper's Weekly,* June 6, 1863. For his leadership on the successful April–May raid, which diverted the Confederates and demonstrated that Union troops could operate without a supply line, Benjamin H. Grierson (1826–1911) was promoted to brigadier general.

The Army of the Potomac Crossing the Rappahannock River on a Pontoon Bridge at Night, Near Rappahannock Station. Drawing by Edwin Forbes, October 1863.

APRIL
1 2 3 4 5 6 7 8 9 10 11 12 13 14 15 16 17 18 19 20 21 22 23 24 25 26 27 28 **29** 30

and, also, in themselves. . . . What the result will be, time and coming events will unfold. Gen. Hooker has not, as yet . . . conducted an active campaign." Today, Hooker begins to move against Robert E. Lee's Army of Northern Virginia.[140]

APRIL 29, 1863: "The enemy crossed the Rappahannock today in large numbers," Robert E. Lee wires President Davis, from his headquarters at Fredericksburg, Virginia. "Their intention I presume is to turn our left & probably to get into our rear. Our scattered condition favors their operations. I hope if any reinforcements can be sent they may be forwarded

immediately." This evening, Fighting Joe Hooker joins the three Union army corps that have crossed the river at their camp near the large house owned by the Chancellor family in an area known, for good reason, as the Wilderness. Armed with more accurate information on his enemy than previous Army of the Potomac commanders have enjoyed, aware that his forces outnumber Lee's and that Lee's are scattered, Hooker still has the air of confidence that led him, days earlier, to say to some of his officers: "My plans are perfect, and when I start to carry them out, may God have mercy on General Lee, for I will have none."[141]

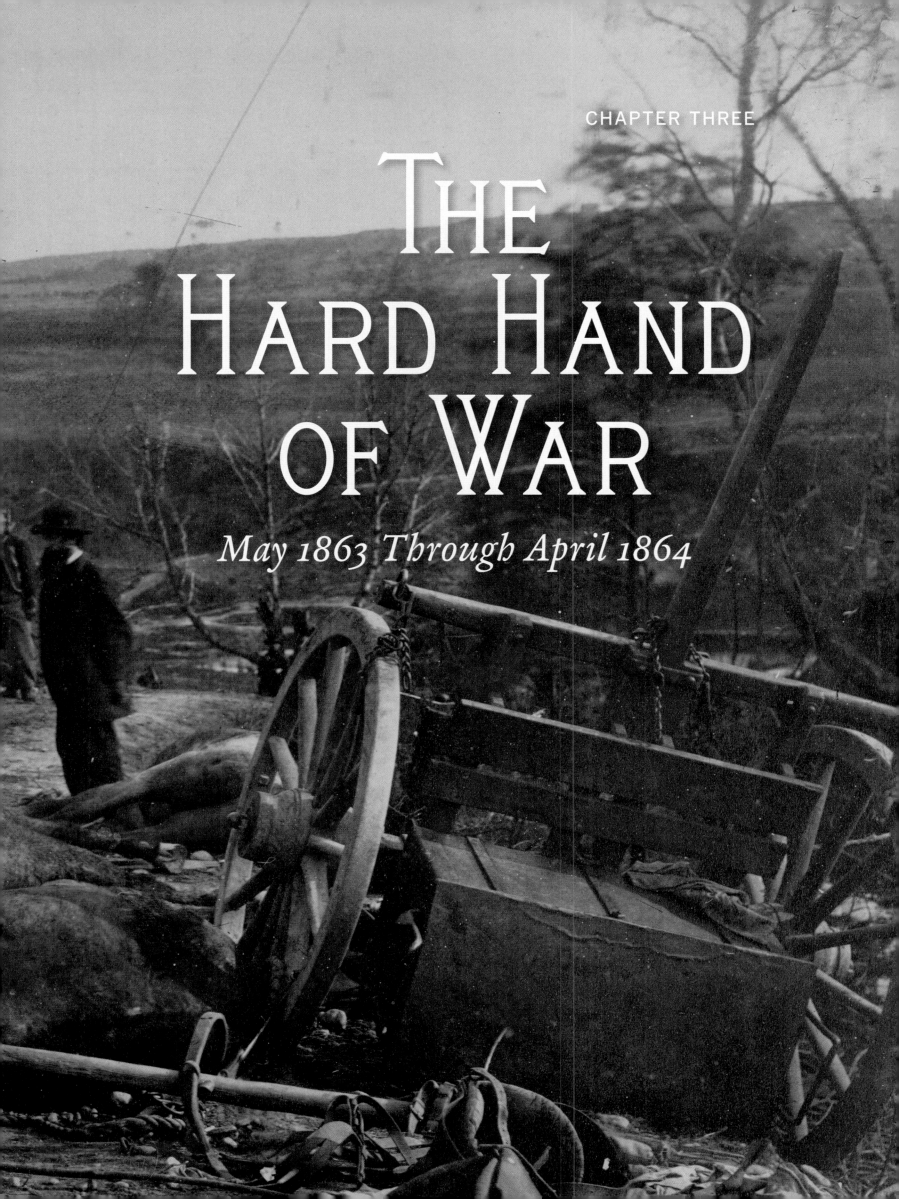

CHAPTER THREE

THE HARD HAND OF WAR

May 1863 Through April 1864

"*We have a great many wounded; the same old story — men mutilated in every possible way....I am sick at heart at these scenes, and there seems to be little prospect of a change.*"

KATE CUMMING, NURSE, ARMY OF TENNESSEE, CSA, DIARY ENTRY, JUNE 27, 1863[1]

"*One's heart grows sick of war, after all, when you see what it really is; every once in a while I feel so horrified and disgusted — it seems to me like a great slaughter-house and the men mutually butchering each other — then I feel how impossible it appears, again, to retire from this contest, until we have carried our points.*"

WALT WHITMAN, USA, LETTER TO HIS MOTHER, SEPTEMBER 8, 1863[2]

"The army like General Hooker," Lieutenant Colonel Rufus Dawes observed, as his new commanding officer performed wonders reorganizing and revivifying the Union's Army of the Potomac. "They like him because he is 'fighting Joe Hooker.' They like him because of the onions and potatoes he has furnished, and ... because ... they expect him to lead them to victory." That was Hooker's expectation as well, as he crossed the Rappahannock River the night of April 30, 1863, and joined the vanguard of his army at its camp in a seventy-acre clearing around the George Chancellor house (Chancellorsville). Hooker's formidable force, primed and ready for battle, outnumbered by two to one the sixty-two thousand men of Robert E. Lee's Army of Northern Virginia who were arrayed against it. It seemed the time had come for an Army of the Potomac victory, "the glory and blessing of which," Dawes believed, "will repay us for the disasters

Captain Charles F. Morse (1839–1926), USA. Frontispiece from Charles F. Morse, *Letters Written During the Civil War, 1861–1865,* 1898. One of many eloquent and opinionated wartime letter-writers, Morse was furious at Major General Joe Hooker's decision to withdraw from the field at Chancellorsville. Hooker, he deduced, "gained his position [as commander of the Army of the Potomac] by merely brag and blow."

Major General Joseph Hooker (1814–1879), USA. Although he had done an exceptional job reorganizing the Army of the Potomac upon assuming its command, by June of 1863, many were beginning to wonder if Hooker was becoming "another McClellan."

and sufferings of the past." Yet Hooker had begun his operations without a true appreciation for the character of the countryside in which he had chosen to fight. Chancellorsville was situated in one of the few cleared portions of the "Wilderness" — seventy square miles of tangled, ravine-pocked terrain centering on a nearly impenetrable forest that one Union infantryman would call "the most god forsaken looking place I ever saw."

As Hooker awoke to his geographical problems on the morning of May 1, in the western theater David Dixon Porter's naval fleet was ferrying Ulysses S. Grant and his forty-four-thousand-man army to a point on the eastern bank of the Mississippi River well below Vicksburg. From there, the ques-tion was how best to proceed. Grant's daring decision worried his subordinates, including Fifteenth Corps commander William Sherman, as well as General in Chief Halleck and President Lincoln in Washington. Taking with them only a minimum of supplies, Grant's men will not depend on the vulnerable supply line extending from U.S. encampments above Vicksburg; they will live off the land for what is bound to be a significant period of time as they move inland on a circuitous route. Vicksburg has been Grant's primary objective since October 1862, and he remains bound to take the city. "One of my superstitions had always been," he will write after the war, "when I started to go anywhere or to do anything, not to turn back, or stop until the thing intended was accomplished."[3]

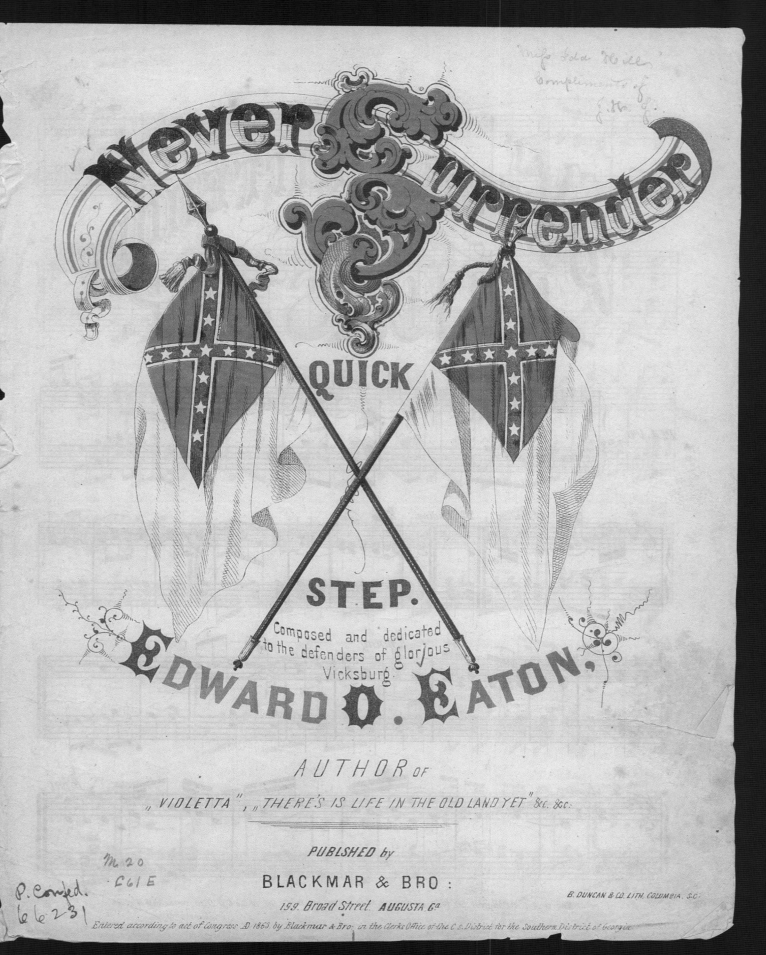

"Never Surrender, Quick Step," composed by Edward O. Eaton, published by Blackmar & Bro., Augusta, Georgia, 1863. The song was "dedicated to the defenders of glorious Vicksburg," who repulsed two Union attempts to breach the city's formidable defenses on May 19 and May 22, 1863.

THE PARTING "Buy us too".

The Parting—"Buy Us Too." Color lithograph by Henry Louis Stephens, from *Album Varieties No. 3: The Slave in 1863*, 1863. "[T]he handcuff, the lash—the tearing away of children from parents, of husbands from wives," actress and former Georgia resident Fanny Kemble wrote in her diary, "these are the realities which belong to the system [of American slavery]."

May 1863 Through April 1864

MAY 1863

MAY 1, 1863: The Confederate Congress passes a resolution declaring that captured officers of black regiments who are "deemed as inciting servile insurrection" should be "put to death or be otherwise punished at the discretion" of a military tribunal. Black enlisted men are to "be delivered to the authorities of the State or States in which they shall be captured to be dealt with according to the present or future laws of such State or States." The prisoner exchange cartel established in July of 1862, and based on the equal treatment of the men of both armies, begins to break down. *In England,* noted actress Frances Anne (Fanny) Kemble, former wife of a Southern slave owner, this month publishes her *Journal of a Residence on a Georgian Plantation* in an effort to persuade the English government *not* to support the Confederacy. An account of the cruelty of slavery as she perceives it (marked by "Scorn, derision, insult, menace — the handcuff, the lash — the tearing away of children from parents"), the *Journal* will have such an effect that portions will be read aloud in the House of Commons. In July, when an American edition is published, it will be equally well received — in the Union. *In Mount Vernon, Ohio,* leading Copperhead (Peace Democrat) Clement Vallandigham delivers a fiery speech before a large audience (which includes two army captains, dressed as civilians and taking careful notes). Denouncing "this wicked, cruel and unnecessary war . . . for the freedom of the blacks and the enslavement of the whites," Vallandigham also lambastes Ambrose Burnside's

General Order No. 38 (see April 13, 1863) as "a base usurpation of arbitrary authority." His subsequent arrest by soldiers who break down the door of his house in the middle of the night will cause a riot during which his angry supporters set fire to the offices of a Republican newspaper — and inadvertently destroy both the paper and a half block of adjoining buildings. *In Virginia,* Robert E. Lee leaves Major General Jubal Early, with some ten thousand men and limited artillery support, to protect the city of Fredericksburg and advances to meet Joseph Hooker's army. Hooker, meanwhile, begins the day cautiously. It is nearly 11:00 AM when he orders an advance by three Union columns over three different routes. After they run into heavy Confederate resistance (as well as the treacheries of Wilderness terrain), Hooker's caution deepens to a timidity that stuns some of his subordinates and startles Lee: in midafternoon Hooker recalls the columns and forms a defensive line around Chancellorsville, thus surrendering the initiative to Lee. "The men went back disappointed," Union brigadier general Alpheus S. Williams will report, "not without grumbling." As night falls and the Federals entrench, Lee meets with Stonewall Jackson and develops, for the following day, a risky plan that violates a principal tenet of military tactics.[4]

MAY 2-4, 1863: Outnumbered by the enemy, and already separated from Jubal Early's men protecting Fredericksburg, Lee divides his army again, sending Stonewall Jackson and

127

Fanny Kemble (1809–1893). Steel engraving, ca. 1873. A celebrated actress who abhorred what she had seen of American slavery as the former wife of Georgia slave owner Pierce Butler, Kemble published the diary of her experiences in the South primarily to discourage the British government from recognizing the Confederacy.

Battle of Chancellorville. Color lithograph by Kurz & Allison, 1889–90. This view of the battle includes, at right, a depiction of the mortal wounding of Stonewall Jackson. Hit in the right hand, the left wrist, and above the left elbow, Jackson was taken to Dr. Hunter McGuire, who amputated his arm just below the shoulder. But the doctor could not prevent pneumonia from invading the lungs of the weakened general.

his troops on a fourteen-mile march to attack the Union right flank, which Jeb Stuart's reconnaissance has shown to be vulnerable. After marching most of the day, Jackson's men smash into General Oliver O. Howard's Eleventh Corps at about 6:00 PM, as many of Howard's men are cooking their dinner. Rebel yells, stunned Union soldiers, and the cries of the wounded and dying turn the once placid evening into a nightmare as the Union corps buckles and falls back, pell-mell, to Chancellorsville. "Men on foot on horseback on mules & in teams were rushing & piling back," Union soldier Charles Parker will report some days later. "Some had no caps some not coats all going for dear life." For the Confederates, the night's triumph is tempered by a terrible accident: riding forward with a small party at about 9:00 PM on this shadow-filled, moonlit night, Jackson is caught in an encounter between a Federal unit and a Confederate brigade and is shot by mistake by his own men. He is carried to the rear for medical attention; Jeb Stuart assumes temporary command of Jackson's troops.[5]

MAY 3, 1863: "Where is Gen. Hooker?" an anxious President Lincoln wires to Hooker's chief of staff, Major General Daniel A. Butterfield. Hooker and his men entrenched around the Chancellor house are being hit hard on the right of their line by Jeb Stuart's Confederates — infantry pressing forward under heavy fire while Confederate artillery, perfectly positioned on high ground, rakes the Union line with shells. One shell splits the pillar on the Chancellor house porch next

to which Hooker is standing, briefly knocking him out and making him shaky for the rest of the day. Other shells set fire to the house. As Lee orders all his troops to press forward, and Major General Darius N. Couch, acting for Hooker, orders a Union retreat, the Federals hastily evacuate their wounded from the house, along with the Chancellor family and other civilians who have been sheltering in the basement. "At our last look," fourteen-year-old Sue Chancellor will later remember, "our old home was completely enveloped in flames." While Hooker's men establish a new line anchored by the Rapidan and Rappahannock rivers, other Union troops, under Major General John Sedgwick, assault Jubal Early's Confederates at Fredericksburg. After confusion, delays, and ferocious fighting, the Northerners gain possession of the high ground above the city that so many of their comrades died trying to attain just a few months before (see December 13, 1862). This causes Lee to postpone a final assault on Hooker; dividing his force yet again, he sends men to reinforce Early. Lee also takes a moment to respond to a note from the wounded Stonewall Jackson: "Could I have directed events," Lee writes, "I should have chosen for the good of the country to have been disabled in your stead."[6]

MAY 4, 1863: The battle of Chancellorsville comes to an end as Confederate troops regain their lost ground at Fredericksburg (General Sedgwick and his Federal troops withdraw across the Rappahannock after nightfall) while, near Chancel-

Thomas Jonathan ("Stonewall") Jackson (1824–1863), CSA. Photographic print on *carte de visite* mount, date unknown. By 1863 a near-legendary military commander, Jackson was deeply mourned throughout the Confederacy. "Would that the battle of Chancellorsville had never have been fought," the *Knoxville Register* editorialized, "if the brilliant victory have [*sic*] cost us the life of Stonewall Jackson."

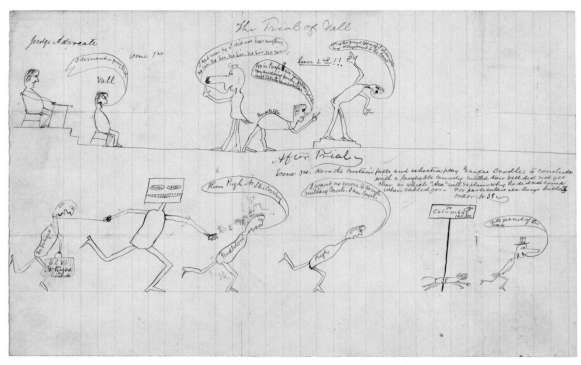

The Trial of Vall. Ink drawing on lined paper, ca. 1863. This eccentric political cartoon depicts, in three primitively drawn scenes, the controversial trial of Copperhead leader Clement Vallandigham and its aftermath. Above, left, Vallandigham demands of the military judge that he be tried by a jury; above, right, the military trial proceeds; bottom, Vallandigham (extreme left) is dragged off to prison in the Dry Tortugas (a fate that did not actually befall him).

MAY

1 2 3 4 5 **6 7** 8 9 **10** 11 12 13 14 15 16 17 18 19 20 21 22 23 24 25 26 27 28 29 30 31

lorsville, an uncertain Hooker does nothing — to the everlasting frustration of many of his men. Among some, frustration will deepen to anger the night of May 5–6, when they, too, are ordered to recross the Rappahannock. "When the time came to show himself, [Hooker] was found without the qualities necessary for a general," an irate Captain Charles F. Morse, of the Second Massachusetts Infantry, will write home on May 7. "I doubt if, ever in the history of this war, another chance will be given us to fight the enemy with such odds in our favor as we had last Sunday, and that chance has been worse than lost to us." Against all odds, and at rending cost to both armies (some thirty thousand men killed, wounded, or missing), Robert E. Lee has won his most brilliant victory of the Civil War.[7]

MAY 6, 1863: In Washington, where he has been anxiously awaiting news of the Army of the Potomac, Lincoln learns, via a telegram from Major General Daniel Butterfield, that Hooker has suffered a stunning defeat at Chancellorsville. Lincoln's friend newsman Noah Brooks is with the president when he receives the wire. "I shall never forget that picture of despair," Brooks will later report. "Clasping his hands behind his back, he walked up and down the room, saying, 'My God! My God! What will the country say! What will the country say!'"[8]

MAY 7, 1863: In Cincinnati, Ohio, a military commission convicts noted civilian Clement Vallandigham of having expressed "disloyal sentiments and opinions, with the object . . . of weak-

ening the power of the Government in its effort to suppress the unlawful rebellion" and orders him imprisoned for the duration of the war. Because of General Burnside's sparse communication, President Lincoln is forced to follow the case largely by newspaper accounts — many of them peppered with thunderous protests and a host of new epithets directed against the president (including "demagogue," "Caesar," and "despot"). "A crime has been committed against the most vital right of the poor and the rich . . . the right to think, to speak, to live," the *Dubuque Herald* will thunder editorially on May 14. Troubled by Burnside's actions, the protests, and the constitutional questions provoked by this episode, Lincoln will commute Vallandigham's sentence to exile in the Confederacy. On May 26, the Copperhead leader will be placed in Confederate hands at Murfreesboro, Tennessee. He will eventually travel to Canada, where he will continue his campaign for governor of Ohio by mail.[9]

MAY 10, 1863: "It becomes my melancholy duty to announce to you the death of Genl. Jackson," Secretary of War Seddon wires Robert E. Lee. "He expired at three and a quarter p.m. today. His body will be conveyed to Richmond in the train tomorrow." A terrible blow to Lee (who will say, "I know not how to replace him"), Stonewall Jackson's death from pneumonia after the amputation of his wounded arm (see May 2, 1863) plunges the entire Confederacy into mourning. "How can I record the sorrow which has befallen our country!" Virginian Judith McGuire will write in her diary on May 12. "The good,

the great, the glorious Stonewall Jackson is numbered with the dead! . . . The body lies in state to-day at the Capitol, wrapped in the Confederate flag, and literally covered with lilies of the valley and other beautiful Spring flowers. Tomorrow the sad *cortège* will wend its way to Lexington, where he will be buried, according to his dying request, in the 'Valley of Virginia.' "[10]

MAY 14, 1863: On the move and living off the land in Mississippi, Grant's army has clashed with Confederates at Port Gibson (May 1) and Raymond (May 12). Today, two Union columns under James B. McPherson and William T. Sherman battle with troops covering the Confederate withdrawal from the Mississippi state capital, Jackson. Ordered by Confederate general Joseph E. Johnston, recently appointed area commander, the retreat will soon prove controversial. After fighting that results in 290 Federal casualties and 845 Confederate killed, wounded, and captured, Union forces enter the town, raise the Stars and Stripes, and indulge in a celebration hosted by General Grant, who has been traveling with Sherman's troops. A blow to Southern morale, Jackson's fall further isolates Vicksburg: before leaving, the Federals will burn part of the town and sever the railroad lines that connect the two cities. *In Vicksburg,* Northern-born Confederate lieutenant general John C. Pemberton is caught between two imperatives: both he and President Davis believe it is essential to defend the city at all costs; General Johnston believes the city is indefensible and has ordered Pemberton to evacuate his troops and join up with Johnston's men. Pemberton elects to remain with the city, and will conduct raids against Union communications — or attempt to.[11]

MAY 15, 1863: Having earlier spoken against a suggestion that two of his divisions be sent to reinforce Pemberton at Vicksburg, a move that would weaken his already outnumbered army as it faces the still strong Army of the Potomac, Robert E. Lee today outlines a daring plan at a strategy conference in Richmond: after receiving reinforcements, he will invade Pennsylvania. Such a bold move will draw Union forces out of Virginia — and meeting and defeating the Federals on their home ground, Lee believes, will deal a blow to Northern morale and to the Republican Party, strengthen the hand of the Union's Peace Democrats, and increase Confederate chances of European recognition. The post-Chancellorsville glow surrounding Lee and the Army of Northern Virginia leads the cabinet to approve Lee's plan.[12]

MAY 16, 1863: Grant's forces, principally the corps led by James B. McPherson, engage Pemberton's Confederates, who are occupying Champion Hill, a seventy-foot-high ridge overlooking the surrounding Mississippi countryside. Several hours of skirmishing precede four hours of all-out fighting; the hill and an adjoining crossroads change hands three times, until finally Pemberton's men are forced to withdraw — with McPherson pursuing until it grows too dark to see. This

ABOVE: Lieutenant General John C. Pemberton (1814–1881), CSA, n.d. The Confederate commander at Vicksburg, Pemberton had served with Ulysses S. Grant during the 1846–48 Mexican War. "I knew him very well, therefore," Grant wrote in his postwar memoirs, "and greeted him [when negotiations for Vicksburg's surrender began] as an old acquaintance."

OPPOSITE: *Battle of Jackson, Mississippi — Gallant Charge of the 17th Iowa, 80th Ohio and 10th Missouri, Supported by the First and Third Brigades of the Seventh Division.* Lithograph published by Middleton, Strobridge & Co., ca. 1863.

RIGHT: *Marching Prisoners over the Mountains to Frederick, M.D.* Pencil and Chinese white drawing by Alfred R. Waud, 1863. In a letter to his father, Union sergeant Warren H. Freeman disputed the general belief that Rebel prisoners were ragged and half-starved. "Those that I saw," he reported, "were fully equal in looks and condition to the average of our men."

MAY

1 2 3 4 5 6 7 8 9 10 11 12 13 14 15 16 **17 18 19 20 21 22** 23 24 25 26 27 28 29 30 31

crucial victory nets the Union some twenty-seven pieces of Confederate artillery and hundreds of prisoners, and it further weakens Pemberton by cutting off one of his divisions (which will later join up with Johnston). Pushing on toward Vicksburg behind Pemberton and McPherson, Grant and some of his staff bed down after dark on the porch of a house being used as a Confederate hospital, now filled with some of the thirty-eight hundred Southern casualties from Champion Hill. "While a battle is raging one can see his enemy mowed down by the thousands, or the ten thousand with great composure," Grant will write in his memoirs, "but after the battle these scenes are distressing, and one is naturally disposed to do as much to alleviate the suffering of an enemy as a friend."[13]

MAY 17, 1863: Grant's forces deal Pemberton's Confederates another jolting blow at Big Black River Bridge, within ten miles of Vicksburg, sending the battered and footsore Southerners reeling back into the city. Close behind them are Grant's troops, now, after their stunning seventeen-day campaign, right on top of their objective. But Vicksburg is surrounded by some of the most formidable fortifications constructed during the war, and within them Pemberton's men will regain their fighting spirit. *The following day, in Virginia,* Sergeant Warren Freeman, of the Thirteenth Massachusetts Infantry, will describe other Confederate soldiers, captured during the Chancellorsville Campaign, in a letter to his father: "Our papers speak about the prisoners that we take as looking half-starved, ragged, etc.

Now I could never see this. Those that I saw, and I should think there were 2,000 of them, were fully equal in looks and condition to the average of our men; they say we can never subdue them, that they will fight till there is not a man left."[14]

MAY 18, 1863: From Vicksburg, Lieutenant General John C. Pemberton answers a May 17 communiqué from General Joseph Johnston ordering him to avoid "losing both troops and place" by evacuating Vicksburg "[i]f it is not too late." "I have decided to hold Vicksburg as long as is possible," Pemberton writes, "with the firm hope that the government may yet be able to assist me in keeping this obstruction to the enemy's free navigation of the Mississippi River. I still conceive it to be the most important point in the Confederacy."[15]

MAY 19–22, 1863: Buoyed by his army's success and convinced that Pemberton's Confederates are demoralized by their recent battering, General Grant orders an assault on Vicksburg at 2:00 PM on May 19. It is repulsed, although, as Grant will later report, "it resulted in securing more advanced positions for all our troops where they were fully covered from the fire of the enemy." After working to strengthen their position over the following two days, on May 22, aware that Johnston's Confederates are some fifty miles to the rear of his army and might advance to Vicksburg's rescue at any time, Grant attempts to breach Vicksburg's defenses with another assault. After a furious cannonade that sets the air "ablaze

An unidentified volunteer in the United States Colored Troops (USCT), probably with his wife and two daughters. Ambrotype, between 1863 and 1865. Despite the hardships it caused them and their families, many black soldiers reacted to the U.S. government's sudden determination that they would be paid less than white troops by refusing to accept any pay until the decision was reversed.

MAY

1 2 3 4 5 6 7 8 9 10 11 12 13 14 15 16 17 18 19 20 21 **22** 23 24 25 26 **27** 28 29 30 31

with burning and bursting shells, darting like fiery serpents across the sky," as Captain James H. Jones, of the Thirty-eighth Mississippi Infantry, inside the city, will write, Grant's men move on the Confederate works — where they are met with murderous rifle and artillery fire. "Still, they never faltered, but came bravely on," Jones will report. "Surely no more desperate courage than this could be displayed by mortal men." This second Federal assault also fails. As Grant begins laying siege to the city, General in Chief Halleck sends reinforcements to help secure the Union position.[16]

MAY 22, 1863: The U.S. War Department issues General Orders, No. 143, establishing the Bureau of Colored Troops to coordinate and administer the raising of African American regiments in every part of the country. The order also establishes boards to examine candidates for commissions to command black troops (Section III); stipulates that no recruiting of African Americans can be conducted by unauthorized persons (Section IV); and specifies that noncommissioned officers of Colored Troops be selected and appointed "from the best men of their number in the usual mode of appointing noncommissioned officers"(Section VIII). Major Charles F. Foster, Assistant Adjutant General of U.S. Volunteers, will be appointed chief of the bureau and will serve in that position until October 1867.[17]

MAY 27, 1863: Union forces make the first of two all-out assaults on the Confederate Mississippi River bastion of Port Hudson, Louisiana, 240 miles south of Vicksburg, which has been under Union siege since May 23. In this harrowing action, soldiers of the First Louisiana Native Guards (later, the Seventy-third U.S. Colored Infantry; see September 27, 1862) and the Third Louisiana Native Guards (later, the Seventy-fifth U.S. Colored Infantry) conduct themselves with extreme and costly heroism: some 20 percent of the two regiments are casualties, including two of the regiment's black officers, Captain André Cailloux and sixteen-year-old lieutenant John H. Crowder, both killed in action. Reporting on this battle, the *New York Times* will state, on June 11, "It is no longer possible to doubt the bravery and steadiness of the colored race, when rightly led." *In New York City,* a government agent enrolling eligible men for the Federal draft (draftees will be selected by lottery from the enrollment lists) arrests an auctioneer named Thomas Gaffney for forcibly resisting enrollment. In this heavily Democratic city rife with tensions between rich and poor, abolitionists and anti-abolitionists, immigrants and native-born, and black people and white, sentiment against the draft is high. Yet, despite a few such incidents, most New Yorkers remain calm, believing that the state's Democratic politicians will find some way to prevent the Federal government from actually conscripting men from the city.[18]

The Battle at Milliken's Bend. Wood engraving based on a drawing by Theodore R. Davis, published in *Harper's Weekly,* July 4, 1863. Union general Elias S. Dennis, who witnessed the battle, later reported, "It is impossible for men to show greater gallantry than the negro troops in that fight."

JUNE

1   2   **3**   **4**   5   6   **7**   **8**   9   10   11   12   13   14   15   16   17   18   19   20   21   22   23   24   25   26   27   28   29   30

JUNE 1863

JUNE 3, 1863: A "peace convention" organized by former mayor Fernando Wood, a Copperhead, takes place in New York City. In its coverage the following day, the *New York Times* will call the gathering "one of the largest recently held in the City" and declare that it is characterized by "its open, straight-forward, avowed sympathy with the principles and the cause of the Secessionists."[19]

JUNE 4, 1863: The U.S. War Department devastates the morale of black soldiers already in uniform and hinders the recruitment of black soldiers when it announces that, in line with a provision of the Militia Act of July 17, 1862, specifying pay for black *laborers,* African American soldiers will henceforth be paid less than their white counterparts: $10 a month (white soldiers receive $13), out of which $3 is to be used for clothing (white soldiers receive a clothing bonus). This announcement, which directly counters the policy of equal pay that the War Department established in August 1862, elicits a storm of protest from black soldiers, their white officers, and many civilians. Yet black soldiers are *not* given the option of leaving the service if they object to this radical and discrimina-tory revision of rules. Many determine that their only recourse is to refuse to accept any pay until the discriminatory policy is reversed — despite the hardship this will cause them and the even greater hardship it will cause their families, many

of whom will be turned away from white-run charities in the North as the pay strike continues.[20]

JUNE 7, 1863: At Milliken's Bend, on the Mississippi River above Vicksburg, two newly formed regiments of "contraband" African American soldiers, as yet untrained, armed only with old muskets, and assisted by the gunboats USS *Lexington* and USS *Choctaw,* drive off a Confederate brigade attempting to disrupt Grant's supply line. One of the regiments' white officers will later describe the brutal clash as "a horrible fight, the worst I was ever engaged in, not even excepting Shiloh" — and he unstintingly praises his men. "They met death coolly, bravely – not rashly did they expose themselves, but all were steady and obedient to orders." The black regiments sustain 35 percent casualties; some captured black soldiers are report-edly murdered. The valor of black troops in this engagement, recently appointed assistant secretary of war Charles A. Dana will note, "completely revolutionized the sentiment of the army with regard to the employment of negro troops. I heard prominent officers who formerly in private had sneered at the idea of the negroes fighting express themselves after that as heartily in favor of it."[21]

JUNE 8, 1863: "There is always hazard in military move-ments," Robert E. Lee writes Secretary of War James Seddon today, "but we must decide between the positive loss of inactivity and the risk of action." As he writes, his men are

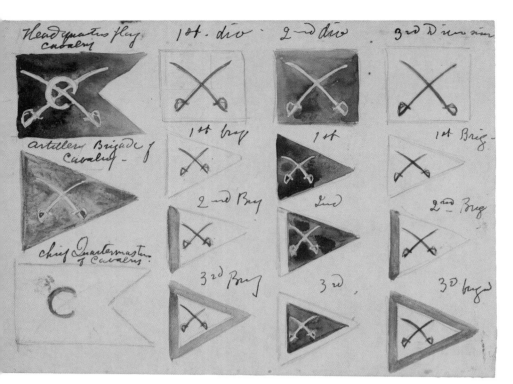

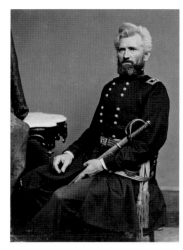

Military Standards of the Cavalry During the American Civil War. Pencil, black ink, and watercolor drawing, between 1860 and 1865, artist unknown. At the June 9, 1863, battle of Brandy Station, Virginia, Union horsemen for the first time more than held their own against Jeb Stuart's storied mounted troops.

Lieutenant General Richard S. Ewell (1817–1872), CSA, between 1860 and 1865. Victorious at the second battle of Winchester, Ewell then led his troops of the Army of Northern Virginia's Second Corps across the Potomac and into Maryland.

Major General Robert H. Milroy (1816–1890), USA, between 1860 and 1865. After Milroy's defeat at Second Winchester, he never again held a field command.

concealing their preparations for the Army of Northern Virginia's move into Pennsylvania so successfully that Joseph Hooker is growing increasingly eager to secure evidence of Lee's intentions, for a major offensive is rumored to be afoot. A reconnaissance attempt by an infantry corps on June 5 was unfruitful. Today, Hooker dispatches General Alfred Pleasonton and the Army of the Potomac cavalry on another attempt. They head toward Culpeper, Virginia — unbeknownst to them, the area where most of Lee's army is encamped, protected by Jeb Stuart's cavalry.

JUNE 9, 1863: Crossing the Rappahannock River in two columns, Alfred Pleasonton and his Union cavalry surprise Jeb Stuart and initiate the greatest cavalry battle of the war at Brandy Station, Virginia. Through charges and counter-charges, men and horses mix in the dusty havoc of all-out fighting until Pleasonton is finally forced to withdraw because of approaching Confederate infantry. The Federals had found Lee's army — and had emerged from this battle with Stuart's storied cavalry with a new sense of pride in their own abilities. Stuart and his cavalry will screen the Army of Northern Virginia's right flank from prying Union eyes as Lee's army moves north (while Stuart will smart for some time from critical Southern newspaper accounts that claim he was "disgracefully surprised" at Brandy Station).[22]

JUNE 10, 1863: President Lincoln, concerned by a telegram from General Hooker proposing a move against Richmond rather than pursuit of Lee's army, wires the general:

> If left to me, I would not go South of the Rappahannock, upon Lee's moving North of it. If you had Richmond invested to-day, you would not be able to take it in twenty days; meanwhile, your communications, and with them, your army would be ruined. I think *Lee's* Army, and not *Richmond,* is your true objective point. If he comes toward the Upper Potomac, follow on this flank, and on the inside track, shortening your lines, whilst he lengthens his. Fight him when oppertunity [*sic*] offers. If he stays where he is, fret him, and fret him.[23]

JUNE 13, 1863: Having received what he considers reliable reports that Lee's army is, in fact, moving north through the Shenandoah Valley, Joseph Hooker orders the Army of the Potomac to pursue, in a manner that will keep his force always between Lee and Washington. Heat, dust, lice, nagging thirst — and excellent foraging from secessionist Virginians — are what many of Hooker's soldiers will remember about the next few days of hard marching.[24]

JUNE 14, 1863: Union general Nathaniel Banks calls on the seven thousand Confederates under siege in Port Hudson, Louisiana, to surrender — and when they do not, he orders a

ABOVE: *Cave Life in Vicksburg.* Etching by Adalbert J. Volck (1828–1912), included in *Sketches from the Civil War in North America, 1861, '62, '63,* by V. Blada (a Volck pseudonym), 1863–1864. Mrs. Mary Loughborough's residential cave was "in the first line of hills back of the heights," as she reported in 1864, "and, of course . . . being so near, many [shells] that passed over the first line of hills would fall directly around us."

LEFT: Brigadier General George A. Custer (1838–1876), USA, between 1863 and 1865. His courage in leading a heroic charge at Aldie, Virginia, resulted in his promotion, at age twenty-three, to brigadier general.

JUNE

1 2 3 4 5 6 7 8 9 10 11 12 13 14 15 **16** **17** 18 19 20 21 22 23 24 25 26 27 28 29 30

second all-out assault on the Confederacy's second remaining Mississippi River bastion by some six thousand Federal troops. It is as unsuccessful as the first (see May 27, 1863), resulting principally in 1,792 killed, wounded, and missing Union soldiers versus 47 Confederate casualties. The siege of Port Hudson continues. *In Virginia,* Richard Ewell's corps of Lee's army meets and defeats more than six thousand Federals under Major General Robert H. Milroy (who did not believe, until too late, that Confederates were approaching in force) at the second battle of Winchester, Virginia. After nearly overrunning the Federal garrison during fighting that begins at 6:00 PM, Ewell's men intercept the Union troops as they are attempting to withdraw from the town in the postmidnight dark. The Confederates take some four thousand prisoners, confiscate wagons, stores, and cannon, and clear the way for the remainder of Lee's men to move untroubled into Union territory.[25]

JUNE 16, 1863: In a day of heavy communication between President Lincoln and Joseph Hooker, the president again presses Hooker to move aggressively against Lee's army (see June 10, 1863): "As it looks to me, Lee's now returning toward Harper's Ferry gives you back the chance that I thought McClellan lost last fall." Lincoln finds he must also deal with the bad relations between Hooker and General in Chief Halleck. At 10:00 PM he telegraphs Hooker: "To remove all misunderstanding, I now place you in the strict military relation to Gen. Halleck, of a commander of one of the armies, to the General-in-Chief of all the armies. . . . I shall direct him to give you orders, and you to obey them."[26]

JUNE 17, 1863: In Georgia, the Confederate ironclad CSS *Atlanta* runs aground after a brief battle with the Union warships *Weehawken* and *Nahant* at the mouth of the Wilmington River and is forced to surrender. The loss of *Atlanta,* a ship considered superior to the revered ironclad *Virginia* (*Merrimac*), is a blow to Confederate pride. Adding insult to injury, the Union navy will incorporate *Atlanta* into its own blockading squadron. *At Aldie, Virginia,* where Federal cavalry, trying to keep track of Lee's northward movement, battle successfully to dislodge Confederates from the village, George Armstrong Custer leads a heroic charge that will shortly result in his promotion, at age twenty-three, to brigadier general — making Custer, for a time, the youngest Union general. *From "inconveniently near the rebel works, in view of Vicksburg,"* Union lieutenant Cyrus E. Dickey writes to his sister in Illinois: "This is a queer phase of war to us all; the ground around Vicksburg is a network of ravines running parallel to the rebel works. Our troops are occupying these ravines, have terraced the slopes, and dug caves for tents. During a bombardment from the enemy these caves are at a premium. The timid boys who have not dug caves for themselves try to buy out others who have dug their holes. Good caves today run up to $250." *At about this same time, in Vicksburg,* Mrs. Mary Webster Loughborough,

Major General Daniel Butterfield (1831–1901), USA. Army of the Potomac chief of staff Butterfield, with his bugler, Oliver Willcox Norton, turned a prewar bugle call, "Extinguish Lights," into the haunting "Taps." Yet Butterfield's temper and officiousness earned him the nickname Little Napoleon.

Drawing Number 1 in *Sketches with Co B, 8th Reg. Pa. Ma. Under the Officers of the Old "Southwark Gaurd [sic] in Harrisburg, Pa."* Watercolor and graphite drawing by James Fuller Queen (1820/21–1886). As Lee's army moved through Maryland and into Pennsylvania, Pennsylvania governor Andrew Curtin deployed state troops and called for more volunteers to repel the invasion.

JUNE

1 2 3 4 5 6 7 8 9 10 11 12 13 14 15 16 17 **18** 19 **20** **21** 22 23 24 25 26 27 28 29 30

occupying one of the many caves in which the city's civilians have taken refuge, is suffering through a heavier than usual Union bombardment when she is startled by shouts and

a most fearful jar and rocking of the earth, followed by a deafening explosion, such as I had never heard before. The cave filled instantly with powder, smoke and dust. I stood with a tingling, prickling sensation in my head, hands, and feet, and with a confused brain. Yet alive!—was the first glad thought that came to me;—child, servants, all here, and saved! . . . A mortar shell had struck the corner of the cave, fortunately so near the brow of the hill, that it had gone obliquely into the earth, exploding as it went, breaking large masses from the side of the hill. . . . A portion of earth from the roof of my cave had been dislodged and fallen. Saving this, it remained intact.[27]

JUNE 18, 1863: "They are asking me," an irritated General in Chief Halleck wires Joseph Hooker today, "why does not General Hooker tell where Lee's army is; he is nearest to it." Despite the efficiency of the Army of the Potomac's own intelligence arm, the Bureau of Military Information, which Hooker established, and despite the ample evidence provided by the second battle of Winchester that Lee's men are moving northward through the Shenandoah Valley, there is still confusion surrounding what part of Lee's army is where. Hooker and his chief of staff, Daniel Butterfield, claim that they cannot, in

Butterfield's words, "go boggling around until we know what we are going after." Yet some of Hooker's subordinate officers consider Hooker's own lack of heart to be at the heart of the problem. Provost Marshal Marsena Patrick will confide to his diary that Hooker "acts like a man without a plan and is entirely at a loss what to do, or how to match the enemy, or counteract his movements."[28]

JUNE 20, 1863: Pursuant to a December 31, 1862, act of Congress and a presidential proclamation of April 20, 1863, fifty western counties formerly part of the Confederate state of Virginia are today admitted to the Union as the state of West Virginia — under a state constitution stipulating that children born of slaves after July 4, 1863, are free and all other slaves are free as of their twenty-fifth birthday. As Arthur Boreman assumes the governorship of the new state, Francis H. Pierpont, head of the "restored [Unionist] government" of the state of Virginia, moves his headquarters to Union-occupied Alexandria, directly across the river from Washington, DC (see May 26, June 11, 1861).[29]

JUNE 21, 1863: "Yankeedom is in a great fright at the advance of Lee's army to the Potomac, and considers this part of Pennsylvania south of the Susquehanna as good as gone," Confederate War Department official Robert Kean writes in his journal. "The public records have been removed from Harrisburg. I hope they might be destroyed, and all the public buildings

Engineers Filling Bombs, 1864. Illustration from *The Army and Navy of the United States from the Period of the Revolution to the Present Day,* by William Walton, 1889–1895, Vol. 1. At Vicksburg on June 22, 1863, Union engineers exploded mines they had placed in tunnels under the Confederate defenses, creating a huge crater that became a bloody battlefield.

Major General William S. Rosecrans (1819–1898), USA. Steel engraving, based on a photograph by H. Wright Smith, in *The Southern Rebellion: Being a History of the United States from the Commencement of President Buchanan's Administration through the War for the Suppression of the Rebellion,* by William A. Crafts, Vol. 1, 1865.

JUNE

1 2 3 4 5 6 7 8 9 10 11 12 13 14 15 16 17 18 19 20 21 **22** **23** 24 **25** **26** 27 28 29 30

also, as they did at Jackson [see May 14, 1863]. . . . Why some energy cannot be infused into the western operations is hard to understand."[30]

JUNE 22, 1863: The Army of Northern Virginia begins to cross the Potomac River, one corps under Richard Ewell moving today toward Hagerstown, Maryland. Corps commanders A. P. Hill and James Longstreet will have their men across within two days. *At Vicksburg,* where both Union besiegers and Confederate besieged have been digging tunnels in which to lay mines, Union forces set off a massive explosion under one section of Confederate fortifications, which "commenced an upward movement," Grant's chief engineer, Andrew Hickenlooper, will report, "gradually breaking into fragments . . . until it looked like an immense fountain of finely pulverized earth, mingled with flashes of fire and clouds of smoke, through which could occasionally be caught a glimpse of some dark objects, — men, gun-carriages, shelters, etc." When the dust settles, Federal troops rush into the huge resulting crater and begin a bloody struggle against Confederates. "[H]and-to-hand conflict rages for hours," Illinois soldier Wilbur F. Crummer will later recall; "hand grenades and loaded shells are lighted and thrown over the parapet [and down on the Union troops] as you would play ball . . . as many as a dozen men being killed and wounded at one explosion. . . . Many a brave hero laid down his life in that death hole, or, as we most appropriately called it, 'Fort Hell.'" For forty-eight

hours, the Federals pay a terrible price to hold the crater and attempt to move past it, but it proves impossible to further breach the Confederate lines and they finally withdraw. The siege continues.[31]

JUNE 23, 1863: Having regrouped and built up his army after the grueling battle of Murfreesboro (see December 31, 1862–January 2, 1863), Union major general William S. Rosecrans begins his Tullahoma Campaign, which will prevent Braxton Bragg from detaching any of his Tennessee-based force to go to the aid of Vicksburg and will, by July 3, force Bragg to withdraw from middle Tennessee to Chattanooga.[32]

JUNE 25, 1863: Finally convinced that Lee has moved north of the Potomac River, General Hooker begins sending his own men into Maryland.[33]

JUNE 26, 1863: At midafternoon, the calm routine of Gettysburg, Pennsylvania, professor and minister Michaels Jacobs is rudely disrupted when Confederate general Jubal Early and about two hundred men ride into town, "shouting and yelling like so many savages from the wilds of the Rocky Mountains," the irate professor will later report; "firing their pistols, not caring whether they killed or maimed man, woman, or child." Soon after, an additional five thousand Southern infantrymen appear, many of whom are in need of new clothes and good (or any) shoes. Lee's incursion into Union territory is a quest for

Generals of the Army of the Potomac: from left, Gouverneur K. Warren, William H. French, Army of the Potomac commander George G. Meade, Henry J. Hunt, Andrew A. Humphreys, and George Sykes, September 1863. "You know how reluctant we both have been to see me placed in this position," Meade wrote to his wife after he was selected to replace Joseph Hooker, "[but], as a soldier I had nothing to do but accept."

A Short History of General J. A. [Jubal Anderson] Early. Booklet in a series designed to be included in cigarette packs, 1888. Early's "visit" to Gettysburg with some five thousand Confederates on June 26 presaged the pivotal battle that would take place there.

needed supplies as well as a military/political campaign, and Early demands that the townspeople provide his men with a list of goods or five thousand dollars in cash. After city leaders prove to Early's satisfaction that Gettysburg is unable to comply with either demand, Rebel troops confiscate all available liquor, damage the railroad, and move on. At the same time, larger elements of Lee's army converge on Chambersburg and threaten the state capital of Harrisburg — sending all the black people they capture during their march south into slavery. As Pennsylvania governor Andrew Curtin calls for sixty thousand volunteers to repel the invasion, General Hooker reports that the Army of the Potomac is nearing Frederick, Maryland.[34]

JUNE 27, 1863: A dispute between General Hooker and General in Chief Halleck about whether Union troops should evacuate Harpers Ferry and reinforce the Army of the Potomac in Maryland leads Hooker to request "that I may at once be relieved from the position I occupy" — most probably to pressure Halleck into giving him the Harpers Ferry troops. Instead, Halleck passes the general's request on to President Lincoln, providing the president a ready opportunity to deal with a growing concern. As Lincoln will explain to his cabinet the following morning (and Gideon Welles will record in his diary), he has recently "observed in Hooker the same failings that were witnessed in McClellan after the Battle of Antietam. — A want of alacrity to obey, and a greedy call for more

troops which could not, and ought not to be taken from other points." Though at this stage in the building military crisis it is a risky act, the president removes Hooker from command of the Army of the Potomac.[35]

JUNE 28, 1863: Dispatched from Washington to Fifth Corps headquarters near Frederick, Maryland, Brigadier General James Hardie brings Major General George Gordon Meade orders to assume command of the Army of the Potomac. An 1835 graduate of West Point whose spectacles and sometimes prickly personality have led some of his troops to call him "that damned old goggle-eyed snapping turtle," Meade has also been dubbed "Old Reliable" for his steadiness on the battlefield and his competence in command. As news of the change travels through the army and is generally well received, Meade makes plans to advance toward the Susquehanna River in Pennsylvania, making certain his troops will remain able to cover both Washington and Baltimore, should that become necessary. *In Vicksburg,* where lack of proper food has become an even greater concern than Union bombardments from gunships on the river and land-based cannon, "Many Soldiers" send their commanding general, John C. Pemberton, a letter: "Our rations have been cut down to one biscuit and a small bit of bacon per day, not enough scarcely to keep soul and body together, much less to stand the hardships we are called upon to stand. . . . If you can't feed us, you had better surrender, horrible as the idea is, than suffer this noble army to disgrace

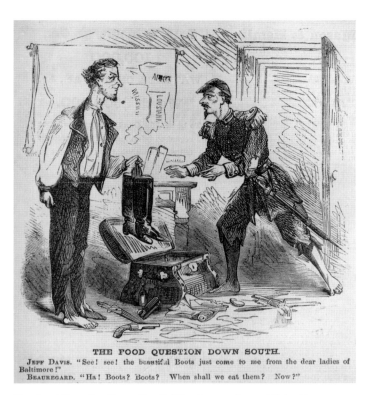

The Food Question Down South. Wood engraving published in *Harper's Weekly*, May 9, 1863. In this editorial cartoon, Confederate president Jefferson Davis offers a new pair of boots to General P. G. T. Beauregard—who would much rather have food for his troops. While the Union cartoonist might have exaggerated the condition of Beauregard's command, in besieged Vicksburg, General John Pemberton's troops had such meager rations there was some talk of mutiny.

Administration Escort of the President, 1865. Illustration from *The Army and Navy of the United States from the Period of the Revolution to the Present Day,* by William Walton, 1889–1895, vol. 1. Looking out from his window on June 30, 1863, Walt Whitman described, in a letter to his mother, President Lincoln's escort, including "about thirty cavalry."

themselves by desertion. . . . This army is now ripe for mutiny, unless it can be fed."[36]

JUNE 29, 1863: "It is reported that the Rebels are 110,000 strong in infantry, with 20,000 cavalry," Army of the Potomac brigadier general Alpheus S. ("Old Pap") Williams writes to his daughters. "I think the report is greatly exaggerated, but they have been all winter recruiting by conscription, while we have been all winter running down. Still, I don't despair. On the contrary, now with a gentleman and a soldier in command I have renewed confidence that we shall at least do enough to preserve our honor and the safety of the Republic. But we run a fearful risk, because upon this small army everything depends."[37]

JUNE 30, 1863: Writing to his mother from Washington, Walt Whitman reports on one of the prominent citizens of the city:

> Mr. Lincoln passes here (14th St.) every evening on his way out [to the Soldiers' Home, where the Lincolns spend the hot summer evenings]. I noted him last evening about half-past 6 — he was in his barouche, two horses, guarded by about thirty cavalry. . . . He looks more careworn even than usual, his face with deep cut lines, seams, and his *complexion gray* through very dark skin — a curious looking man, very sad. . . . He was alone yesterday. As he came

up, he first drove over to the house of the Sec. of War, on K st., about 300 feet from here; sat in his carriage while Stanton came out and had a 15 minutes interview with him (I can see from my window), and then wheeled around the corner and up Fourteenth st., the cavalry after him. I really think it would be safer for him just now to stop [spend his nights] at the White House, but I expect he is too proud to abandon the former custom.

In Pennsylvania, as Union intelligence indicates that Lee's army is concentrating around Chambersburg or Gettysburg, with the latter being most likely, General Meade orders Major General John F. Reynolds to take two army corps to Gettysburg. Brigadier General John Buford and two cavalry brigades have already arrived in the town and are keeping a watchful eye on all ten roads leading into it. Their activities are observed from afar by a Confederate brigade, whose commander reports to his division commander and General A. P. Hill that Army of the Potomac horsemen are in Gettysburg. Hill determines to move in that direction the following day.[38]

ABOVE: *Soldier's Home, Washington, D.C.* Color lithograph published by Charles Magnus, ca. 1868. For refuge from Washington's oppressive summer weather, the Lincolns would often spend nights in the two-story Anderson Cottage on the 300-acre campus of the Soldier's Home, which had been established in the 1850s as a retirement community for disabled veterans.

OPPOSITE: *Plan of the Gettysburg Battle Ground.* Color map by Charles Wellington Reed (1841–1926), Ninth Massachusetts Light Artillery Battery, USA, ca. 1864. The map shows Union positions in black and Confederate positions in red. Himself a combatant at Gettysburg, Reed was awarded the Medal of Honor for the conspicuous bravery he exhibited in saving the life of Captain John Bigelow during the second day of that battle.

"Unless the siege of Vicksburg is raised, or supplies are thrown in, it will become necessary very shortly to evacuate the place."

—GENERAL JOHN PEMBERTON,
JULY 1, 1863

JULY 1863

JULY 1, 1863: A limited engagement between Major General Henry Heth's division of A. P. Hill's Confederates and John Buford's dismounted Union cavalry begins the three-day battle of Gettysburg. As Buford's men delay the Southerners' progress, General John Reynolds arrives, sends men to hold McPherson's ridge west of the town, and, shouting "Forward men, forward, for God's sake," leads a Wisconsin regiment to clear nearby Herbst woods, where Confederate riflemen who are "howling like demons" meet the assault with deadly volleys that mortally wound the general. Bitter fighting temporarily secures McPherson's ridge for the Union. But after a mid-afternoon lull (as Robert E. Lee arrives and more troops of both sides converge on the battlefield), the Confederates renew their assault, igniting combat so intense one Union lieutenant will remember men falling around him "like ripe apples in a storm." Retreating through the town, the Union troops regroup to its south, by late that evening forming part of what will eventually be a fishhook-shaped line along Cemetery Ridge embracing places that will soon become legendary: Cemetery Hill, Big and Little Round Top, and Culp's Hill. In the evening, as General Meade arrives on one side of the battlefield, on the other, Robert E. Lee determines to renew the battle the following day, "in view of the valuable results that would ensue from the defeat of the army of General Meade." *In Vicksburg*, General John Pemberton sends a message to each of his four division commanders: "Unless the siege of Vicksburg is raised, or supplies are thrown in, it will become necessary very shortly to evacuate the place. . . . You are, therefore, requested to inform me . . . as to the condition of your troops and their ability . . . to accomplish a successful evacuation." The division commanders report that evacuation will not be possible; two of the generals advise Pemberton to surrender.[39]

JULY 2, 1863: Leading twenty-five hundred Confederate cavalrymen, Brigadier General John Hunt Morgan begins the longest cavalry raid of the war, impelled by his conviction that only by taking the war into the Northern homeland, and thus augmenting the influence of Union Copperheads, could pressure on the Confederacy be relieved. During twenty-five days of almost constant combat, covering more than seven hundred miles (through Kentucky, southeast Indiana, and southern and eastern Ohio), Morgan and his "Terrible Men" will make no distinction between enemies and potential allies as they hold businesses for ransom; destroy commercial buildings, railroads, and bridges; loot local treasures — and garner the undying enmity of the Northerners in their path. They will also divert some 14,000 Federal troops from other duties and spark the call-up of 120,000 militia before Union troops under Brigadier General Edward H. Hobson hand them a costly defeat at Buffington Island (Morgan's troops suffer 850 casualties plus 700 men captured). Finally captured with his remaining 364 men less than 100 miles from Cleveland, Morgan will be sent to the Ohio state penitentiary — but that

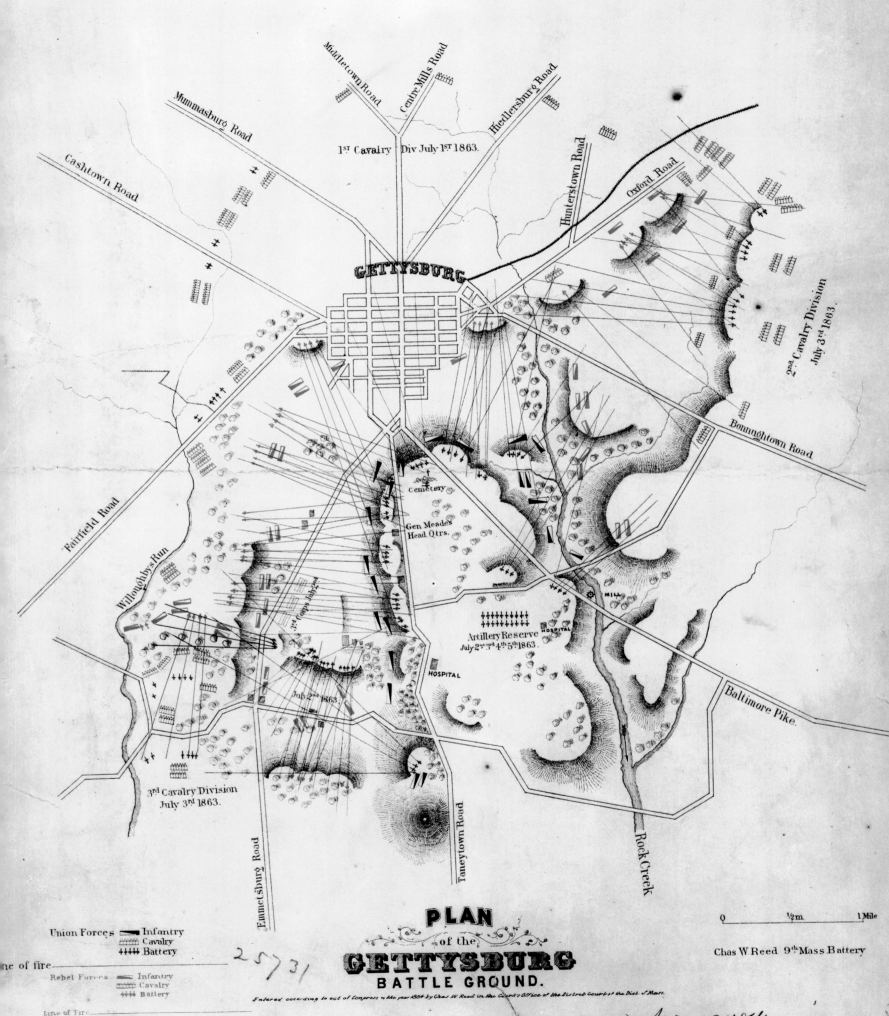

PLAN
of the
GETTYSBURG
BATTLE GROUND.

Chas W. Reed 9th Mass Battery

Union Forces — Infantry — Cavalry — Battery
Line of fire
Rebel Forces — Infantry — Cavalry — Battery
Line of Fire

Deposited April 28. 1864
Recorded Vol. 39. Page 108

0   ½m   1 Mile

Hancock at Gettysburg. Pencil and watercolor drawing
by Alfred R. Waud, ca. July 1–3, 1863. A Union hero of the
battle, Major General Winfield Scott Hancock (1824–1886)
was instrumental in selecting excellent Union positions on
day one, led the successful stand that thwarted Lee's attempt
to turn the Union left flank on day two, and was wounded
(but refused to leave the field) as his men withstood Pickett's
Charge on day three.

The Story of Gettysburg. Watercolor over graphite
design for a sheet-music cover by James Fuller
Queen, ca. 1863. The pivotal three-day battle of
Gettysburg would yield endless stories of the suffering and valor of men on both sides. Though it was a
Union victory that caused Lee to retreat, as Union
officer Charles Francis Adams Jr. noted in a letter on
July 12, Lee "has lots of fight left and this war is not
over yet."

will not end his Civil War story (see November 27, 1863, and
September 4, 1864). *At Gettysburg,* despite objections from
Lieutenant General James Longstreet (who favors a turning
movement), Lee orders an attack against the left of the Federal
line, which begins, under Longstreet's command, at about
4:00 PM. Through air sizzling with musket and rifle fire, over
ground erupting from exploding artillery shells, Confederate and Union forces grapple in what one Texan will term
"a devil's carnival." Bloody struggles engulf new battlefield
landmarks: the Wheatfield, the Devil's Den, and the Peach
Orchard. College professor Joshua Chamberlain, now colonel
of the Twentieth Maine, leads a bayonet charge to repulse
Confederates charging Little Round Top after his men run
out of ammunition. On Culp's Hill, five thousand screaming
Confederates repeatedly smash up against field fortifications
painstakingly erected by fourteen hundred Union defenders
led by sixty-two-year-old George S. Greene. Finally, the firing
subsides. Both armies have suffered terribly; neither has gained
an appreciable advantage. The night air fills with the odor
of death, an eerie hum from moaning wounded — and, from
behind Federal lines, band music played to mask screams from
the Union hospitals. Ghostlike figures walk the battlefield
searching for comrades. At their respective headquarters,
Meade decides to maintain a defensive position, while Lee
determines to renew his attack the next day.[40]

JULY 3, 1863: In Richmond, Confederate vice president Alexander H. Stephens boards a boat bearing a flag of truce and
sails toward the Union lines around Norfolk. Bearing letters
from Jefferson Davis to Abraham Lincoln, and acting with full
approval of Davis and the Confederate cabinet, Stephens hopes
to exploit Grant's failure to take Vicksburg and Lee's daring
incursion into the North by bringing peace proposals to the
Union leader, whom he has known since they served together
in the U.S. Congress. *In Mississippi,* Confederate general John
Pemberton emerges from Vicksburg under a flag of truce. Near
a stunted oak tree a few hundred feet from the Confederate
lines, he confers with General Grant, an old friend from their
service together in the Mexican War. Grant reiterates his
demand, made in an earlier message, that the Confederates
surrender unconditionally; Pemberton is reluctant. After the
interview ends, negotiations continue, via letter, until late into
the night. *At Gettysburg,* Union artillery fire rips into Confederate positions at the base of Culp's Hill, beginning a seven-hour
struggle for that position, the Southerners' repeated attempts
to gain the heights leaving the hillside slippery with blood. To
the east of the main battlefield, Union cavalry led by Brigadier
General George A. Custer and Colonel John B. McIntosh
repulse Jeb Stuart's formidable horsemen. At the same time, a
terrible drama unfolds at the center of the Union line, where
Lee has decided to make a frontal assault that will live in
memory as Pickett's Charge. Preceded by forty-five minutes of
soul-shattering cannon fire (which falls far short of ravaging

The Battle of Gettysburg. Engraving by John Sartain (1808–1897), after a painting by Peter Frederick Rothermel (1812–1895), ca. 1872. The scene depicted in Rothermel's painting may be Pickett's Charge.

JULY

1 2 **4** 5 6 7 8 9 10 11 12 13 14 15 16 17 18 19 20 21 22 23 24 25 26 27 28 29 30 31

Union artillery batteries, as Lee believes it will), the assault begins with 13,500 Confederates, in line, battle flags flying, moving forward — until their order disintegrates under volleys of furious Union fire. "Come on, Come to Death," some Federals shout, and despite fearful losses, the Rebels press on until the survivors can endure it no longer. Many are taken prisoner; many others stream back toward the Confederate lines on Seminary Ridge — where Robert E. Lee tells them, "It was not your fault this time. It was all mine." From Union lines on Cemetery Ridge, "cheer upon cheer arose from our troops," staff officer Adolphus Cavada will recall, "and spread right & left like wild fire."[41]

JULY 4, 1863: Exhausted troops and overwhelmed medical workers survey the carnage at Gettysburg: over the past three days some fifty-one thousand men of both sides have been killed, wounded, or gone missing. "[E]verywhere wounded men were lying in the streets on heaps of blood-stained straw," Union nurse Sophronia Bucklin will write about her arrival after the battle, "everywhere there was hurry and confusion, while soldiers were groaning and suffering." As evening descends and rain, falling since midday, grows heavier, Lee's army withdraws from the battlefield, miles of marching men, their wounded and supplies in wagons, struggling along miry roads. By then, President Lincoln has announced to the country that "news from the Army of the Potomac . . . is such as to cover that Army with the highest honor, [and] to promise a great success to the cause of the Union." As more details of the battle circulate, the surge in Northern morale is reflected in ecstatic newspaper headlines, including the *Philadelphia Inquirer*'s "Victory! Waterloo Eclipsed!" *In Mississippi,* John Pemberton and his Confederate garrison march out of Vicksburg, stack their arms, and surrender to Ulysses S. Grant and the Federal army that has had Vicksburg in its sights for nearly a year. Securing the city is so important a victory that General Grant will later write in his memoirs, "The fate of the Confederacy was sealed when Vicksburg fell." His commander in chief also appreciates the magnitude of the western army's achievements — and the quality of its commander. "Grant is my man," President Lincoln will state on July 5, "and I am his the rest of the war." *In Washington,* after a cabinet discussion of Alexander Stephens's proposed visit to Washington (see July 3, 1863), and with good news from Gettysburg in hand, Lincoln denies the Confederate vice president's request for a pass through Union lines to meet with Lincoln in Washington. *In New York City,* New York's Democratic governor, Horatio Seymour, gives a fiery speech at an antidraft rally. Dismissing the Lincoln administration's claim of military necessity for emancipation and conscription, Seymour thunders, "Remember this — that the bloody and treasonable doctrine of public necessity can be proclaimed by a mob as well as by a government."[42]

Civil War induction officer with a draft lottery box.
Sixth-plate ambrotype, ca. 1863.

The American Ram. Lithograph cover by H. F. Greene for a patriotic song
by R. S. Frary, published by Henry Tolman & Co., 1863. A celebration of
the long-awaited victories at Vicksburg and Port Hudson, which brought
the entire Mississippi River under Union control, the song is dedicated
to U.S. Secretary of the Navy Gideon Welles, who was responsible for
ushering the Union navy into the age of ironclad steamers.

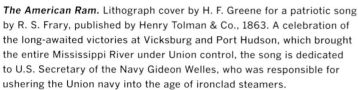

JULY

1 2 3 4 5 6 7 8 **9 10 11** 12 **13 14 15 16 17** 18 19 20 21 22 23 24 25 26 27 28 29 30 31

JULY 9, 1863: With Vicksburg now in Union hands, the
Confederates 240 miles to the south at Port Hudson, recognizing that their situation is hopeless, surrender this last Southern
bastion on the Mississippi River. "The father of waters again
goes unvexed to the sea," President Lincoln will declare. The
Confederacy is split in two.[43]

JULY 10, 1863: Beginning another attempt to take Charleston, South Carolina (see April 7, 1863), Union infantry under
Brigadier General George Crockett Strong, supported by naval
guns and Union artillery on Folly Island, land on the south end
of Morris Island, at the mouth of Charleston Harbor. Their
objective: Fort (Battery) Wagner, one of the harbor's main
defenses. Their first assault on the fort, July 11, will be unsuccessful. Within a week, with considerable reinforcements, they
will try again (see July 18, 1863).[44]

JULY 11, 1863: Draft officers begin drawing names in heavily
Democratic New York City, where sentiment against abolition
and conscription runs high. This is especially the case among
hardscrabble Irish workers already struggling against lagging
wages and confined with their families in seething tenements
that are seedbeds of crime and disease. Many Irishmen are still
boiling with resentment at being replaced by black stevedores
during a bitter longshoremen's strike in June, and they worry
about the same thing happening if they are drafted: at this
time, black men are not considered citizens and thus are not

eligible for the draft. Moreover, the three-hundred-dollar fee
the government requires for legally evading the draft is, for
the vast majority of Irish laborers, an impossible amount to
raise. Today's lottery goes smoothly — but the following day, a
Sunday, crowds of angry people, some of them fueled by cheap
liquor and all of them now aware that the state's Democratic
administration cannot protect New York from the draft, will
plot to stop the drawings.[45]

JULY 13, 1863: President Lincoln composes a note to Ulysses
S. Grant, "as a grateful acknowledgement for the almost
inestimable service you have done the country." He goes on
to make a small confession: "When you got below, and took
Port-Gibson, Grand Gulf, and vicinity, I thought you should go
down the river and join Gen. [Nathaniel] Banks; and when you
turned Northward East of the Big Black [River], I feared it was
a mistake. I now wish to make the personal acknowledgment
that you were right, and I was wrong."[46]

JULY 13-17, 1863: New York erupts into four of the bloodiest
days of mob violence in United States history, an uprising that
begins with thousands of people forgoing work to demonstrate outside the draft office on Third Avenue. Someone hurls
a stone through an office window, someone else fires a pistol,
and the demonstration transforms to a riot — initially led by
members of a company of firemen, one of whom has just been
drafted. Surging into the office, the rioters smash everything

The Riots in New York: The Mob Lynching a Negro in Clarkson-Street.
Engraving published in the *Illustrated London News*, August 8, 1863. "[A] stout clothes-line . . . was attached to the negro's neck," the correspondent from the *News* reported, "and he was drawn up several feet. Some of them then set his shirt on fire, and the sight presented was a frightful one. The body remained hanging, surrounded by a dense crowd of people, who shouted and yelled, pursuing every negro who made his appearance."

The Sinking of the Japanese Ships. Wood engraving based on a drawing by W. Taber, published in *The Century Illustrated Monthly* magazine, April 1892. Occurring only three years after the first visit of Japanese diplomats to Washington, DC, the U.S. Navy's defeat of attacking Japanese vessels in the Shimonoseki Straits strained relations between the two countries at a time when the war at home required most of the government's, and the navy's, attention.

JULY

1 2 3 4 5 6 7 8 9 10 11 12 13 14 15 **16** 17 **18** 19 20 21 22 23 24 25 26 27 28 29 30 31

inside, the draft officials barely escaping with their lives as the mob sets fire to the building (imperiling hundreds of people who live on the floors above). Outside, as the firemen watch the building burn, rioters cut telegraph wires and attack the small force of police and soldiers that city authorities can muster to stop them (most city-based regiments are still with the Army of the Potomac in Pennsylvania). The mob's fury builds and widens to include Republicans, soldiers, the wealthy, and, especially, black people and the businesses that employ them. "One of the first victims to the insane fury of the rioters," *Harper's Weekly* will report, "was a negro cartman residing in Carmine Street," who is beaten, hanged, and set afire. Colonel Henry F. O'Brien of the Eleventh New York Infantry is another victim, beaten, shot, and pummeled with stones as he is dragged through the streets before he finally dies. The mob attacks the headquarters of the *New York Times* (where they are turned away by borrowed Gatling guns); besiege Horace Greeley in the *Tribune* offices, setting the first floor afire; and loot and burn the four-story Colored Orphan Asylum (its staff and 233 children escaping to safety) before troops fresh from the carnage at Gettysburg arrive in the city and help restore order. The draft is temporarily suspended in New York City as the government sends more troops and the human cost of the violence becomes clear: hundreds have been injured; at least 105 people — including eleven African Americans, eight soldiers, two police officers, and dozens of rioters — have been killed.[47]

JULY 16, 1863: In the Straits of Shimonoseki, Japan, USS *Wyoming*, on patrol against Confederate commerce raiders, emerges victorious from a battle with the makeshift fleet of a Japanese warlord who is intent on driving foreigners from those well-traveled waters. This marks the first U.S. naval engagement with Japanese forces since Commodore Matthew Perry and his warships were instrumental in opening Japan to American and European vessels in 1854. The situation will remain volatile: "Our relations with Japan have been brought into serious jeopardy," President Lincoln will state in his December message to Congress, "through the perverse opposition of the hereditary aristocracy of the empire, to the enlightened and liberal policy of the Tycoon designed to bring the country into the society of nations. It is hoped, although not with entire confidence, that these difficulties may be peacefully overcome."[48]

JULY 18, 1863: Six thousand Union troops commanded by Brigadier General Truman Seymour make a frontal assault on the formidable Fort Wagner at Morris Island in Charleston Harbor (see July 10, 1863). In the vanguard of the attack is the Fifty-fourth Massachusetts, an African American infantry regiment that had arrived on the island earlier in the day. Surging forward through withering fire that includes shells from nearby Confederate batteries and rifle fire that sweeps them at times from three sides, the regiment manages to seize one small angle of the fort. But the hold is tenuous,

Colonel Robert G. Shaw (1837–1863), USA. Upon learning that the U.S. Army was attempting to retrieve Shaw's body from the common grave Confederates had made for him and his soldiers, Shaw's father asked that the colonel's body remain with those of his men.

Sergeant William H. Carney (1840–1908), USA. Reproduction of a photograph, ca. 1900, published in *Deeds of Valor: How Our Soldier-Heroes Won the Medal of Honor*, 1901. Carney earned his Medal of Honor at Fort Wagner, where he rescued the Union colors in the midst of a hail of bullets, proudly telling fellow survivors of the Fifty-fourth Massachusetts, "Boys, the old flag never touched the ground."

Louisa May Alcott (1832–1888). Photogravure print by A. W. Elson & Co., reproduced in *Louisa May Alcott, Her Life, Letters, and Journals*, 1889. Alcott's six weeks as a volunteer nurse in Washington ended when she contracted typhoid fever, which permanently weakened her health.

and the cost is too great. "Men fell all around me," Frederick Douglass's son Lewis will write to his future wife, Amelia. "A shell would explode and clear a space of twenty feet, our men would close up again, but it was no use." Taking more casualties, the Fifty-fourth is forced to fall back, and the Union assault fails. Later, when Union men, under a flag of truce, attempt to retrieve the body of Colonel Robert Gould Shaw, the regiment's white commanding officer, they are reportedly told by a Confederate, "We have buried him with his niggers!" Intended as an insult, this will become a rallying cry in the North, where the Fifty-fourth's valor will be widely celebrated. "This regiment has established its reputation as a fighting regiment," Lewis Douglass will write. "I wish we had a hundred thousand colored troops we would put an end to this war."[49]

JULY 30, 1863: Grappling with the problem of how to ensure the safety of black soldiers and their white officers captured by Confederate forces, President Lincoln states an eye-for-an-eye policy: "The government of the United States will give the same protection to all its soldiers, and if the enemy shall sell or enslave anyone because of his color, the offense shall be punished by retaliation upon the enemy's prisoners in our possession. It is therefore ordered that for every soldier of the United States killed in violation of the laws of war, a rebel soldier shall be executed; and for every one enslaved by the enemy or sold into slavery, a rebel soldier shall be placed at hard labor

on the public works." Unacceptable to many, and impractical to enforce, the policy will fade from view. The problem will remain.[50]

AUGUST 1863

AUGUST 8, 1863: In a letter to the editor of the *Floridian & Journal*, Confederate congressman Robert Hilton defends the Southern government's less popular wartime measures, particularly suspension of habeas corpus. Even though the president and military authorities "have been compelled for the defense of all that men hold dear — our wives, our homes, our children, our altars — to place temporary restraint at periods of great danger, upon the inhabitants of certain localities," he writes, "the sufferers, if good citizens, will not complain; if disloyal to our cause, who shall sympathize with them?"[51]

AUGUST 10, 1863: Meeting with President Lincoln, Frederick Douglass vehemently protests the disparity of pay between white and black soldiers — a policy only recently instituted in violation of assurances originally made to potential African American recruits (see June 4, 1863, August 25, 1862). The president responds, Douglass will report in a postwar auto-

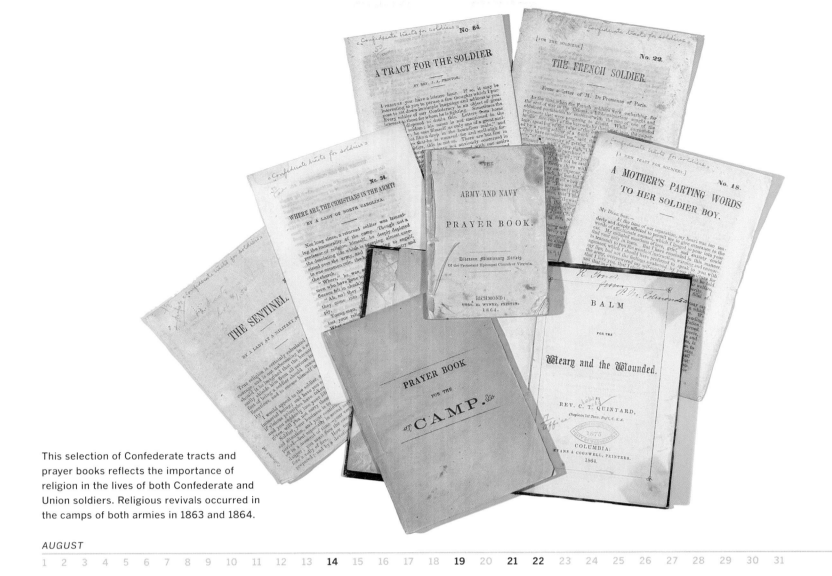

This selection of Confederate tracts and prayer books reflects the importance of religion in the lives of both Confederate and Union soldiers. Religious revivals occurred in the camps of both armies in 1863 and 1864.

biography, that in view of the prevailing racial prejudice, "the fact that they were not to receive the same pay as white soldiers seemed a necessary concession to smooth the way to their employment at all as soldiers, but that ultimately they would receive the same." Given past promises, and the needs of their families, "ultimately" is not a satisfactory time frame for most United States Colored Troops (USCT).[52]

AUGUST 14, 1863: In Missouri, from the 1850s the scene of particularly vicious guerrilla warfare that sharply escalated with the declaration of war, another tragic chapter begins with a terrible accident: five women, the wives and sisters of men fighting under Confederate guerrilla William Quantrill, are killed in the collapse of a Kansas City building in which Union authorities have confined them for aiding the enemy. Enraged, scattered guerrilla bands begin to come together; Quantrill, future postwar outlaws Cole Younger and Frank James, and more than four hundred others determine to exact vengeance for the deaths.[53]

AUGUST 19, 1863: With six thousand Federal troops now on hand, the draft — suspended after the July riots — resumes in New York City.[54]

AUGUST 21, 1863: "This is a fast day, proclaimed by the President of the Confederate States, and has been observed as a Sabbath in the Camp," Army of Northern Virginia mapmaker

Jedediah Hotchkiss writes in his diary. "Mr. Lacy preached at our headquarters and nearly a thousand soldiers and many officers came to hear him. . . . [He] gave us a noble discourse in which he handled, unsparingly, our sins as an army and people, but held out that God must be on our side because we are in the right as proven by our deeds, and our enemies had shown themselves cruel and blood-thirsty. . . . General Lee, I noticed, spoke to each lady there and to all the children." *In the North,* this month, Louisa May Alcott, previously a writer of undistinguished fairy tales, gothic sagas, and short stories, establishes her literary reputation with the publication of *Hospital Sketches,* a 102-page fictionalized account of the six weeks she served as a nurse in a Washington hospital, until illness forced her to leave. "There they were! 'our brave boys,' as the papers justly call them, for cowards could hardly have been so riddled with shot and shell, so torn and shattered, nor have borne suffering for which we have no name, with an uncomplaining fortitude," one passage reads. "The sight of several stretchers, each with its legless, armless, or desperately wounded occupant, entering my ward, admonished me that I was there to work, not to wonder or weep; so I corked up my feelings, and returned to the path of duty, which was rather 'a hard road to travel' just then."[55]

AUGUST 21–22, 1863: Issuing orders to "kill every male and burn every house," William Quantrill leads a force of 450 Confederate guerrillas in an attack on the prewar free-soil bastion

The Destruction of the City of Lawrence, Kansas, and the Massacre of Its Inhabitants by the Rebel Guerrillas, August 21, 1863. Wood engraving published in *Harper's Weekly*, September 5, 1863.

of Lawrence, Kansas, where they murder more than 180 men and burn 185 buildings before moving back into Missouri, hotly pursued by Union cavalry. This act of vengeance (see August 14, 1863) will beget reciprocal vengeance. The raid so enrages the area's Union commander, General Thomas Ewing, that on August 25 he will issue General Orders, No. 11, under which Union forces will sweep four western Missouri counties clear of all but the most certainly loyal inhabitants, turning more than ten thousand suspected Confederate sympathizers out on the roads, with only the goods they can carry, as the smoke from their own burning houses rises behind them. The bitterness this Federal action inspires will last long after the war.[56]

AUGUST 29, 1863: The third of the Confederacy's experimental submarines, *H. L. Hunley* (named after the government businessman and inventor who is financing its development), sinks in Charleston Harbor when it is swamped by the wake of a passing vessel as it maneuvers on the surface with an open hatch. Five crewmen are lost; three survive. Unlike its two predecessors, however, *Hunley* will be recovered, and the South will continue trying to develop it as a combat vessel.[57]

AUGUST 30, 1863: "Oh these vexatious postal delays," Union soldier David Lane complains, in his diary, after receiving a letter dated more than two weeks before. "They are the bane of my life. I wonder if postmasters are human beings, with live hearts inside their jackets, beating in sympathetic unison with other hearts." Mail is vital, to Lane and to hundreds of thousands of other soldiers, North and South: it bolsters courage and brings the reassurance of familiar "voices" to men fighting their way through dangerous and unfamiliar ground. No news can be worrisome, particularly for Confederate soldiers whose families are in the line of Union advance. "Why don't some one from home write to me?" Lieutenant James Billingslea Mitchell will write his mother in October. "I have not received a line since I left Chattanooga. I am beginning to fear the Yankees have come up from Florida & there has been a battle at home, as there seems to be a perfect cessation of all communication. You must not forget that I am always as anxious to hear from home as you are to hear from me."[58]

SEPTEMBER 1863

SEPTEMBER 2, 1863: As Union forces under General William Rosecrans move toward strategically important Chattanooga, Tennessee, crossroads of the only rail lines still linking the eastern and western parts of the Confederacy, Ambrose Burnside's Union Army of the Ohio occupies Knoxville, which has been evacuated by the Confederates (the division that

ABOVE: *Army Mail Leaving Hd. Qts. Post Office. Army Potomac.* Pencil and Chinese white drawing by Alfred R. Waud, ca. March 1863. "We are only a mile and a half from the steamboat landing," Army of the Potomac lieutenant colonel Alfred B. McCalmont wrote his brother in February 1863, "but our letters go first to Brigade Headquarters, then to Division Headquarters, one mile due west; then to Corps Headquarters, three miles further west; then to Grand Division Headquarters . . . and finally to the Headquarters of the Army of the Potomac . . . [after which] they are sent down to Falmouth and thence by rail over to the Potomac river from which they started. . . . There is a great deal more of method for the sake of method in the army, than of method for the sake of substance."

RIGHT: Mail was crucially important to the people of both sides, but in the Confederate States, paper was among the materials not to be wasted. Thus, at times, to make the most of each sheet, correspondents would first write north-to-south, then turn the paper and continue writing west-to-east. As can be seen in this example from the papers of Burton Harrison, secretary to Jefferson Davis, deciphering the result took a high degree of concentration.

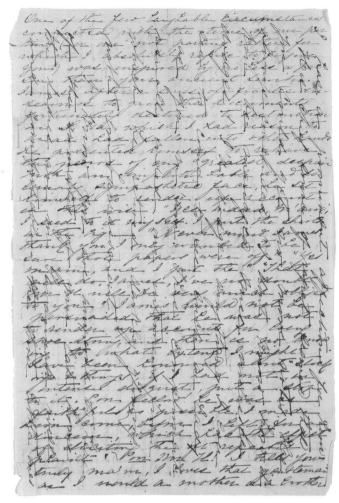

SEPTEMBER

1   2   3   4   **5**   **6**   7   **8**   **9**   10   11   12   13   14   15   16   17   18   19   20   21   22   23   24   25   26   27   28   29   30

had occupied the town heading toward Chattanooga to join Braxton Bragg).[59]

SEPTEMBER 5, 1863: United States ambassador to Great Britain Charles Francis Adams writes a stern warning to the British foreign minister, Lord John Russell, on the subject of what have come to be called the Laird Rams — two powerful vessels equipped with subsurface iron extensions designed to pierce the hulls of enemy vessels below the line of their iron plating. Built by the British company John Laird & Sons, the rams were contracted for by James D. Bulloch, the South's naval agent in England, and are slated to become potent new weapons in the North/South naval war. British law officers, however, have been claiming they have no evidence that the ships are being built for the Confederacy and thus cannot seize them as violations of British neutrality. Adams knows better. However, he does not know that, two days earlier, Lord Russell decided to have British authorities seize the two vessels, thus avoiding a diplomatic crisis with the United States. The rams will eventually be commissioned in the British navy.[60]

SEPTEMBER 6, 1863: In South Carolina, Confederates vacate Fort Wagner after intensive naval bombardment and in anticipation of an imminent infantry assault. The first Union regiment to move into the fortification will be the Fifty-fourth Massachusetts, the African American regiment that was

severely battered leading the unsuccessful Union attack on the fort almost two months earlier (see July 18, 1863).[61]

SEPTEMBER 8, 1863: As the Confederate division that recently evacuated Knoxville arrives in Chattanooga, joining more than ten thousand other reinforcements that have arrived from Mississippi, Braxton Bragg, leery of becoming trapped should William Rosecrans's approaching Federals secure the surrounding mountains, leads the Rebel force out of the city. After Union troops occupy Chattanooga the following day, a despondent President Davis will declare, "We are now at the darkest hour of our political existence." *At Sabine Pass on the Texas-Louisiana border,* Confederates employing deadly accurate artillery fire hand an embarrassing defeat to a Union expedition (four gunboats escorting seven troop transports) attempting to overwhelm the Southerners' small fort. Though a minor victory, the action provides a great morale boost to Confederates; President Davis will later refer to it as the "Thermopylae of the Civil War."[62]

SEPTEMBER 9, 1863: A brigade of Confederate soldiers plunders the offices, in Raleigh, of the *North Carolina Standard,* published by William H. Holden, whom many Confederates now regard as a traitor. Holden has reached the conclusion that the South cannot win the war and has been acting on that assumption — organizing antiwar meetings and printing editorials advocating a negotiated peace with the North. *At*

Longstreet's Soldiers Debarking from the Trains Below Ringgold, September 18, 1863. Reproduction of a drawing by Alfred R. Waud, published in *The Mountain Campaigns in Georgia* by Joseph M. Brown, 1886. Dispatched over General Lee's objections, Longstreet's soldiers were to play a crucial role in the battle of Chickamauga.

The First Gun at Chickamauga. Pencil, Chinese white, and black ink wash drawing on tan paper by Alfred R. Waud, ca. September 18, 1863. After searching for each other for some time, by September 18, 1863, Bragg's Confederates and Rosecrans's Federals were firing preliminary salvos to what would be the bloodiest battle of the war in the western theater.

SEPTEMBER

1 2 3 4 5 6 7 8 9 **10** 11 **12** 13 14 15 16 17 18 **19 20** 21 22 23 24 25 26 27 28 29 30

Charleston, South Carolina, United States Marines and sailors attempt a night landing at Fort Sumter in Charleston Harbor and are turned back with heavy casualties. The attempt fails, in part, because Confederates, using a codebook recovered from USS *Keokuk,* wrecked during the navy's earlier assault on Charleston (see April 7, 1863), are able to read flag signals between the Union commanders during the operation's planning. *In Virginia,* President Davis overrides the objections of Robert E. Lee and sends General James Longstreet and two Army of Northern Virginia divisions to reinforce Bragg near Chattanooga. Because Union forces now hold the rail hub of Knoxville, these twelve thousand reinforcements will have to take a roundabout route; about six thousand will arrive in time to join Bragg's army in a bitter fight with the Federals (see September 19–20, 1863).[63]

SEPTEMBER 10, 1863: Little Rock, Arkansas, falls to the Union, a loss that severely threatens the entire Confederate Trans-Mississippi Department, already cut off from the rest of the Confederacy by the fall of Vicksburg and Port Hudson. The Confederate state government that withdraws from the city with Rebel forces today will reestablish itself in the city of Washington, to the southwest. Unionist Arkansans will establish their own state government early in 1864. These two opposing governments will hold sway over different sections of the state (divided roughly by the Arkansas River) for the remainder of the war — one factor that will contribute to

an upsurge in Arkansas guerrilla warfare. *In Raleigh, North Carolina,* supporters of newspaper editor and prominent state political leader William H. Holden, whose newspaper offices were wrecked by Confederate troops the previous day (see September 9, 1863), return the "favor" by trashing the offices of the local pro-administration newspaper.[64]

SEPTEMBER 12, 1863: As three scattered columns of William Rosecrans's Union army, their supply lines increasingly vulnerable, search for Braxton Bragg's Confederates in wooded and mountainous north Georgia (facing the growing danger that Bragg will attack each Federal column in turn), Union brigadier general John Beatty writes in his diary: "The roads up and down the mountains are extremely bad; our progress has therefore been slow and the march hither a tedious one. The brigade lies in the open field before me in battle line. The boys have had no time to rest during the day and have done much night work, but they hold up well." *Six days later,* as the Union columns converge and Beatty moves his men up to a position on Chickamauga Creek, he will note: "Occasional shots along the line indicated that the enemy was in our immediate front."[65]

SEPTEMBER 19–20, 1863: The bloodiest battle of the war in the western theater takes place in hostile, wooded terrain near Chickamauga Creek in north Georgia, as sixty-six thousand Confederates under Braxton Bragg clash with the sixty thousand Federals of William Rosecrans's Army of the Cumberland.

Major General George H. Thomas (1816–1870), USA, between 1862 and 1865. Thomas's decision to remain loyal to the Union alienated him from his family in Virginia; and his Virginia roots led some in the North to distrust him—despite his excellent record as a Civil War general.

John Clem: A Drummer Boy of 12 Years of Age Who Shot a Rebel Colonel upon the Battle Field of Chickamauga, Ga., Sept. 20, 1863, from the series *Album Sketches of the Great Southern Campaign.* Color lithograph based on a drawing by James Fuller Queen, ca. 1863. Nine years old when he was allowed to tag along with the Twenty-second Michigan regiment in 1861, Clem was first mentioned in news reports as "Johnny Shiloh" after that 1862 battle before his fame increased in 1863 as "the drummer boy of Chickamauga." Eventually a career army man, he retired as a general in 1915.

SEPTEMBER

1 2 3 4 5 6 7 8 9 10 11 12 13 14 15 16 17 18 19 20 21 22 **23 24** 25 26 27 28 29 30

Union troops hold their own through the first day of bitter combat. But midway through day two, Confederates exploit a gap in the Union line, sundering the Federal army. Striking at its flanks and rear, the Rebels push most of Rosecrans's men, and Rosecrans himself, into a full-scale retreat toward Chattanooga. (In the midst of this confusion and carnage, Union drummer boy Johnny Clem, advancing against orders to stay in the rear, picks up the gun of a slain comrade and takes part in the battle, his age and his conduct under fire making him a Union hero.) Throughout the battle, Major General George Henry Thomas, a Virginian who remains a staunch Unionist, has held the Union left; as the Union line breaks, he and his men, assisted by reserve units under Gordon Granger, continue to hold, saving this Federal defeat from becoming a complete disaster. Henceforth known as the "rock of Chickamauga," Thomas does not withdraw his troops from the field until nightfall—and their subsequent march, Brigadier General John Beatty will note in his diary, is "a melancholy one. All along the road, for miles, wounded men were lying. They had crawled or hobbled slowly away from the fury of the battle, become exhausted, and lain down by the roadside to die. . . . What must have been their agony, mental and physical, as they lay in the dreary woods, sensible that there was no one to comfort or to care for them and that in a few hours more their career on earth would be ended!" Casualties from Chickamauga will exceed thirty-four thousand Union and Confederate soldiers killed, wounded, or missing. Braxton Bragg,

shaken at the cost of his tactical victory, will not press after the Federals. After the Army of the Cumberland reaches Chattanooga, Bragg's battered force will occupy the surrounding heights, including Lookout Mountain and Missionary Ridge, and besiege the city.[66]

SEPTEMBER 23, 1863: President Lincoln is summoned to a nighttime meeting at the War Department by Secretary of War Stanton, who has received a long message from Major General Rosecrans giving details of and reasons for his Chickamauga defeat. ("I know the reasons well enough," Stanton grumbles. "Rosecrans ran away from his fighting men and did not stop for 13 miles.") With Rosecrans's army now trapped in Chattanooga, Lincoln, Stanton, General in Chief Halleck, and other advisers decide that they must send reinforcements. Their decision sets in motion the longest and largest movement of troops to occur before the twentieth century. Performing bureaucratic miracles, Stanton organizes the immediate transport, by rail, of more than twenty thousand men from the Army of the Potomac—their equipment, horses, and artillery. Led by Major General Joseph Hooker (no longer commanding the entire Army of the Potomac but still very much on active duty), the reinforcements will complete the 1,233-mile journey to the vicinity of Chattanooga within eleven days.[67]

SEPTEMBER 24, 1863: Abraham Lincoln writes to his wife, Mary Todd Lincoln, currently staying at the Fifth Avenue

Brigadier General Benjamin H. Helm (1831–1863), CSA, between 1860 and 1863. Married to Mary Todd Lincoln's half-sister, Emily, Helm refused a commission in the Union army offered to him in 1861 by President Lincoln, choosing instead to serve the Confederate States.

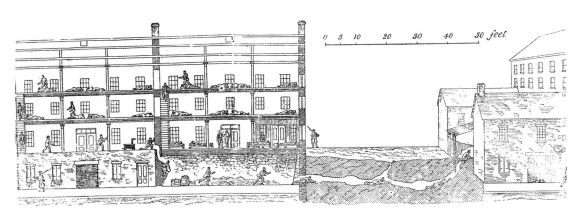

Sectional View of Libby Prison, showing Diagram of the Tunnel.

Sectional View of Libby Prison, Showing Diagram of the Tunnel. Illustration from *Col. Rose's Story of the Famous Tunnel Escape from Libby Prison,* by Thomas E. Rose, ca. 1890. Richmond's Libby Prison, intensely overcrowded after the arrival of prisoners from Chickamauga, was the site of a daring February 9, 1864, escape by 109 of the prisoners. Eventually 48 of the men were recaptured, including the ringleader, Colonel Thomas E. Rose, of the Seventy-seventh Pennsylvania Volunteers. (Rose rejoined William T. Sherman's Union army after a July 1864 prisoner exchange.)

Hotel in New York City: "We now have a tolerably accurate summing up of the late battle between Rosecrans and Bragg. The result is that we are worsted, if at all, only in the fact that we, after the main fighting was over, yielded the ground, thus leaving considerable of our artillery and wounded to fall into the enemies' hands. . . . Of the [Confederate generals] killed, one Major Genl. and five Brigadiers, including your brother-in-law, [Ben Hardin] Helm." This news adds to the growing burden of anguish pressing upon Kentucky-born Mary and her family: she and Abraham have lost two of their own sons to illness, and three of Mary's brothers have perished fighting for the South (Sam Todd at Shiloh, David at Vicksburg, and young Alexander at Baton Rouge). Now her sister Emilie's husband has been killed — heartrending news to both Mary and Abraham. "I never saw Mr. Lincoln more moved than when he heard that his young brother-in-law, Ben Hardin Helm, scarcely thirty-two years of age, had been killed," Lincoln's friend Judge David Davis will recall after the war. "I saw how grief-stricken he was . . . so I closed the door and left him alone."[68]

OCTOBER 1863

OCTOBER 1, 1863: In the midst of shortages and other wartime problems, including a growing population of Southern refugees, the *Richmond Examiner* publishes a satire based on Jonathan Swift's "Modest Proposal" penned by correspondent George W. Bagby. Among its harshly tongue-in-cheek proposals: that poor people and refugees who have flocked to the South's major cities be crammed into "elegant and commodious" homes made out of empty tobacco and whiskey barrels, and that food shortages be solved by resorting to cannibalism. ("The common repugnance to human food is but a foolish prejudice born of modern philosophy and political economy.") Slaves would be among the few not condemned to be eaten, both because of racial prejudice and because it would be foolish to destroy such valuable property.[69] *There are some Union prisoners in Richmond* who are in no mood for Confederate satire. Colonel Caleb Carolton, of the Eighty-ninth Ohio Volunteers, writes his wife, Sadie, from the city's Libby Prison: "My regiment (that is what had not been killed, wounded, or missing) was captured just after dark on Sunday night, 20th Sept. I escaped as usual without a wound, my horse was killed under me early in the engagement. . . . I received a couple of pretty sharp raps from spent bullets which in addition to loss of sleep, poor food and general disgust, renders me sore cross and very much dissatisfied with my situation." He asks her to send clothes — and books and a chess game, for "we are going to find it troublesome to pass

Brigadier General John Beatty (1828–1914), USA. After service in the Union army, the eloquent Ohioan served in the U.S. House of Representatives from 1868 to 1873. His wartime journals, first published as *The Citizen Soldier* in 1879 and later reissued as *Memoirs of a Volunteer,* were dedicated to "Kinsmen of the coming centuries."

Unidentified Union sailor. Hand-colored quarter-plate tintype, between 1861 and 1865.

OCTOBER

1 2 **3** 4 **5** **6** 7 8 9 10 11 12 13 14 15 16 17 18 19 20 21 22 23 24 25 26 27 28 29 30 31

the time here, five hundred or more officers in the three rooms with nothing to do."[70]

OCTOBER 3, 1863: With the Union army under siege in Chattanooga, Brigadier General John Beatty takes advantage of a quiet moment to write in his diary:

> The two armies are lying face to face. The Federal and Confederate sentinels walk their beats in sight of each other. The quarters of the rebel generals may be seen from our camps with the naked eye. The tents of their troops dot the hillsides. . . . Their long lines of campfires almost encompass us. But the campfires of the Army of the Cumberland are burning also. Bruised and torn by a two days' unequal contest, its flags are still up and its men still unwhipped. It has taken its position here, and here, by God's help, it will remain.

Two days later, he will record something he sees during an hours-long bombardment from Confederate artillery ensconced on Lookout Mountain: "A shell entered the door of a dog tent, near which two soldiers of the Eighteenth Ohio were standing, and buried itself in the ground, when one of the soldiers turned very coolly to the other and said: 'There, you damn fool, you see what you get by leaving your door open!'"[71]

OCTOBER 5, 1863: The formidable Union fleet blockading Charleston Harbor becomes painfully aware of a new element in naval warfare when the steam-driven, cigar-shaped Confederate torpedo boat *David,* riding so low in the water it can hardly be discerned, rams a torpedo into the side of USS *New Ironsides.* The Union's saltwater armored warship, though damaged, is able to remain on station. *David,* meanwhile, almost succumbs to its own attack: water showering in after the explosion douses its power plant. But the boat's engineer saves the day, and *David* escapes.[72]

OCTOBER 6, 1863: With the U.S. draft now in force, but without any provision for conscientious objection (see March 31 and September 27, 1862, and February 24, 1864), some draftees face heavy consequences for their nonviolent beliefs. Today, Vermont Quaker Cyrus Pringle describes his rough treatment in a diary entry:

> Two sergeants soon called for me, and taking me a little aside, bid me lie down on my back and stretching my limbs apart tied cords to my wrists and ankles and these to four stakes driven in the ground somewhat in the form of an X. I was very quiet in my mind as I lay there on the ground [soaked] with the rain of the previous day, exposed to the heat of the sun, and suffering keenly from the cords binding my wrists and straining my muscles. . . . I wept, not so much from my own suffering as from sorrow that such

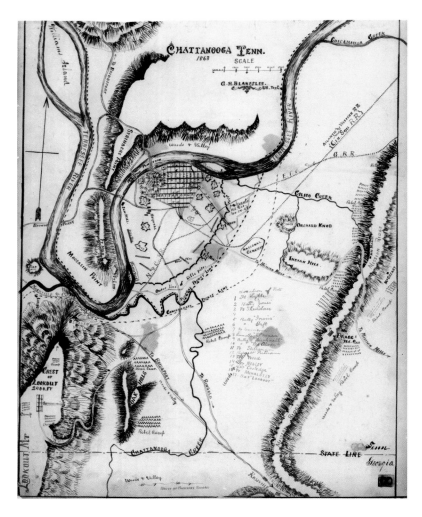

LEFT: *Chattanooga Tenn.* Color map by G. H. Blakeslee, U.S. Topographical Engineers, 1863.

OPPOSITE, LEFT: *A Quaker Letter to Lincoln.* Music by E. M. Bruce with words by Elmer Ruán Coates; music cover art by James Fuller Queen, May 1863. Many Quaker men in the Union, opposed to war on religious grounds, appealed to the president for assistance. "For those appealing to me on conscientious grounds," Lincoln wrote to Quaker Eliza P. Gurney in September 1864, "I have done, and shall do, the best I could and can, in my own conscience, under my oath to the law."

OPPOSITE, RIGHT: *Great Central Fair for the Sanitary Commission.* Original watercolor-and-graphite drawing for letterhead, and color lithograph proof for the printed letterhead. Design by James Fuller Queen, 1864. Ambitious in scope, often grand in presentation, sanitary fairs became a prime method of raising funds to assist Union soldiers.

things should be in our own country, where Justice and Freedom and Liberty of Conscience have been the annual boast of Fourth-of-July orators so many years.[73]

OCTOBER 8, 1863: "General Longstreet has written to the Secretary of War a letter which has filled me with concern," Confederate War Department official Robert Kean writes in his diary. "He says [General Braxton] Bragg has done but one thing he ought to have done since he (General Longstreet) has been out there and that was the order to attack on September 18 [precipitating the battle of Chickamauga] . . . [and] he expressed the opinion that nothing will be effected under Bragg's command." General Bragg has long had contentious relations with his fellow officers, but his actions in the wake of Chickamauga have created particular ire — and President Davis's efforts to encourage harmony among his snarling western generals (extending even to a visit to Bragg's headquarters for a face-to-face meeting) will have little positive effect. On October 29, Davis will approve irate cavalryman Nathan Bedford Forrest's request to be detached from Bragg's army for an independent command in Mississippi and west Tennessee. Longstreet will remain restive.[74]

OCTOBER 13, 1863: Having run his campaign by mail while in exile in Canada, Copperhead Clement Vallandigham (see May 1 and May 7, 1863) is soundly defeated in the contest for governor of Ohio by War Democrat John Brough. Pro-Union

candidates prevail in other state elections this day as well. The election results stem in part from the Union triumphs at Gettysburg and Vicksburg. Moreover, in the wake of sympathy stirred by the anti-black riots in New York City and elsewhere and public recognition of the valor of black regiments, including the Fifty-fourth Massachusetts (see July 18, 1863), emancipation, roundly attacked by Democrats, has also become less controversial to many Northern whites. *In the South,* suffering from shortages, inflation, and the losses at Gettysburg and Vicksburg, 1863 congressional elections will change the nature of Confederate politics by bringing more conservative and negotiation-prone legislators (known as reconstructionists or tories) to Richmond and to the governorships of several Southern states. A further faction that supports the war but does not support Jefferson Davis will also gather strength.[75]

OCTOBER 15, 1863: Inventor H. L. Hunley is among eight men who die when the Confederate submarine *H. L. Hunley* sinks (for the second time; see August 29, 1863) during a practice dive in Charleston Harbor.[76]

OCTOBER 17, 1863: In Indianapolis, on his way to Louisville, Kentucky, to receive new orders, General Ulysses S. Grant encounters Secretary of War Edwin Stanton, who is en route to see him. As a result of their encounter, the following day Grant will assume command of the new Military Division of the Mississippi, encompassing the Departments of the Ohio

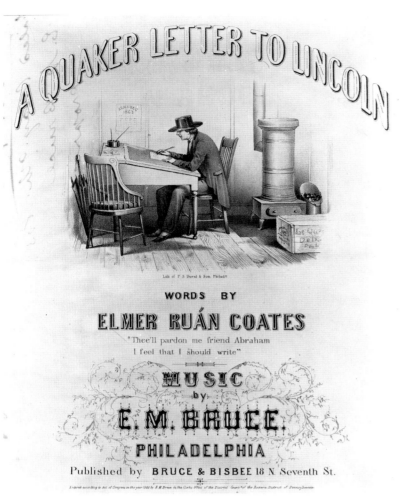

OCTOBER–NOVEMBER

24 25 26 **27** **28** **29** **30** **31** **1** **2** **3** **4** **5** **6** **7** 8 9 10 11 12 13 14 15 16 17 18 19 20 21 22 23

(Ambrose Burnside, commanding), the Tennessee (William T. Sherman to be named commander), and the Cumberland. Stanton allows Grant to choose whether or not to retain William Rosecrans as Department of the Cumberland commander; Grant opts to replace him with Major General George H. Thomas, whom he orders to hold Chattanooga at all costs. As Grant sets out on a difficult journey to Chattanooga, he receives Thomas's answer: "We will hold the town until we starve."[77]

OCTOBER 24, 1863: Having arrived at Chattanooga the previous night, General Grant, accompanied by General Thomas and a party of staff officers, inspects the area. At Brown's Ferry on the Tennessee River west of the city, they come so close to the enemy lines that they are in full view of Confederate pickets. "They did not fire upon us nor seem to be disturbed by our presence," Grant will write in his memoirs. "They must have seen that we were all commissioned officers. But, I suppose, they looked upon the garrison of Chattanooga as prisoners of war . . . and thought it would be inhuman to kill any of them except in self-defense." In the evening, Grant issues orders to open the way to Bridgeport, Alabama, establishing a supply line, or "*a cracker line,* as the soldiers appropriately termed it," Grant will write. "They had been so long on short rations that my first thought was the establishment of a line over which food might reach them." The general and his officers next turn their attention to breaking the Confederate siege.[78]

OCTOBER 27–NOVEMBER 7, 1863: Chicago hosts the first "sanitary fair," a multistate Grand North-Western Fair organized to raise money, as a Chicago Sanitary Commission booklet notes, "to obtain comforts and necessaries for the sick and wounded of our army." The two-week extravaganza begins with a procession some three miles long, which everyone can watch, since the mayor has proclaimed opening day a holiday. It proceeds to draw some five thousand people a day, their seventy-five-cent tickets admitting them to a wonderland of exhibition areas, food concessions, entertainment, and halls where donated items are offered for sale. The most precious item auctioned, donated by President Lincoln, is the original draft of the final Emancipation Proclamation, which sells for $3,000. The buyer, Thomas B. Bryan, will give the document to another Chicago Sanitary Commission project, the Soldiers' Home. This refuge for thousands of soldiers traveling between hospitals, camps, and battlefields will eventually become a permanent home for Civil War veterans. (The document will be destroyed in the 1871 Chicago fire, though the Soldiers' Home will survive.)[79]

"TO CARE FOR HIM WHO SHALL HAVE BORNE THE BATTLE"

"Mrs. Harris, Mrs. Barnes, Mrs. Auld and myself went to the [railroad] cars, on their arrival from the front," Georgia-based Confederate nurse Kate Cumming wrote in her diary, in May 1864, "and O, what a sight we there beheld! No less than three long trains filled, outside and in, with wounded. Nearly all seemed to be wounded in the head, face, and hands. I asked some one near why this was. They replied, because our men had fought behind breastworks [temporary chest-high fortifications]. There were ladies at the depot with baskets filled with edibles of all kinds, and buckets of milk, coffee, and lemonade; and I noticed many had wines," Cumming added. "The ladies in Atlanta have been doing this work ever since the commencement of the war."

Ladies and civilian gentlemen, army and navy doctors, members of such large organizations as the U.S. Sanitary Commission and Christian Commission in the North, and smaller state and local organizations in both North and South—all pitched in throughout this war that quickly grew into a medical nightmare for which neither side was prepared. Occurring, in the postwar words of former Union surgeon general William A. Hammond, "at the end of the medical Middle Ages," the Civil War brought hundreds of thousands of sick and maimed men into hospitals and soldiers'

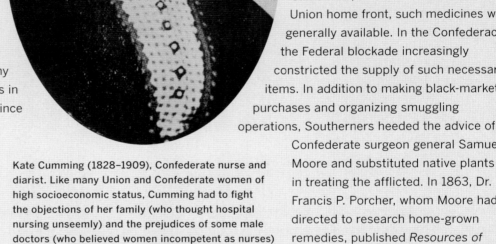

Kate Cumming (1828–1909), Confederate nurse and diarist. Like many Union and Confederate women of high socioeconomic status, Cumming had to fight the objections of her family (who thought hospital nursing unseemly) and the prejudices of some male doctors (who believed women incompetent as nurses) to achieve a permanent position as a nurse with the Confederate army.

homes and strained the capacities of both sides to provide proper treatment.

Home front general hospitals, field hospitals, and hospital trains and ships were built, converted, and improvised. Federal and Confederate armies set up regimental medicine wagons to supply surgeons in the field with anesthetics, antiseptics, narcotics, purgatives/cathartics (to clean out body poisons), diaphoretics (to increase perspiration), stimulants, and skin irritants. On the Union home front, such medicines were generally available. In the Confederacy, the Federal blockade increasingly constricted the supply of such necessary items. In addition to making black-market purchases and organizing smuggling operations, Southerners heeded the advice of Confederate surgeon general Samuel P. Moore and substituted native plants in treating the afflicted. In 1863, Dr. Francis P. Porcher, whom Moore had directed to research home-grown remedies, published *Resources of Southern Fields and Forests, Medical, Economical, and Agricultural*, listing more than 400 useful plants (including skunk cabbage, white willow, cranesbill, and pipissewa).

Illnesses and infections accounted for nearly two-thirds of the 620,000 military deaths in the war, but battle wounds abounded, the .58-caliber minié ball, artillery fire, and other

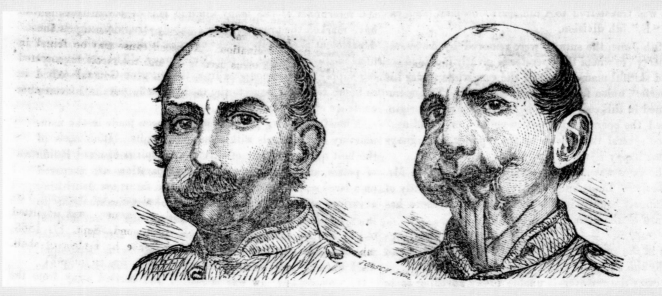

Illustrations depicting surgical reconstruction after facial wounds from *Confederate States Medical & Surgical Journal*, published in Richmond, Virginia, by Ayres & Wade, 1864–1865.

Union Volunteer Refreshment Saloon and Hospital. Lithograph-with-watercolor receipt, designed by James Fuller Queen, and filled out for Master George Morton Moore by J. B. Wade, 1862. Refreshment saloons throughout the Union offered meals and accommodations to soldiers who were on leave, who were on the way home to recuperate from illness or wounds, or who had been released from hospitals and were returning to camp. In the South, similar "wayside homes" were operated by volunteer aid societies.

implements of destruction wreaking havoc on the human body. Amputations were common, as was gangrene: "We have some dreadful cases of that awful disease," Kate Cumming wrote in November 1863, and cited the case of a man named Deal, "a large, fine-looking Texan, who was wounded at Chickamauga. We thought it was impossible to cast a cloud o'er his spirits. . . . Since he has had gangrene he is grave enough. . . . The doctors are fearful they will not be able to stop the gangrene on his back before it eats inwardly and reaches some vital part; nor on his knee at all, and that he will likely lose his leg." The only Confederacy-wide relief organization established during the war was the Association for the Relief of Maimed Soldiers, which supplied artificial limbs to Confederate servicemen.

Many veterans of the war were able to resume normal lives. Many others carried physical and emotional scars. In the South, both during and for years after the war, disabled soldiers could only turn to volunteer groups for assistance. In the North, the Federal government passed a Pension Act, amended in 1864, that provided some monetary compensation to men with permanent physical impairments; and, shortly after the war, the U.S. government built a system of National Homes for Disabled Volunteer Soldiers. Yet money and housing, though important, could not compensate for all that some veterans lost in this terrible war, or exorcise the ghosts of experience for soldiers or their caretakers: "It is curious, when I am present at the most appalling things—deaths, operations, sickening wounds (perhaps full of maggots)—I do not fail, although my sympathies are very much excited, but keep singularly cool," Union nurse Walt Whitman wrote to his mother in October 1863, "but often hours afterward, perhaps when I am home or out walking alone, I feel sick and actually tremble when I recall the thing and have it in my mind again before me."[80]

The Great Russian Ball at the Academy of Music, November 5, 1863. Wood engraving published in *Harper's Weekly*, November 21, 1863. Although Russian motives for sending their fleet to visit the Union cities of New York and San Francisco were mixed, the Union celebrated this apparent show of support from a friendly European power.

Edward Everett (1794–1865). Engraving by Henry W. Smith (b. 1828), ca. 1858. A former president of Harvard University, U.S. representative from Massachusetts, minister to Great Britain, and U.S. secretary of state, Everett wrote to Lincoln a day after the Gettysburg ceremony: "I should be glad, if I could flatter myself that I came as near to the central idea of the occasion in two hours, as you did in two minutes."

NOVEMBER

1 **2** 3 **4** **5** **6** 7 8 9 10 11 12 13 14 15 16 17 18 19 20 21 22 23 24 25 26 27 28 29 30

NOVEMBER 1863

NOVEMBER 2, 1863: President Lincoln receives an invitation to make a "few appropriate remarks" at the November 19 dedication of the new Gettysburg National Cemetery. Despite the short notice, the president accepts.[81]

NOVEMBER 4, 1863: At President Davis's suggestion, Braxton Bragg detaches some fifteen thousand men under General James Longstreet from his Army of Tennessee and sends them to Knoxville, where they will besiege that Union-occupied railroad hub in what will be an unsuccessful effort to retake the city and reestablish rail links with Virginia. (The siege will end by December 4.) While this move puts a comfortable distance between Bragg and his unhappy subordinate general (see October 8, 1863), it also weakens the Confederate siege of Chattanooga.[82]

NOVEMBER 5, 1863: At New York City's Academy of Music, Americans put on a grand ball in honor of Russian diplomats and personnel of the Russian fleet, which arrived in U.S. East Coast ports in September, with other vessels docking in San Francisco in October. The United States has enjoyed cordial relations with Russia for more than a decade, Czar Alexander II being both friend and inspiration to the Lincoln administration (in 1861, the czar emancipated the Russian serfs). Although the fleet has been deployed to be well placed for action should European tensions over events in Russian

Poland erupt into war, its visit has been viewed as a gesture of support for the Union, and the effect on Northern morale has been electric. Naval facilities have been placed at the Russians' disposal, and the Russians have been honored at many social events. The Russians, in turn, won the enduring thanks of San Franciscans when they helped extinguish, at the cost of several Russian lives, a roaring fire in late October. "Russia . . . has our friendship," Secretary of State William H. Seward will write on December 23, "because she always wishes us well, and leaves us to conduct our affairs as we think best." The fleet will remain in American ports through April 1864.[83]

NOVEMBER 6, 1863: Having completed the journey to assume his new duties in Louisiana, Lieutenant Lawrence Van Alstyne, formerly a sergeant with the 128th New York, records in his diary what he has seen on a routine day spent organizing his new command, Company D, Ninetieth U.S. Colored Infantry, a unit comprising recently liberated slaves.

> My company was examined and almost every one proved to be sound enough for soldiers. A dozen at a time were taken into a tent, where they stripped and were put through the usual gymnastic performance, after which they were measured for shoes and a suit, and then another dozen called in. Some of them were scarred from head to foot where they had been whipped. One man's back was nearly all one scar, as if the skin had been chopped up and

The earliest of the five known drafts of the Gettysburg Address in Abraham Lincoln's handwriting. Known as the Nicolay copy, because it was owned by one of Lincoln's secretaries, John Nicolay, this is presumed to be the only working, or predelivery, draft of the speech. The second page, on different paper from the first, was probably drafted in Gettysburg on November 18, during Lincoln's overnight stay at the home of Judge David Wills.

left to heal in ridges. Another had scars on the back of his neck, and from that all the way to his heels every little ways; but that was not such a sight as the one with the great solid mass of ridges, from his shoulders to his hips. That beat all the anti-slavery sermons ever yet preached.[84]

NOVEMBER 18, 1863: President Lincoln, Secretary of State Seward, and a party from Washington, including Lincoln's two secretaries, John Hay and John Nicolay, arrive in Gettysburg, Pennsylvania, a town now "filled to overflowing," as the *New York Times* will report, with people awaiting the dedication of the National Cemetery the following day. The president goes to the home of prominent local attorney David Wills, a moving force behind the establishment of the cemetery and an organizer of the dedication ceremonies. Declining an opportunity to address a crowd that comes to the house, Lincoln retires to his second-floor room, where he puts the finishing touches on the short remarks he will deliver the following day, after the day's main address by Massachusetts statesman, scholar, and celebrated orator Edward Everett.[85]

NOVEMBER 19, 1863: After making final changes to his remarks, President Lincoln mounts a horse for the short ride to the cemetery. "The procession formed itself in an orphanly sort of way & moved out with very little help from anybody," Lincoln's secretary John Hay will write in his diary, "& after a little delay Mr. Everett took his place on the stand — and

Mr. Stockton made a prayer which thought it was an oration; and Mr. Everett spoke as he always does, perfectly." Everett's oration, a description of the three-day Gettysburg battle that he delivered from memory, took two hours (and will meet with mixed critical reviews). President Lincoln's remarks take about two minutes — but Lincoln has been pondering the underlying idea for years. "The central idea pervading this struggle," he told John Hay in 1861, "is the necessity that is upon us, of proving that popular government is not an absurdity. . . . If we fail it will go far to prove the incapability of the people to govern themselves." Now, adjusting his spectacles and looking out over the huge crowd, he salutes, with ringing eloquence, the thousands who have died so that the United States might have a "new birth of freedom" and calls on all those present to "highly resolve . . . that government of the people, by the people, for the people, shall not perish from the earth."[86]

NOVEMBER 22, 1863: Major General William T. Sherman arrives at Chattanooga with seventeen thousand troops — and the formidable U.S. Sanitary Commission nurse "Mother" Mary Ann Bickerdyke (see May 26, 1861, and February 15, 1862), who spent most of the difficult march to Chattanooga treating soldiers' feet and the aches, pains, and chills caused by unexpectedly cold weather. Grant's preparations to break the Confederate siege of the city are nearly complete.[87]

Triumphant Union soldiers atop Lookout Mountain, near Chattanooga, Tennessee. Color lithograph based on a drawing by James Fuller Queen, ca. 1863. After stunning action by Union troops at Lookout Mountain and Missionary Ridge broke the Confederate siege of Chattanooga, General Grant "rode the length of the lines," as Charles Dana reported, and "the men, who were frantic with joy and enthusiasm over the victory, received him with tumultuous shouts."

NOVEMBER

1 2 3 4 5 6 7 8 9 10 11 12 13 14 15 16 17 18 19 20 21 22 **23 24 25** 26 **27** 28 29 30

NOVEMBER 23, 1863: As Grant begins his siege-breaking operations, Union troops knock Confederates off Orchard Knob, their forward position on Missionary Ridge.[88]

NOVEMBER 24, 1863: Encouraged by Union commander Ulysses S. Grant to show initiative as Federal forces at Chattanooga launch their breakout attempt, General Joe Hooker leads three divisions against Confederates holding Lookout Mountain, southwest of the city. One small Confederate division under General Carter Stevenson holds the summit, supported by troops under Generals Edward C. Walthall and John C. Moore protecting the slopes. Fog that moves in as the Federals begin their assault at about 8:00 AM continues to inhibit both forces — and observers at Grant's headquarters. Much of this "battle above the clouds" is heard but not seen. By 8:00 PM, however — Stevenson having been ordered to withdraw to reinforce Confederates battling Sherman's troops to the northeast — the mountain belongs to the Union. By then, the field hospital below is crowded with wounded from two days' fighting. Mother Bickerdyke is helping doctors treat the wounded, who seem to occupy every bit of available ground. With few drugs available, she flexes her belief in temperance enough to fix the men in her charge her own peculiar brew of whiskey diluted with hot water, sweetened with brown sugar, and thickened with crumpled hardtack. Tough as nails, she makes certain that, as men die, their bodies are taken outside so living soldiers can have their beds; always looking

out for her soldiers, she comforts amputees who plead that their severed limbs be decently buried. It is a familiar request, though the men know perfectly well that, like animals that die in military service, amputated limbs are doused with kerosene and burned.[89]

NOVEMBER 25, 1863: The men of Major General George H. Thomas's Army of the Cumberland perform the "miracle of Missionary Ridge" when they exceed their orders for a limited frontal assault and sweep Braxton Bragg's Confederates completely off the ridge. "Glory to God! The day is decisively ours," Assistant Secretary of War Charles A. Dana, on the scene, wires to Secretary Stanton. "No man who climbs the ascent by any of the roads that wind along its front can believe that eighteen thousand men were moved in tolerably good order up its broken and crumbling face unless it was his fortune to witness the deed," he will later write in his memoirs. "It seemed as awful as a visible interposition of God." With this action, the siege of Chattanooga is lifted, and the door to Georgia is open to the Union army. Confederate official Hugh Lawson Clay reflects the general mood in the Confederacy at the news when he terms the defeat a "calamity . . . defeat . . . utter ruin. Unless something is done . . . we are irretrievably gone."[90]

NOVEMBER 27, 1863: Mississippi civilian William Delay writes to Governor Charles Clark, protesting an unhappy situation. Mississippians who crossed the Tallahatchie River to

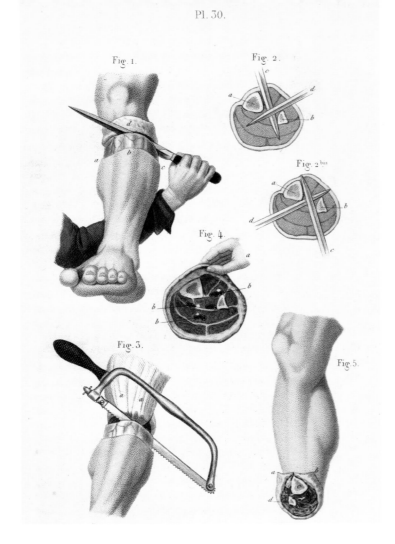

Pl. 30.

Fig. 1.   Fig. 2.

Fig. 2 bis

Fig. 4.

Fig. 3.   Fig. 5.

Brigadier General John Hunt Morgan (1825–1864), CSA. Ink brush over graphite drawing, artist and date unknown. The daring cavalryman and raider was commended by the Confederate Congress for his "varied, heroic and invaluable services."

LEFT: Plate 30, "Amputation of the Leg," from *Illustrated Manual of Operative Surgery and Surgical Anatomy,* by Claude Bernard, 1852. Dr. Stephen Smith adapted and compressed Bernard's work into the pocket-size *Hand-Book of Surgical Operations* in 1862, specifically for Union army doctors. There was no manual, however, that could help the thousands of amputees on both sides of the conflict deal with the loss of their limbs.

buy much-needed supplies from Southern civilians living in a Union-occupied area of the state returned to their side of the river only to have the materials they had purchased confiscated by Confederate troops. The military claimed the supplies under a Confederate sequestration law allowing the seizure of "estates, property, and effects of alien enemies," a measure that clearly does not apply in this case — but the soldiers, low on supplies themselves, refused to return the goods even under pressure of legal writs from local civil authorities. "Can the civil law be enforced," Delay writes in frustration, "or can the military authorities overrule and disregard all civil law?" *In Ohio,* Confederate cavalryman John Hunt Morgan, captured during the stunning raid he led into Northern states (see July 2, 1863), makes a daring escape from the state penitentiary at Columbus. He will make his way back to Southern lines. *In Virginia,* Confederates and Federals skirmish at several locations as George Gordon Meade leads the Army of the Potomac in an attempt to surprise Robert E. Lee's army and turn its right flank. But Meade's slow progress (due to harsh weather and the tentativeness of Meade's lead corps, commanded by William H. French) has allowed Lee to establish strong field fortifications along the west bank of Mine Run, just south of the Wilderness. Discovering this, Meade will withdraw, much to Lee's disgust. "I am too old to command this army," he will say, when he realizes the Federals have gone. "I should never have permitted those people to get away."[91]

NOVEMBER 30, 1863: General Braxton Bragg sends the first of several messages to Jefferson Davis, calling his defeat at Chattanooga "justly disparaging to me as a commander" and submitting his resignation (while also noting that the "warfare" that his subordinate officers have been carrying on against him "has been carried on successfully and the fruits are bitter"). Bitterly disappointed at the debacle in the west, Davis will accept Bragg's resignation. But he is left with a dilemma: whom shall he send in Bragg's place to restore order and morale in his premier western army? The officer that Bragg has left in temporary command, Lieutenant General William J. Hardee, a veteran professional soldier, does not want the job permanently. In fact, he will ask Davis to send to his army "our greatest and best leader . . . yourself, if practicable."[92]

DECEMBER 1863

DECEMBER 7, 1863: As the Thirty-eighth U.S. Congress convenes in Washington, the *Atlantic Monthly* publishes a narrative that is destined to become a classic American story. Written by Unitarian minister Edward Everett Hale, a staunch Unionist and member of the Boston Union Club, "The Man Without a Country" is intended by Hale to be taken as the true

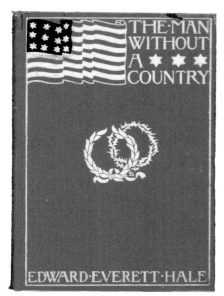

Cover of *The Man Without a Country* by Edward Everett Hale. Illustrated by L. J. Bridgman and published by Dana Estes & Company, 1897, this is only one of many printed editions of Hale's now famous 1863 story, which also became a 1937 movie and was filmed for television in 1973.

RIGHT: *Negroes Leaving the Plough.* Pencil and Chinese white drawing by Alfred R. Waud, March 1864. Lincoln's Proclamation of Amnesty and Reconstruction stipulated that seceded states would have to create a constitution that abolished slavery before they would be allowed to rejoin the Union. Since early in the war, meanwhile, slaves had been freeing themselves and seeking refuge behind Union lines, tens of thousands of the men subsequently serving in the Union armed forces.

account of the life of Philip Nolan, a court-martialed army officer who, in a moment of disgust and frustration, shouted, "Damn the United States! I wish I may never hear of the United States again!" — and was thereupon condemned to sail for the rest of his life on a series of U.S. Navy vessels whose crews were forbidden to speak of the United States in his presence. In line with the mission of the North's Union Leagues, Hale intends this story as an object lesson for those Northerners who may be insufficiently aware of the importance of loyalty to the Union. "Deny the duty of loving your country," the Reverend Joseph Fransioli will declare, in a widely circulated sermon this July, "and you deny your own feelings; you deny mankind itself."[93]

DECEMBER 8, 1863: Aware of unrest among some Confederates over Jefferson Davis's policies and of the growing agitation for a negotiated peace, President Lincoln issues the Proclamation of Amnesty and Reconstruction. Offering pardon and amnesty to any secessionist (with some notable exceptions) who takes an oath of allegiance to the United States and all of its laws and proclamations relating to slavery, Lincoln's document also outlines conditions under which seceded states might rejoin the Union; it becomes known as the Ten-Percent Plan, from the stipulation that a state might form a loyal state government (and create a constitution that abolishes slavery) when one-tenth of its voting population, as tabulated in the 1860 census, has taken a loyalty oath to the United States. "But why any proclamation now upon this

subject?" Lincoln will ask rhetorically, in his annual message to Congress, also delivered this day. "By the proclamation a plan is presented which may be accepted by [the several states] as a rallying point, and which they are assured in advance will not be rejected here. This may bring them to act sooner than they otherwise would." The proclamation is the first indication of Lincoln's moderate approach to Reconstruction, which will place him at odds with the more punitively minded Radical Republicans. *The president also writes* a short letter to Ulysses S. Grant: "Understanding that your lodgment at Chattanooga and Knoxville is now secure, I wish to tender you, and all under your command, my . . . profoundest gratitude — for the skill, courage, and perseverance, with which you and they, over so great difficulties, have effected that important object. God bless you all."[94]

DECEMBER 9, 1863: "I am called to Richmond this morning by the President," Robert E. Lee writes to Jeb Stuart. "My heart and thought will always be with this army." Lee is aware that Davis is on the brink of appointing him to replace Braxton Bragg as commander of the Army of Tennessee, a move Lee, for a variety of reasons, is exceedingly reluctant to make. After several days of discussion in Richmond, however, Davis will decide that Lee must remain in Virginia.[95]

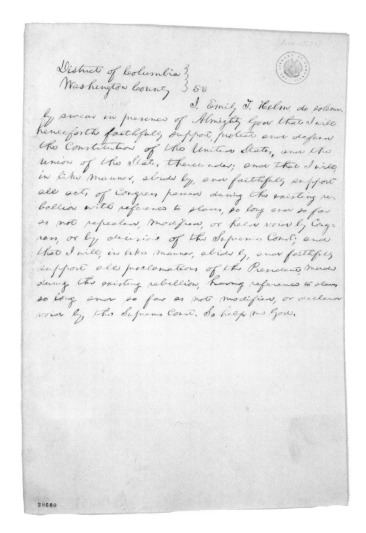

> *"You should not have that rebel*
>
> *in your house."*
>
> —GENERAL DANIEL E. SICKLES
> TO PRESIDENT LINCOLN,
> DECEMBER 14, 1863

Abraham Lincoln. Loyalty Oath for Emilie (Emily) Todd Helm, December 14, 1863. Lincoln wrote out the loyalty oath for Mrs. Helm at the White House, and she took the document with her when she left. She never signed it, however, and her refusal created a permanent rift with the Lincolns.

DECEMBER

1   2   3   4   5   6   7   8   9   10   11   12   13   **14**   15   **16**   17   18   19   20   21   22   23   24   25   **26**   **27**   28   29   30   31

DECEMBER 14, 1863: President Lincoln writes out an amnesty declaration for his sister-in-law, Emilie Helm, whose husband was killed fighting for the Confederacy at Chickamauga (see September 24, 1863); the amnesty will become effective if and when she signs the oath of loyalty to the Union (she never does). Mrs. Helm is staying at the White House, a visit that Emilie and the Lincolns have hoped to keep as private as possible. But as the days go by, the pleasure of having her sister with her moves Mary Lincoln to invite Emilie to join the Lincolns as they entertain two friends, General Daniel E. Sickles and Senator Ira Harris. War enters the room as the men encounter Emilie's still strong Southern pride, Sickles snapping to the president, "You should not have that rebel in your house." The unhappy evening prompts Emilie to end her visit and Mary to sigh, "Oh Emilie, will we ever awake from this hideous nightmare?"[96]

DECEMBER 16, 1863: President Davis orders General Joseph E. Johnston to assume command of the Army of Tennessee. Though Davis believes Johnston to be the best choice, under the circumstances — and it is a popular one, favored by Lee and Secretary of War Seddon, among others — the president does not fully trust Johnston and does not relish making the appointment.[97]

DECEMBER 26, 1863: The Free Military School for Applicants for the Command of Colored Troops opens its doors

at 1210 Chestnut Street, Philadelphia. The brainchild of Thomas Webster, who has helped raise several black units in Pennsylvania, the school has been established to help officer candidates — all white men at this time, many of them veterans of white regiments — pass the rigorous examination required for service as officers in black regiments. Nearly 50 percent of those who have taken the exam to date have failed. Later dubbed the "grandfather of the Officer Candidate School" by historian Dudley Cornish, the Free Military School, supervised by chief preceptor Colonel John H. Taggart, will provide a rigorous thirty-day course (though many students will stay longer) that includes both military subjects and such other courses as arithmetic, algebra, geography, and ancient history. Before it ceases operation on September 15, 1864, a total of 484 of its graduates will pass their examinations. The stringent requirements for officer candidates in the United States Colored Troops will make most of these men (some political appointees notably excepted) among the best-prepared military officers in the United States.[98]

DECEMBER 27, 1863: A grieving Robert E. Lee writes his wife upon learning of the death, the previous day, of their daughter-in-law, Charlotte: "It has pleased God to take from us one exceedingly dear to us & we must be resigned to His holy will. . . . I loved her with a father's love, & my sorrow is heightened by the thought of the anguish her death will cause our dear son [Brigadier General William H. F. "Rooney" Lee, now

ABOVE: *The Soldier's Memorial.* Hand-colored lithograph published by Currier & Ives, 1863.

RIGHT: *Officers and Soldiers on the Battlefield of Second Bull Run, Attempting to Recognize the Remains of Their Comrades.* Pencil drawing by Edwin Forbes, 1863.

"I saw battle-corpses, myriads of them, / . . . I saw the debris and debris of all the slain soldiers of the war, / But I saw they were not as was thought, / They themselves were fully at rest — they suffer'd not, / The living remain'd and suffer'd — the mother suffer'd / And the wife and the child, and the musing comrade suffer'd, / And the armies that remain'd suffer'd."

—Walt Whitman, "When Lilacs Last in the Door-yard Bloom'd," 1866

a prisoner of war], & the poignancy it will give to the bars of his prison." *In northern Georgia,* Brigadier General John Beatty writes pensively in his diary:

> Today we picked up, on the battle-field . . . the skull of a man who had been shot in the head. . . . A little over three months ago this skull was full of life, hope, and ambition. He who carried it into battle had, doubtless, mother, sisters, friends, whose happiness was, to some extent, dependent upon him. They mourn for him now, unless, possibly, they hope still to hear that he is safe and well. Vain hope. Sun, rain, and crows have united in the work of stripping the flesh from his bones, and while the greater part of these lay whitening where they fell, the skull has been rolling about the field the sport and plaything of the winds. This is war, and amid such scenes we are supposed to think of the amount of our salary, and of what the newspapers may say of us.[99]

DECEMBER 28, 1863: The Confederate Congress abolishes the practice of hiring substitutes for military service. Faced with military manpower shortages, the legislators are considering additional methods to fill the Confederate ranks.[100]

1864

JANUARY

JANUARY 2, 1864: As his Army of Tennessee commander, Joseph Johnston, calls for greater impressment of slaves to support the Confederate war effort, Irish-born Major General Patrick R. Cleburne (admiringly called "the Stonewall of the West") proposes freeing slaves and recruiting them for service in the Confederate army. The idea touches off a bitter debate among Southern military and political leaders but yields no result (save to hinder Cleburne's military advancement).[101]

JANUARY 4, 1864: In southwest Georgia, some planters have begun to hoard food, in some cases because they hope that the approaching Yankees will pay more for it than their neighbors can. "They have plenty of corn, but solemnly declare they have none to spare and refuse to sell a bushel," Georgian Carey Stiles writes to Governor Joseph Brown. "Hundreds of thousands are now without a particle of bread, and under this state of things they must starve or, driven to desperation by hungry starvation, resort to the violence of *bread riots* and mobocracy. . . . If something is not done, and quickly to force these corn cormorants to open their cribs to the poor & the non producers it will burst in all its fury."[102]

Major General Patrick R. Cleburne (1828–1864), CSA. Born in Ireland, Cleburne proved to be a supremely effective battlefield commander who held the respect of his men by demonstrating his concern for their welfare and his own unrelenting courage under fire.

Southern Women Feeling the Effects of the Rebellion, and Creating Bread Riots. *Wood engraving published in* Frank Leslie's Illustrated Newspaper, *May 23, 1863. By 1864, Richmond and other cities had already experienced bread riots, and in his letter to the governor of Georgia (see text for January 4, 1864), Carey Stiles cautioned that conditions in the state might spark others.*

JANUARY

1 2 3 4 **5** 6 **7** 8 **9** **10** **11** **12** **13** 14 15 **16** 17 18 19 20 21 22 23 24 25 26 27 28 29 30 31

JANUARY 5, 1864: Black citizens of New Orleans draw up a petition addressed to President Lincoln and the U.S. Congress asking for the right to vote. The petition bears the signatures of more than a thousand men, twenty-seven of whom fought under Andrew Jackson at the battle of New Orleans in 1815. Two of the signers, Jean Baptiste Roudanez and Arnold Bertonneau, are selected to carry the petition to Washington (see March 12, 1864).[103]

JANUARY 7, 1864: President Davis names William Preston, former U.S. ambassador to Spain, Confederate envoy to Mexico, where the French, long sympathetic to the Confederacy, are fighting to displace President Benito Juárez with a puppet emperor, Maximilian, a prince of the Austro-Hungarian empire. The Union opposes the French action. The Confederacy supports it, chiefly because it increases the likelihood of French recognition (Maximilian has told more than one Southern visitor to Europe that he supports Confederate independence). Preston, in Cuba, will await notification that he is to assume his new post.[104]

JANUARY 9–12, 1864: Sergeant William Walker, of the Twenty-first U.S. Colored Infantry, is tried before a court-martial for inciting a mutiny after he refused to perform military duties because the U.S. government is discriminating against black soldiers regarding pay. He is convicted — and is executed before President Lincoln has a chance to review the

case. "The Government which found no law to pay him except as a nondescript and a contraband," Massachusetts governor John A. Andrew will later say, "nevertheless found law enough to shoot him as a soldier."[105]

JANUARY 13, 1864: "It makes me hate public life," Secretary of the Treasury Salmon Chase writes to President Lincoln, "when I realize how powerless are the most faithful labors and the most upright conduct to protect any man from carping envy or malignant denunciations." Chase's apparently wounded pride stems from inquiries surrounding a rosy biographical sketch of the secretary recently published in the Philadelphia-based *American Exchange and Review* and the financial backing that made its publication possible. In fact, the article is one step Chase has taken toward realizing his presidential ambitions. Thwarted when Lincoln was chosen at the 1860 Republican convention, they have never subsided; and Chase has been assiduously maintaining correspondence and connections with people who can help him win the 1864 nomination. Moreover, he has not been reticent about criticizing the incumbent. In early February Secretary of the Navy Gideon Welles will note in his diary that in his presence Chase "lamented the want of energy and force by the President, which he said paralyzed everything."[106]

JANUARY 16, 1864: At the behest of admiring Republicans in Washington (Vice President Hannibal Hamlin, twenty-three

Anna E. Dickinson (1832–1932). Dickinson's feisty eloquence in support of the Union cause won her the nickname America's Joan of Arc.

ABOVE: *Burning the Rappahannock Railway Bridge, Oct. 13th 1863.* Pencil and Chinese white drawing by Alfred R. Waud, October 13, 1863. The Civil War was the first conflict in which railroads were used extensively. Both sides depended on rail transport of troops, supplies, and casualties; and both made persistent efforts to disrupt the enemy's rail systems, as Sherman's troops did during their Meridian, Mississippi, campaign.

OPPOSITE, LEFT: Paper currency of the Confederate States of America. Though impressively designed, Confederate paper money became increasingly worthless as inflation ballooned during the war. When civilian Jacob Thompson was sent to Canada to engage in plots complementing Captain Thomas Hines's espionage adventures, he was backed by $1 million in Confederate gold.

senators, and seventy-eight representatives signed the note inviting her to speak), celebrated abolitionist-orator Anna E. Dickinson delivers a fiery address before an impressive assemblage of government officials, journalists, and other public figures — including President and Mrs. Lincoln — in the U.S. House of Representatives. Speaking on "The Perils of the Hour," the twenty-one-year-old Radical Republican rakes Lincoln over the coals for his moderate policies but receives great applause (and a smile from the president) when she finally states that, in the nation's hour of peril, she does support him, despite his faults. The address will enhance Dickinson's growing reputation and spark many more invitations to speak. It will also inspire verbal barrages from her many critics. "Among the excrescences upon the body politic is one which may be best described by its Greek name Gynaekokracy, which manifests itself in the absurd endeavors of women to usurp the places and execute the functions of the male sex," the *Geneva (New York) Gazette* will editorialize. "It is a moral and social monstrosity — an inversion . . . of the laws of nature." This particular social inversion will be a benefaction to some: accepting the legislators' invitation to speak, Dickinson specified that all proceeds should be used to support "the suffering freedmen."[107]

FEBRUARY 1864

FEBRUARY 1, 1864: Major General William T. Sherman launches a campaign to secure Meridian, Mississippi, the state's largest remaining railroad center, by ordering Memphis-based cavalry under Brigadier General William Sooy Smith to conduct a sweeping raid and meet up with the main force at Meridian. Leaving Vicksburg on February 3 with twenty thousand men in two columns (led by Generals Stephen A. Hurlbut and James B. McPherson), Sherman's main force creates such consternation on the way to its objective that Lieutenant General Leonidas Polk will order Confederate forces to evacuate Meridian on February 14. Over the following five days, Sherman's troops will wreck some 115 miles of railroad track, 61 bridges, 20 locomotives, an arsenal, and assorted warehouses and other facilities of military value. In addition to confiscating or destroying supplies potentially useful to Confederate armies, the Federals will escort some five thousand slaves and one thousand white refugees back to Vicksburg.[108]

FEBRUARY 2, 1864: Fifty-three North Carolina men, former Confederate soldiers who are now serving as Company F, Second North Carolina Union Volunteer Infantry, are taken into custody by Confederates under the command of George E. Pickett. While the U.S. government considers these men Federal soldiers, thus due to be treated as prisoners of war, the Confederates deem them deserters. Desertion has become

THE HARD HAND OF WAR

Major General George E. Pickett (1825–1875), CSA. His name forever associated with the costly and futile frontal assault Lee's army made on the third day of the battle of Gettysburg, Pickett later outraged North Carolinians and people throughout the Union when he treated former North Carolina soldiers who had joined the Union army as deserters and put them on trial for their lives.

FEBRUARY

1 2 3 4 5 6 7 8 9 **10** 11 12 13 14 **15** 16 **17** 18 19 20 21 22 23 24 25 26 27 28 29

a formidable problem in Pickett's military department, as it has throughout the Confederacy. ("I will venture to say that there are more deserters in this county today than was here when the cavalry came here," a Mississippi sheriff will write to Governor Charles Clark this month, "& they are in formidable gangs a doing mischief . . . & destroying the property of all loyal citizens such as will not sympathize with them.") Pickett's decision to maintain proper discipline in his department by court-martialing some of these prisoners as deserters, and the outcome of their case, will add to Southern tragedy — and Northern fury (see March 6, 1864).[109]

FEBRUARY 10, 1864: When flames are spotted at the president's stables near the White House, Abraham Lincoln dashes outside, leaping over an intervening boxwood hedge "like a deer," presidential bodyguard Robert McBride will recall, and "with his own hands burst open the stable door. . . . [H]e would apparently have tried to enter the burning building had not those standing near caught and restrained him." The fast-moving fire, which will prove to be the work of an arsonist, kills six horses, including the pony that belonged to Lincoln's beloved Willie, who died two years before. The tragedy, including the loss of an animal so dear to his son, leaves Lincoln in tears.[110]

FEBRUARY 15, 1864: In a secret session, the Confederate Congress appropriates $5 million for Canadian-based sabotage operations against the North. Former cavalryman Thomas C. Hines, who had proposed the espionage idea, will be dispatched to Canada to carry out "appropriate enterprises of war against our enemies." Rebel agents will have many meetings with Northern Peace Democrats in Canada in the coming summer, when Union home front morale is low and sentiments for peace are high.[111]

FEBRUARY 17, 1864: Responding to a February 3 speech by Jefferson Davis pleading for authority to once again suspend the writ of habeas corpus, the Confederate Congress again, and with reluctance, authorizes the president to suspend the writ to suppress disloyalty and enforce the draft (see also February 27, 1862). Vice President Alexander Stephens is one of several powerful Georgians to protest the decision — with such vehemence that the actions of the protesters will create a patriotic backlash; the Georgia legislature will pass a resolution declaring the state's support for the war. The Southern legislators also expand the draft, allowing conscription of white men between the ages of seventeen and fifty; and they repeal the Partisan Ranger Act, passed nearly two years earlier (see April 21, 1862). By this time, however, numerous ranger/guerrilla bands are operating in Southern territory — well outside the scope of Confederate government or military control. *In Charleston Harbor,* the Confederate submarine *Hunley,* captained by Lieutenant George Dixon, goes into action against a Union steam-driven sloop of war, USS *Housatonic.* Operating

Samuel C. Pomeroy (1816–1891), between 1855 and 1865. While he was serving as a U.S. senator from Kansas (1861–1873), Pomeroy stirred up a political hornet's nest by issuing a circular touting Salmon Chase as the best Republican candidate for president in 1864.

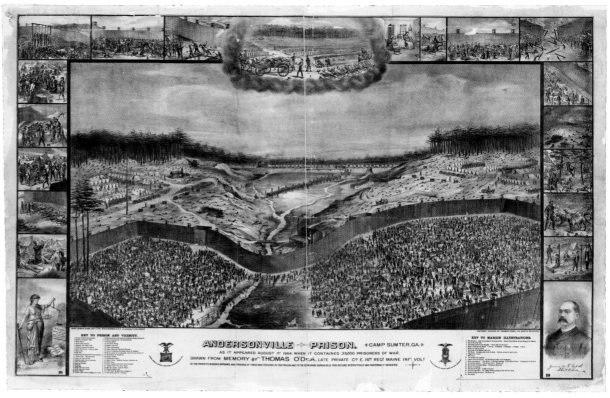

Andersonville Prison, Camp Sumter, Ga., as It Appeared August 1st 1864 When It Contained 35,000 Prisoners of War. Lithograph by Henry Selbert & Bros., ca. 1864, based on a drawing, from memory, by Andersonville prisoner Thomas O'Dea, Sixteenth Maine Volunteer Infantry. "Rebels say they have no medicine for us," John Ransom wrote, in his *Andersonville Diary,* less than a month after arriving at the prison. "We have stopped wondering at suffering or being surprised at anything. . . . Can see a dozen most any morning laying around dead."

under orders from the area commander, General P. G. T. Beauregard, to proceed only partially submerged (because of the vessel's unhappy safety record: see August 29 and October 15, 1863), *Hunley* rams a spar-mounted torpedo into the side of the Union vessel, which quickly sinks. Although *Hunley* thus earns a place in naval history as the first submarine to sink an enemy vessel, the honor comes at an exorbitant price: after successfully disengaging from its victim, *Hunley* sinks en route to its base, with the loss of all eight crewmen. (More than 130 years later, on August 8, 2000, salvagers will raise the Confederate submarine.)[112]

FEBRUARY 22, 1864: An underground movement to replace Abraham Lincoln with Secretary of the Treasury Salmon Chase as the Republican candidate for president in the 1864 elections comes out in the open when a Chase-for-president committee headed by Kansas senator Samuel Pomeroy sends what comes to be known as the "Pomeroy Circular" to one hundred select Republicans (it rapidly reaches a much wider audience). The circular seeks to generate support for Chase by blasting the president, whose reelection, "even were [it] . . . desirable . . . is practically impossible," the circular notes, given the current feeling among the electorate. Even should he be elected, "his manifest tendency toward compromises and temporary expedients of policy will become stronger during a second term than it has been in the first." A man of Chase's unique qualities is needed to "vindicate the honor

of the republic" and put energy into a languishing war effort. The ensuing backlash from Lincoln supporters effectively ends Chase's quest for the Oval Office (though it does not still the secretary's ambition).[113]

FEBRUARY 24, 1864: The U.S. Congress responds to the vigorous petitions of the Quakers and other pacifist churches and passes legislation permitting exemptions from military service for conscientious objectors. (An estimated twelve hundred to fifteen hundred men of both sides were conscientious objectors during the war; see March 31 and September 27, 1862 and October 6, 1863.)[114]

FEBRUARY 27, 1864: The first Union prisoners of war arrive at Camp Sumter, near Andersonville, Georgia. Built with slave labor, the camp will quickly become known simply, and unhappily, as "Andersonville." Sergeant John Ransom, late of the Ninth Michigan Cavalry, will shortly attempt to settle into its discomforts, arriving in a cold rain after a long train ride from another prison in Richmond and "marched into our pen," he will write in his clandestine diary, "between a strong guard carrying lighted pitch-pine knots, to prevent our crawling off in the dark." His impression of his new prison: "a dismal hole." The "hole" will rapidly deteriorate into something infinitely worse, an unhealthy morass without any shelters for its inmates, thirty-three thousand of whom will, within five months, be crammed into space intended for less than one-third that number.[115]

Execution of Five Deserters in the 5th Corps. Pencil and Chinese white drawing by Alfred R. Waud, August 29, 1863. Although execution for desertion was unusual at the beginning of the war, it became much more common in 1863 and 1864. President Lincoln contributed to the relatively low wartime total of 147 Union executions for desertion by commuting the sentences of many soldiers whose cases were brought to his attention. He could do nothing, of course, to mitigate the sentences in the North Carolina cases (see March 6, 1864). The wartime total of Confederate executions for desertion is unknown.

FEBRUARY 28, 1864: Brigadier General Hugh Judson Kilpatrick and Colonel Ulric Dahlgren lead four thousand Union troops in a daring attempt to enter Richmond and release Union prisoners of war. The raid will bring greater damage to the Union than the Confederacy, however. Papers found on the body of Colonel Dahlgren, killed in an ambush by Major General Fitzhugh Lee's cavalry, outline plans for the released prisoners to hold the city and wait for Union reinforcements; to burn Richmond thereafter; and to murder Jefferson Davis and his cabinet. Amid a firestorm of Southern indignation, Robert E. Lee will write to George Gordon Meade, his letter sparking an investigation that will settle blame on the deceased Colonel Dahlgren. Meanwhile, Lee will respond to an inquiry from Secretary of War Seddon counseling against executing prisoners captured during the raid who may not have known the contents of the captured documents. "I do not think that reason & reflection would justify such a course. I think it better to do right, even if we suffer in so doing, than to incur the reproach of our consciences & Posterity."[116]

MARCH 1864

MARCH 2, 1864: As of this date, Major General Ulysses S. Grant is promoted to lieutenant general, a rank recently revived by Congress with Grant in mind and one held by only George Washington before him (although former U.S. general in chief Winfield Scott was brevetted lieutenant general—that is, given the rank temporarily, in 1855). Grant receives orders to report to Washington.[117]

MARCH 6, 1864: Twenty-two of the fifty-three North Carolina men who were captured while serving in the Union army (see February 2, 1864), having been tried by court-martial, are publicly hanged by Confederate authorities in Kinston, North Carolina. On March 11, the *New York Times* will carry a *Raleigh Confederate* correspondent's account of the event:

> The prisoners . . . ascended the scaffold with a firm and elastic step, and met their fate with unflinching fortitude and determination. They asked for no quarter, and scornfully spurned all overtures of concession on condition of returning to duty in the Confederate service. After making their peace with their God, they fearlessly proclaimed their readiness to die for their country, against which they said they had been forcibly conscripted to fight. A more sublime exhibition of loyalty to the old flag was never witnessed. The multitude were moved to tears, and openly denounced this cruel massacre, which is causing

Lieutenant General Ulysses S. Grant (1822–1885), USA. Acknowledging his promotion as the first lieutenant general in the U.S. Army since George Washington, and aware he would soon be Union general in chief, Grant told President Lincoln, "It will be my earnest endeavor not to disappoint your expectations. I feel the full weight of the responsibilities now devolving on me."

Antonia Ford Willard (1838–1871), date unknown. Named an honorary aide to Confederate general Jeb Stuart, Antonia Ford fell in love with Joseph Willard, the Yankee who escorted her to prison. They married soon after Willard resigned from the Union army.

desertions from the Confederate service by the wholesale, and creating an indignation which, it is feared, will be uncontrolable [*sic*].[118]

MARCH 8, 1864: The Twenty-ninth Connecticut Volunteer Infantry (Colored) is officially mustered into U.S. service. One of its organizers has been Mary Ann Shadd Cary, a free black woman and tireless activist who will also help organize the Twenty-eighth Colored Infantry (Indiana), assist freedmen and women as an agent of the Colored Ladies' Freedmen's Aid Society, headquartered in Chicago — and who, in 1870, will become the first African American woman to earn a law degree, graduating from Howard University in Washington, DC. *This evening in Washington,* General Grant reports to President Lincoln at the White House, where the president is engaged in his weekly reception — and the crowd heartily applauds the victorious general of the western armies. The following day, before a smaller gathering of officials at the White House, Lincoln formally promotes Grant to lieutenant general. "With this high honor devolves upon you also, a corresponding responsibility. As the country herein trusts you, so, under God, it will sustain you," the president says in his short remarks. The general's reply includes a salute to "the noble armies that have fought on so many fields for our common country.... I feel the full weight of the responsibilities now devolving on me and know that if they are met it will be due to those armies, and above all to the favor of the Providence which leads both Nations and men."[119]

MARCH 10, 1864: Jeb Stuart's former honorary aide, Antonia Ford (see March 13, 1863), marries civilian Joseph Willard, who, one year before, was the Union army officer who escorted her to the Old Capitol Prison in Washington. Her charms had intrigued him from the first, and she gradually returned his affections. But she would not marry him while he was in uniform: "[My] parents and relatives would be mortified to death," she had written; "acquaintances would disown me." The ceremony takes place at Washington's Metropolitan Hotel. *Nearby, at the White House,* President Lincoln writes an executive order: "Lieutenant-General Ulysses S. Grant, U.S. Army, is assigned to the command of the armies of the United States."[120]

MARCH 11, 1864: The U.S. Congress passes the Ambulance Corps Act, which applies the improved system of battlefield care for the wounded developed by Army of the Potomac medical director Dr. Jonathan Letterman (see September 18, 1862) to all U.S. armies. (In the South, Dr. Hunter H. McGuire developed a successful "infirmary corps" for Stonewall Jackson's troops. Yet the absence of a comparable Confederacy-wide ambulance corps, as well as a shortage of ambulances in the resource-strapped South, will result, throughout the war, in greater confusion and suffering for Confederate wounded.)[121]

MARCH 12, 1864: Major General Nathaniel Banks and Rear Admiral David D. Porter launch the Red River Campaign

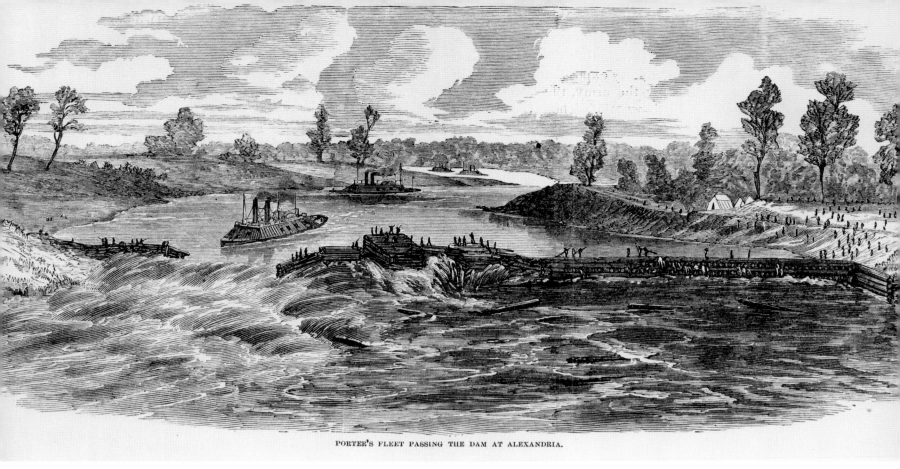

PORTER'S FLEET PASSING THE DAM AT ALEXANDRIA.

Porter's Fleet Passing the Dam at Alexandria. Wood engraving published in *Harper's Pictorial History of the Civil War,* Vol. 2, 1894. Commanding the naval contingent of the Union's abortive Red River Campaign, Porter encountered more than a few vexing challenges, including falling water levels that made it necessary for his men to construct a dam in order to make it back to the Mississippi River.

MARCH–APRIL

23 24 25 26 27 28 29 30 31 1 2 3 **4** 5 6 7 8 9 10 11 12 13 14 15 16 17 18 19 20 21 22

in Louisiana, seeking to block the flow of supplies from Shreveport, Louisiana (headquarters of Confederate Trans-Mississippi Department commander Edmund Kirby Smith), into Texas. Approved directly by President Lincoln, the campaign will interrupt a plan General Grant has developed to move against Mobile, Alabama, the base of Confederate forces that could be sent to reinforce General Joseph Johnston. Banks and Porter will have some initial successes: their men will remove river obstructions; capture the South's Fort DeRussy, built to defend the Red River; and occupy Alexandria, Louisiana. But the problem-plagued expedition will quickly fall behind schedule (see March 23 and April 8, 1864). *In Washington,* Jean Baptiste Roudanez and Arnold Bertonneau present President Lincoln with a petition requesting the right to vote (see January 5, 1864). They have added a paragraph to the original petition, which sought voting rights only for "the citizens of Louisiana of African descent, born free." The new paragraph asks that "suffrage may be extended . . . to all others, whether born slave or free, especially those who have vindicated their right to vote by bearing arms, subject only to such qualifications as shall equally affect the white and colored citizens." Greatly impressed, Lincoln will, the following day, write to Michael Hahn, governor of (occupied) Louisiana, suggesting that the convention that is to meet in April to draw up a new state constitution consider "whether some of the colored people may not be let in [allowed to vote] — as, for instance, the very intelligent, and especially those who have fought

gallantly in our ranks." The constitution that emerges will not itself extend suffrage to black men but will include a clause allowing the legislature to enfranchise blacks in the future.[122]

MARCH 23, 1864: Major General Frederick Steele embarks on the Camden Expedition in Arkansas to assist Nathaniel Banks's planned assault on Shreveport (see Red River Campaign, March 12, 1864) by diverting Confederate cavalry from that city. Like Banks's expedition, Steele's quickly runs into problems, as well as the Southern cavalry it was sent to draw out. It will end in miserable failure the first week in May.[123]

APRIL 1864

APRIL 4, 1864: Lieutenant General Ulysses S. Grant, newly appointed U.S. Army general in chief, writes Major General William T. Sherman: "It is my design, if the enemy keep quiet and allow me to take the initiative in the spring campaign, to work all parts of the army together. . . . You I propose to move against Johnston's army [in Georgia], to break it up and to get into the interior of the enemy's country as far as you can, inflicting all the damage you can against their war resources." As part of his coordinated movement against all Confederate

Ferdinand Maximilian von Habsburg (1832–1867). A grandson of Austrian emperor Francis II, in 1864 Maximilian became Emperor Maximilian I of Mexico after the throne was offered to him by Napoleon III of France.

THE WAR IN TENNESSEE—REBEL MASSACRE OF THE UNION TROOPS AFTER THE SURRENDER AT FORT PILLOW, APRIL 12.—SEE PAGE 16[?]

ABOVE: *The War in Tennessee — Rebel Massacre of the Union Troops After the Surrender at Fort Pillow, April 12.* Wood engraving published in *Frank Leslie's Scenes and Portraits of the Civil War,* 1894. Inciting outrage throughout the North, the murder of surrendered Union troops, most of them black, on April 12, also inspired a new battle cry among U.S. Colored Troops: "Remember Fort Pillow!"

OPPOSITE: *Federal Encampment on the Pamunkey River, Cumberland Landing, Virginia.* Photograph by James Gibson, May 1862. After the relative inaction of winter, each spring brought the prospect of hard and costly campaigning. "The 'Army of the Potomac' is now commanded by a general who has never known defeat," Union sergeant Warren H. Freeman wrote his father on May 2, 1864. "Opposed to him is the first general in the rebel service. . . . Who can predict the results of the impending contest?"

armies, Grant deems it crucial that Nathaniel Banks "finish up his present expedition against Shreveport with all dispatch . . . turn over the defence of Red River to General Steele and the navy," and, taking command of a substantial force, "commence operations against Mobile as soon as he can."[124]

APRIL 8, 1864: Eight thousand Confederates under Major General Richard Taylor defeat Federals led by Nathaniel Banks at the battle of Mansfield (Pleasant Grove; Sabine Cross Roads), causing Banks to order a retreat that he will continue despite besting Taylor in a clash at Pleasant Hill the next day; there will be no assault on Shreveport. Failing in all its objectives — and inciting the ire of civilians from whom supplies have been expropriated along the way — the Red River Campaign will also create problems for other Union commanders. Banks will never move on Mobile, and Confederate forces from that city will reinforce Joseph Johnston in Georgia.[125]

APRIL 10, 1864: Napoleon III persuades the Austro-Hungarian prince Maximilian to become emperor of Mexico, his wife, Carlota, to become empress. Maximilian is convinced, at least in part, by the results of what was almost certainly a rigged plebiscite election that occurred July 1863 (under the watchful eye of French occupation troops), in which 99 percent of the people supposedly voted in favor of the new royal house. The new monarchs will leave Europe for Mexico within a week.[126]

APRIL 12, 1864: While raiding important Federal communications facilities and posts in west Kentucky and Tennessee, Confederate cavalry commanded by Nathan Bedford Forrest attack and capture Fort Pillow, Tennessee, on the Mississippi River. Many of the United States Colored Troops defending the fort are murdered after they surrender, as are some white defenders and the fort's commander, Major William F. Bradford — "shot while trying to escape." News of this massacre will rage through the Union like a storm. "Let the fate of the Fort Pillow prisoners overtake a like number of rebel prisoners in our hands," the *Indianapolis Daily Journal* will declare, "and their blood be upon the heads of the Fort Pillow butchers." Members of the Joint Committee on the Conduct of the War will travel to Fort Pillow (evacuated by Forrest's troops the night of the battle) to see the aftermath and interview survivors. President Lincoln and his cabinet will deliberate on how the Federal government should respond. If an investigation conclusively proves a massacre took place, he will tell people attending a Sanitary Fair in Baltimore on April 18, "it will be matter of grave consideration in what exact course to apply the retribution; but in the supposed case, it must come." Many Union soldiers, particularly black soldiers, meanwhile will adopt "Remember Fort Pillow" as a battle cry.[127]

APRIL 17, 1864: "No distinction whatever will be made in the exchange between white and colored prisoners" is the most pressing of two conditions General in Chief Grant makes

for prisoner exchanges to continue. Confederate authorities do not agree to the conditions, and the exchanges cease. But the taking of prisoners does not, putting a severe strain on prisoner-of-war facilities.[128]

APRIL 18, 1864: At Poison Springs, Arkansas, 1,200 Union troops on a foraging expedition — 438 of them troopers from the First Kansas Colored Volunteers — are attacked by nearly 3,400 Confederates under Brigadier General John S. Marmaduke and badly defeated. Over half the Union casualties are black, and witnesses will later report that some of them were murdered. Although Confederates will deny the charge, evidence will support it.[129]

APRIL 30, 1864: At Jenkins Ferry, on the Sabine River in Arkansas, a charge by the Second Kansas Colored Volunteers shouting "Remember Poison Springs!" overwhelms a Confederate battery and results in numerous Rebel casualties — during an engagement that is an overall Union defeat. Other black troops will also reciprocate Confederate brutality "under the black flag" (that is, giving no quarter). *In Richmond,* on this pleasant Saturday afternoon, five-year-old Joe Davis slips while playing on a high porch at the Confederate White House and plunges twelve feet to the brick pavement below, breaking both his legs and fracturing his skull. Summoned from the president's office in the Customs House, Jefferson and Varina Davis arrive in time to hold their young son as he dies. Both parents are overwhelmed by grief, the president, waving away a courier bearing state business, saying, "I must have this day with my little child." *From his Union army camp at Mitchell's Station, Virginia,* Sergeant Warren Freeman, a veteran of many eastern theater battles, writes to his father:

> We can see the rebels drilling across the river; they have been fortifying the hills for some time. . . . [A]ll the advantages are on their side, for they are protected behind fortifications, entrenchments, and rifle-pits — and we are to be the attacking party along the whole line. Should we force them back from their first line of works, I suppose they have a second line to occupy and defend; but we will know all about it very soon, for to judge from what is going on around here the forward movement is to be made immediately.[130]

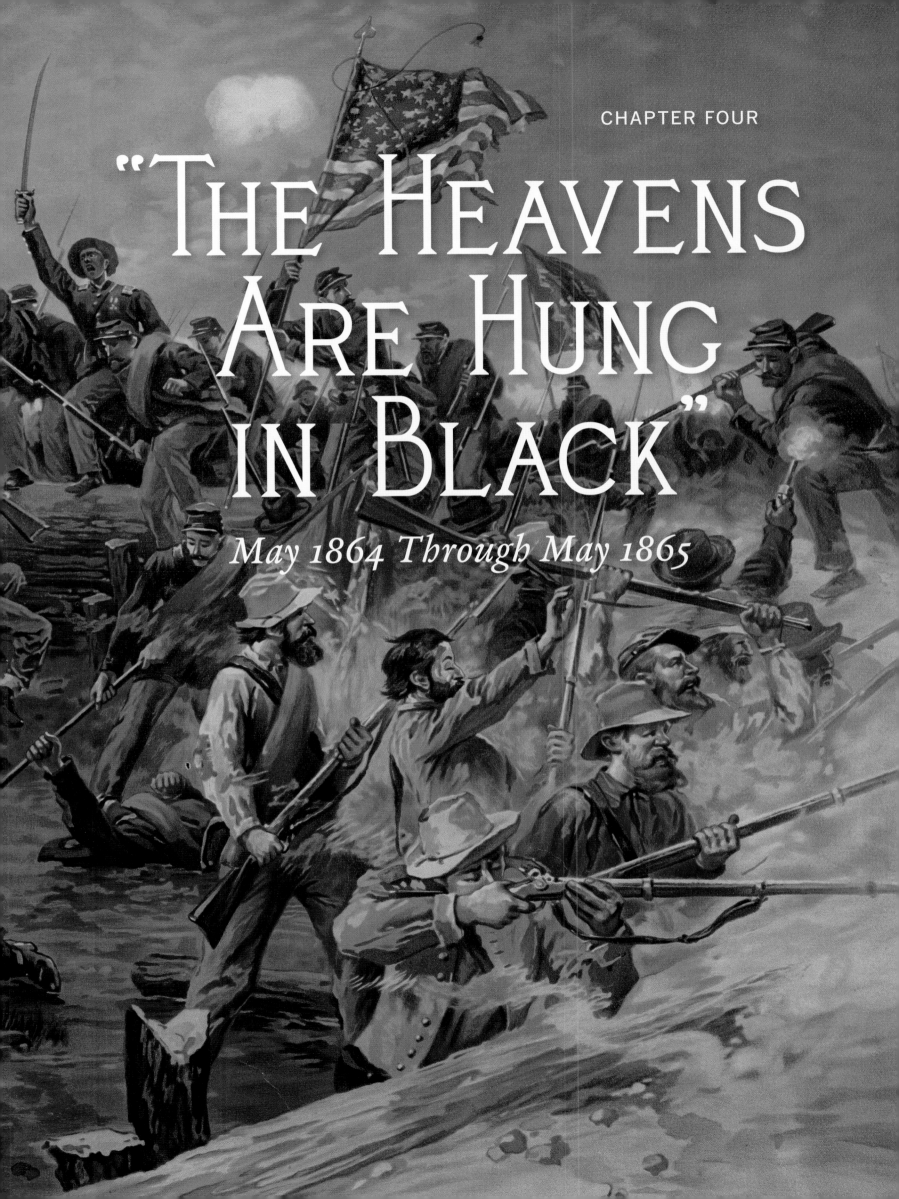

CHAPTER FOUR

"The Heavens Are Hung in Black"

May 1864 Through May 1865

"I propose to fight it out on this line if it takes all summer."

LIEUTENANT GENERAL ULYSSES S. GRANT, USA,
DISPATCH, MAY 11, 1864[1]

"We must destroy this army of Grant's before it gets to the James River. If he gets there it will become a siege, and then it will be a mere question of time."

GENERAL ROBERT E. LEE, CSA,
CONVERSATION WITH LIEUTENANT GENERAL
JUBAL A. EARLY, SPRING 1864[2]

"We cannot change the hearts of those people of the South," Major General William T. Sherman wrote to Ulysses S. Grant late in 1862, "but we can make war so terrible . . . [and] make them so sick of war that generations would pass away before they would again appeal to it."[3] Nearly two years later, as the Union and the Confederacy braced for the spring 1864 campaigns that would open a fourth year of fighting, the horrors of war had become amply apparent to the people in both regions. Casualty lists had grown to the hundreds of thousands, and civilians on both sides strained to help their governments cope with never-ending waves of sick and wounded — as well as the white and black refugees fleeing before armies or following in their wake. In the South, where most military battlegrounds lay, civilians already beset by shortages, impressment, and encroachments by the detested Yankees regarded the onset of another year with a mixture of fear and faith — and a determination that would be severely tested by coming trials. "The very air is rent with the groans of the wounded and dying," Confederate nurse Kate Cumming would write, in December 1864. "Although woe and desolation stare

PRECEDING OVERLEAF: *Battle of Spottsylvania [sic].* Color lithograph published by L. Prang & Co., 1887.

LEFT: *Hospital Attendants — Collecting the Wounded after the Engagement — within Our Lines near Hatchers Run.* Pencil, Chinese white, and black ink drawing on brown paper by William Waud, September–October, 1864. Launched by General in Chief Grant, the February 1865 battle of Hatcher's Run, near Petersburg, Virginia, did extend Union lines (and force the Rebels to do the same), as Grant intended — but at a cost of more than 1,500 Union casualties.

PLATE V.

105th REGT NY VOLS.
Cedar Mountain Aug 9? 1862.
RAPPAHANOCK STATION Aug 13th 1862.
Thoroughfare Gap Aug 28th
2nd BULL RUN Aug 3
Chantilly
SOUTH MOUNTAIN
1862

FAMOUS UNION BATTLE-FLAGS.
1 First N.J. Cavalry.   2. Forty-eighth N.Y.Regt.
3. One hundred and fiftieth Penn. Regt. ("Bucktails")
4. Eighty third Penn Regt.   5. Ninth N.J. Regt.   6 One hundred and fifth N.Y. Regt.
For Descriptions see pages 40-47.
PHOTOGRAPHED AND PAINTED FROM THE ORIGINAL FLAGS EXPRESSLY FOR THIS WORK.

Famous Union Battle-Flags. Illustration in *My Story of the War: A Woman's Narrative,* by Mary A. Livermore, 1888.

at us every way we turn, the heart of the patriot is as firm as ever, and determined that, come what may he will never yield."[4]

Not all had Cumming's stubborn spirit. In both warring regions, cries for accommodation and peace grew louder as death and destruction surged to new levels and neither side looked capable of achieving a clear military victory. In the Union, as the presidential election of 1864 approached, Lincoln's administration seemed about to topple, to be replaced by an administration that might settle for disunion and negate the Emancipation Proclamation. In the Confederacy, as casualties and army desertions increased, state and national legislators debated a war measure that had

once been unthinkable: "As to calling out the negro men and placing them in the army, with the promise that they shall be free at the end of the war," Confederate congressman Warren Akin wrote to a friend in October 1864, "I can only say it is a question of fearful magnitude. Can we prevent subjugation, confiscation, degradation and slavery without it. If not will our condition or that of the negro, be any worse by calling them into service."[5]

Two men in uniform stood at the center of the military struggle that so closely influenced, and was influenced by, the political debates and the rise and fall of morale at home. General Robert E. Lee, who would become general in chief

Confederate standards. Illustration on the inside front cover of the postwar scrapbook compiled by former Confederate general Jubal A. Early.

of all Confederate armies, remained a beacon of hope for civilians throughout the Confederacy and an inspiration to his troops; and he retained the absolute confidence of his volatile commander in chief, Jefferson Davis. Appointed general in chief of all Union armies in March 1864, Ulysses S. Grant had achieved great victories in the west, but it remained uncertain, as the spring campaigns began, whether the traits that had served him so well at Fort Donelson, Vicksburg, and Chattanooga would serve the nation well on this larger stage. Establishing his headquarters in the east, he did make a favorable first impression on most officers and men of the Army of the Potomac. But they had turned hopefully toward

commanding generals before and been bitterly disappointed. "I have unbounded confidence in Grant, but he puzzles me as much as he appears to [puzzle] the rebels," Captain Charles Francis Adams Jr. wrote to his father, the U.S. minister to Britain, in June 1864. "He fights when we expect him to march, waits when we look for motion, and moves when we expect him to fight. Grant will take Richmond, if only he is left alone; of that I feel more and more sure. His tenacity and his strength, combined with his skill, must, on every general principle, prove too much for them in the end. Yet I often feel discouraged."[6]

May 1864
Through
May 1865

MAY 1864

MAY 2, 1864: The Second Confederate Congress convenes in Richmond. In the wake of the fall 1863 elections, its makeup has changed from overwhelmingly secessionist to a legislature that includes a near balance of ardent secessionists and more conservative former Whigs and Unionists. Some members represent areas under Union control — a phenomenon that will expand as the war continues. The more conservative members of Congress, as well as a number of state officials, will continue to object to some of President Davis's war policies as conflicting with states' rights as the war moves into its fourth year. Meanwhile, both the Confederate military and Southern civilians will face increasing shortages and the relentless encroachments of Federal armies.[7]

MAY 4, 1864: Just after midnight the Army of the Potomac begins to move forward, embarking on Lieutenant General Ulysses S. Grant's Overland Campaign. Headquartered with this army, which is still under the command of Major General George Gordon Meade, Grant has also directed Major General Franz Sigel and his troops to move southward up Virginia's Shenandoah Valley while Major General Benjamin Butler begins a campaign south of Richmond; at the same time, Major General William T. Sherman is to begin operations against General Joseph Johnston's Army of Tennessee in Georgia. Abraham Lincoln's new general in chief is thus finally realizing the coordinated multifront operation against Confederate

forces that the president has long advocated. Grant's plan for confronting Lee's Army of Northern Virginia is to move around the Confederate right flank, quickly traversing the treacherous Wilderness area in which the battle of Chancellorsville took place a year earlier (see May 2–4, 1863), and, having placed the Army of the Potomac between Lee's army and Richmond, fight Lee in open territory. Yet Meade's huge army, with all its accoutrements, moves slowly. When Meade calls a halt to marching for the day (believing, erroneously, that Lee's army is still miles away behind its fortifications), the Army of the Potomac is still in the Wilderness.[8]

MAY 5, 1864: Having embarked from Fort Monroe the day before and left garrisons at key locations along the way, Major General Benjamin F. Butler and thirty thousand of his thirty-nine-thousand-man Army of the James arrive at Bermuda Hundred Landing. A large neck of land just fifteen miles south of Richmond, Bermuda Hundred is strategically important because of the Richmond & Petersburg Railroad, a vital connection between the Confederate capital and points south — particularly the important railroad center of Petersburg, only seven miles distant. Butler and his troops begin pushing westward, but their progress is ponderously slow (see May 7, 9, 13, and 16, 1864). *Some miles to the northwest, Grant's plan to reach open ground before meeting Lee comes to naught when elements of Lee's Army of Northern Virginia engage the Army of the Potomac, beginning the harrowing*

Wounded Escaping from the Burning Woods of the Wilderness. Pencil and Chinese white drawing by Alfred R. Waud, May 5–7, 1864. Despite rescue efforts by many of their comrades, some wounded soldiers perished in the flames. "This is one of the horrors of fighting in dense woods," Union soldier Josiah Marshall Favill wrote after the Wilderness battle, "where the bursting shells invariably in dry weather set fire to the dead leaves and branches."

MAY

1   2   3   4   5   **6   7**   8   9   10   11   12   13   14   15   16   17   18   19   20   21   22   23   24   25   26   27   28   29   30   31

two-day battle of the Wilderness. "If any opportunity presents itself of pitching into a part of Lee's army," Grant orders Meade after he learns of the Confederates' surprise appearance, "do so without giving time for disposition." Union officers move more slowly in getting their men into battle than their Confederate counterparts, but before long, as one Federal will write, "these hitherto quiet woods seemed to be lifted up, shook, rent, and torn asunder." Storms of musket fire and bursting artillery shells set patches of underbrush in the dry woods ablaze as the battle becomes, in one Confederate's description, "a butchery pure and simple." Both sides suffer heavy casualties, and some of the wounded, lying helpless in the paths of the crackling fires where no one can reach them, perish in the flames, their anguished cries continuing to haunt the Wilderness after fighting stops for the night. As exhausted soldiers of both sides huddle in the flickering darkness, Grant plans to take the initiative the following day.[9]

MAY 6, 1864: At 5:00 AM, the Wilderness erupts into action as some thirty thousand Federals smash into Lieutenant General A. P. Hill's weakened Third Corps on the right flank of the Army of Northern Virginia. Having suffered heavily in the previous day's fighting, and unprepared for the attack, the Confederates fall back — until elements of Lieutenant General James Longstreet's First Corps, General Robert E. Lee in their midst (but prevented by his worried soldiers from actually leading the attack), arrive in the nick of time. Slamming into

the Union troops, the Confederates precipitate a two-hour spate of intense fighting, forcing Union troops under Major General Winfield Scott Hancock and Brigadier General James S. Wadsworth to fall back and regroup. Wadsworth is mortally wounded while rallying his men — and the Confederates also suffer bitter losses among their top officers. Only four miles from where Stonewall Jackson was mortally wounded during the battle of Chancellorsville (see May 2–4, 1863), General Longstreet is seriously wounded by Confederates who mistake the First Corps commander and the men riding with him for Union officers. (Two of Longstreet's staff officers and Confederate brigadier general Micah Jenkins are killed by the same "friendly fire.") Major General Richard H. Anderson assumes Longstreet's command, but the Confederate counterattack against the left of the Union line is stalled. A renewal of the assault later in the day proves ineffective, as does an attack on the Union right by three Southern brigades under Brigadier General John Brown Gordon. Although the Confederates end the day preparing for a third day of fighting, this first clash of the Overland Campaign ends with the coming of dark. Generally regarded as a tactical draw, the battle of the Wilderness has cost the Union 17,600 killed, wounded, and captured; the Confederates have suffered nearly 11,000 casualties.[10]

MAY 7, 1864: Pushing slowly toward the Richmond & Petersburg Railroad from Bermuda Hundred Landing, an eight-thousand-man contingent of Major General Benjamin

LEFT: *A Short History of J. [James] Longstreet.* Booklet in a series designed to be included in cigarette packs, 1888. Commander of the First Corps of the Army of Northern Virginia during the battle of the Wilderness, Lieutenant General Longstreet was seriously wounded by Confederates who mistook him for an enemy.

RIGHT: Brigadier General James S. Wadsworth (1807–1864), USA. Photograph by the Brady National Photographic Art Gallery, between 1860 and 1864. A wealthy philanthropist who kept a firm eye on the welfare of his troops, Wadsworth was described by Illinois senator Orville H. Browning as "firm in his hostility to slavery and rebellion." He was killed at the battle of the Wilderness.

Charles A. Dana (1819–1897), assistant secretary of war, USA, at Cold Harbor, Virginia, July 11 or 12, 1864. Photographer unknown. The former managing editor of Horace Greeley's *New York Tribune*, Dana was an ardent and eloquent Unionist. As assistant secretary of war, he often went into the field to observe operations firsthand.

MAY

1 2 3 4 5 6 7 **8** 9 10 11 12 13 14 15 16 17 18 19 20 21 22 23 24 25 26 27 28 29 30 31

Butler's Union Army of the James meets twenty-six hundred Confederate troops under Brigadier General Bushrod Johnson and pushes them back. Meanwhile, Butler's cavalry, under Brigadier General August Kautz, is engaged in the first of several raids to destroy Confederate supplies and disrupt the enemy's communications. (The raids will prove to be largely ineffective, as the Confederates will quickly repair most of the damage done.) *In Georgia,* Major General William T. Sherman's one-hundred-thousand-man force — comprising the Army of the Tennessee under Major General James B. McPherson, the Army of the Cumberland under Major General George H. Thomas, and the Army of the Ohio under Major General John M. Schofield — begins in earnest its campaign against General Joseph E. Johnston's sixty-thousand-man Army of Tennessee, which is so well entrenched on high ground at Dalton, Georgia, that Sherman decides against a frontal assault. He will, instead, attempt to turn Johnston's left flank. *In the Wilderness,* after a day marked by probing clashes between Union and Confederate skirmishers and, to the south of the main armies, a nearly daylong clash between Union and Confederate cavalry, Grant withdraws his forces under cover of darkness and starts them marching — in a direction that both surprises and elates his army and people throughout the North. "The previous history of the Army of the Potomac had been to advance and fight a battle, then either to retreat or to lie still, and finally to go into winter quarters," Charles A. Dana will write after the war. "As the army began to realize that we were

really moving south . . . the spirits of men and officers rose to the highest pitch of animation. On every hand I heard the cry, 'On to Richmond!'" Unbeknownst to his troops, Grant has promised Lincoln that "whatever happens, there will be no turning back." Yet his enemy is equally determined. "[T]here were to be a great many more obstacles to our reaching Richmond than General Grant himself, I presume, realized on May 8, 1864," Dana will write. "We met one that very morning; for when our advance reached Spottsylvania [*sic*] Courthouse it found Lee's troops there, ready to dispute the right of way with us."[11]

MAY 8, 1864: Finding Lee's First Corps under Richard Anderson digging in at Spotsylvania when he and his men arrive at about 8:00 AM, the Army of the Potomac Fifth Corps commander, Major General Gouverneur Warren, launches a series of unsuccessful piecemeal attacks against Anderson's position before being joined first by Major General John Sedgwick's Sixth Corps and slowly by other elements of the Union force. In the evening, after Confederates repulse a final assault on their works, General Meade orders that "the army will remain quiet to-morrow." They will be quiet but active, entrenching and building field fortifications. Grant, meanwhile, has become concerned over what he deems the insufficient aggressiveness of the Army of the Potomac's leading officers, an attitude that had been ingrained by two and a half years of cautious leadership and battlefield setbacks. "Oh, I am heartily tired of hearing about what Lee is going to do," he had said, two days before, to

ABOVE: Major General John Sedgwick (1813–1864), USA. Photograph by the Brady National Photographic Art Gallery, between 1860 and 1864. A West Point graduate and veteran of the Mexican War, Sedgwick was among the most beloved officers of the Army of the Potomac, which deeply mourned his death from sniper fire.

LEFT: General Robert E. Lee (1807–1870), CSA. Photograph by Julian Vannerson, March 1864. With his Army of Northern Virginia, Lee formed the heart of the Confederate military effort. His reputation caused some Union officers to regard him as having almost superhuman qualities (see May 8, 1864). "But I had known him personally and knew that he was mortal," Ulysses S. Grant wrote in his memoirs, "and it was just as well that I felt this."

officers worrying about the Confederate commander's intent. "Some of you always seem to think he is suddenly going to turn a double somersault, and land in our rear and on both of our flanks at the same time. Go back to your command, and try to think what we are going to do ourselves, instead of what Lee is going to do." In the evening, Grant agrees to a course of action suggested by the Army of the Potomac's cavalry commander, Major General Phil Sheridan: he orders Sheridan to take his ten thousand horsemen (leaving one regiment with the army) and "proceed against the enemy's cavalry."[12]

MAY 9, 1864: As Sherman's army continues to probe the Confederate Army of Tennessee's defenses at Dalton, Georgia (some of the probes resembling full-scale attacks), Butler's Federals are repulsed by Confederates at Swift's Creek. After Butler timidly orders a withdrawal behind fortifications on Bermuda Hundred, the more disgruntled of his men dub this campaign their "stationary advance." *Some miles to the north,* the Army of the Potomac and the Army of Northern Virginia have a relatively quiet day, though it is one punctuated by gunfire. In the morning, Union Sixth Corps commander John Sedgwick, seeing a man flinch from the Confederate shooting, says, "Why, what are you dodging for. They could not hit an elephant at that distance." An instant later, an enemy bullet smashes into his head below the left eye, killing him instantly. "'Uncle John' was loved by his men as no other corps commander ever was in this army," Colonel Charles S.

Wainwright will note in his diary. For the Federals, this "quiet" day becomes a day of mourning.[13]

MAY 10, 1864: Probing for weaknesses in the Confederate fortifications at Spotsylvania, Grant launches attacks against Lee's well-entrenched troops, initiating combat in which intense firing traps the battling soldiers in a storm of lethal metal. Refusing to give up despite the growing cost of these assaults, the Union general in chief approves a plan proposed by twenty-four-year-old Colonel Emory Upton, a West Point graduate and a sharp and ambitious student of military tactics. Upton believes that attacking in columns several soldiers deep, rather than in single lines, will provide the punch required to breach the Confederate defenses. Now, given twelve of the best regiments in the Army of the Potomac's Sixth Corps, he vows to General David A. Russell, "I will carry those works. If I don't, I will not come back." Forming the regiments in three columns, each column four lines deep, Upton explains to the men that he is going to lead them in an assault on the salient (forward protrusion) in Southern lines known as the Mule Shoe. "I felt my gorge rise, and my stomach and intestines shrink together in a knot," one New Yorker will later remember. "I looked about in the faces of the boys around me, and they told the tale of expected death." A fury of Confederate fire lashes into the columns as they near the Rebel lines, but the Federals have been ordered to push on no matter what, and they do; the first lines take a brutal pounding in hand-to-hand

Major General Emory Upton (1839–1881), USA. Photograph by the Brady National Photographic Art Gallery, circa 1865. After graduating from West Point in May 1861 with the rank of lieutenant, Upton rapidly rose through the ranks, promoted to brigadier general for his service at Spotsylvania and becoming a major general by the end of the war.

Major General James Ewell Brown (Jeb) Stuart (1833–1864), CSA, between 1861 and 1864. After resigning from the U.S. Army, Stuart commanded the cavalry that were the eyes of Lee's Army of Northern Virginia. He twice led his men on raids that thoroughly embarrassed the Federal Army of the Potomac.

fighting, but those behind them surge over the fortifications. Yet this is just a temporary victory; when support from other Union troops does not materialize as planned, Confederate reinforcements surge forward and push Upton's troops back. It is a bitter pill for the surviving Federals to swallow. The attack has cost the Union about one thousand killed and wounded; the Confederates have lost a similar number, plus some twelve hundred prisoners. Still, this assault has shown Grant and his officers that a strong enemy position can be overcome with ample concentration of — properly supported — force. Upton will shortly receive a promotion to brigadier general.[14]

MAY 11, 1864: During a lull in the fighting at Spotsylvania, the people of Richmond are seized by convulsions of worry as they learn that a Union force is approaching the city. Notices go up all over the city: "The enemy . . . may be expected at any hour, with a view to [Richmond's] capture, its pillage and its destruction. The strongest consideration of self and duty to the country, calls every man to arms!" Only six miles to the north, at Yellow Tavern, Virginia, Jeb Stuart and three thousand Confederate horsemen (half the Rebel cavalry remain with Lee at Spotsylvania) manage to interpose themselves between Sheridan's cavalry and the Confederate capital. In the ensuing helter-skelter battle, a bullet fired by a soldier of George A. Custer's Michigan Brigade strikes Stuart in the abdomen. As the two forces disengage, Stuart's men carry him back to Richmond by a circuitous route, avoiding the advanc-

ing Federals; Sheridan's men move on and bump up against the city's defenses (Sheridan determining it would be too costly to take the city) before heading off to the east.[15]

MAY 12, 1864: Enticed from behind Union fortifications by Confederate movements along the James River, Major General Benjamin Butler leads fifteen thousand of his Army of the James infantry toward Drewry's Bluff, which is only eight miles below Richmond, on the James River. *At Spotsylvania*, the apex of the Mule Shoe salient (see May 10, 1864) becomes known as the "Bloody Angle" during a rain-drenched day of brutal hand-to-hand fighting that commences at 4:30 AM, when twenty thousand massed Union troops under Major General Winfield Scott Hancock surge out of the fog, over the Confederate fortifications, and into the Rebel soldiers firing from their trenches. By the end of this epically bloody day, which Private John Haley, of the Seventeenth Maine, will describe as "a seething, bubbling, roaring hell of hate and murder," the Confederates have fallen back to a new line at the base of the salient — and survivors on both sides are shaken by the terrible fighting they have just been through: "It was the most desperate struggle of the war," veteran campaigner Dr. Spencer Glasgow Welch, of the Thirteenth South Carolina Volunteers, will write to his wife the next day. "I do not know that it is ended . . . but I hope the Yankees are gone and that I shall never again witness such a terrible day as yesterday was." The Yankees are not gone. There will be two more all-out clashes (May 18 and 19) — bringing

Corporal Alvin B. Williams, Company F, Eleventh Regiment, New Hampshire Volunteers, killed at age eighteen near Spotsylvania Court House, Virginia, May 12, 1864 — three weeks after his brother, Oscar, also serving in the Eleventh New Hampshire, died in an army hospital of pneumonia. Hand-colored ambrotype, date and photographer unknown. Above: Corporal Alvin Williams's dogtag.

LEFT: Brigadier General Franz Sigel (1824–1902), USA. Photographic print on a *carte de visite* mount, circa 1861. A German immigrant and military academy graduate, Sigel proved to be a less than distinguished Civil War battlefield commander and retired from the service after the battle of New Market. His greatest service to the United States was in rallying German Americans to the Union cause.

MAY

1 2 3 4 5 6 7 8 9 10 11 12 **13** 14 **15** **16** 17 18 19 20 21 22 23 24 25 26 27 28 29 30 31

the total number of Spotsylvania killed, wounded, and missing to some eighteen thousand Federals and twelve thousand Confederates — before Grant withdraws to try again to push forward around Lee's right flank. *In Richmond,* after suffering through the day and calmly setting his affairs in order, at 7:38 PM thirty-one-year-old Jeb Stuart dies of his wound at the home of his brother-in-law, Dr. Charles Brewer. Newspapers quickly publish accounts of his last hours; but it will be eight days before a grieving Robert E. Lee is able to issue General Orders, No. 44, announcing Stuart's death to his men: "His grateful countrymen will mourn his loss and cherish his memory. To his comrades in arms he has left the proud recollection of his deeds, and the inspiring influence of his example."[16]

MAY 13, 1864: Having pushed Confederates back from their forward positions and into their main lines at Drewry's Bluff (see May 12, 1864), Major General Benjamin Butler does not press after them but holds his fifteen thousand Union troops in a defensive position. As he ponders his next move, Confederate reinforcements will arrive from Richmond and North Carolina. *From Washington,* Walt Whitman writes his mother: "Yesterday and to-day the badly wounded are coming in. . . . I steadily believe Grant is going to succeed, and that we shall have Richmond — but O what a price to pay for it."[17]

MAY 15, 1864: Confederates led by Major General John C. Breckinridge, a former U.S. vice president, defeat Union troops

under General Franz Sigel at the battle of New Market, in the Shenandoah Valley. In this encounter, which allows Confederates to hold on a little longer to the valley, widely known as the "Breadbasket of the Confederacy," Breckinridge's troops include 247 Virginia Military Institute cadets whose courageous charge makes them instant Southern heroes. Disappointed in this Federal loss, General in Chief Grant and Chief of Staff Henry Halleck will urge President Lincoln to replace Sigel, who, the two officers believe, "will do nothing but run; he never did anything else." On May 21, Major General David Hunter will assume command in the valley.[18]

MAY 16, 1864: At 4:45 AM, Confederates under General P. G. T. Beauregard burst from their lines and hit Major General Benjamin Butler's Union troops, beginning the second battle of Drewry's Bluff. Though the attack's organization is partially confounded by heavy fog, the Confederates are able to force the Federals back, Butler leading them to the Bermuda Hundred fortifications they had left not long before. The following morning, Confederate troops will arrive and position themselves across the narrow neck of land opposite those fortifications, making it impossible for the Army of the James to move forward. The Federal commander, who has been known, at least in Southern circles, as Beast Butler, since the infamous "women's order" he issued in New Orleans (see May 15, 1862), now becomes known as Bottled Up Butler.[19]

"THE HEAVENS ARE HUNG IN BLACK"

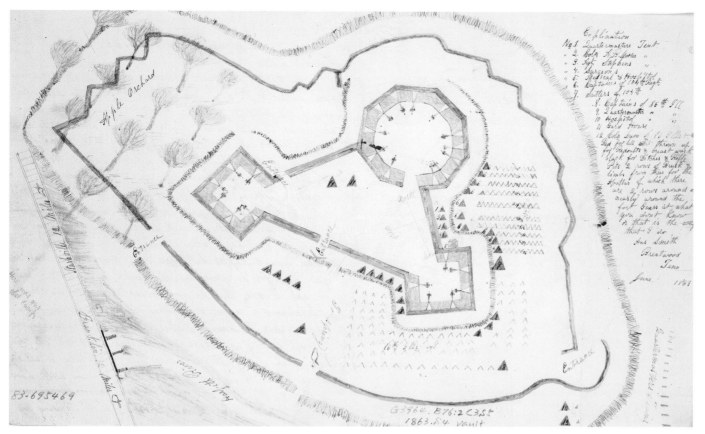

As the war progressed, armies of each side became adept at entrenching and erecting field fortifications, such as the ones Lee's Army of Northern Virginia hastily erected at the North Anna River, discouraging Union assault (see May 23–26, 1864). This sketch, by Union soldier Anson Smith, depicts a Union fortification that his regiment, the 104th Illinois, constructed in Tennessee to guard the strategically vital Louisville and Nashville Railroad.

MAY

1 2 3 4 5 6 7 8 9 10 11 12 13 14 15 16 17 18 19 **20** 21 22 **23** **24** **25** **26** 27 **28** 29 30 31

MAY 20, 1864: Weary in body and spirit from the near-ceaseless pounding they have been taking and the loss of so many in their ranks, yet still stubbornly determined, the men of the Army of the Potomac begin to withdraw from their lines at Spotsylvania. They continue their movement south, Grant believing (erroneously) that he might be able to catch the equally battered and determined men of the Army of Northern Virginia in the open as Lee maneuvers to keep his force between Grant's army and Richmond. The Federals forage as they march, exhibiting little of the consideration for the property of Confederate civilians that characterized the first year of the war. Meanwhile, after crossing the North Anna River, Lee will order his army to halt and quickly erect field fortifications — something at which they have become surpassing experts during this brutal campaign.[20]

MAY 23–26, 1864: Leaving some of their men to guard the north bank, Grant and Meade send the bulk of the Army of the Potomac across the North Anna River — where the Union force immediately runs up against Lee's entrenched Confederates, whose inverted-V-shaped lines pose difficult tactical problems. After some piecemeal attempts to penetrate the Rebel position, Grant and his officers decide, as Grant informs Washington, that "to make a direct attack from either wing [each Union wing facing one side of the Confederate V] would cause a slaughter of our men that even success would not justify." Grant decides to recross the North Anna and move

around Lee's flank, making "one more effort," as he will write in his memoirs, "to get between him and Richmond. I had no expectation now, however, of succeeding in this; but I did expect to hold him far enough west to enable me to reach the James River high up." During the North Anna operations, Phil Sheridan and his cavalry, their two-week raid concluded (see May 8 and 11, 1864), rejoin the Army of the Potomac.[21]

MAY 26, 1864: Despite shortages of manufactured goods throughout the Confederacy, "blockade-running," or sneaking through the Federal blockade of the Southern ports to sell goods for immense profit, becomes widespread enough for Jefferson Davis to complain in a speech that "50 or 60 millions have gone into blockade-running while not a new dollar has gone into manufacturing."[22]

MAY 28, 1864: General Lee reports to President Davis that his best guess at the enemy's route has led him "to take position on the ridge between the Totopotomoi [*sic*] and Beaver Dam Creeks, so as to intercept his march to Richmond," yet "the want of information" now leads him to doubt if his calculations are correct. As he writes, Army of the Potomac cavalry searching for Lee collide with Confederate cavalry searching for Grant at Haw's Shop near Hanovertown. During the fight, George A. Custer leads his dismounted Michigan Brigade in a charge that routs the Rebels — not the first time the young Union general has demonstrated effective leadership under

fire. "So brave a man I never saw and as competent as brave," one of his officers writes. "Under *him* our men can achieve wonders." For the next few days, Federals and Confederates will clash intermittently as Grant continues to move his troops toward the James River.[23]

MAY 31, 1864: A group of some four hundred white radicals who have formed the Radical Democracy Party meet in Cleveland, Ohio, and nominate famed explorer and former Union general John C. Frémont as their candidate for president of the United States (see August 30, 1861). The party platform stipulates that there must be no compromise with the Confederacy and supports equal rights for blacks in the South and a constitutional amendment banning slavery. Although a majority of blacks unswervingly support Lincoln, several influential African American leaders, including Frederick Douglass, initially lean toward Frémont, feeling that the president is too cautious and lenient in his terms for Reconstruction. *In Virginia,* Army of the Potomac cavalry units occupy Old Cold Harbor. They have been ordered to hold this position until their infantry arrives. As Confederate troops from Lee's Totopotomoy Creek position as well as from Richmond arrive in the area, the Union horsemen comply with their orders, repulsing Rebel attempts to dislodge them. Meanwhile, the Confederates form a new line just east of New Cold Harbor — and only a dozen miles from the Confederate capital.[24]

JUNE 1864

JUNE 1, 1864: The battle of Cold Harbor begins late in the day as two newly arrived Federal infantry corps, ordered forward by General Meade, attack Lee's entrenched Confederates — and are repulsed with some two thousand casualties. As the survivors return to the lengthening Union lines, Major General Winfield Scott Hancock's Army of the Potomac Second Corps, still some distance from Cold Harbor, begins a forced march in order to be in position for a full-scale assault that Grant has ordered for the following day. It is a difficult night for men already worn down from a month of brutal campaigning. When Hancock's men arrive at Cold Harbor on June 2, Grant will postpone his planned attack for a day "by reason of the exhausted state of the 2nd Corps." Confederates have been on the march, too; Lee has received reinforcements from Bermuda Hundred and the Shenandoah Valley. *In Mississippi,* Major General Nathan Bedford Forrest leads his cavalry out of Tupelo, heading northeast into Alabama and toward the Nashville & Chattanooga Railroad, the supply lifeline for Major General William T. Sherman's one-hundred-thousand-man force now pursuing General Joseph Johnston's Confederate army in Georgia. Uncomfortably aware of Forrest's expertise at disrupting Federal supply lines, as he had done effectively during the first Union campaign for Vicksburg (see December 21, 1862), Sherman has already ordered Brigadier General Samuel D. Sturgis to distract Forrest by threatening northern Mississippi. Sturgis will lead eighty-one hundred Union troops out of Memphis on June 2.[25]

Cold Harbor, Virginia (vicinity). Collecting Remains of Dead on the Battlefield. Photograph by John Reekie, April 1865. The site of a three-day battle during the Union's costly Overland Campaign, Cold Harbor included a final, hour-long frontal assault on Confederate entrenchments that caused more than three thousand Federal casualties; casualty estimates for the entire battle exceed seventeen thousand men killed, wounded, and missing.

JUNE

1 2 **3** 4 5 **6 7 8** 9 10 11 12 13 14 15 16 17 18 19 20 21 22 23 24 25 26 27 28 29 30

JUNE 3, 1864: At 4:30 AM, infantrymen of the Second, Sixth, and Eighteenth Corps of the Army of the Potomac advance on the Army of Northern Virginia's formidable lines at Cold Harbor — and are met by a wall of lacerating musket and artillery fire that fells ranks of men "like rows of blocks or bricks pushed over by striking against each other," as one survivor will remember. After one searing hour, during which thirty-five hundred Federal soldiers are killed or wounded, the assault fails. Yet gunfire does not cease. Thousands of Union soldiers, both unhurt and wounded, lie trapped in the open between Federal and Confederate lines; their slightest movement sparks Rebel fire that causes more than a thousand additional casualties before darkness brings an end to this terrible day. "I have always regretted that the last assault at Cold Harbor was ever made," Grant will write in his memoirs. "[N]o advantage whatever was gained to compensate for the heavy loss we sustained." As both armies work to strengthen their positions, Grant and Lee will begin an exchange of messages about the men of both armies who are suffering between the lines. Marked by delays and misunderstandings, the negotiations will take more than forty-eight hours; during that time, as Grant will later note, "all but two of the wounded had died."[26]

JUNE 6, 1864: William T. Sherman's ploy to keep Confederate cavalry commander Nathan Bedford Forrest away from his army's vital railroad supply line proves effective when Major General Stephen D. Lee recalls Forrest from his raid. Forrest

and his men are to find and intercept Samuel D. Sturgis's Union column, which is threatening northeastern Mississippi. (See June 1 and 10, 1864.)[27]

JUNE 7, 1864: Both to harass the enemy and to divert attention from the next phase of his Overland Campaign, General in Chief Grant sends Phil Sheridan and nine thousand cavalrymen on a mission to destroy as much as possible of the Virginia Central Railroad, then move on to Charlottesville to connect, if feasible, with David Hunter's Shenandoah Valley contingent (Hunter will actually remain in the valley; see June 11–12, 1864). Sheridan departs while somber music from Union bands echoes in the air: the Federals are burying the dead they have finally been able to retrieve from the killing ground between Union and Confederate lines (see June 3, 1864). *In Washington,* Walt Whitman writes to his mother about "one new feature" of the wounded soldiers crowding the city's hospitals: "Many of the poor afflicted young men are crazy. Every ward has some in it that are wandering. They have suffered too much, and it is perhaps a privilege that they are out of their senses."[28]

JUNE 8, 1864: In Baltimore, delegates from twenty-five states attend the Republican Party Convention (redesignated the National Union Party Convention this year, to attract War Democrats). Although there has been some agitation to replace Abraham Lincoln as the party's candidate (see, for example, January 13 and February 22, 1864), his nomination is a foregone

Major General Nathan Bedford
Forrest (1821–1877), CSA.
A prewar slave trader, Forrest
became one of the Confederacy's
most talented and resourceful
cavalry commanders. His victory
at Brice's Crossroads brought
him the official thanks of the
Confederate Congress.

*Jones' Landing, Va., vicinity. Pontoon Bridge over the James, from
the North Bank,* date and photographer unknown. Reaching the James
River at the end of the Overland Campaign, engineers of the Army of the
Potomac built a pontoon bridge that allowed Grant's huge army to cross.
It would remain the longest floating bridge ever erected until the record
was broken during World War II.

conclusion. When it is achieved, a band erupts with a rousing
"Star-Spangled Banner" and, as the *National Republican* will
report, "the audience rose *en masse,* and such an enthusiastic
demonstration was scarcely ever paralleled." Delegates then
bump Vice President Hannibal Hamlin from the ticket, replacing him with Tennessee Unionist Andrew Johnson (see July 11,
1861). *In Washington,* Lincoln is following convention events as
best he can from the War Department telegraph office. He will
not be officially notified of his renomination, however, until a
delegation calls at the White House the following day.[29]

JUNE 10, 1864: Confederates under Nathan Bedford Forrest
trounce Samuel Sturgis's Union force at the battle of Brice's
Crossroads, Mississippi. Defeating the thirty-three-hundred-
man Union cavalry first, the Confederates then duel Sturgis's
infantry for four hours before the Federals break and run. They
are saved from total disaster by action of one brigade, comprising three regiments of U. S. Colored Troops. Often fighting
hand-to-hand, with almost no assistance from white volunteers,
the black soldiers hold the Confederates back long enough to
allow the balance of the Federal force to escape. *In the North
Atlantic,* having by now taken some sixty-five Union vessels
as prizes, Raphael Semmes, captain of the famed and feared
Confederate commerce raider CSS *Alabama,* welcomes an experienced English Channel pilot aboard his vessel as it enters the
channel en route to getting a much-needed refit in France. "I felt
great relief to have him on board," Semmes writes in his diary.

"And thus, thanks to an all-wise Providence, we have brought
the cruise of the Alabama to a successful termination." Yet it is
too soon for Semmes to relax; *Alabama* is being pursued.[30]

JUNE 11–12, 1864: More than six thousand Confederate
cavalrymen led by Major General Wade Hampton intercept
Phil Sheridan's Union cavalry at Trevilian Station, Virginia,
precipitating a two-day battle that will become the bloodiest
cavalry clash of the war. Action on June 11 includes a desperate
three-hour struggle for survival by George Custer's surrounded
Michigan Brigade, which is finally relieved when other Federal
troops punch a hole in the Confederate line. On June 12, after
Confederates repulse seven charges by Sheridan's dismounted
men throughout the day, Sheridan decides to withdraw
toward Cold Harbor, taking with him as many as possible of
his one thousand wounded, plus prisoners and runaway slaves.
Hampton's Confederates, who have suffered eleven hundred
casualties, have put an end to the Union raid before it has truly
started. *Over these same two days, in the Shenandoah Valley,* David
Hunter's Union troops storm into Lexington, Virginia, site
of the Virginia Military Institute (VMI), whose cadets won
plaudits for joining in the battle of New Market the previous
month (see May 15, 1864). Harassed for a month by Rebel guerrillas, who have prevented most of their supply wagons from
getting through to them, the Yankees are hungry and incensed
at civilians they believe are supporting the irregulars. Today,
they forage with a vengeance — and for good measure burn

The War in Virginia—a Regiment of the 18th Corps Carrying a Portion of Beauregard's Line in Front of Petersburg.
Wood engraving based on a sketch by E. F. Mullen, published in *Frank Leslie's Illustrated Newspaper*, July 23, 1864.
Although they vastly outnumbered the city's Confederate garrison when they arrived at Petersburg in mid-June,
Grant's battered troops, wary after weeks of brutal campaigning, failed to take this vital rail hub. Instead, Petersburg became the object of a Union siege that lasted for months.

JUNE

1 2 3 4 5 6 7 8 9 10 11 **12** 13 **14** **15** 16 17 18 19 20 21 22 23 24 25 26 27 28 29 30

down VMI and the home of Virginia governor John Letcher, who recently issued what Hunter will describe as "a violent and inflammatory proclamation . . . inciting the population . . . to rise and wage a guerrilla warfare on my troops." As Hunter leads his troops toward Lynchburg, Robert E. Lee orders Jubal Early to lead the Second Corps of the Army of Northern Virginia into the valley to neutralize this Union threat.[31]

JUNE 12, 1864: General Grant begins one of the most remarkable troop movements of the war. Withdrawing the Army of the Potomac from its lines at Cold Harbor after dark, he leads the huge force across the Virginia Peninsula. By June 14, it will arrive at the north bank of the James River — which Lee had told Jubal Early it was essential to keep the Federals from crossing. As some Federals cross the water by boat, Grant's engineers construct a 2,170-foot pontoon bridge — the longest floating bridge erected before World War II. When, at 11:00 PM, they finish assembling this marvel, bands play, drummers drum, and troops begin streaming across the new span, an operation that will continue for nearly two days. It is, as Colonel Horace Porter, of Grant's staff, will later say, "a matchless pageant that could not fail to inspire all beholders with the grandeur of achievement and the majesty of military power."[32]

JUNE 14, 1864: Reporting to Washington on his movements, Grant wires Chief of Staff Halleck: "The enemy show no signs yet of having brought troops to the south side of Richmond. I will have Petersburg secured, if possible, before they get there in much force." This will bring an optimistic response from the president: "I begin to see it. You will succeed. God bless you all." *In the North Atlantic*, the warship USS *Kearsarge* arrives in the waters off Cherbourg, France, where CSS *Alabama* has just arrived for a refit. On board *Alabama*, Raphael Semmes immediately sends for one hundred tons of coal and prepares to go out and engage his pursuer.[33]

JUNE 15, 1864: The Thirteenth Amendment to the U.S. Constitution (abolishing slavery), which the U.S. Senate approved on April 8, falls thirteen votes short of passing the House of Representatives by the required two-thirds majority. Congress does finally pass legislation granting equal pay to black soldiers, some of whom have, for many months, been refusing to accept any pay until the inequity was rectified. Retroactive to January 1, 1864, the legislation does not, however, apply to all of the nation's black soldiers; it covers only those who were free as of April 19, 1861. Tens of thousands of ex-slaves in the U.S. Army are thus excluded from this remedial measure. Efforts on their behalf will continue (see March 3, 1865). *In Virginia*, General Lee sends one infantry division to reinforce P. G. T. Beauregard, who is currently both defending Petersburg and keeping Benjamin Butler's Union Army of the James bottled up on Bermuda Hundred with only fifty-four hundred troops. Yet the Federal units that are arriving at Petersburg's defenses do not know that Beauregard's force

THE COPPERHEAD PARTY.—IN FAVOR OF *A VIGOROUS PROSECUTION OF PEACE!*

ABOVE: *The Copperhead Party. — In Favor of a Vigorous Prosecution of Peace!* Wood engraving published in *Harper's Weekly*, February 28, 1863. Distress over the "butcher's bill" of casualties suffered by Federal troops during Grant's Overland Campaign lent strength to the arguments of Copperheads eager to make peace with the Confederacy — perhaps even at the cost of the Union itself.

LEFT: This color plate from *History of the Brooklyn and Long Island Fair, February 22, 1864,* published that same year, illustrates the elaborate and patriotic nature of the fund-raising "sanitary fairs" sponsored by individual chapters of the United States Sanitary Commission. On June 16, 1864, President Lincoln praised these efforts when he spoke at the Great Central Sanitary Fair in Philadelphia.

is so small, and, like Grant's entire army, they are wary and exhausted by their experiences from the Wilderness through Cold Harbor. Though today they begin a series of attacks on the city's defenses, the assaults will not be sufficiently forceful or coordinated to breach the Confederates' inner lines. The attacks will, however, increase by nearly ten thousand casualties the "butcher's bill" that the Union has been paying during this costly campaign. "Yesterday afternoon another horrid massacre of our corps was enacted," Colonel Rufus Dawes, of the Sixth Wisconsin, will write to his wife on June 18. "It is awfully disheartening to think we have Generals who will send their men to such sure destruction."[34]

JUNE 16, 1864: "War at the best, is terrible, and this war of ours, in its magnitude and in its duration, is one of the most terrible," President Lincoln says, in a speech at the Great Central Sanitary Fair in Philadelphia. "It has carried mourning to almost every home, until it can almost be said that the 'heavens are hung in black.'" After praising the "benevolent labors" of the men and women of the Sanitary Commission, its sister organization, the Christian Commission, and the soldiers these organizations assist, Lincoln addresses the oft-asked question, when will the war end? "Speaking of the present campaign, General Grant is reported to have said, I am going through on this line if it takes all summer. This war has taken three years; it was begun or accepted upon the line of restoring the national authority over the whole national domain, and

for the American people, as far as my knowledge enables me to speak, I say we are going through on this line if it takes three years more."[35]

JUNE 17, 1864: Volatile materials explode at the Federal arsenal in Washington, igniting a conflagration. "The scene was horrible beyond description," the capital city's *Daily National Intelligencer* will report. "Under the metal roof of the building were seething bodies and limbs, mangled, scorched, and charred beyond the possibility of identification. . . . The square in front of the Arsenal gate presents a most distressing spectacle. . . . Sisters, husbands, and fathers are there waiting for sisters, wives, and daughters. The anxiety and sorrow exhibited is beyond all description." As was the case with a similar accident the previous year in Richmond, where more than sixty people died, most of the twenty-one people killed at the Washington Arsenal are women who had entered the workforce to assist in the war effort.[36]

JUNE 18, 1864: Federal troops under David Hunter probe the Confederate defenses at Lynchburg, Virginia, and find that John C. Breckinridge's troops have been reinforced by the Army of Northern Virginia corps under Jubal Early that Lee has sent to counter the Union threat in the Shenandoah Valley (see June 11–12, 1864). In the evening, Hunter, deciding a full-scale assault will be unsuccessful given the reinforced Confederate garrison, begins to withdraw his men. Early

Kearsarge and Alabama. Color lithograph published by L. Prang & Co., 1887. A particularly painful thorn in the Union's paw, Confederate commerce raider Raphael Semmes's vessel CSS *Alabama* was finally caught and destroyed, an event that caused mourning throughout the South. *Alabama*'s nemesis, USS *Kearsarge,* was captained by John A. Winslow, who had been a friend and shipmate of Semmes during the Mexican War.

and his troops will soon be in pursuit, eventually chasing Hunter completely out of the Shenandoah Valley. The route to Northern territory will thus lie open. *At Petersburg, Virginia,* a series of frontal assaults on the city's defenses having failed (see June 15, 1864), the 110,000-man Army of the Potomac begins digging in to besiege that crucially important railroad hub less than twenty-five miles from Richmond. Morale among Grant's battered and exhausted troops is at a low ebb (and thousands of these exhausted veterans, having reached the end of their three-year enlistment, are leaving the ranks). But war-weariness isn't confined to the trenches. At home on sick leave, Union general John H. Martindale writes to Major General Benjamin Butler that there is "great discouragement over the North, great reluctance to recruiting, strong disposition for peace." The price of gold rises, reflecting the pessimism of Northern financial markets. With casualty rolls listing 65,000 Federal soldiers killed, wounded, or missing since the Overland Campaign began on May 4, Democrats are denouncing Grant as a "butcher." (Confederate casualties, some 35,000, constitute approximately the same percentage of their smaller force.)[37]

JUNE 19, 1864: A host of civilians observe from the shoreline cliffs of Cherbourg, France, as CSS *Alabama* battles USS *Kearsarge* in the war's greatest ship-to-ship combat in open seas. Circling and firing, the two vessels draw closer together, with *Kearsarge* taking the offensive. Outgunned and not yet repaired and refitted, *Alabama* very quickly suffers critical damage. "Our

decks were now covered with the dead and the wounded," Semmes's executive officer, Lieutenant John McIntosh Kell, will report, "and the ship was careening heavily to starboard from the effects of the shot-holes on her waterline." Semmes is forced to strike his colors in order to rescue the wounded before his ship sinks. Nine *Alabama* crewmen are killed and thirty are wounded; but Semmes and some of his officers manage to escape to England aboard the yacht of wealthy Englishman John Lancaster, who had sailed out to observe the encounter. "[T]he Alabama, our pride & our hope has been sunk off Cherburgh," North Carolina's Catherine Edmondston will write in her diary on July 14. "Not a vestige of the Alabama fell into the hands of the Victors! Everything went down & she has left only her fame behind her."[38]

JUNE 22, 1864: Seeking to cut the Confederates' supply lines and extend Union lines, Grant dispatches two Union cavalry divisions under Brigadier General James H. Wilson and Brigadier General August Kautz on a raid against the Southside Railroad, while three infantry corps push south and west toward the Weldon railroad. The infantry corps almost immediately run into trouble. Lee's Confederates exploit a gap in their lines to shatter one division and threaten others before the Federals manage to regroup. The day's fighting costs them twenty-four hundred casualties, including seventeen hundred prisoners. The cavalry will have greater success — for a while. Although in the course of a week they will destroy sixty miles

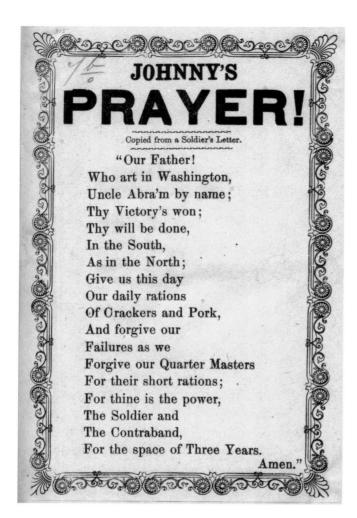

JOHNNY'S
PRAYER!
Copied from a Soldier's Letter.

"Our Father!
Who art in Washington,
Uncle Abra'm by name;
Thy Victory's won;
Thy will be done,
In the South,
As in the North;
Give us this day
Our daily rations
Of Crackers and Pork,
And forgive our
Failures as we
Forgive our Quarter Masters
For their short rations;
For thine is the power,
The Soldier and
The Contraband,
For the space of Three Years.
Amen."

LEFT AND ABOVE: The Union music broadside *Johnny's Prayer!* and the cover of the 1864 Confederate song *Short Rations* shine satirically humorous lights on the subject of army food. Despite copious complaints, Federal soldiers were comparatively well fed, but lack of adequate, nourishing rations became a serious problem for many Rebels.

OPPOSITE, LEFT: *Kennesaw's Bombardment, 64.* Pencil, Chinese white, and black ink wash drawing by Alfred R. Waud, 1864. Major General William T. Sherman's attack at Kennesaw Mountain, Georgia, was a costly failure that raised civilian morale — in the Confederacy.

JUNE

1 2 3 4 5 6 7 8 9 10 11 12 13 14 15 16 17 18 19 20 21 22 **23** **24** **25** 26 **27** 28 29 30

of railroad track (which will be quickly repaired), in doing so, they excite the attentions of Wade Hampton's Confederate cavalry and three of Lee's infantry brigades. Outnumbered and nearly surrounded, Wilson and Kautz will be forced to burn their wagons and leave artillery and their wounded behind to escape total disaster. *While these events are unfolding,* General Grant meets with President Lincoln at City Point, Virginia. The president will tour the Petersburg lines on horseback and then, with Grant, travel by boat to meet with Major General Butler before returning to Washington, tired but optimistic, having been impressed by Grant's quiet confidence.[39]

JUNE 23, 1864: Having chased David Hunter and his Federal troops into West Virginia (see June 18, 1864), Jubal Early turns his men northward. Some thirteen thousand Confederates begin marching through dust and scorching heat down the now undefended Shenandoah Valley toward the Potomac River and Union territory. Low on food, the troops chant "bread, bread, bread" when their officers ride by. But, despite their hunger, they keep on going.[40]

JUNE 24, 1864: "Carpenter, the artist, who is painting the picture of 'Reading the [Emancipation] Proclamation' says that [Secretary of State William H.] Seward protested earnestly against that act being taken as the central and crowning act of the Administration," President Lincoln's secretary, John Hay, notes in his diary.

[Seward] says . . . the formation of the Republican Party destroyed slavery; the anti-slavery acts of this administration are merely incidental. Their great work is the preservation of the Union, and in that, the saving of popular government for the world. The scene which should have been taken was the Cabinet Meeting in the Navy Department where it was resolved to relieve Fort Sumter. That was the significant act of the Administration. The act which determined the fact that Republican institutions were worth fighting for.[41]

JUNE 25, 1864: At Petersburg, Virginia, Union lieutenant colonel Henry Pleasants, a prewar civil and mining engineer, embarks on a project he has suggested and Army of the Potomac Ninth Corps commander Major General Ambrose Burnside has approved: with men of the Forty-eighth Pennsylvania Infantry, a regiment comprising many experienced coal miners, he begins digging a tunnel that will end under the Confederate lines.[42]

JUNE 27, 1864: Secretary of the Treasury Salmon P. Chase nominates Maunsell Field to be assistant treasurer of New York. Though he has been cautioned by President Lincoln to appoint a qualified individual approved by prominent New York Republicans, Chase has chosen a wholly unqualified crony. This is one of many posts Chase has been filling with people who might be useful to him in what President Lincoln,

Kennesaw's Bombardment 64
MAP ON OTHER SIDE—

Miss Kate Chase (1840–1899), between 1855 and 1865. The daughter of Lincoln's ambitious secretary of the treasury, Salmon P. Chase, the bright, attractive, and vivacious Kate served as her father's hostess, confidante, and ally in his unsuccessful quest for the presidency. "Diplomats and statesmen felt it an honor to be her guests," one reporter wrote of her exceptional skills as a Washington hostess.

Salmon P. Chase (1808–1873). Photograph by the Brady National Photographic Art Gallery, between 1860 and 1865.

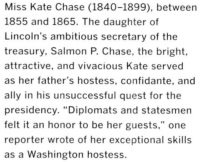

JUNE

1 2 3 4 5 6 7 8 9 10 11 12 13 14 15 16 17 18 19 20 21 22 23 24 25 26 27 **28 29** 30

with some amusement, once called, "Chase's mad hunt after the presidency." *In Georgia,* Major General William T. Sherman, now within thirty miles of Atlanta but still frustrated by Joseph Johnston's reluctance to commit his Confederates to battle, orders his men to assault the entrenched center of Johnston's army at Kennesaw Mountain. Trying to advance uphill in hundred-degree heat, the Union troops are repulsed at great cost. Reports of the defeat will increase the frustration building on the Union home front. In the South, morale will soar. An Atlanta paper predicts that Sherman's army will soon be "cut to pieces."[43]

JUNE 28, 1864: On the day he signs congressional legislation that finally repeals the Fugitive Slave Law, the president also sends a note to Secretary of the Treasury Chase regarding Chase's nomination of the unqualified Maunsell Field the previous day: "I can not, without much embarrassment, make this appointment," the president writes, and asks that Chase submit another name. This directive from the chief executive stings Chase's considerable ego, an aspect of the secretary's personality that sharp-tongued Radical Republican Senator Benjamin Wade has remarked upon in his singularly pithy fashion: "Chase is a good man, but his theology is unsound," Wade has said. "He thinks there is a fourth Person in the Trinity, S. P. C. [Salmon P. Chase]."[44]

JUNE 29, 1864: Having maneuvered successfully to solve the crisis that his appointment of Maunsell Field has caused among New York Republicans (by asking the man Field was to have replaced to serve some months longer), Treasury Secretary Chase then goes one step too far. Convinced that he is irreplaceable, he seeks to confirm his value as a cabinet officer and assert his right to nominate whomsoever he chooses by submitting his resignation — something he has done, for equally manipulative reasons, three times before. Lincoln, however, understands perfectly well what Chase is truly up to and, after three years, he has had enough of the secretary's machinations. "Your resignation of the office of Secretary of the Treasury, sent me yesterday, is accepted," he will write Chase June 30. "Of all I have said in commendation of your ability and fidelity, I have nothing to unsay; and yet you and I have reached a point of mutual embarrassment in our official relation which it seems can not be overcome, or longer sustained, consistently with the public service." Chase's departure will alarm many in the Union capital — until Lincoln finds a perfect replacement, Republican senator William Pitt Fessenden, chairman of the Senate Finance Committee. Fessenden's appointment will be confirmed on July 1.[45]

Invasion of Maryland, 1864: Driving off Cattle and Plunder Taken from the Farmers by Early's Cavalry. Wood engraving from a sketch by Edwin Forbes, published in *American Soldier in the Civil War: A Pictorial History*, 1895. Making their way toward Washington and on their return, Early's Confederates sought both sustenance and revenge for damage Union troops under David Hunter had done in the Shenandoah Valley.

JULY 1864

JULY 2, 1864: Congress passes the Wade-Davis Bill, which stipulates certain conditions that seceded states must fulfill before rejoining the Union. President Lincoln views these as retaliatory against the South and a refutation of his own more moderate approach to reconstructing the Union. The president's pocket veto of the bill [failure to sign it within the constitutionally mandated ten days] will underline the growing rift between Lincoln and congressional Radical Republicans over Reconstruction policy. Reacting to the veto, the sponsors of the bill, Senator Benjamin F. Wade and Representative Henry Winter Davis, will issue a manifesto calling the president's action a "studied outrage upon the legislative authority of the people."[46]

JULY 4, 1864: President Lincoln signs into law a repeal of certain exemption clauses of the Enrollment [Draft] Act of 1863, including the provision allowing payment of a commutation fee of $300 ("blood money" to its many opponents) instead of being drafted. On the other end of Pennsylvania Avenue, Congress passes the Pension Act of 1864, which, among other provisions, allows special, if limited, monetary compensation to those who have been blinded or who have lost both arms or both legs during their wartime service. *In Richmond*, newspapers print a roster of more than six hundred recaptured slaves and ask their owners to reclaim them. *At Harpers Ferry, West Virginia*, Jubal Early's hungry Confederate troops, still heading north (see June 23, 1864), occupy the heights around the town, displacing Union troops. "The Yankees made a great preparation for a July [Fourth] dinner," one delighted Confederate soldier will write, "so we had the pleasure of eating it for them." Early will not attempt to take the well-fortified town and Union arsenal, however. The following day, his men will begin crossing the Potomac River into Maryland — spurring alarmed Union officials to call for twenty-four thousand Maryland, New York, and Pennsylvania militia to help defend against this third Confederate incursion into Union territory.[47]

JULY 5, 1864: With Nathan Bedford Forrest's cavalry still posing a major threat to his supply lines (see June 10, 1864), William T. Sherman has ordered Major General Andrew J. Smith to "follow Forrest to the death, if it cost 10,000 lives and breaks the Treasury." Today, Smith leads fourteen thousand infantry and cavalry out of La Grange, Tennessee, and toward Forrest's base in north Mississippi. On their way, the Union force will wreck everything they find that might be useful to the Confederate military. *In Canada*, an obscure U.S. peace advocate named W. C. Jewett has been meeting with Confederate emissaries who are ostensibly seeking peace but who are, in truth, more interested in seeing Lincoln defeated in the forthcoming presidential election. Today, Jewett writes to an influential acquaintance, Horace Greeley: "I am authorized to state to you . . . that two ambassadors of Davis & Co. are now in Canada, with full and complete powers for a peace." He

Sisters Lucretia Electa and Louisa Ellen Crossett, probably mill workers, holding weaving shuttles. Photograph by Alfred Hall, September 26, 1859. During the war, textile mills in both the North and the South supplied a range of essential materials to the warring armies. So valuable were their contributions to the war effort that in July 1864 William T. Sherman ordered Georgia mill workers transported to Union territory to deprive the Confederacy of their skills.

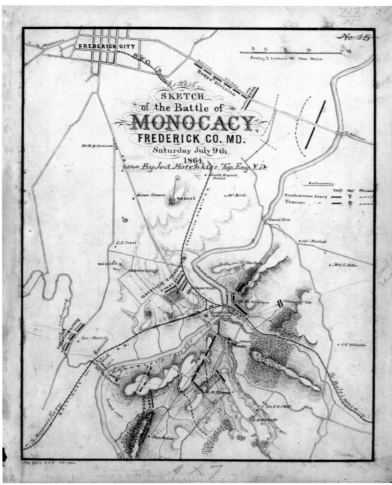

ABOVE: Major General Lewis (Lew) Wallace (1827–1905), USA. A veteran of the Mexican War and a prewar lawyer and politician, Wallace commanded the patchwork Union force that dueled with Jubal Early's Confederates at the battle of Monocacy.

LEFT: *Sketch of the Battle of Monocacy, Frederick Co. Md. Saturday July 9th, 1864.* Color map by Jedediah Hotchkiss, included in his *Report of the Camps, Marches and Engagements, of the Second Corps, A.N.V. and of the Army of the Valley Dist., of the Department of Northern Virginia; during the Campaign of 1864,* December 1864.

JULY

1 2 3 4 5 **6** 7 8 **9** 10 11 12 13 14 15 16 17 18 19 20 21 22 23 24 25 26 27 28 29 30 31

includes an invitation for Greeley to meet with the "ambassadors," one of whom, George N. Sanders, has assured him that "the whole matter can be consummated by me, you, them [the ambassadors], and President Lincoln." Though Greeley is skeptical that the emissaries have the full powers Jewett says that they do (and Greeley is correct, they do not), on July 7 he will forward the note to Lincoln. In his own covering letter, he will remind the president "that our bleeding, bankrupt, almost dying country also longs for peace — shudders at the prospect of fresh conscriptions, of further wholesale devastations, and of new rivers of human blood," and he begs the president to "submit overtures for pacification to the Southern insurgents."[48]

JULY 6, 1864: Under orders from William T. Sherman, Brigadier General Kenner Garrard burns the cotton and textile mills of Roswell, Georgia, after discovering that the mills, operating under the neutral French flag, have been supplying rope, tent cloth, and material for uniforms to the Confederate army. Some four hundred Roswell mill workers (all women), and other female and male workers from a nearby town, are transported, via several intermediate stops, to Indiana to "prevent them," as Sherman says, "from renewing their efforts on behalf of the Confederacy." Very few of these unwilling deportees will ever find their way back to Georgia; some will settle in the North; others will die there.[49]

JULY 9, 1864: Having driven on after his defeat at Kennesaw Mountain, William T. Sherman has outflanked Joseph Johnston and pushed the Confederates back to a position only four miles from downtown Atlanta. Progress has been slow thus far, and the road ahead promises to be even more difficult. "The whole country is one vast fort," Sherman writes to General Henry Halleck, "and Johnston must have at least fifty miles of connected trenches, with abattis [field defenses] and finished batteries." Despite these extensive fortifications, with the large Union army at their gates, citizens of Atlanta begin leaving. Meanwhile, President Davis, increasingly distressed at what he deems Johnston's insufficient aggressiveness against the encroaching Yankees, sends his military adviser, Braxton Bragg, to Georgia on a fact-finding mission; Bragg will recommend to the president that Johnston be replaced. *At the Monocacy River near Frederick, Maryland,* Jubal Early's thirteen thousand Confederate troops, now heading toward Washington, DC, meet a hastily assembled Federal force led by Major General Lew Wallace (who will achieve postwar literary fame with his novel *Ben-Hur*). Except for a contingent of battle-hardened troops (the vanguard of reinforcements Grant has sent north from Petersburg to help protect the capital), the six thousand Federals who engage the invading Confederates at the battle of Monocacy are predominantly inexperienced and no match for Early's larger force of combat veterans. But before Wallace orders his men to withdraw, his troops do manage, at a cost of more than eighteen hundred casualties, to buy valuable

Major General Horatio G. Wright (1820–1899), USA. In command of the Sixth Corps of the Army of the Potomac, which relieved Washington when the capital was threatened by Jubal Early's Confederates, Wright respectfully but firmly curbed President Lincoln's enthusiasm for viewing the enemy at Fort Stevens. After the war, as chief of army engineers, Wright was involved in completing the Washington Monument.

JULY

1 2 3 4 5 6 7 8 9 **10 11 12** 13 14 15 16 17 18 19 20 21 22 23 24 25 26 27 28 29 30 31

time. As Early pushes on toward Washington, his troops do not treat Yankee property gently. Among the dwellings they ransack and destroy is the Silver Spring, Maryland, home of Postmaster General Montgomery Blair. When they begin the same process in the nearby home of Blair's parents, however, they are stopped by one of their officers, General John C. Breckinridge, toward whom the elder Blairs had acted with great kindness before the war. Breckinridge will leave a note on the elder Blairs' mantel: "a confederate officer, for himself & all his comrades, regrets exceedingly that damage & pilfering was committed in this house."[50]

JULY 10, 1864: Federal authorities and the tense people of Washington continue to prepare for unwanted Confederate callers as refugee civilians from outlying areas pour into the capital city. Militia, ambulatory soldiers convalescing in Washington's hospitals, and government clerks are armed and sent to the forts defending the capital. President Lincoln, who remains an island of calm in this furious sea of activity, takes time from pressing military matters to wend through the streets in an open carriage with Secretary of War Stanton, in an effective effort to prevent panic. Morale rises considerably when the main body of the reinforcements Grant has dispatched from Petersburg, Major General Horatio Wright's Sixth Corps, arrives in the city. Crowds rush to the wharves to cheer the blue-coated soldiers as they debark from their naval transports.[51]

JULY 11–12, 1864: Now on the outskirts of Washington, within sight of the U.S. Capitol's recently completed cast-iron dome, Jubal Early and his thirteen thousand Confederates survey the city's fortifications, which Early will later report are "exceedingly strong." But having come this far, he refuses to withdraw without militarily thumbing his nose at the enemy. He sends a detachment to attack Fort Stevens, only five miles from the White House, and they keep its defenders busy for two days. On both, the U.S. commander in chief is present, evincing, as Horatio Wright will report, "a remarkable coolness and disregard of danger." Too great a disregard, for some: when Lincoln, wearing his trademark stovepipe hat, keeps popping up to get a good look at the Confederates over the defenses, an irritated young officer (and future U.S. Supreme Court justice), Captain Oliver Wendell Holmes Jr., not realizing who the offending civilian is, shouts, "Get down, you damn fool, before you get shot!" General Wright expresses his own concern for the chief executive's safety by respectfully threatening to have Lincoln removed under guard if he doesn't stop exposing himself to enemy fire. "In consideration of my earnestness in the matter," Wright will report, "[Lincoln] agreed to compromise by sitting behind the parapet instead of standing upon it." The danger is very real; some nine hundred men on both sides are killed or wounded in the fighting around Fort Stevens before the irascible Early withdraws toward the Shenandoah Valley, declaring to one of his officers (with only partial accuracy), "We didn't take Washington, but we scared Abe Lincoln like hell!"[52]

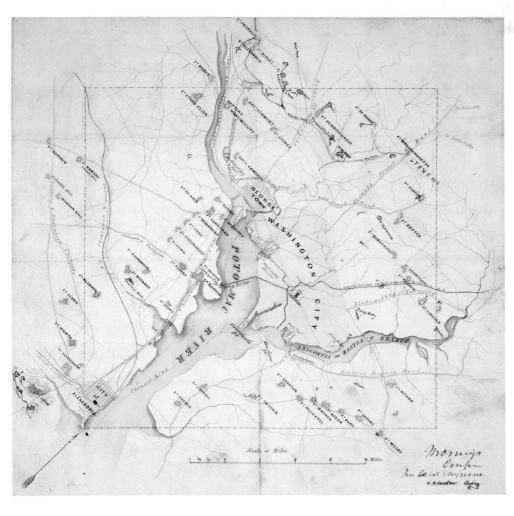

ABOVE: *Confederate General John Bell Hood.* Pencil drawing on olive paper by Alfred R. Waud, between 1862 and 1865. Known for his aggressive leadership, Hood (1831–1879) was appointed by President Davis to replace General Joe Johnston at Atlanta, as William T. Sherman's Federals closed in on the city.

LEFT: *Washington, D.C., and Forts.* Color map by R. K. Sneden, circa 1863. Fort Stevens, where President Lincoln came under Confederate fire, can be seen in the upper right of the map.

JULY

1 2 3 4 5 6 7 8 9 10 11 12 13 **14** 15 16 **17** **18** 19 **20** 21 22 23 24 25 26 27 28 29 30 31

JULY 14, 1864: At Tupelo, Mississippi, eight thousand Confederates under Lieutenant General Stephen D. Lee and Major General Nathan Bedford Forrest engage the fourteen-thousand-man Union force William T. Sherman dispatched to smash Forrest (see July 5, 1864). Confederate assaults on Andrew Smith's Federals are disjointed, however, and the Union troops repel them, inflicting many casualties, including Forrest, who is wounded. Finally, Lee orders a withdrawal. Although Sherman will not be happy that Smith fails to follow and destroy the Rebel force, Smith's victory at the battle of Tupelo does at least give Sherman temporary relief from the fear that Forrest will sever his railroad supply line.[53]

JULY 17, 1864: "As you have failed to arrest the advance of the enemy to the vicinity of Atlanta, far in the interior of Georgia, and express no confidence that you can defeat or repel him," President Davis writes to General Joseph Johnston, "you are hereby relieved from the command of the Army and Department of Tennessee." Following the recommendation of his military adviser, General Braxton Bragg (see July 9, 1864), Davis replaces Johnston with General John Bell Hood. The action will stir controversy in the Confederacy but will please General Sherman, who believes that Hood will come out and fight in the open, something Johnston would not do.[54]

JULY 18, 1864: President Lincoln issues a new call, for five hundred thousand men. Coming just after Jubal Early's raid

into Maryland, and in the midst of the costly stalemate in Virginia and Sherman's slow progress at Atlanta, it is an unpopular plea that sets his prospects for reelection in November even lower. *In Niagara Falls, Canada,* editor Horace Greeley (who will be joined in two days by Lincoln's secretary, John Hay) opens negotiations with Confederate agents Clement Clay and James Holcombe (see July 5, 1864). Greeley and Hay will convey to the agents a presidential safe conduct for travel to Washington to discuss peace, as long as the proposition conveyed by the agents, Lincoln states in the safe conduct, "comes by and with an authority that can control the armies now at war against the United States," and providing the peace under discussion guarantees "the integrity of the whole Union, and the abandonment of slavery." But, as Greeley had suspected, the agents are not empowered to negotiate — and the Davis administration is only prepared to discuss a peace that will maintain Confederate independence and slavery. The failure of this Canadian encounter will become a potent piece of anti-Lincoln propaganda.[55]

JULY 20, 1864: The new Confederate commander at Atlanta, General John Bell Hood, fulfills William T. Sherman's expectations (and those of President Davis) and launches an attack on Major General George H. Thomas's Army of the Cumberland, beginning the battle of Peachtree Creek. Led by Lieutenant General William J. Hardee, the spirited Confederate assault lacks coordination and fails in the

A scene from **The Myriopticon: A Historical Panorama of the Rebellion,** manufactured by Milton Bradley & Co. before 1890. Turning the wheel inserted in the box changes the scenes and gives viewers a primitive "motion picture" account of the Civil War. Here, an anonymous Union officer succumbs to enemy fire, but his men continue their assault — something that happened during the battle of Atlanta, a Union victory despite the death of Major General James B. McPherson.

Major General James B. McPherson (1828–1864), USA. Steel engraving published in *Commanders of the Army of the Tennessee,* 1884. Regarded as one of the most promising young officers in the army after his 1853 graduation from West Point, McPherson proved to be an excellent wartime battlefield commander. His death was deeply mourned by his men, and by his friend and commanding officer, William T. Sherman.

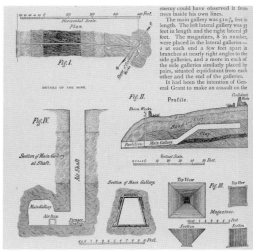

Diagram of the tunnel dug by Union troops led by Lieutenant Colonel Henry Pleasants. Illustration in "The Tragedy of the Crater," published in *Century* magazine, volume 34, 1887.

face of equally spirited Union resistance. The Confederates pay a high price for this failure: 4,796 of Hardee's 19,000-man force are killed or wounded versus 1,710 of the 21,000 Federal soldiers engaged.[56]

JULY 22, 1864: Undaunted by his army's failure at the battle of Peachtree Creek, General John B. Hood launches another attack, this time focusing his efforts on the Army of the Tennessee, led by Major General James B. McPherson, Hood's former West Point roommate. Hitting McPherson's men when they are less than three miles from the city, Hood ignites the battle of Atlanta, a day of fierce fighting that badly shakes the Federals; but it does not break them — even after the Army of the Tennessee loses its commander. Riding forward to deal with a gap in Union lines, McPherson is killed by Confederate skirmishers — becoming one of thirty-seven hundred Federals and eight thousand Confederates killed or wounded in this bloody encounter that is another costly failure for Hood.[57]

JULY 23, 1864: Lieutenant Colonel Henry Pleasants and the coal miners of the Forty-eighth Pennsylvania Infantry finish the tunnel they have been digging under the Confederate lines at Petersburg, Virginia (see June 25, 1864). Extending 525 feet, the tunnel has two side galleries, which, on June 27, Pleasants and his men will start packing with twenty-five-pound kegs of gunpowder.[58]

JULY 24, 1864: Having largely eluded the Union troops that followed him from Washington (see July 11–12, 1864), whose pursuit was hampered, General Grant will later report, by "constant and contrary orders . . . from Washington," Jubal Early and his Army of Northern Virginia Second Corps rout eighty-five hundred Federals at the second battle of Kernstown, near Winchester, Virginia. Once again, the lower Shenandoah Valley is open to the Confederates and Early heads north, toward the Potomac.[59]

JULY 28, 1864: At the battle of Ezra Church, outside Atlanta, John B. Hood's Confederates stop a Union attempt to cut Atlanta's last railroad supply line — but they suffer 5,000 casualties in the process (versus the Union's 562). Combined with the losses sustained at the battles of Peachtree Creek and Atlanta, this so weakens Hood's army that the general will be forced henceforth to remain on the defensive.[60]

JULY 30, 1864: Brigadier General John McCausland and twenty-six hundred cavalry dispatched from Jubal Early's force arrive at Chambersburg in southern Pennsylvania with Early's demand for $100,000 in gold or $500,000 in greenbacks as compensation for property David Hunter's Union troops destroyed in the Shenandoah Valley (see June 11–12, 1864). After Chambersburg citizens refuse to pay, McCausland's troopers set fire to the town, destroying some four hundred buildings and leaving nearly three hundred families without

Colonel Delevan Bates at "The Crater" (Petersburg). Illustration in *Deeds of Valor*, Volume 1, 1901–1902.
Commander of the Thirtieth U.S. Colored Infantry, Bates was wounded in the head as he led his troops into what
was described as "a perfect maelstrom of rebel lead." Ten officers and 212 enlisted men of this regiment alone
were killed, wounded, or taken prisoner during the bitter fighting at the Crater.

AUGUST

1 2 3 **4** 5 6 7 8 9 10 11 12 13 14 15 16 17 18 19 20 21 22 23 24 25 26 27 28 29 30 31

homes. Within a few days, General Grant will form a new military force, the Army of the Shenandoah, and place Major General Phil Sheridan at its head. Sheridan's objectives: first, to destroy Early's army; second, to destroy the fertile valley's capacity to be the "Breadbasket of the Confederacy" (feeding among others, Lee's army at Petersburg and guerrillas operating in the valley). "Take all provisions, forage and stock wanted for the use of your command," Grant orders Sheridan. "Such as cannot be consumed, destroy," leaving the area so deprived that "crows flying over it . . . will have to carry their provender with them." *At Petersburg,* Lieutenant Colonel Pleasants's inspired plan for breaching Confederate defenses (see June 25 and July 23, 1864) reaches its climax as four tons of gunpowder placed in the finished tunnel explodes in a lethal fountain of red sand, earth, and Rebel fortifications. The blast kills or wounds nearly three hundred Confederates, creates a huge gap in the Petersburg defenses, and gouges a crater, 30 feet deep and 170 feet long, in the ground over which Union troops are set to attack. That assault devolves into a misdirected muddle during which many Federal troops tumble into the crater rather than go around it and are trapped in murderous Confederate musket and mortar fire. The subsequent Rebel counterattack is one of the earliest occasions "on which any of the Army of Northern Virginia came in contact with Negro troops," Confederate brigadier general Porter Alexander will later write, "and the general feeling of the men toward their employment was very bitter." The fighting turns vicious. "This

day was the jubilee of fiends in human shape, and without souls," one Rebel soldier will say. Federal casualties are high, particularly among black soldiers, some of whom are killed as they try to surrender. Grant will call the abortive battle of the Crater "the saddest affair I have witnessed in the war."[61]

AUGUST 1864

AUGUST 1, 1864: The Confederate legislative act of February 17, 1864, which renewed President Davis's authority to suspend the writ of habeas corpus, expires. Despite intensifying Union pressure and the growing influence of Southern peace societies, the Confederate Congress will never again give Davis the authority to suspend the writ.[62]

AUGUST 4, 1864: The London *Times* carries a dispatch from its Richmond-based correspondent, Francis Lawley, who has lately been impressed by the relative calm of the Confederate capital: "If a man were landed here from a balloon after six months' absence . . . and told that two enormous armies are lying a few miles off and disputing its possession, he would deem his informant a lunatic. . . . Richmond trusts and believes in St. Lee as much as Mecca in Mahomet." Lawley seems to

ABOVE: *Lashed to the Shrouds—Farragut Passing the Forts at Mobile, in His Flagship Hartford.* Color lithograph published by L. Prang & Co., 1870–1871. The highest-ranking officer in the Union navy during the war, Farragut led his fleet to victory through a minefield and intense Confederate fire, closing the port of Mobile to Rebel shipping.

RIGHT: Abraham Lincoln. Memorandum, August 23, 1864. Convinced that it was probable that he would be defeated in the November 1864 presidential election, Lincoln wrote this pledge, folded it, and had his cabinet sign the memorandum without reading it.

AUGUST

1 2 3 4 **5** 6 7 8 9 10 11 12 13 14 15 16 17 18 **19** 20 21 22 **23** 24 25 26 27 28 **29 30 31**

share this faith. Lee, he states, has the initiative "now that his hardy antagonist lay foiled, baffled, and emasculated before him."[63]

AUGUST 5, 1864: Admiral David Farragut, Union hero at New Orleans and veteran of Mississippi River combat, again reflects his personal motto of "Audacity, still more audacity, always audacity" as he leads his Union fleet of fourteen wooden ships and four ironclads into Mobile Bay. Serving Mobile, Alabama, the last blockade-running port in the Gulf of Mexico east of Texas, the bay is guarded by the formidable Fort Morgan and a small naval contingent of three gunboats and the ironclad CSS *Tennessee,* captained by Admiral Franklin Buchanan (see March 8, 1862). It is also laced with underwater mines, called torpedoes. Undaunted, the admiral climbs to a vantage point on a mast of his flagship USS *Hartford* and, shouting "Damn the torpedoes, full speed ahead," he leads his fleet in a duel with the fort and Buchanan's *Tennessee*. At a cost of 145 Union lives, including 93 men on USS *Tecumseh,* which strikes a torpedo and founders, Farragut's fleet takes the fort and the bay, closing the port of Mobile to all shipping (though Mobile itself will continue to hold out; see March 24–25, 1865).[64]

AUGUST 19, 1864: President Lincoln meets with Frederick Douglass, chiefly concerning the effects the current "mad cry" for peace might have on people still held as slaves. The meeting

is a revelation for Douglass, who has often been critical of the president's actions. "The President is a most remarkable man," he will report. "I am satisfied now that he is doing all that circumstances will permit him to do." For his part, the president will tell Union chaplain and commissioner of contrabands John Eaton that, "considering the conditions from which Douglass rose, and the position to which he had attained, he was . . . one of the most meritorious men in America."[65]

AUGUST 23, 1864: The lack of clear Union military victories; adverse reaction to the peace negotiations in Canada, particularly Lincoln's condition that peace will require "abandonment of slavery" (see July 5 and 18, 1864); and intimations from political informants of a movement to replace him as presidential candidate inspire Lincoln to write a memorandum committing his administration to a course of action should its time in office be ending: "It seems exceedingly probable that this Administration will not be re-elected. Then it will be my duty to so co-operate with the President elect, as to save the Union between the election and the inauguration; as he will have secured his election on such ground that he can not possibly save it afterwards." He asks cabinet members to sign this "blind memorandum" without having read it, and they comply.[66]

AUGUST 29–31, 1864: Thousands of excited Democrats gather in Chicago for their national convention, which, on

"The Heavens Are Hung in Black"

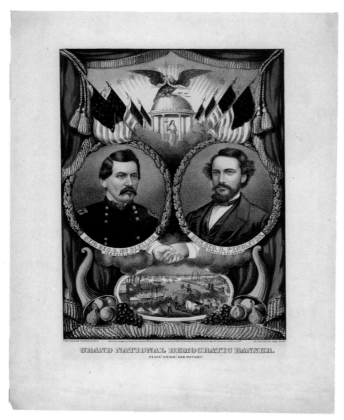

Grand National Democratic Banner. Peace! Union! And Victory!
Lithograph with watercolor, published by Currier & Ives, 1864. Meeting in Chicago, the Democrats chose former Union general in chief George B. McClellan as their presidential candidate and Ohio congressman George H. Pendleton as his running mate.

A Union wagon train viewed across the railroad track on Whitehall Street, in Atlanta, Georgia. Photograph by George N. Barnard, 1864. Sherman's conquest of Atlanta greatly enhanced Lincoln's chances of reelection—and gave Sherman's weary troops a base for resting and accumulating supplies.

SEPTEMBER

1 **2** 3 **4** **5** 6 7 8 9 10 11 12 13 14 15 16 17 18 19 20 21 22 23 24 25 26 27 28 29 30

August 31, will nominate Major General George B. McClellan for president on a platform that is for immediate negotiations for peace (almost certainly leaving the nation divided) and against emancipation. Ohio Peace Democrat George H. Pendleton will complete the ticket as vice presidential candidate. In the background, a plot to stir a Northern uprising from the excitement of the convention, hatched earlier between Copperheads and Confederates in Canada, fails to ignite when the seventy armed Confederate agents who show up in Chicago fail to find the anticipated number of eager Copperhead conspirators.[67]

SEPTEMBER 1864

SEPTEMBER 2, 1864: Having cut the last railroad into the city and bested Hood's forces in two final encounters, General William T. Sherman wires Washington: "Atlanta is ours, and fairly won." In the North spirits soar at this great land victory coming just a month after Farragut's triumph in Mobile Bay (see August 5, 1864). Celebratory cannons boom; Sherman is dubbed the greatest general since Napoleon; and Lincoln's reelection, considered unlikely until the telegram arrives, suddenly looks possible. In the South, Mary Boykin Chesnut will

reflect the gloom induced by the news when she confides to her diary: "Since Atlanta I have felt as if all were dead within me, forever. We are going to be wiped off the earth."[68]

SEPTEMBER 4, 1864: Confederate brigadier general John Hunt Morgan, who led a spectacular 1863 cavalry raid that penetrated deep into Northern territory (see July 2 and November 27, 1863), is killed in an encounter with Union cavalry at Greeneville, Tennessee. He will be given a state funeral in Richmond (an event that will be interrupted when participating military units have to rush off to reinforce Lee's lines against an attempted Federal incursion).[69]

SEPTEMBER 5, 1864: "I have deemed it to the interest of the United States that the citizens now residing in Atlanta should remove, those who prefer it to go South and the rest North." With those words, General Sherman precipitates the evacuation of Atlanta by civilians who had remained during the siege. Given five days to comply (with trains made available to those who wish to go north), nearly sixteen hundred people leave behind their homes, most of their possessions, and terrible resentments that are echoed by outcries against the action in the Confederate press. "War is cruelty and you cannot refine it," Sherman will say to Atlanta's mayor after giving the order. "When peace does come," he adds, "you may call on me for anything. Then will I share with you the last cracker."[70]

LEFT: *Interior View of the Hospital.* Illustration in *Life and Death in Rebel Prisons: Giving a Complete History of the Inhuman and Barbarous Treatment of our Brave Soldiers by Rebel Authorities, Inflicting Terrible Suffering and Frightful Mortality, Principally at Andersonville, Ga., and Florence, S.C.,* by Robert H. Kellogg, 1866.

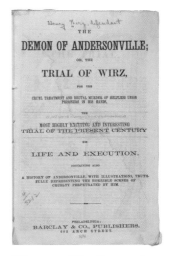

Title page of *The Demon of Andersonville; or, the Trial of Wirz, for the Cruel Treatment and Brutal Murder of Helpless Union Prisoners in His Hands,* 1865. As unprecedented numbers of troops fell into enemy hands, both Confederate and Union captives suffered under prison conditions. Henry Wirz commanded what became the most infamous Civil War prison camp. Designed for ten thousand men, by August 1864, Andersonville held more than thirty-three thousand.

Cattle Raid. Pencil and Chinese white drawing on green paper by Alfred R. Waud, September 16, 1864. In an inscription accompanying the drawing (not shown), Waud wrote that Wade Hampton and his men "suddenly appeared at Coggins point in the rear of the [Union] army [of the Potomac] . . . and carried off the entire beef supply. . . . The rebel soldiers were much inclined to joke with the pickets on the loss of their meat rations; the Union men, on the other hand, thanked them heartily for removing the tough remnant of herds that had been driven behind the army all summer and which were at once replaced by a fresh stock."

SEPTEMBER

1 2 3 4 5 6 **7** **8** 9 10 11 12 13 **14** 15 16 17 **18** 19 20 21 22 23 24 25 26 27 28 29 30

SEPTEMBER 7, 1864: Sherman's success at Atlanta and a fear of Union raids lead authorities at the Andersonville prison camp to begin transferring ambulatory prisoners to other parts of the state. Many of the men transferred, including secret diarist John Ransom (see February 27, 1864), are in terrible physical condition, a result of overcrowding, disease, and insufficient food. Although conditions are far from ideal in many military prisons, North and South, Andersonville will become a symbol of particular cruelty to people in the Union. Its commandant, Swiss-born Henry (Heinrich) Wirz, will become the only Civil War figure tried for what will later be deemed war crimes. Wirz will be executed on November 10, 1865.[71]

SEPTEMBER 8, 1864: In the wake of the Union victories at Mobile Bay and Atlanta (see August 5 and September 2, 1864) and the resulting surge in Union morale — and because of his own personal inclination and political judgment — George B. McClellan includes wording that effectively repudiates the crucial "peace plank" in the 1864 party platform when he publishes his letter officially accepting the Democratic nomination for president: "I could not look in the faces of gallant comrades of the army and navy . . . and tell them that their labor and the sacrifice of our slain and wounded brethren had been in vain. . . . The Union is the one condition of peace — we ask no more." Far from pleased, Peace Democrats will briefly consider agitating to replace McClellan with another nominee; but they will decide against it.[72]

SEPTEMBER 14, 1864: Informed by a scout that a huge herd of cattle is lightly guarded by Union troops six miles south of Union headquarters at City Point, Virginia, Major General Wade Hampton leads some four thousand Army of Northern Virginia cavalrymen on a mission to ease the food shortages Lee's soldiers are suffering in the Petersburg trenches. After traveling by a circuitous route to confuse any Federal observers, Hampton and his men pounce on the surprised Union cowherds on September 16, killing, wounding, or capturing more than two hundred while suffering sixty-one casualties themselves. Fighting off Federal pursuers, they successfully abscond with 2,468 head of cattle, one of the largest rustling capers in American history. "They are certainly the greatest sight in the way of cattle that I ever saw," a delighted South Carolina soldier exclaims when the beeves arrive in Confederate lines. Judiciously distributed, the rustled cattle will provide meat for Lee's army for almost a month — and the cattle hides will be used for much-needed footgear.[73]

SEPTEMBER 18, 1864: Voters in Maryland approve the new state constitution drafted by a constitutional convention that met from April 27 to September 6, 1864. The constitution, which will go into effect on November 1, 1864, abolishes slavery in the state. *In camp near Petersburg, Virginia,* Union soldier David Lane, of the Seventeenth Michigan Volunteer Infantry, reacts in his diary to reports he has received from his wife about some Northerners' passion for peace at any cost:

"The Heavens Are Hung in Black"

Major General Wade Hampton (1818–1902), CSA. Trained as a lawyer, the wealthy South Carolina plantation owner became one of only three Confederates to attain the rank of lieutenant general (1865) without any formal military training.

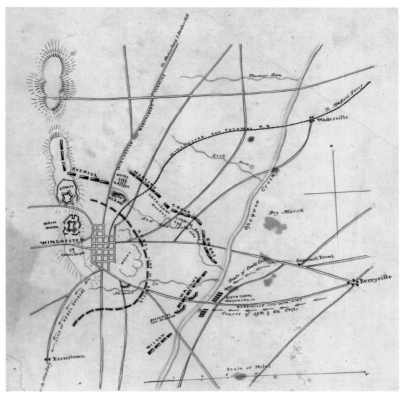

Sketch of the Battle of Winchester, September 19, 1864. Pen-and-ink, pencil, and color pencil map by Jedediah Hotchkiss, 1864. After this first major encounter between the newly formed Union Army of the Shenandoah and Jubal Early's Confederate troops, Major General Sheridan was able to report to General in Chief Grant that his troops had bested the Confederates and sent them "whirling through Winchester."

Montgomery Blair (1813–1883). A respected lawyer and thoughtful presidential adviser, Blair was replaced as Lincoln's postmaster general in the months approaching the presidential election to help heal rifts in the Republican Party. "In parting with Blair," Secretary of the Navy Gideon Welles wrote in his diary, "the President parts with a true friend."

I would like to tell it so that all our friends might hear . . . that we, the soldiers in the army, hold in contempt the man who would accept peace on any other terms than submission to law. We have fought too long; have suffered too much; too many precious lives have been lost, to falter now. The Rebels themselves acknowledge all their hopes are based on a divided North; they are straining every nerve to hold out until after the fall elections, hoping their friends may triumph.[74]

SEPTEMBER 19, 1864: Rebel privateer and special agent John Yates Beall leads a group of Confederates who have taken refuge in Canada on a Great Lakes piracy raid, seizing and plundering two ships on Lake Erie, scuttling one and setting the other adrift, before heading back to Canada. Though insignificant, the raid feeds growing rumors of Rebel conspiracies to release Confederate prisoners held in the North and commit other assaults on Northern soil. *In the Confederate Trans-Mississippi Department,* Texan, Cherokee, and Seminole units led by Brigadier General Richard M. Gano and the Cherokee leader Brigadier General Stand Watie are victorious in the second battle of Cabin Creek in the Indian Territory. Capturing a large Union wagon train and evading pursuit, they make away with an estimated $1.5 million in Federal supplies. *As this occurs,* Confederate major general Sterling Price leads twelve thousand Rebels out of Princeton, Arkansas, beginning what will become known as Price's Missouri Raid. Dogged by

Union pursuers and destroying sections of railroad as they go, Price's men will engage in almost constant skirmishing as they enter Missouri, causing state authorities to mobilize thousands of militia. *In the Shenandoah Valley,* Phil Sheridan's new Union Army of the Shenandoah (see July 30, 1864) has its first major encounter with Jubal Early's Confederates at the third battle of Winchester, Virginia. Outnumbered nearly three to one, the Confederates resist stubbornly — until Union cavalry get beyond their left flank and charge, shattering their ranks. Although he has made some potentially disastrous tactical errors during the battle, Sheridan is able to report to Grant that he has sent Early's forces "whirling through Winchester."[75]

SEPTEMBER 22, 1864: Sheridan's Federals clash with Early's Confederates again at the battle of Fisher's Hill, where the Rebel lines are spread too thin to resist Union assaults on their front, flank, and rear. Sheridan's victory here leaves the northern Shenandoah Valley clear of all but Union troops and — along with the victory at Winchester — provides another boost to Lincoln's reelection prospects.[76]

SEPTEMBER 24, 1864: "You have generously said to me more than once, that whenever your resignation could be a relief to me, it was at my disposal," President Lincoln writes to Postmaster General Montgomery Blair. "The time has come." It has come, almost certainly because of the fast approaching elections; Blair has long been an irritant to Radical

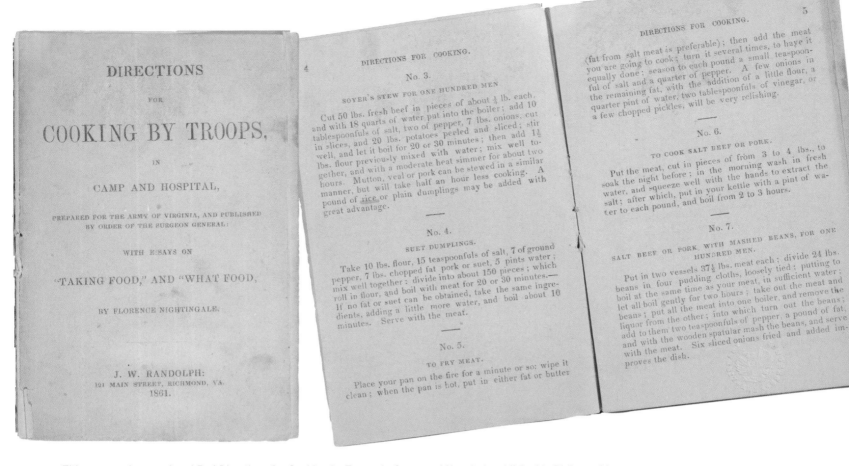

Title page and pages 4 and 5 of *Directions for Cooking by Troops in Camp and Hospital,* published in Richmond in 1861. The recipes on page five are for meat preserved with salt, a commodity sufficiently important to inspire a Union raid on Saltville in southwestern Virginia in October 1864.

Republicans, particularly supporters of John Frémont. Lincoln will immediately appoint former Ohio governor William Dennison to replace Blair.[77]

SEPTEMBER 25, 1864: On this rainy Sunday, a tired and careworn Jefferson Davis arrives at General John Bell Hood's new headquarters at Palmetto, Georgia, southwest of Union-occupied Atlanta. The mood in the camp is somber: some officers criticize Hood; and the men in the ranks, though respectful, do not cheer the president as he rides past their ranks in review. Discussing strategy, Davis agrees with Hood's plan to move his army into northern Georgia, hoping to draw Sherman away from Atlanta; should Sherman turn south, Hood will turn and pursue. Not long after Davis moves on to Montgomery, Alabama (where he will meet with the Department of Alabama and Mississippi commander, Lieutenant General Richard Taylor), Sherman will become aware of Hood's movement north. Fearing for the safety of his railroad supply line, Sherman will leave one corps in Atlanta and lead the balance of his army in pursuit of Hood.[78]

SEPTEMBER 27, 1864: At Fort Davidson, near Pilot Knob, Missouri, Confederate General Sterling Price's invading troops are dealt their first major defeat by General Thomas Ewing's Federals — even as infamous guerrilla "Bloody Bill" Anderson's men are massacring unarmed and wounded Union soldiers and militia during an encounter at Centralia. Price had entered Missouri with the intent of bringing it, finally and actually, into the Confederacy (and by doing so, ensuring the election of Democratic U.S. presidential candidate George B. McClellan). By the end of October, after his defeat at the battle of Westport (October 23), Price will have been driven from the state, Bloody Bill Anderson will be dead, and organized Confederate resistance in Missouri will be at an end (though guerrilla activity in the state will continue).[79]

OCTOBER 1864

OCTOBER 2, 1864: Dispatched to Tennessee by General Sherman, Major General George H. Thomas arrives in Nashville to take charge of the defense of the state against a possible incursion by General Hood's Confederates. *In southwestern Virginia,* some thirty-six hundred Union troops under Brigadier General Stephen G. Burbridge, including four hundred black soldiers of the Fifth U.S. Colored Cavalry, attack twenty-eight hundred Confederate troops at Saltville, the source of the salt without which beef cannot be preserved to feed Robert E. Lee's hungry troops. Protected by stone and log barricades, the Rebels repeatedly repulse the Federal assaults — although a charge by black cavalrymen temporarily

Sheridan's Ride. Chromolithograph of a painting by Thure de Thulstrup (1848–1930). Major General Phil Sheridan's pell-mell ride back to Cedar Creek, where his troops had been badly shaken by a Confederate attack, was the catalyst not only for visual art but also for a seven-stanza poem by Thomas Buchanan Read: "The heart of the steed and the heart of the master / Were beating like prisoners assaulting their walls, / Impatient to be where the battle-field calls."

OCTOBER

1 2 3 **4 5 6 7** 8 9 10 11 **12** 13 14 15 16 17 **18 19** 20 21 22 23 24 25 26 27 28 29 30 31

pushes some Rebels back. During the battle and its aftermath, Confederates murder a number of black soldiers, including the wounded, who fall into their hands.[80]

OCTOBER 4–7, 1864: One hundred forty-four African Americans representing eighteen states, including seven slave states, assemble in Syracuse, New York, for a National Convention of Colored Citizens of the United States, where they organize a National Equal Rights League, with freeborn Ohio attorney John Mercer Langston as president. In an Address to the People of the United States, authored by Frederick Douglass, the convention will declare: "We believe that the highest welfare of this great country will be found in erasing from its statute-books all enactments discriminating in favor of or against any class of its people, and by establishing one law for the white and colored people alike." The National Equal Rights League will quickly spawn auxiliaries to work for equal rights and opportunities at the state level.[81]

OCTOBER 7, 1864: In the harbor at Bahia, Brazil, the Union deals with another notorious Confederate commerce raider. CSS *Florida* has captured thirty-seven U.S. vessels, including *Jacob Bell,* worth, with its cargo, an estimated $1.5 million, the most valuable prize taken by the Rebels. *Florida*'s captain, Lieutenant Charles M. Morris, believes that international law protects *Florida* from U.S. action in the waters of neutral Brazil. Commander Napoleon Collins, captain of the Union

sloop *Wachusett,* also moored in the harbor, has an altogether different opinion. In the wee hours of the morning, his vessel rams *Florida,* captures it, tows it out to sea, and returns it to U.S. waters — where it is rammed again and sunk. The U.S. government will apologize to the government of Brazil for this highly questionable action.[82]

OCTOBER 12, 1864: Chief Justice Roger Taney, 88, dies at his home in Maryland. "Already (before his poor old clay is cold), they are beginning to canvass vigorously for his successor," President Lincoln's secretary, John Hay, will note in his diary the following day. "[Salmon] Chase men say the place is promised to their *magnifico.*" One Chase supporter, sharp-tongued Massachusetts abolitionist Charles Sumner, will write to Lincoln, calling Taney's death "a victory for Liberty & for the Constitution. Thus far the Constitution has been interpreted for Slavery. Thank God! It may now be interpreted surely for Liberty." Yet as Hay writes in his diary, Lincoln "does not think he will make the appointment immediately." The presidential election is less than a month away, its outcome far from certain, and political prudence dictates Lincoln's biding his time in naming a new chief justice.[83]

OCTOBER 18–19, 1864: On his quest to crush Jubal Early in Virginia's Shenandoah Valley, Phil Sheridan rides into legend at the battle of Cedar Creek. After achieving victories at Winchester and Fisher's Hill (see September 19 and 22, 1864),

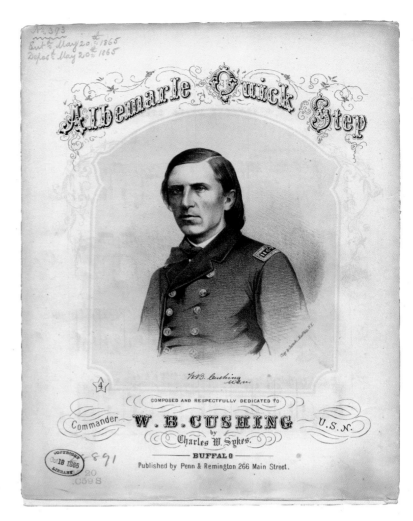

ABOVE: Lieutenant Commander James Iredell Waddell (1824–1886), CSN. A U.S. Naval Academy graduate, Waddell served in the U.S. East Indian Squadron before resigning to join the Confederate navy. Concerned that he and his crew would be arrested for destroying U.S. whaling ships after the war had officially ended (at sea, he did not receive definitive word of the surrender of Confederate armies for months), Waddell sailed his ship *Shenandoah* to Britain, completing a circumnavigation of the globe.

RIGHT: Cover of the sheet music for *Albemarle Quick Step,* composed by Charles W. Sykes, 1865, featuring the likeness of William B. Cushing (1842–1874), USN, for whom the piece was composed and to whom it is "respectfully dedicated." Cushing led the daring raid that finally sank the fearsome Confederate ram CSS *Albemarle* near Plymouth, North Carolina, on October 27, 1864.

OCTOBER

1 2 3 4 5 6 7 8 9 10 11 12 13 14 15 16 17 18 **19** **20** 21 22 23 24 25 26 **27** 28 29 30 31

Sheridan has departed his camp for a strategy conference in Washington when Early attacks so unexpectedly that the army Sheridan has left securely encamped begins a pell-mell retreat. Sheridan's return to the front on his warhorse Rienzi helps turn the morning's humiliating defeat into an afternoon of overwhelming victory — and it generates a patriotic poem, "Sheridan's Ride," that is a pre-election rouser in the North. The Union is now firmly in control of the Shenandoah Valley — and the area is showing the effects of the "hard war" policy Grant has directed Sheridan to embrace (see July 30, 1864). "It is a sad sight to see this beautiful valley desolated as it is," Confederate soldier Richard Habersham will write in November. "All along the route from Staunton to this place, barns are leveled to the ground, stock wantonly destroyed, and horses by the hundred lying scattered over the fields or stretched off on the roadside either killed in Early's last fight or died and left unburied."[84]

OCTOBER 19, 1864: Lieutenant Bennett H. Young and twenty-five disguised Confederate soldiers briefly bring Civil War action to St. Albans, Vermont. Descending the fifteen miles from Canada, they rob three town banks, killing one resisting Vermonter and wounding others, before recrossing the border with some $200,000. Although this is part of a larger plan to pillage a number of Northern towns, the raiders are quickly arrested by Canadian authorities. (They are subsequently tried and set free; St. Albans will recover about $75,000 of its stolen money.) *At the Madeira Archipelago, off Portugal,* the

last of the Southern commerce raiders, CSS *Shenandoah,* enters Confederate service. Captained by James Iredell Waddell, *Shenandoah* will effectively disrupt the New England whaling fleet in the Pacific through June 1865. Belatedly notified that the war is over, Waddell will then sail *Shenandoah* seventeen thousand miles nonstop to Britain, making his ship the only Confederate vessel to circumnavigate the globe.[85]

OCTOBER 20, 1864: Having followed Hood's Army of Tennessee as it veered into Alabama, Sherman halts his army at Gaylesville. Eight days later, he will begin moving again — back into Georgia. He has decided to take his army farther south, minus forces sent to George H. Thomas to defend Tennessee. In a plan reluctantly approved by Grant, after returning to Atlanta to make preparations, Sherman will lead his troops on a march toward Savannah and the sea.[86]

OCTOBER 27, 1864: Since April 1864, when it sank USS *Southfield* and routed three other Union vessels in the waters off Plymouth, North Carolina, the ironclad CSS *Albemarle* has been a thorn in the U.S. Navy's side. Today, twenty-two-year-old U.S. naval lieutenant William B. Cushing and a crew of seven men set in motion a risky plan of Cushing's own devising. Moving stealthily after dark up the Roanoke River to Plymouth in a specially designed vessel inspired by Confederate torpedo boats, Cushing and his men attack and sink the Rebel ironclad with a torpedo fastened to a spar. "The most of

"The Heavens Are Hung in Black"

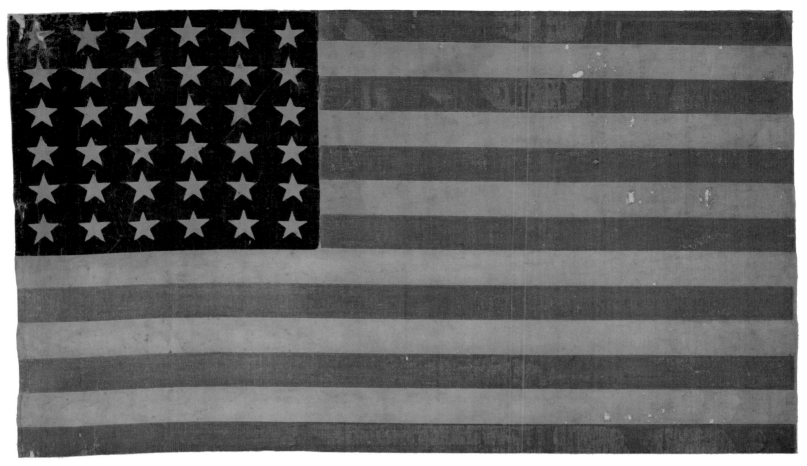

Thirty-six-star United States flag. Color woodcut on linen, between 1865 and 1867. The thirty-sixth star was added to the U.S. flag after the admission of Nevada to the Union on October 31, 1864.

our party were captured, some were drowned, and only one escaped besides myself," Cushing will state in his postaction report. "All the officers and men behaved in the most gallant manner." Without *Albemarle*'s protection, Plymouth will quickly be taken by Union forces.[87]

OCTOBER 29, 1864: African American abolitionist and human rights advocate Sojourner Truth (Isabella Baumfree) and white abolitionist Lucy Colman meet with President Lincoln at the Executive Mansion. Observing the president with a few other civilian petitioners before she speaks with him, Truth is impressed, she will later report, that "he showed as much kindness and consideration to the colored persons as to the white." In Washington to work with the National Freedmen's Relief Association, Truth will show that her dedication to equal rights is matched by a stubborn courage. Shoved and slammed against the door of a streetcar in 1865 by a white conductor who objects to her being on board, she will take the man to court for violating a new District of Columbia statute prohibiting discrimination on those conveyances — and he will lose his job.[88]

OCTOBER 31, 1864: Nevada enters the Union.

NOVEMBER 1864

NOVEMBER 7, 1864: The second session of the Second Congress of the Confederate States convenes in Richmond. The legislators confront, among other matters, a controversial proposal by President Davis that slaves purchased for war work as teamsters and laborers might be freed should they render faithful service. The idea proves less than universally appealing: the *Richmond Whig* will call it "a repudiation of the opinion held by the whole South . . . that servitude is a divinely appointed condition for the highest good of the slave."[89]

NOVEMBER 8, 1864: Election Day in the Union. Renewed confidence in Abraham Lincoln's war policies, instilled by Sherman's victories in Georgia and Sheridan's campaign in the Shenandoah Valley, sweeps Lincoln into office for a second term. Democratic candidate McClellan will characterize his unsuccessful campaign as "a struggle of honor patriotism & truth against deceit selfishness & fanaticism" and declare, "For my country's sake I deplore the result — but the people have decided with their eyes wide open." Many of those open-eyed voters are in Federal uniforms; by election time, nineteen Union states have enacted provisions for soldiers to vote in the field, and among these fighting men, Lincoln wins by a three-to-one margin. "We proposed to fight for peace, not to crawl and beg for it," Corporal Alexander Chisholm will write, explaining his Lincoln vote to his father. The resulting tally, in the army and nationally, elates soldier and Lincoln enthusiast

John Wilkes Booth (1838–1865). Member of a famous family of actors, Booth was a passionate believer in the Confederate cause. After Lincoln's reelection, he wrote a friend, "All hope for peace is dead."

Major General Joseph ("Fightin' Joe") Wheeler (1836–1906), CSA. Commander of the Confederate cavalry in the western theater of operations, Wheeler received the official thanks of the Confederate Congress for an audacious 1863 raid against Federals in Tennessee. With limited resources, he and his men could only harass Sherman's column after it left Atlanta.

The ruins of a depot, blown up by William T. Sherman's troops as they departed from Atlanta, Georgia. Photograph by George Barnard, 1864. Union soldiers went well beyond their orders to destroy everything militarily useful before leaving and wrecked and burned much more, "to the great scandal of our army," wrote a disgusted Federal officer, Orlando M. Poe.

David Lane, who will write in his diary: "The people with a unanimity never equaled, have decided in favor of a united Government. . . . Supported by the moral force of the Nation, [Lincoln] can now proceed, untrammeled, with the great work before him." *At about this same time,* actor and fervent Confederate sympathizer John Wilkes Booth, moved in a wholly other way by Lincoln's reelection, writes to a former friend, John S. Clarke: "For four years have I waited, hoped and prayed, for the dark clouds to break, And for a restoration of our former sunshine, to wait longer would be a crime. All hope for peace is dead, my prayers have proved as idle as my hopes. God's will be done. I go to see, and share the bitter end."[90]

NOVEMBER 14, 1864: Making final preparations to depart from Atlanta, which has been denuded of supplies and equipment, Sherman's men set fire to more than militarily useful buildings, their excess of enthusiasm disgusting Sherman's chief engineer, Captain Orlando M. Poe. There is, he will write, "much destruction of private property by unauthorized persons, to the great scandal of our army and marked detriment of its discipline." Observing from afar, the Confederate western-theater cavalry commander, Major General Joseph ("Fightin' Joe") Wheeler, reports to General Hood that the Yankees are "burning things" in Atlanta. Two days later, Wheeler and his men will follow as Sherman and his sixty-two-thousand-man army (organized in two wings to confuse the enemy) leave the smoldering city behind them and head south. In this "March to

the Sea," undertaken, as Sherman has said, to "demonstrate the vulnerability of the South," the Union troops will travel with a bare minimum of supplies and are to live off the land. Sherman has ordered, however, that his men are to abide by certain rules both when they forage and when they attempt to destroy the area's militarily useful resources:

> In districts and neighborhoods where the army is unmolested, no destruction of such property (as houses, cotton gins, and grist mills) should be permitted; but should guerrillas or bushwhackers molest our march, or should the inhabitants burn bridges, obstruct roads, or otherwise manifest local hostility, then army commanders should order and enforce a devastation more or less relentless, according to the measure of such hostility.

Some of Sherman's subordinates will interpret these orders very broadly.[91]

NOVEMBER 17, 1864: The *New York Times* reports that President Lincoln has accepted Major General George B. McClellan's resignation from the United States Army.[92]

NOVEMBER 30, 1864: Having led his Army of Tennessee out of Georgia and into Tennessee on a quest to secure reinforcements that will allow him to defeat George Thomas's Union army at Nashville, then move on against Grant and Sherman,

"The Heavens Are Hung in Black"

Major General John M. Schofield (1831–1906), USA. An 1853 graduate of West Point (where he later taught philosophy), Schofield commanded the Union force that severely battered John Bell Hood's Confederates at the battle of Franklin, Tennessee.

Here's a Health to the Next One That Dies. Pencil drawing on cream paper by Alfred R. Waud, between 1861 and 1865. From Grant's spring battles in Virginia to Sherman's end-of-the-year campaigns in Georgia, Tennessee, and the Carolinas, 1864 took a heavy toll in soldiers' lives. More than six thousand of the eighty-five hundred casualties in the November 30, 1864, battle of Franklin, Tennessee, were Confederates, including eleven Rebel generals, six of whom were killed, five wounded.

DECEMBER

1 2 **3** 4 5 **6** 7 8 9 10 11 12 13 14 15 16 17 18 19 20 21 22 23 24 25 26 27 28 29 30 31

Confederate general John Bell Hood encounters a Union force under Major General John M. Schofield at the battle of Franklin, Tennessee. Beginning in the afternoon and continuing into the night, the battle features some of the bloodiest fighting of the war, Hood insisting on a disastrous frontal assault on entrenched positions that results in sixty-two hundred casualties. In this bitter Confederate defeat, six Southern generals, including Patrick Cleburne and States Rights Gist, are among the Confederate dead; five other Rebel generals are wounded, and another is captured. (Union casualties are comparatively light.) As Schofield's men withdraw to George H. Thomas's lines at Nashville, Hood decides to pursue, despite the damage his army has suffered. His battered force will entrench four miles south of the city.[93]

DECEMBER 1864

DECEMBER 1, 1864: Major General George Stoneman and fifty-seven hundred Union cavalry and horse artillery embark on a month-long raid from Knoxville, Tennessee, into southwestern Virginia. Meeting and defeating two Confederate forces on the way, Stoneman's Federals will move toward Saltville (see October 2, 1864), destroying every factory, train,

bridge, supply depot, mill, mine, foundry, and warehouse in their path (as well as what Stoneman will call "four pestiferous secession printing-presses"). At Saltville, after brushing aside seven hundred Virginia home guards, they will destroy the salt-works and fifty thousand to one hundred thousand bushels of salt — further straining the dwindling Confederate resources.[94]

DECEMBER 3, 1864: Confederate cavalry commander Joe Wheeler, whose limited forces are doing what they can to harass Sherman's troops marching through Georgia, strike Yankee infantrymen tearing up rail lines at Thomas's Station. The following day, Sherman's cavalry will engage Wheeler's men at Waynesborough and force them to retreat.[95]

DECEMBER 6, 1864: President Lincoln nominates former treasury secretary Salmon Chase as the next chief justice of the U.S. Supreme Court. He also sends his annual message to Congress. "In a great national crisis, like ours, unanimity of action among those seeking a common end is . . . almost indispensable," the president states in this lengthy document. "In this case, the common end is the maintenance of the Union." Then, declaring that the "national resources . . . are unexhausted, and, as we believe, inexhaustible," he considers the nation's future course through the war:

> On careful consideration of all the evidence accessible it seems to me that no attempt at negotiation with the

In Defence [sic] of the Union and the Constitution. This 1861 color lithograph certificate intended to commemorate a volunteer's service to the United States emphasizes the importance of preserving the Union, which, as President Lincoln noted in his December 6, 1864, message to Congress, remained the bedrock principle of all his administration's actions.

ABOVE: Rear Admiral David Dixon Porter (at center, thumb hooked in jacket) with his staff aboard his flagship, USS *Malvern*, at Hampton Roads, Virginia, December 1864. The foster brother of another celebrated Union naval leader, David G. Farragut, the talented and energetic Porter commanded the largest U.S. fleet that had been assembled to that time for the Union assaults on Fort Fisher, North Carolina.

OPPOSITE: *Battle of Nashville.* Color lithograph published by Kurz & Allison, 1891. After thorough preparation, Union general George H. Thomas sent his troops, comprising both white and black regiments, against John Bell Hood's besieging Confederates. The Union force all but destroyed the Rebel Army of Tennessee.

DECEMBER

1 2 3 4 5 6 7 8 9 **10** 11 12 13 14 **15** **16** 17 18 19 20 21 22 23 24 25 26 27 28 29 30 31

insurgent leader [Jefferson Davis] could result in any good. . . . He does not attempt to deceive us. He affords us no excuse to deceive ourselves. He cannot voluntarily reaccept the Union; we cannot voluntarily yield it. . . . What is true, however, of him who heads the insurgent cause, is not necessarily true of those who follow. Although he cannot reaccept the Union, they can. . . . In stating a single condition of peace, I mean simply to say that the war will cease on the part of the [U.S.] government, whenever it shall have ceased on the part of those who began it.

Lincoln also emphatically reiterates his position regarding an important and continuing war-related debate:

I repeat the declaration made a year ago, that "while I remain in my present position I shall not attempt to retract or modify the emancipation proclamation, nor shall I return to slavery any person who is free by the terms of that proclamation, or by any of the Acts of Congress." If the people should . . . make it an Executive duty to re-enslave such persons, another, and not I, must be their instrument to perform it.[96]

DECEMBER 10, 1864: As the Army of the Potomac settles into winter quarters near Petersburg, Union troops again raid the Weldon Railroad (December 7–12), destroying some fifteen miles of this important element in the Army of Northern

Virginia's supply line. *In Georgia,* General William T. Sherman and his troops — and thousands of freedmen, who have fallen in behind the Union columns as they moved through the state — arrive outside Savannah, completing their march to the sea. In the twenty-six days since they have left Atlanta, the general's men, following their orders to confiscate or destroy anything of use to the enemy's military forces, have caused some $100 million in damages. "If the people raise a howl against my barbarity and cruelty," Sherman had written army chief of staff Halleck in September, "I will answer that war is war, and not popularity-seeking. If they want peace, they and their relatives must stop the war."[97]

DECEMBER 15–16, 1864: Having prepared for battle against John B. Hood's besieging Confederates so methodically and for so long that General Grant is chafing and Secretary of War Stanton is fuming, Union general George Thomas finally sends his army charging into Hood's Army of Tennessee, beginning the battle of Nashville. On the first day, the Federals, including both white and black soldiers, push Hood's men back two miles. On the second, they shatter the Confederate lines altogether. Protected by Nathan Bedford Forrest's cavalry, Hood's men fall back through Alabama and into Mississippi, finally stopping at Tupelo. The gravity of this defeat will send shudders of distress through the Confederacy. The decisiveness of the Union victory will restore Grant and Stanton's confidence in their commander at Nashville. And it will answer the

"The Heavens Are Hung in Black"

question Thomas, a native of the slave state of Virginia, had asked Colonel Thomas J. Morgan, the white commander of the Fourteenth U.S. Colored Infantry: would the untested black soldiers in his army fight out in the open, without the protection of field fortifications? "When General Thomas rode over the battle-field and saw the bodies of colored men side by side with the foremost, on the very works of the enemy," Morgan will report in his postwar memoirs, "he turned to his staff, saying: 'Gentlemen, the question is settled; negroes will fight.'"[98]

DECEMBER 18, 1864: A Federal expedition comprising sixty-five hundred infantrymen of the Army of the James under Major General Benjamin F. Butler and more than fifty warships under Admiral David D. Porter converges on Fort Fisher, the most formidable bastion protecting Wilmington, North Carolina, the only major Confederate seaport open to trade with the outside world. The fort is an important target not only because cutting off the supplies flowing through Wilmington would "insure a speedy termination of the war," as General Grant will write in his postwar memoirs, "but also because foreign governments, particularly the British Government, were constantly threatening that unless ours could maintain the blockade of that coast they should cease to recognize any blockade." Grant has specifically informed the expedition commanders "that to effect a landing would be of itself a great victory, and if one should be effected, the foothold must not be relinquished; on the contrary, a regular siege of

the fort must be commenced." The assault on the fort will be delayed by five days of bad weather.[99]

DECEMBER 20, 1864: Lieutenant General William J. Hardee, commander of the Confederate Department of South Carolina, Georgia, and Florida, and in immediate command of the comparatively small force of ten thousand Rebels defending Savannah, orders his men to withdraw from the city. The following day, Sherman's army will march peacefully in, allowing Sherman to wire a most welcome message to President Lincoln on December 22: "I beg to present you, as a Christmas gift, the City of Savannah."[100]

DECEMBER 24–25, 1864: After a massive twelve-hour bombardment by Admiral David D. Porter's naval fleet, a vanguard of twenty-two hundred Union troops under Benjamin Butler debark from their transports and assault Fort Fisher, North Carolina (see December 18, 1864). But the bombardment has not silenced the fort's many cannons, and the Federals are quickly pinned down. Almost as quickly Butler orders a withdrawal (undertaken so eagerly that he temporarily strands seven hundred men in front of the fort) and sails back to Fort Monroe — defying Grant's specific instructions to besiege the fort if his troops secured even a foothold. Porter "complained bitterly of having been abandoned by the army just when the fort was nearly in our possession," Grant will write in his memoirs. Furious at Butler's decision to retreat, Grant will soon

relieve the general from duty; he will select Brigadier General Alfred H. Terry to command the land force in a second attempt to take the fort (see January 12, 1865).[101]

1865

JANUARY 1865

JANUARY 10, 1865: North Carolina's governor, Zebulon Vance, receives a letter signed only "A Poor Woman," from a citizen who has obviously seen more than enough of war: "It is impossible to whip the Yankees. If we are to bee [*sic*] slaves, let us all bee slaves together, for there is, I see no other chance." She believes there has been far too much suffering and tells the governor, "You and some of the rest of those big bugs will have to answer for the blood of our dear ones who have been slain."[102]

JANUARY 11, 1865: Francis P. Blair Sr., father of Lincoln's former postmaster general (see September 24, 1864), arrives in Richmond, Virginia, ostensibly to track property confiscated by Jubal Early's Confederates (see July 9, 1864) but actually, as he has written to his old friend Jefferson Davis, to discuss "the state of the affairs of our country." Although Blair proposes a totally unworkable plan (suspending the war while North

and South ally to expel the French from Mexico), he does secure a letter from Davis in which the Confederate leader agrees to send peace commissioners to Washington "with a view to secure peace to the two Countries." Lincoln will reply, via Blair, "I have constantly been, am now, and shall continue, ready to receive any agent whom he, or any other influential person now resisting the national authority, may informally send to me, with the view of securing peace to the people of our one common country." Despite this fundamental difference, Davis will appoint three peace commissioners — Vice President Alexander Stephens, president *pro tem* of the Confederate senate (and former U.S. senator) R. M. T. Hunter, and Assistant Secretary of War John A. Campbell, a former U.S. Supreme Court justice — and dispatch them to the Union stronghold, Fort Monroe. *In Missouri,* the state constitutional convention abolishes slavery.[103]

JANUARY 12, 1865: Moved by rumors of indifference and ill-treatment of contrabands by General William T. Sherman's army, Secretary of War Stanton has traveled to Savannah, Georgia, where, today, he and Sherman meet with twenty black church officials, most of whom are former slaves. One of the questions asked during this interview is how former slaves can best support themselves and their families in freedom. The answer: "We want to be placed on land until we are able to buy it, and make it our own." *At sea off Wilmington, North Carolina,* Admiral David D. Porter returns to Fort Fisher with

ABOVE: Major General Galusha Pennypacker (1844–1916), USA. Frontispiece of the commemorative pamphlet *Galusha Pennypacker, America's Youngest General*, 1917. Elected captain of his regiment in 1861 (and soon promoted to major), Pennypacker served with distinction in the battles of Fort Wagner and Cold Harbor and in the trenches near Petersburg before leading the charge at Fort Fisher that brought his promotion to brigadier general at age twenty-one. In March 1865, he was brevetted (given the temporary rank) major general.

OPPOSITE: *Capture of Fort Fisher.* Color lithograph of a painting by J. (Julian) O. Davidson (1853–1894), published by L. Prang & Co., 1887. After an abortive first attempt in December 1864, Union forces captured this powerful bastion in January 1865, thus closing the port city of Wilmington, North Carolina, to Confederate blockade runners and depriving Robert E. Lee's army of much-needed supplies.

Circular announcing the "Grand Exhibition of Left-Hand Penmanship," circa 1866, with photographs of two of the exhibition participants, George C. Bucknan, formerly of the Third Massachusetts Battery, and Henry Helsel, Company I, Fifty-fourth Pennsylvania Volunteers. A creative effort to assist veterans and to learn from them (see January 17, 1865) was instigated by William Oland Bourne, editor of the periodical *The Soldier's Friend* and a chaplain at Central Park Hospital in New York City. Bourne sponsored two contests in which Union soldiers and sailors who lost their right arms during the war were invited to submit samples of their penmanship using their left hands; many of these soldiers wrote of the battles in which they had been wounded. The first exhibition, in 1866, awarded cash prizes totaling $1,000.

a fleet of nearly sixty ships and eight thousand infantry under Brigadier General Alfred Terry (see December 24–25, 1864). At dawn on January 13, more than six hundred naval guns will begin a near-continuous bombardment of the formidable fort as Terry's men land under Confederate fire and begin to entrench. Fort Fisher will fall to the Union on January 15, after sixteen hundred sailors and four hundred U.S. Marines stage an abortive but distracting land assault and Terry's U.S. infantrymen launch an all-out attack that precipitates some of the bitterest hand-to-hand fighting of the war. (One young officer who leads a charge toward the fort, Colonel Galusha Pennypacker, will later be awarded the Medal of Honor; when he is promoted in February, he will become, at age twenty-one, the youngest general in the Civil War.) Federal forces will soon occupy Wilmington, depriving the hungry and beleaguered Army of Northern Virginia of its last avenue for receiving supplies by ship. Morale plummets; in February Lee will report, "Hundreds of men are deserting nightly."[104]

JANUARY 16, 1865: General William T. Sherman issues Special Field Order No. 15, designating the coastline and riverbank thirty miles inland from Charleston, South Carolina, to Jacksonville, Florida, as an area for settlement exclusively by black people and specifying that "the sole and exclusive management of affairs will be left to the freed people themselves, subject only to the United States military authority and the acts of Congress." Though more than forty thousand freedmen

will have moved onto new farms carved out of this formerly Confederate land by June 1865, President Andrew Johnson will cause their eviction when, in August, he restores the land Sherman had set aside to its former Confederate owners.[105]

JANUARY 17, 1865: Frederick Knapp, head of the U.S. Sanitary Commission's Special Relief Department, writes to commission president Henry W. Bellows about the many thousands of needy Union veterans returning from the service: "Our statistics . . . and my own *eyes* resting daily on these men helpless or half helpless from disease or wounds, tell me that although it is to be scattered all over the country, yet there will be in the aggregate, a vast amount of *suffering & poverty & toil* among these men . . . unless some wise provision is made for them now, while the sympathies of the people are all alive." Knapp's urgent proposal that the USSC establish "sanitaria" for these veterans is unsuccessful. Most Sanitary Commission leaders believe that the veterans' families and local communities will provide whatever care the returning veterans need.[106]

JANUARY 18, 1865: Confederate congressman Duncan F. Kenner, a wealthy slaveholder from Louisiana, slips out of Richmond on a secret mission that Kenner himself suggested nearly two years before but which was only recently, and reluctantly, approved by President Davis, his cabinet, and leading members of Congress. Traveling in disguise to a seaport in the

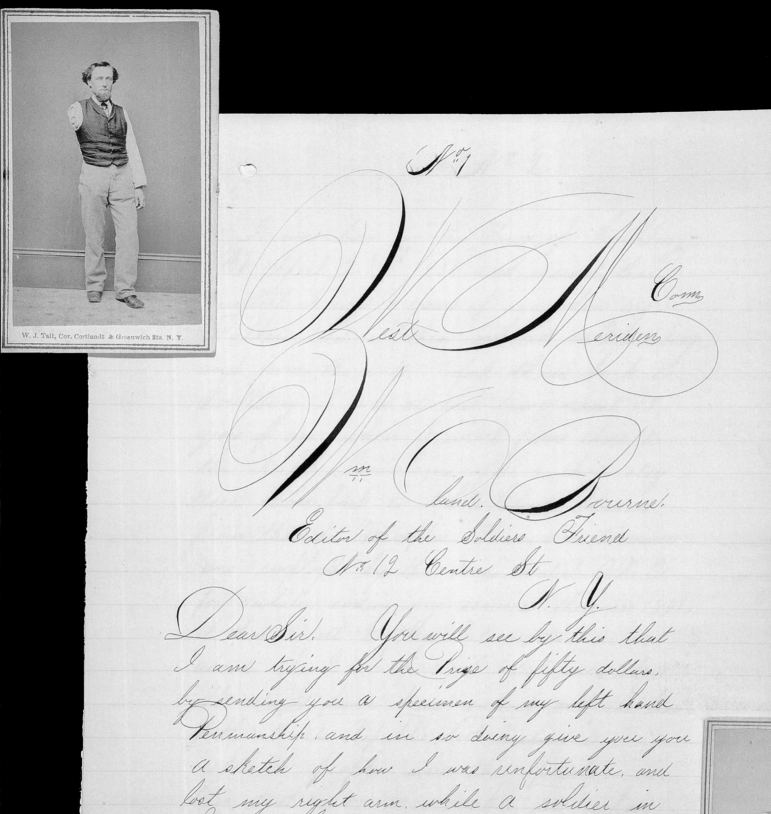

West Meriden Com

Wm Bland. Bourne.

Editor of the Soldiers Friend
Nº 12 Centre St
N. Y.

Dear Sir! You will see by this that
I am trying for the Prize of fifty dollars.
by sending you a specimen of my left hand
Penmanship. and in so doing give you
a sketch of how I was unfortunate. and
lost my right arm. while a soldier in
Uncle Sams Army.

One former Union soldier, Burritt Stiles (pictured here), submitted a letter to the Left-Hand Penmanship Exhibition (see illustration, page 215), "trying for the Prize of fifty dollars." In New Orleans when the war broke out, Stiles pluckily made his way north, via Cuba, and enlisted in Company A, Fourteenth Connecticut Volunteers. In the letter, the first page of which is shown here, Stiles describes his experience in the battle of the Wilderness, where he received the wound that resulted in the amputation of his arm.

Exciting Scene in the House of Representatives, January 31st 1865, on the Announcement of the Passage of the Amendment to Abolish Slavery Forever. Wood engraving published in *American Soldier in the Civil War: A Pictorial History*, 1895. "I have felt, ever since the vote," one Republican congressman wrote, "as if I were in a new country."

hostile North, Kenner will travel to Europe, where he has full authority to secure British and French recognition for the Confederate States by guaranteeing that the Davis administration will abolish slavery. On February 24, he will arrive in France, where he will outline this plan to the Confederacy's official envoys to Britain and France, James Mason and John Slidell.[107]

JANUARY 23, 1865: In the aftermath of the loss of Fort Fisher (which provoked such criticism that Secretary of War James Seddon resigned) and aware that confidence in his leadership is waning, President Jefferson Davis bolsters Confederate resolve by signing an act providing for the appointment of a general in chief of all Confederate armies — and on January 31 he will appoint the revered general Robert E. Lee to the post. (Lee will officially assume these responsibilities February 6.) *In another command change,* Confederate general John Bell Hood, whose Army of Tennessee was defeated at Atlanta and nearly shattered at Nashville, resigns his command. One of his soldiers, Douglas Cater of the Nineteenth Louisiana Volunteers, will write of the general: "I had never had the faith in him that I always desire to have in a general. . . . I like him for his bravery and untiring energy but he lacked caution and seemed to care nothing for the lives of his men."[108]

JANUARY 29, 1865: The Confederate peace commissioners (see January 11, 1865) arrive under a flag of truce at Petersburg, Virginia, sparking celebrations among both Federals and

Confederates hopeful that peace may be in the offing. The commissioners are escorted to General Grant's headquarters at City Point.[109]

JANUARY 31, 1865: After long delay and a tense debate, the U.S. House of Representatives passes the Thirteenth Amendment to the Constitution, abolishing slavery (it had been passed by the Senate April 8, 1864). When the 119–56 vote is announced, celebrations erupt in the House, and artillery salvos fired on Capitol Hill to signal the measure's passage beget joyful demonstrations in Washington's streets. "I have felt, ever since the vote," a Republican congressman will write in his diary, "as if I were in a new country." In Boston, fervent abolitionist William Lloyd Garrison will ask a celebrating throng to whom they are most indebted for this great event, and the people will cheer when he gives the answer: "to the humble railsplitter of Illinois — to the Presidential chainbreaker for millions of the oppressed — to Abraham Lincoln." On February 1, Lincoln's home state of Illinois will become the first state to ratify the amendment; ratification by the required two-thirds of the states will make the Thirteenth Amendment law on December 18, 1865.[110]

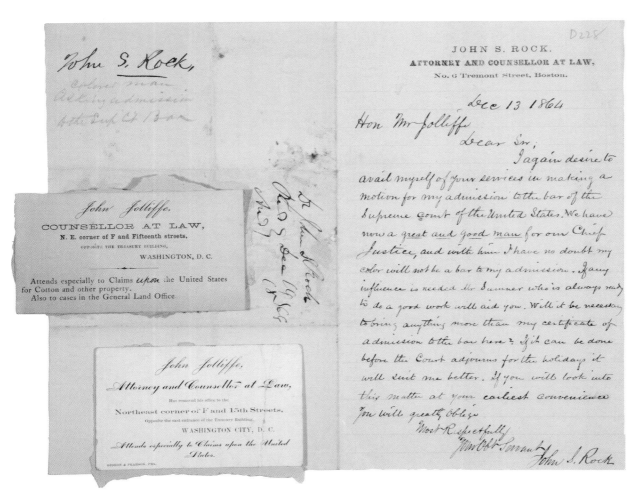

FEBRUARY

1 **2** 3 4 5 6 7 8 9 10 11 12 13 14 15 16 17 18 19 20 21 22 23 24 25 26 27 28

FEBRUARY 1865

FEBRUARY 1, 1865: "Why don't you go over to South Carolina and serve them this way," Georgians had reportedly asked General Sherman. "They started it." The idea had already occurred to the general (who had, on January 19, dispatched some troops in that direction) and today, Sherman leads sixty thousand troops away from Savannah. His goal: to move north, through both Carolinas, destroying all war resources in his path, and come up on the rear of the Army of Northern Virginia, which would then be caught between two large Union forces. A much longer and more difficult campaign than Sherman's march to the sea, this expedition will carve a corridor of destruction through the heart of South Carolina, the leading secessionist state, against which, Sherman reports to Halleck, "the whole army is burning with an insatiable desire to wreak vengeance." *In Washington,* Chief Justice Salmon P. Chase and his associate justices listen with special attentiveness as Senator Charles Sumner of Massachusetts stands before them and moves "that John S. Rock, a member of the Supreme Court of the State of Massachusetts, be admitted to practice as a member of this Court." When Chase grants Sumner's motion, Rock becomes the first African American admitted to practice before the U.S. Supreme Court — the same court that, in 1857 under Chief Justice Taney, had issued the Dred Scott decision, denying that any black person could be a citizen of the United States.[111]

FEBRUARY 2, 1865: Secretary of State Seward's negotiations with the Confederate peace commissioners (see January 11 and 29, 1865) are almost aborted when President Lincoln learns that the commissioners have instructions to negotiate as if the Confederate States are a separate country. Lincoln is moved, however, by a wire in which General Grant expresses his conviction that the commissioners' "intentions are good and their desire sincere to restore peace and union," and he agrees to meet personally with the Confederate delegation. The following day, aboard the Union steamer *River Queen* at Hampton Roads, off Fort Monroe, Virginia, Lincoln and Seward confer for several hours with commissioners Alexander Stephens, Robert Hunter, and John A. Campbell. Although an armistice is discussed, Lincoln makes it clear that the United States considers unconditional Confederate surrender the only acceptable means of ending the war. The Hampton Roads Conference ends in an impasse. "The 'peace commissioners' returned on Sunday, & with the answer I expected — no terms save Submission will be listened to," Confederate chief of ordnance Josiah Gorgas will write in his diary a few days later. "It has had a good effect on the country. . . . The war feeling has blazed out afresh in Richmond, & the spirit will I hope spread thro' the land." In the North, Lincoln's detailed report on the conference and related events will relieve Radical Republicans, who had feared that, to achieve peace, the president would surrender "the political fruits which had been already gathered from the long and exhausting military struggle."[112]

FEBRUARY 5–7, 1865: Grant launches another offensive against the Confederate lines at Petersburg, precipitating the battle of Hatcher's Run. The Confederates' spirited response results in what one Union officer describes as "the greatest skedaddle that has taken place yet" among some of the Union troops. But the Federals recover and manage to extend their lines another three miles — thus forcing the already straining Rebels to extend their own. The two sides now face each other along a thirty-seven-mile front.[113]

FEBRUARY 9, 1865: Riding a wave of public outrage at the outcome of the Hampton Roads Conference, for the second time in three days Jefferson Davis electrifies a crowd in Richmond with a speech excoriating "His Majesty Abraham [Lincoln] the First," condemning congressional passage of the Thirteenth Amendment to the U.S. Constitution, and predicting, despite current circumstances, the ultimate triumph of the Confederate cause. Even Vice President Alexander Stephens, no admirer of Davis, is moved by the president's fiery rhetoric, although the canny Georgian believes Davis's prediction of Confederate triumph to be "the emanation of a demented brain."[114]

FEBRUARY 12, 1865: Meeting in Washington, the Electoral College confirms Lincoln's election by a vote of 212 to 21. *In South Carolina,* Federal troops brush aside Confederate skirmishers at the North Edisto River as Sherman's army

pushes deeper into the state. By February 16, the Federals will almost completely surround the capital city, Columbia, announcing their presence with occasional artillery fire. At the same time, in Charleston, Lieutenant General William J. Hardee, having already been forced to cede Savannah (see December 20, 1864) and leery of being trapped by Sherman's advancing forces, prepares to evacuate the city where the war began.[115]

FEBRUARY 17, 1865: As small units of Confederate cavalry withdraw from Columbia, South Carolina (leaving burning bales of cotton behind them), Sherman and his troops enter, escorted by the mayor and other city officials who have surrendered the city. Although the Union occupation begins in an orderly fashion, liberated Federal prisoners, slaves newly transformed to freedmen, and the discovery by Union troops of the city's liquor stores combine to loosen military discipline. At night, fires break out in several areas of the city and, fanned by high winds, spread until much of Columbia is in flames. In the following few days, Sherman's troops will add to the city's misery by destroying railroad facilities, supply depots, and other buildings deemed militarily useful to the enemy. *One hundred miles to the southeast:* Confederate troops, along with some wealthy civilians, evacuate Charleston, leaving behind them fires started to destroy supplies that might be useful to the enemy.[116]

Susie King Taylor (1848–1912). Born a slave, Taylor circumvented Georgia law and learned to read before escaping to freedom behind Union lines in 1862. She became a laundress, teacher, and nurse to the First South Carolina Volunteer Infantry (Colored) and was with the Union troops that occupied Charleston, South Carolina, in February 1865.

The final page of the manuscript text of the second inaugural address includes the eloquent concluding passage expressing Lincoln's intention to preserve the Union "with malice toward none; with charity for all."

FEBRUARY 18, 1865: Union troops commanded by Brigadier General Alexander Schimmelfennig — and including, near the van, the Twenty-first U.S. Colored Troops and two companies of the Fifty-fourth Massachusetts — enter Charleston, South Carolina. In a reversal of events in Columbia, the Federal troops work to extinguish the fires the Confederates set as they left. Susie King Taylor, an African American nurse and laundress, will arrive in the city within a few days with elements of the First South Carolina Volunteers. "When we landed . . . our regiment went to work assisting the citizens in subduing the flames," she will write in a postwar memoir. "For three or four days the men fought the fire, saving the property and effects of the people, yet these white men and women could not tolerate our black Union soldiers, for many of them had formerly been their slaves; and although these brave men risked life and limb to assist them in their distress, men and even women would sneer and molest them whenever they met them." Charleston, the "fire-eater" stronghold where the first salvos of the war were fired, has become a city of resentments and despair, described by one Northern reporter as "silent, mournful, in deepest humiliation."[117]

FEBRUARY 22, 1865: Tennessee voters approve an amendment to the state constitution abolishing slavery.[118]

MARCH 1865

MARCH 3, 1865: The U.S. Congress enacts legislation establishing a Bureau of Refugees, Freedmen, and Abandoned Lands, the first national social welfare agency. Assigned supervisory and management responsibilities for all abandoned lands in former Confederate territory, the Freedmen's Bureau is to have "control of all subjects relating to refugees and freedmen from rebel States." Related acts passed this day establish the Freedmen's Savings and Trust Company and finally extend equal pay to *all* U.S. Colored Troops (see June 15, 1864), while a "Resolution to encourage Enlistments and to promote the Efficiency of the military Forces of the United States" declares that the wives and children of black soldiers will henceforth "be forever free." Approving a bill introduced March 1 by Senator Henry Wilson and inspired by the work of philanthropist Delphine Baker, Congress also incorporates the National Asylum of Disabled Volunteer Soldiers (NADVS). The beginning of a system of shelters for totally disabled veterans that will become known collectively as the National Home, the effort will suffer from organizational flaws and will not start to become effective for more than a year.[119]

MARCH 4, 1865: Some fifty thousand people converge on the United States Capitol on this rainy morning to witness the second inauguration of Abraham Lincoln. Preliminary ceremonies include a graceful farewell address by retiring vice president Hannibal Hamlin in the Senate Chamber, where

Abraham Lincoln delivering his second inaugural address as president of the United States at the U.S. Capitol.
Photograph by Alexander Gardner, March 4, 1865.

new vice president Andrew Johnson also takes his oath of office. Johnson's inaugural address is far from graceful. Tired after his journey from Nashville and not feeling well, he fortified himself with three glasses of whiskey before the ceremony; and his rambling, nearly incoherent speech (which Lincoln will characterize later as nothing other than a "bad slip") moves the recently appointed attorney general, James Speed, to whisper to Secretary of the Navy Gideon Welles, "The man is certainly deranged." Things become both literally and figuratively brighter when the dignitaries move outside for the presidential oath-taking and speech. The sun breaks through the dissipating cloud cover and Lincoln's second inaugural address, much shorter than his first, proves to be a conciliatory speech of surpassing eloquence, most notably in its concluding paragraph:

> With malice toward none; with charity for all; with firmness in the right, as God gives us to see the right, let us strive on to finish the work we are in, to bind up the nation's wounds, to care for him who shall have borne the battle and for his widow and his orphan, to do all which may achieve and cherish a just, and a lasting peace, among ourselves, and with all nations.

In the evening, at a huge post-inaugural White House reception during which the president shakes the hands of more than five thousand people, Lincoln warmly greets Frederick Douglass — the first time an African American is a guest at a social event in the Executive Mansion. "Taking me by the hand, he said ' . . . I saw you in the crowd today, listening to my inaugural address; how did you like it?' " Douglass will later report. His answer: "Mr. Lincoln, that was a sacred effort."[120]

MARCH 7, 1865: Crossing from South Carolina into North Carolina, Sherman's troops undergo an attitude change: resentments and the urge to punish fade. "Not a house was burned," a Union officer will later report, "and the army gave to the people more than it took from them." Sherman and his men concentrate on finding and defeating the remaining Confederate forces in the state before moving on toward Richmond. All Rebel troops in the Carolinas and south of Petersburg, Virginia, are now under the command of General Joseph E. Johnston, who is preparing his limited forces to meet Sherman as well as Federal units advancing from Union-held New Bern, North Carolina.[121]

MARCH 13, 1865: "It is now becoming daily more evident to all reflecting persons that we are reduced to choosing whether the negroes shall fight for us or against us," President Davis had written a friend in February. Today, despite continuing opposition, the Confederate Congress passes and Davis signs a bill authorizing the enlistment of slaves as soldiers. The law does not guarantee emancipation for slaves who serve in the Confederate army; their freedom remains subject to the consent

Major General James H. Wilson (1837–1925), USA. A second lieutenant when the war began, Wilson became one of Grant's staff officers during the campaign for Vicksburg and led the cavalry that pursued John Bell Hood's troops after their defeat at Nashville before leading the largest cavalry operation of the war in 1865. He was promoted to major general on May 6, 1865.

Robert Todd Lincoln (1843–1926). A student for much of the war, the Lincolns' eldest son pressed his parents to allow him to join the army, and the president finally asked General in Chief Grant if "without embarrassment to you, or detriment to the service" Robert might "go into your Military family with some nominal rank." Captain Lincoln subsequently served on Grant's staff.

The Peacemakers. Photographic print of an 1868 painting by G. P. A. (George Peter Alexander) Healy (1813–1894). From left: William T. Sherman, Ulysses S. Grant, President Lincoln, and David Dixon Porter. At this meeting aboard *River Queen* on March 27, 1865, Lincoln directed that defeated Rebels be treated with consideration. "I want no one punished. . . . We want those people to return to their allegiance to the Union."

MARCH

1 2 3 4 5 6 7 8 9 10 11 12 13 **14** 15 16 17 18 **19 20 21 22 23 24 25** 26 27 28 29 30 31

of their owners and the states in which the slave soldiers live. As events will prove, this long-debated measure is enacted too late to have any significant impact on the Confederate war effort.[122]

MARCH 14, 1865: Duncan F. Kenner's special mission, a final attempt to secure European recognition for the Confederacy, predicated on the South's embracing its own policy of emancipation (see January 18, 1865), collapses when Britain's Lord Palmerston informs Confederate envoy James Mason that Britain cannot recognize the Confederate States as an independent nation "when the events of a few weeks might prove [the South's attempt at independence] a failure."[123]

MARCH 19–21, 1865: Three days after the Union defeat of Confederates under Joe Johnston at Averasboro, North Carolina, thirty thousand Federals of Sherman's army, on their way to resupply and regroup at Goldsboro, North Carolina, before a final thrust into Virginia, fight twenty thousand Rebels in the three-day battle of Bentonville. By this time, there are nearly one hundred thousand Federal troops in the state, and there is virtually no chance of any success for Johnston's force. Although the Confederate commander does manage to maintain his position during the battle, he will later fall back. Bentonville will prove to be the last significant effort made to halt Sherman's progress.[124]

MARCH 22, 1865: In Alabama, the largest Union mounted force assembled during the war embarks on a raid aimed at the important munitions and manufacturing center of Selma. Led by twenty-seven-year-old Brigadier General James H. Wilson, this 13,480-man force comprises three columns led by Wilson's division commanders: Brigadier General Edward M. McCook, Major General Eli Long, and Major General Emory Upton. Opposing them are scattered Confederate forces, some eight thousand to nine thousand strong, under Lieutenant General Nathan Bedford Forrest.[125]

MARCH 23, 1865: On this blustery day, President Lincoln, accompanied by his wife, Mary, and their son Tad, departs Washington by boat. Aware that the war is almost certainly nearing its end, Lincoln is in fine humor, despite the rough voyage. "He was almost boyish, in his mirth," Mrs. Lincoln will later recall, "& reminded me, of his original nature, what I had always remembered of him, in our own home — free from care, surrounded by those he loved so well." The presidential party will arrive at General Grant's City Point, Virginia, headquarters the next morning. Meeting them at the boat, the general will be escorted by a new member of his staff, Captain Robert T. Lincoln, the president's eldest son.[126]

MARCH 24–25, 1865: With his beleaguered 55,000-man army facing Grant's 120,000, and expecting Sherman's 60,000 to arrive at his rear very soon, Robert E. Lee determines to

The Last Night Bombardment of Petersburg, Va., April 1, 1865 Preparatory to a General Assault. Wood engraving published in *American Soldier in the Civil War*, 1895. "[A]ll the [Union] batteries were opened and kept at work throughout the night," the illustration's caption notes. Mortar shells could be distinguished "by the thread of white light trailing behind them, and as answering shots were sent back by the Confederate batteries, two shells would occasionally strike each other . . . and, bursting, send down fiery fragments over both lines."

MARCH

1 2 3 4 5 6 7 8 9 10 11 12 13 14 15 16 17 18 19 20 21 22 23 24 25 26 **27** 28 29 **30** 31

break out of the siege at Petersburg and combine forces with Joseph Johnston — thus losing Petersburg and Richmond but preserving the Confederate army. In a plan suggested by General John B. Gordon, the attempted breakout begins with an attack on Fort Stedman, east of Petersburg, that completely surprises and overruns the Federal defenders. Gordon then attempts to enlarge this break in the Union lines, but his men are stopped by stubborn Union resistance spearheaded by Pennsylvania regiments, including band members who drop their instruments and pick up available weapons. After four hours of fierce fighting, Union troops charge Fort Stedman from three directions and force the Confederates to retreat. Lee pays a heavy price for this battlefield gamble: he loses part of his own forward line, and nearly 10 percent of his already depleted army are killed, wounded, or taken prisoner. "I am here within five miles of the scene of this morning's action," President Lincoln wires Secretary of War Stanton on March 25. "I have seen the [Confederate] prisoners myself and they look like there might be the number Meade states — 1,600." Though the commander in chief's proximity to combat unsettles Stanton, it bolsters the morale of Grant's troops, demonstrating that "he was not afraid to show himself among them," as the *New York Herald* will report, "and willing to share their dangers here, as often, far away, he had shared the joy of their triumphs." *On the Gulf of Mexico*, thirty-two thousand Federals besiege the twenty-eight hundred Confederates defending Mobile, Alabama. The Rebels will soon be forced to abandon

Spanish Fort and Fort Blakely, two key defensive positions, and on April 12, they will surrender the city.[127]

MARCH 27, 1865: Having driven Jubal Early from the Shenandoah Valley, as ordered, Major General Phil Sheridan rejoins the Army of the Potomac at Petersburg, bringing with him two cavalry divisions led by George Custer and Wesley Merritt. General Sherman also arrives at City Point, Virginia, today to consult with Grant and President Lincoln. After a brief meeting aboard the president's boat, *River Queen*, the three men will reconvene the following day, joined by Admiral David D. Porter. To Sherman's question "What was to be done with the rebel armies," Lincoln replies that all he wants, after Federal troops defeat the Rebels, is "to . . . get the men composing the Confederate armies back to their homes. . . . Let them have their horses to plow with, and, if you like, their guns to shoot crows with. I want no one punished; treat them liberally all round. We want those people to return to their allegiance to the Union and submit to the laws." Sherman will then leave to return to his troops in North Carolina, taking with him an impression of Lincoln that he will describe after the war: "Of all the men I ever met, he seemed to possess more of the elements of greatness, combined with goodness, than any other."[128]

MARCH 30, 1865: "I begin to feel I ought to be at home," President Lincoln wires Secretary of War Stanton, "and yet I dislike to leave without seeing nearer to the end of General

The Fall of Richmond, Va., on the Night of April 2d. 1865. Hand-colored lithograph published by Currier & Ives, 1865.

APRIL

1 **2** 3 4 5 6 7 8 9 10 11 12 13 14 15 16 17 18 19 20 21 22 23 24 25 26 27 28 29 30

Grant's present movement." Stanton agrees. "I hope you will stay to see it out," he replies. "I have strong faith that your presence will have great influence in inducing exertions that will bring Richmond [into Union hands]."[129]

APRIL 1865

APRIL 1, 1865: "No doubt a few days more will settle the fate of Petersburg," a Union soldier declared at the end of March. Today, his prediction begins to come true when Union forces led by Major General Phil Sheridan and Major General Gouverneur Warren attack Five Forks, Virginia, a key position on what was to be Robert E. Lee's route of retreat from Petersburg. Though Lee had ordered Major General George Pickett to "hold Five Forks at all hazards," this proves to be impossible. The left flank of the outnumbered Confederates crumbles, and a division of Union cavalry, charging the Confederate rear, captures over a thousand prisoners. *Also today,* Mary Lincoln returns to Washington; the president remains at City Point, pacing *River Queen*'s deck, awaiting news from the battlefront. *In Alabama,* moving toward Selma, James Wilson's Union cavalrymen (see March 22, 1865) defeat Confederates in a clash at Ebenezer Church.[130]

APRIL 2, 1865: General in Chief Grant launches an all-out assault by the Army of the Potomac on the Confederate lines around Petersburg. Preceded by several hours of Union artillery fire, the attack begins at 4:40 AM, and, within an hour, the Federals, fighting "like Lions," as one soldier will write, effect a breakthrough at one part of the line against Confederates of A. P. Hill's corps, who are fighting "like Tigers." (Riding forward to rally his troops, Hill is killed by a bullet through his heart.) Throughout a day of costly combat, the Confederate lines surrounding Petersburg are breached in several places, their Rebel defenders retreating to the north and west — while, before retreating from the city, Lee sends word to President Davis that "all preparation be made for leaving Richmond tonight." By 11:00 PM Davis and most of his cabinet have heeded Lee and abandoned Richmond, and behind them the city is descending into chaos. Fires started to destroy important papers and supplies or set by looters soon burn out of control; the center of the city becomes an inferno rocked by the explosions of shells in the arsenal and gunboats being scuttled on the river. Richmond's proud role as the capital of a hopeful Confederacy has come to a fiery end. *In Alabama,* employing a three-pronged assault, James Wilson's raiders overcome extensive fortifications, heavy guns, and an estimated five thousand Confederate troops (augmented by civilians impressed into service) to capture Selma, taking twenty-seven hundred prisoners, 102 cannon, and an immense store of supplies. Over the next five weeks, as Wilson's men range through middle

224   *"The Heavens Are Hung in Black"*

President Lincoln Riding Through Richmond, April 4, Amid the Enthusiastic Cheers of the Inhabitants. Wood engraving based on a sketch by J. Becker, published in *Frank Leslie's Illustrated Newspaper,* April 22, 1865. Many of Richmond's white inhabitants were far from enthusiastic about Lincoln's visit, but African Americans in the city crowded around him.

APRIL

1 2 **3** **4** 5 **6** 7 8 9 10 11 12 13 14 15 16 17 18 19 20 21 22 23 24 25 26 27 28 29 30

Georgia, continuing to demonstrate the intense vulnerability of the Southern interior, they will capture five cities, hundreds of artillery pieces, and nearly seven thousand prisoners (including five generals), and either capture or destroy a host of other valuable Confederate resources (see May 10, 1865).[131]

APRIL 3, 1865: On his way to meet General Grant in Petersburg, President Lincoln, his face a mask of sorrow, rides across ground strewn with the bodies of Rebels and Yankees who died deciding the city's fate. When he joins Grant, his spirits rise; the grateful president shakes his leading general's hand for a long time. Back at City Point, Lincoln learns that Richmond is now occupied by Union forces, among them U.S. Colored Troops. Turning to Admiral Porter, he says, "Thank God that I have lived to see this. It seems to me that I have been dreaming a horrid dream for four years, and now the nightmare is over." As the news spreads, igniting huge celebrations in Washington and throughout the North, Lincoln determines to visit Richmond. He reaches the city on April 4 through a harbor clogged with the detritus of war. As he walks through the streets of what had been, just two days before, the enemy capital, accompanied by a nervous Admiral Porter, who fears for the president's safety, Lincoln is surrounded by black people reaching out to touch him to make certain he is really in their midst. Some of them kneel. "Don't kneel to me," he tells them, "that is not right. You must kneel to God only, and thank him for the liberty you will hereafter enjoy." The only

black correspondent to write for a major Northern newspaper during the war, Thomas Morris Chester, witnesses the scene. He will write: "What a wonderful change has come over the spirit of Southern dreams."[132]

APRIL 4, 1865: Stopping in Danville, Virginia, Jefferson Davis, still determined that the Confederacy will prevail, issues a proclamation to the Confederate people. "It is my purpose to maintain your cause with my whole heart and soul," he declares, before setting the seceded states' current dilemma in the best of all possible lights: "Relieved from the necessity of guarding cities . . . with our army free to move from point to point . . . and where the foe will be far removed from his own base . . . nothing is now needed to render our triumph certain, but . . . our own unquenchable resolve."[133]

APRIL 6, 1865: Heading west through Virginia, Lee's faltering Army of Northern Virginia has been closely pursued by Union troops. Today, in the valley of Sayler's Creek, a tributary of the Appomattox River, Federal forces led by Phil Sheridan and George G. Meade hit the Confederates in three separate engagements, turning the day into what the Rebels will term "Black Thursday." Some eight thousand men, at least one-fourth of Lee's remaining force, are overwhelmed and captured by the Federals (Lee's eldest son, George Washington Custis Lee, is among the prisoners). Now outnumbered nearly three to one, Lee has few options left.[134]

The Room in the McLean House, at Appomattox C.H., in Which Gen. Lee Surrendered to Gen. Grant. Lithograph published by the Major & Knapp Eng. Mfg. & Litho. Co., circa 1867. Among the officers surrounding the two generals in chief (seated at center) discussing the terms of Lee's surrender are Phil Sheridan (between Lee and Grant) and George Gordon Meade (standing beside Grant, on the right).

APRIL 7, 1865: Responding to a message from Grant, which calls upon him to surrender because of the "hopelessness of further resistance on the part of the Army of Northern Virginia in this struggle," Lee states that he is not convinced the situation is hopeless. But he asks for Grant's terms. "*Peace* being my great desire, there is but one condition I would insist upon," Grant replies, "namely That the men and officers surrendered shall be disqualified for taking up arms against the Government of the United States until properly exchanged." There will be a further exchange of messages.[135]

APRIL 9, 1865: Meeting at the home of Wilbur McLean in the village of Appomattox Court House, Virginia, General Robert E. Lee surrenders the remaining thirty thousand men of the Army of Northern Virginia to Ulysses S. Grant. Formal surrender ceremonies will take place on April 12 — four years to the day from the Confederate bombardment of Fort Sumter—but at this meeting the two military commanders agree on the terms of surrender, which comport with President Lincoln's wishes, expressed at City Point (see March 27, 1865). After pledging not to take up arms until exchanged, officers and men will be allowed to return to their homes and officers will be allowed to keep their sidearms, their own personal baggage, and their horses. (Later, aware that many of the surrendering soldiers are farmers and will not be able to put in crops without horses, Grant will instruct his officers to "let any Confederate, officer or not, who claimed to own a

horse or mule take the animal to his home." Grant will also agree to provide food for Lee's hungry troops.) Many of Lee's soldiers are bitter about the surrender. Others accept it with magnanimity, cheering their deeply moved general, one man speaking for many when he says, "I love you just as well as ever, General Lee." Beyond Army of Northern Virginia ranks, news of the surrender devastates the already reeling Confederacy. "Oh, I wish we were all dead!" a young Floridian will write in her diary. "It is as if the very earth had crumbled beneath our feet." In the North, barely calmed down after the boisterous celebrations following the fall of Richmond, a happy pandemonium ensues. "The nation seems delirious with joy," Secretary of the Navy Gideon Welles notes in his diary. "Guns are firing, bells ringing, flags flying, men laughing, children cheering — all, all jubilant. This surrender of the great Rebel captain and the most formidable and reliable army of the Secessionists virtually terminates the Rebellion." A crowd converges on the White House, where Lincoln draws cheers when he asks a band to play "Dixie," saying, "It is good to show the rebels that they will be free to hear it again."[136]

APRIL 11, 1865: "We meet this evening, not in sorrow, but in gladness of heart," Lincoln states to a crowd gathered on the White House lawn. In what will be a longer and more sober speech than many in the audience expect, the president addresses what he has termed "the greatest question ever presented to practical statesmanship": reconstructing the

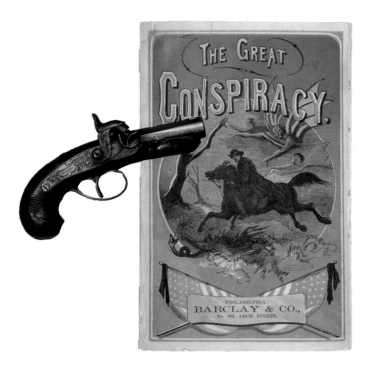

Cover of *The Great Conspiracy,* 1866. After shooting President Lincoln at Ford's Theatre (while a fellow conspirator wounded Secretary of State Seward and members of his household), the injured John Wilkes Booth escaped to Virginia on horseback, beginning a manhunt that was to culminate in his death on April 26.

The derringer John Wilkes Booth used to assassinate Abraham Lincoln, from the museum collection of the National Park Service, Ford's Theatre National Historic Site, photograph by Carol M. Highsmith, May 28, 2008.

The ceremony at Fort Sumter, April 14, 1865, during which General Robert Anderson raised the flag he had been forced to take down exactly four years before.

Union. After asking everyone to "join in doing the acts necessary to restoring the proper practical relations between these [seceded] States and the Union," he considers the specific case of Louisiana, a state partially occupied by the Union army since 1862, and one that has long had a literate and cosmopolitan free black population. "It is also unsatisfactory to some that the elective franchise [the right to vote] is not given to the colored man. I would myself prefer that it were now conferred on the very intelligent, and on those who serve our cause as soldiers." Those words so enrage one man in the crowd that he vows this will be Lincoln's final speech. The man's name is John Wilkes Booth (see November 8, 1864).[137]

APRIL 14, 1865: Four years to the day after surrendering the Union garrison at Fort Sumter, Robert Anderson, now a general, participates in a happier Fort Sumter ceremony, hoisting over the reclaimed bastion the same flag he was forced to lower in 1861. The Reverend Henry Ward Beecher, brother of *Uncle Tom's Cabin* author Harriet Beecher Stowe, delivers a speech before the gathering of Union officers and dignitaries, and the solemn yet joyful ceremonies continue into the evening. *As the Fort Sumter commemoration concludes with fireworks,* President Lincoln, in Washington, arrives at Ford's Theatre to see a performance of the comedy *Our American Cousin.* Accompanied by Mary Lincoln, Clara Harris, the daughter of one of Mary's friends, and Clara's fiancé, Major Henry Rathbone, Lincoln is heartily enjoying the performance

when John Wilkes Booth enters the presidential box and shoots the president in the head, fatally wounding him. (At the same time, Booth's fellow conspirator Lewis Paine assaults Secretary of State Seward in his home, wounding Seward and several members of his household.) Shouting "*Sic semper tyrannis*" (Thus always to tyrants) as he leaps to the stage (breaking his leg in the process), Booth manages to escape from the theater and, on horseback, crosses a bridge over the Potomac River into Virginia. In the theater, meanwhile, all is chaos. "The shrill cry of murder from Mrs. Lincoln first roused the horrified audience," witness James S. Knox will write to his father, "and in an instant the uproar was terrible. . . . Strong men wept, and cursed, and tore the seats in the impotence of their anger." The wounded president is carried across Tenth Street to a boardinghouse. When he dies there, at 7:22 the following morning, a grieving Secretary of War Stanton whispers, "Now he belongs to the ages."[138]

APRIL 15, 1865: As grief sweeps through the Union and U.S. authorities begin a manhunt for the president's assassin and his co-conspirators, Attorney General James Speed calls on Vice President Andrew Johnson at his rooms in the Kirkwood House hotel, delivers a letter signed by members of the cabinet outlining the events of the previous night, and declares: "By the death of President Lincoln, the office of President has devolved, under the Constitution, upon you." Johnson chooses to have Chief Justice Salmon Chase administer the oath of

The Surrender of Genl. Joe Johnston near Greensboro N.C., April 26th 1865. Hand-colored lithograph published by Currier & Ives, 1865.

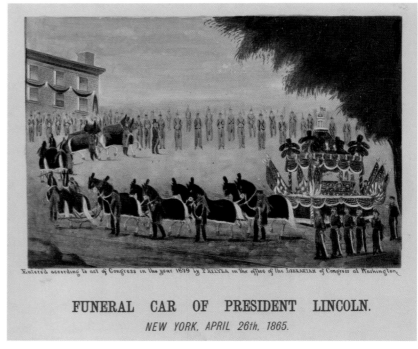

FUNERAL CAR OF PRESIDENT LINCOLN.
NEW YORK, APRIL 26th, 1865.

Funeral Car of President Lincoln. New York, April 26th, 1865. Hand-colored photograph of a painting by P. Relyea, circa 1879. On the same day Confederate troops in North Carolina surrendered and Federal troops cornered John Wilkes Booth, tens of thousands of mourners in New York City were completing their final farewells to President Lincoln, as his funeral train prepared to move on in its sad journey to Illinois.

APRIL

1 2 3 4 5 6 7 8 9 10 11 12 13 14 15 16 17 **18 19** 20 21 22 23 24 25 **26 27** 28 29 30

office in his rooms, with a few cabinet officers and congressmen present. In the Confederate states, there is little rejoicing. Many realize that Lincoln's moderate policies would have eased their way to rejoining the Union; the *Richmond Whig* refers to the Union leader's death as "the heaviest blow which has ever fallen upon the people of the South."[139]

APRIL 18, 1865: After two days of surrender negotiations in North Carolina, Major General William T. Sherman and General Joseph E. Johnston sign a "memorandum or basis of agreement" calling for an armistice of *all* armies remaining in the field. On April 24, Sherman will be informed that President Johnson has rejected this far-reaching and controversial document; further, he will be ordered to inform Johnston that should he not surrender within forty-eight hours, Sherman will resume hostilities against his army.[140]

APRIL 19, 1865: Funeral services are held for President Lincoln at the White House, with only the Lincolns' eldest son, Robert, present to represent the family. Too grief-stricken to attend, Mary and Tad Lincoln remain sequestered as the brief service concludes and the president's body is moved to the rotunda of the Capitol, where a steady stream of mourners will move past it over the next two days. On April 21, the body will be placed aboard a train to begin a remarkable journey, a sad echo of President-elect Lincoln's journey to Washington in 1861. Grieving citizens will wait in long lines to view the body

in the eleven cities (in Maryland, Pennsylvania, New York, Ohio, Indiana, and Illinois) where the train will stop along the way from Washington to Springfield, Illinois. Thousands more will line the train tracks. "In out-of-the-way places, little villages, or single farm-houses, people came out to the side of the track and watched," an 1865 publication, *The Lincoln Memorial,* will report, "some on foot and some in carriages, wearing badges of sorrow, and many evidently having come a long distance to pay this little tribute of respect, the only one in their power, to the memory of the murdered president."[141]

APRIL 26, 1865: Early in the morning, Federal troops surround a barn outside Port Royal, Virginia, to which they have tracked John Wilkes Booth and his fellow conspirator David Herold. They order the two fugitives to surrender, but only Herold complies. Seeking to flush Booth out of the barn, the troops set it on fire. The first presidential assassin in American history is then killed by a single shot fired into the burning building, against orders, by Sergeant Boston Corbett. *Near Durham Station, North Carolina,* General Sherman accepts the surrender of the Confederate troops commanded by Joseph E. Johnston. Confederate forces in Alabama and Mississippi will surrender on May 4, and other Confederate army and navy forces will continue to surrender through June.[142]

APRIL 27, 1865: Hundreds of just-released Union prisoners of war are among the victims of the worst maritime disaster

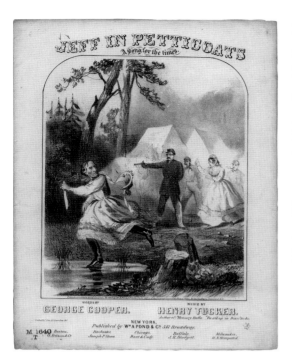

Jeff in Petticoats. Cover of a song composed by Henry Tucker, with lyrics by George Cooper, 1865. Erroneous reports that Jefferson Davis was disguised in a woman's dress when he was apprehended by Union cavalry on May 10, 1865, were eagerly seized upon by Northern cartoonists and songwriters.

The Casemate, Fortress Monroe, Jeff Davis in Prison. Pencil and Chinese white drawing on tan paper by Alfred R. Waud, 1865. Though he was imprisoned for two years at Fort Monroe, Davis was never prosecuted for treason as originally intended. After traveling abroad, he settled in Mississippi, where he wrote *The Rise and Fall of the Confederate Government* (1881).

MAY

1 2 3 4 5 6 7 8 9 **10** 11 12 13 14 15 16 17 18 19 20 21 22 23 24 25 26 27 28 29 30 31

in U.S. history when four boilers on the severely overloaded Mississippi River steamboat *Sultana* explode, destroying the ship and setting its larger remnants afire. Passengers who are not killed outright are plunged into the river. Many of the men cannot swim, and nearly all of them are weak from long months of debilitating captivity; large numbers drown in the muddy current. Because nearly 2,000 people had been crammed onto a boat designed to carry 376, it will be difficult to determine the exact number of casualties, but it will be estimated that between 1,500 and 1,700 people died in this terrible accident.[143]

MAY 1865

MAY 10, 1865: The Fourth Michigan Cavalry, one element of the force that General James H. Wilson led into Alabama (see March 22 and April 2, 1865), receives intelligence that Jefferson Davis is in their vicinity, near Irwinville, Georgia. Moving in on his camp, the Union soldiers surround Davis as he attempts to escape. He surrenders, saying simply, "God's will be done." A rumor will quickly spread that Davis was disguised as a woman when he was captured, and Northern cartoonists will gleefully portray the scene. "Much was said at the time about the garb

Mr. Davis was wearing when he was captured," Ulysses S. Grant will write in his memoirs. "I cannot settle this question from personal knowledge of the facts; but I have been under the belief, from information given to me by General Wilson shortly after the event, that when Mr. Davis learned that he was surrounded by our cavalry he was in his tent dressed in a gentleman's dressing gown." Davis will be imprisoned at Fort Monroe. *Also on this day,* the Union blockade of Southern ports is partially lifted. In Kentucky, former Confederate guerrilla William Quantrill is mortally wounded. Other guerrillas will be pursued by Union army units for much of the year. *At the White House,* President Andrew Johnson proclaims armed resistance at an end (though one more small land engagement will be fought, on May 12 at Palmito Ranch, Texas). *Elsewhere in Washington,* a military tribunal convenes to try those charged as accomplices in the Lincoln assassination: David Herold, Lewis Paine, Samuel Arnold, George Atzerodt (whom Booth had assigned to kill Vice President Johnson), Michael O'Laughlin, Dr. Samuel Mudd (who set Booth's broken leg the day after the assassination and did not inform authorities that he had treated him), Edmund Spangler, and Mary Surratt (owner of the boardinghouse where Booth's cohorts, including Mary's son, John, plotted the assassination). Each will be convicted; Atzerodt, Herold, Paine, and Mary Surratt will be hanged on July 7.[144]

The bodies of those sentenced to death for conspiring to assassinate President Lincoln hang from the scaffold in Washington. Photograph by Alexander Gardner, July 7, 1865.

Andrew Johnson (1808–1875), seventeenth president of the United States. On May 29, 1865, Johnson granted amnesty to most persons who participated in "the existing rebellion." More than a year later, on August 20, 1866, he officially proclaimed "that the said insurrection is at an end, and that peace, order, and tranquillity [sic] and civil authority now exist throughout the whole United States of America."

MAY

1 2 3 4 5 6 7 8 9 10 11 12 13 14 15 16 17 18 19 20 21 22 **23** **24** 25 26 27 28 **29** 30 31

MAY 23–24, 1865: As the military tribunal tries the accused Lincoln assassination conspirators, people flood into Washington for a happier event: the Grand Review. During the huge celebration of the Union's preservation, regiment after regiment of the Grand Armies of the Republic parade along Pennsylvania Avenue and read the banner attached to the Capitol: "The only national debt we never can pay is the debt we owe to the victorious soldiers." The Army of the Potomac marches the first day; General William T. Sherman's troops (informally known as "Sherman's bummers") parade on May 24. Although more than 160 African American regiments were formed during the war, and the courage and accomplishments of black soldiers have been widely celebrated by the Northern press, no black regiments are included in this massive celebration. Within a year, the U.S. Army will be reduced from one

million men to about eighty thousand, on its way to a regular peacetime strength of about twenty-seven thousand. Most of those initially mustered out will be white; a disproportionate number of black units will remain in service as part of an army of occupation in the South.[145]

MAY 29, 1865: By proclamation, President Johnson grants amnesty and pardon to all persons who directly or indirectly participated in "the existing rebellion" — with some exceptions — upon the taking of an oath declaring their allegiance to the U.S. Constitution and laws. The proclamation indicates that Johnson will pursue a moderate Reconstruction policy; Radical Republican objections to some of its provisions indicate that there will be troubled waters ahead.

OPPOSITE: During the Grand Review of the Union troops in Washington, spectators gather beside the Capitol, where the flag remains at half-staff for President Lincoln, and the building itself is hung with black crepe. Photograph by Mathew Brady, May 1865.

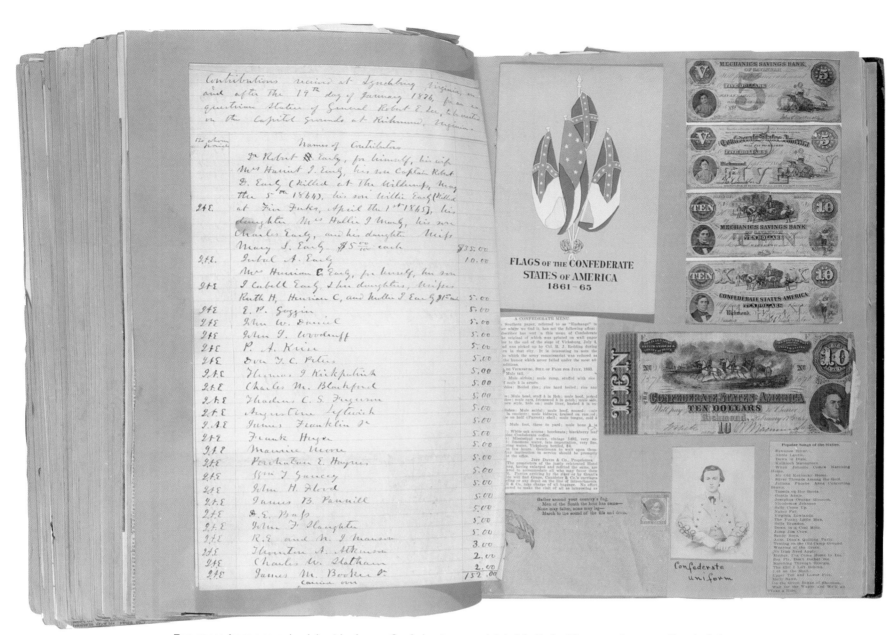

Two pages from a scrapbook kept by former Confederate general Jubal A. Early. After spending some time in Cuba and Canada, Early returned to the United States and reestablished his law practice. Never reconciled to defeat, he was a firm supporter of the "Lost Cause" mythology that idealized Southern life and the Confederate cause. The left-hand page features a list of contributors from one Virginia town "for an equestrian statue of General Robert E. Lee, to be erected in the Capitol grounds at Richmond."

OPPOSITE: *The Stars and Stripes Must Cover the Whole.* Published in 1861, the year Iowa senator James W. Grimes asked "whether we have a country, whether or not this is a nation," this envelope reflects the ultimate answer, achieved at a terrible cost.

EPILOGUE

The United States in 1865 was far different from the country of 1860. Whole areas of the South were in ruins and fully one-quarter of its military-age white men were dead. The region was occupied by Union troops, its economy was shattered, and the potent political influence the South had wielded before the war was gone. North and South, the Civil War took more American lives than all other conflicts *combined,* through Vietnam.[146] It had shaken assumptions, shattered illusions, and added fuel to the fires of social reform movements — from suffrage to labor unions — that had been kindled in the prewar North. In the South, it also gave birth to the gripping mythology encompassed in the term "Lost Cause."

Four million Americans who had been considered property in 1860 were now recognized as human beings and American citizens. But that fact had not erased prejudice; nor would measures taken to assist in the education and integration of these freedmen and women into the larger society, and to erase barriers faced by all people of color in most parts of the nation, be as persistent or effective as their advocates hoped.

Even before the Civil War ended, violence erupted in the South against the freedmen and those who tried to help them. Difficulties escalated during the period of Congressional Reconstruction (1865–1877), as Radical Republicans overrode President Johnson's vetoes of Reconstruction legislation, and that legislation sparked violent reaction among many Southern whites — particularly ex-Confederates, planters, and other men of influence and power. These men were determined to "redeem" their states from Republican influence (and from what they termed "Negro rule," something that never existed), and they succeeded. By 1877, all eleven Confederate states had been readmitted to the Union, and white conservative Democrats controlled those state governments. As these "redeemed" Southern states continued to recover from the ravages of war, the limited progress that some black Southerners had made toward equality during the immediate postwar years was largely reversed.

Terror was one potent weapon in this process of white "redemption"; secret societies, most prominent among them the Ku Klux Klan, employed tactics ranging from psychological intimidation to arson, whippings, and murder to create a climate in which black citizens feared to exercise their rights and sympathetic whites feared to help them. In the late 1860s, Klansmen murdered white Republican congressman James M. Hinds of Arkansas, three South Carolina state legislators, and some two hundred African Americans in one Louisiana parish alone. Louisiana and Georgia went to the Democrats in the 1868 presidential election (won by Republican Ulysses S. Grant) because Republican voters had been so intimidated that they stayed away from the polls. It would be more than a century before the promises of equal rights embodied in the Thirteenth, Fourteenth, and Fifteenth Amendments to the U.S. Constitution would begin to be fully realized for people of color in the South and throughout the country.[147]

Yet the Civil War did resolve the two primary issues that sparked it: It eradicated slavery in the United States. And it preserved the unique American experiment in democracy — "government of the people, by the people, for the people" — answering unequivocally the question articulated by James W. Grimes, U.S. senator from Iowa, as the first Southern states were attempting to fulfill their threats to dismember the Union so painfully birthed in hope and promise less than a century before. "The question before the country, it seems to me, has assumed gigantic proportions," Grimes wrote, in January 1861. "The issue now before us is, whether we have a country, whether or not this is a nation."[148] The answer — inscribed in the blood and sacrifice of the people on both sides of this terrible conflict, and never thereafter challenged — was *yes.*

NOTES

CHAPTER 1

1. Abraham Lincoln Papers, Library of Congress (hereinafter Lincoln Papers, LC).
2. William C. Davis, *Look Away! A History of the Confederate States of America* (New York: The Free Press, 2002), 31, citing letter in a private collection.
3. William J. Cooper Jr., *Jefferson Davis, American* (New York: Alfred A. Knopf, 2000), 328–29.
4. James M. McPherson, *Ordeal by Fire: The Civil War and Reconstruction*, 2nd ed. (New York: McGraw-Hill, 1992), 177.
5. Varina Davis, *Jefferson Davis, Ex-President of the Confederate States of America: A Memoir by His Wife* (New York: Belford Company, 1890), 2: 33.
6. Dunbar Rowland, ed., *Jefferson Davis, Constitutionalist: His Letters, Papers, and Speeches* (Jackson, MS: Mississippi Department of Archives and History, 1923), 47–48 (hereinafter *Davis, Constitutionalist*).
7. Roy P. Basler, ed., *The Collected Works of Abraham Lincoln* (New Brunswick, NJ: Rutgers University Press, 1953), 4: 262–71; Lincoln Papers, LC.
8. Doris Kearns Goodwin, *Team of Rivals: The Political Genius of Abraham Lincoln* (New York: Simon & Schuster, 2005), 306–9 and endnotes for those pages.
9. James M. McPherson, *Battle Cry of Freedom: The Civil War Era* (New York: Oxford University Press, 1988), 254; Allan Nevins, *Ordeal of the Union* (New York: Macmillan, 1992) 2, part 2:411–13, and 3, part 1:14–15.
10. Alan Axelrod, *Political History of America's Wars* (Washington, DC: CQ Press, 2007), 160–61; http://www.desertusa.com/ind1/Cochise.html.
11. E. B. Long with Barbara Long, *The Civil War Day by Day: An Almanac, 1861–1865* (Garden City, NY: Doubleday & Company, 1971), 33.
12. McPherson, *Battle Cry*, 259; *Davis, Constitutionalist*, 51; Margaret E. Wagner, *The American Civil War: 365 Days* (New York: Harry N. Abrams, 2006), January 20 (hereinafter *Civil War: 365*).
13. Margaret E. Wagner, Gary W. Gallagher, and Paul Finkelman, eds., *The Library of Congress Civil War Desk Reference* (New York: Simon & Schuster, 2002), 524 (hereinafter *CWDR*).
14. Howard Jones, *Blue and Gray Diplomacy: A History of Union and Confederate Foreign Relations* (Chapel Hill: University of North Carolina Press, 2010), 17–18.
15. Brian McGinty, *Lincoln and the Court* (Cambridge, MA: Harvard University Press, 2009), 22.
16. Goodwin, *Team of Rivals*, 311; Davis, *Look Away!*, 39.
17. Long, *Day by Day*, 23, 42.
18. *CWDR*, 376, 387; Nevins, *Ordeal of the Union* 3, part 1:17–18.
19. Nevins, *Ordeal of the Union* 3, part 1:30–33.
20. Long, *Day by Day*, 45; Edwin C. Fishel, *The Secret War for the Union* (Boston: Houghton Mifflin, 1996), 15 (security precautions); Basler, *Collected Works*, 4: 262–71.
21. Nevins, *Ordeal of the Union* 3, part 1:18.
22. *CWDR*, 176–77, 524.
23. Nevins, *Ordeal of the Union* 3, part 1:32.
24. Ibid., 3:11, n. 1.
25. Davis, *Look Away!*, 80; *CWDR*, 181–86.
26. William Howard Russell, *My Diary North and South* (New York: Harper & Brothers, 1954), 26–30; Jones, *Diplomacy*, 9, 31.
27. Long, *Day by Day*, 51–52; Nevins, *Ordeal of the Union* 3, part 1:60.
28. Goodwin, *Team of Rivals*, 341–43.
29. Fishel, *Secret War*, 16; Basler, *Collected Works*, 4: 323–24.
30. McGinty, *Lincoln and the Court*, 94–95.
31. Maury Klein, *Days of Defiance: Sumter, Secession, and the Coming of the Civil War* (New York: Alfred A. Knopf, 1997), 408.
32. Wagner, *Civil War: 365*, Jan. 26, 27.
33. McPherson, *Battle Cry*, 318; *CWDR*, 376.
34. McPherson, *Battle Cry*, 279; *CWDR*, 143; Long, *Day by Day*, 60–61.
35. *New York Times*, "An Important Document: Jeff. Davis' Letters-of-Marque," May 24, 1861; McGinty, *Lincoln and the Court*, 120.
36. John David Hoptak, "A Forgotten Hero of the Civil War," article on the Pennsylvania Historical & Museum Commission website at http://www.portal.state.pa.us/portal/server.pt/community/beginnings/18088/nick_biddle/689875, originally published in *Pennsylvania Heritage*, Spring 2010; *CWDR*, 427.
37. Herman Hattaway and Archer Jones, *How the North Won: A Military History of the Civil War* (Urbana: University of Illinois Press, 1983), 28; Clifford Dowdey, ed. *The Wartime Papers of R. E. Lee* (Boston: Little, Brown, 1961), 8–9.
38. Stephen W. Sears, *George McClellan: The Young Napoleon* (New York: Da Capo Press, 1999), 66.
39. *CWDR*, 243–44.
40. Wagner, *Civil War: 365*, Feb. 3; Kathryn Allamong Jacob, *King of the Lobby: The Life and Times of Sam Ward, Man-About-Washington in the Gilded Age* (Baltimore: Johns Hopkins University Press, 2009), 48.
41. *CWDR*, 143; McGinty, *Lincoln and the Court*, 118; Basler, *Collected Works*, 4: 338–39.
42. *CWDR*, 525; "A Brief History of the United States Naval Academy," at http://www.usna.edu/VirtualTour/150years/1860.htm.
43. McPherson, *Battle Cry*, 103; Long, *Day by Day*, 64.
44. Fishel, *Secret War*, 18.
45. McGinty, *Lincoln and the Court*, 67–68.
46. Bruce Tap, *Over Lincoln's Shoulder: The Committee on the Conduct of the War* (Lawrence: University Press of Kansas, 1998), 11.
47. Sears, *McClellan*, 69–71.
48. Basler, *Collected Works*, 4: 342–43.
49. Harry J. Maihafer, *The General and the Journalists: Ulysses S. Grant, Horace Greeley, and Charles Dana* (Washington, DC: Brassey's Books, 2001), 66.
50. *CWDR*, 143; McGinty, *Lincoln and the Court*, 68–71.
51. McPherson, *Battle Cry*, 480; William Quentin Maxwell, *Lincoln's Fifth Wheel: The Political History of the United States Sanitary Commission* (New York: Longmans, Green & Co., 1956), 2.
52. James M. McPherson, *The Negro's Civil War: How American Negroes Felt and Acted During the War for the Union* (New York: Pantheon, 1965), 20.
53. *CWDR*, 143.
54. McGinty, *Lincoln and the Court*, 97.
55. George Hamilton Perkins, *Letters of Capt. Geo. Hamilton Perkins, U.S.N.* (Concord, NH: I. C. Evans, 1886), 97.
56. McPherson, *Battle Cry*, 322; "The American Presidency Project," http://www.presidency.ucsb.edu/ws/index.php?pid=70123 (text of proclamation); Long, *Day by Day*, 69.
57. Sears, *McClellan*, 71.
58. Jones, *Diplomacy*, 32.
59. *CWDR*, 144.
60. Ernest B. Furgurson, *Freedom Rising: Washington in the Civil War* (New York: Alfred A. Knopf, 2004), 87–88, 116n.; Wagner, *Civil War: 365*, Feb. 6.
61. *CWDR*, 8.
62. Long, *Day by Day*, 71–72; Hattaway and Jones, *How the North Won*, 33.
63. McGinty, *Lincoln and the Court*, 71, 125; David Herbert Donald, *Liberty and Union* (Lexington, MA: D. C. Heath and Company, 1978), 107; *CWDR*, 8.
64. Sears, *McClellan*, 72.
65. Long, *Day by Day*, 76.
66. Sears, *McClellan*, 77; *New York Times*, May 22, 1861.
67. *CWDR*, 8, 144.
68. Hattaway and Jones, *How the North Won*, 34, 36; Long, *Day by Day*, 77–78.
69. *CWDR*, 8; *New York Times*, June 1, 1861.
70. Ulysses S. Grant, *Personal Memoirs of U. S. Grant* (New York: Da Capo Press, 1982), 122–23; Sears, *McClellan*, 73.
71. *CWDR*, 144; McGinty, *Lincoln and the Court*, 72.
72. *New York Times*, June 2, 1861.
73. Hattaway and Jones, *How the North Won*, 37; Sears, *McClellan*, 79–80.
74. Nina Brown Baker, *Cyclone in Calico: The Story of Mary Ann Bickerdyke* (Boston: Little, Brown, 1952), 9–10.
75. *CWDR*, 144; McGinty, *Lincoln and the Court*, 72–91.
76. *Davis, Constitutionalist*, 102–3.
77. Michael Shiner diary, LC.
78. Long, *Day by Day*, 82; *CWDR*, 245; Sears, *McClellan*, 80.
79. Lee B. Kennett, *Sherman: A Soldier's Life* (New York: HarperCollins, 2001), 112–15.
80. Long, *Day by Day*, 83.
81. Baker, *Cyclone in Calico*, 37.
82. Allen Johnson and Dumas Malone, eds., *Dictionary of American Biography* (New York: Charles Scribner's Sons, 1943), 5: 323.
83. Wagner, *Civil War: 365*, Feb. 11.

84. Long, *Day by Day*, 84; *CWDR*, 144.
85. McPherson, *Battle Cry*, 481–82; Maxwell, *Lincoln's Fifth Wheel*, 8.
86. Maihafer, *General and Journalists*, 67.
87. Long, *Day by Day*, 86.
88. Basler, *Complete Works*, 4: 449–50.
89. "Francis H. Pierpont (1814–1899)," in *Encyclopedia Virginia*, at http://www.encyclopediavirginia.org/Pierpont_Francis_H_1814–1899; Sears, *McClellan*, 81–83; John H. Eicher and David J. Eicher, *Civil War High Commands* (Stanford, CA: Stanford University Press, 2001), 344.
90. *CWDR*, 235; Mark Grimsley, *The Hard Hand of War: Union Military Policy Toward Southern Civilians, 1861–1865* (New York: Cambridge University Press, 1996), 29–30.
91. *CWDR*, 334; Hattaway and Jones, *How the North Won*, 35; Grimsley, *Hard Hand of War*, 27, 31.
92. Raphael Semmes, *The Cruise of the Alabama and the Sumter* (London: Saunders, Otley, and Co., 1864), 1: 28–29; Long, *Day by Day*, 89; Richard N. Current, ed. in chief, *Encyclopedia of the Confederacy* (New York: Simon & Schuster, 1993) 3: 1392–94.
93. *CWDR*, 145; McGinty, *Lincoln and the Court*, 80–81.
94. Sears, *McClellan*, 88 (to Ellen), 85 (to adjutant).
95. *CWDR*, 244.
96. Harold Melvin Hyman, *Era of the Oath: Northern Loyalty Tests During the Civil War and Reconstruction* (Philadelphia: University of Pennsylvania Press, 1954), 1–4 ; "Potter Report": 37th Cong., 2nd Sess. House of Representatives Report No. 16.
97. McGinty, *Lincoln and the Court*, 125–9; Biographical Directory of Federal Judges, at http://www.fjc.gov/public/home.nsf/hisj.
98. *CWDR*, 145.
99. Davis, *Look Away!*, 43.
100. Sears, *McClellan*, 89–91.
101. Maihafer, *General and Journalists*, 74; *CWDR*, 453: "Before First Bull Run, Southern leaders were able to read detailed information on the composition of Union regiments in and around Washington that had been published in *The Washington National Republican*."
102. Kennett, *Sherman*, 177, 118 (McDowell's dispatch), 119 (Sherman's letter).
103. *CWDR*, 9–10, 246–47; Richard Lewis, *Camp Life of a Confederate Boy, of Bratton's Brigade, Longstreet's Corps, C.S.A.* (Charleston, SC: The News and Courier Book Presses, 1883), 13; Cooper, *Jefferson Davis, American*, 348–50; W. Stanley Hoole, *Vizetelly Covers the Confederacy* (Tuscaloosa, AL: Confederate Publishing Company, 1957), 28–31; Tap, *Over Lincoln's Shoulder*, 15.
104. Sears, *McClellan*, 94.
105. *CWDR*, 10, 145; McPherson, *Battle Cry*, 348.
106. *Dictionary of American Biography* (1943), 2: 18–21.
107. Tap, *Over Lincoln's Shoulder*, 15–16; Walter George Smith, *Life and Letters of Thomas Kilby Smith* (New York: G. P. Putnam's Sons, 1898), 171–72; Maihafer, *General and Journalists*, 70.
108. Sears, *McClellan*, 95; Kennett, *Sherman*, 122–23.
109. *CWDR*, 10.
110. McPherson, *Battle Cry*, 374.
111. McGinty, *Lincoln and the Court*, 100–102.
112. McPherson, *Battle Cry*, 443; *CWDR*, 149; Current, *Encyclopedia of the Confederacy*, 4: 1569–71.
113. *CWDR*, 145; McGinty, *Lincoln and the Court*, 84; Long, *Day by Day*, 105–6; Hyman, *Era of the Oath*, 1–2, appendix.
114. Sears, *McClellan*, 103.
115. *CWDR*, 244; Tap, *Over Lincoln's Shoulder*, 16.
116. *CWDR*, 346, 364; Richard W. Stephenson, *Civil War Maps: An Annotated List of Maps and Atlases in the Library of Congress*, 2nd ed. (Washington, DC: Library of Congress, 1989), 4.
117. Sears, *McClellan*, 98; Kennett, *Sherman*, 124.
118. *CWDR*, 145.
119. Kennett, *Sherman*, 127–29.
120. *CWDR*, 247.
121. Long, *Day by Day*, 112–13; Basler, *Collected Works*, 4: 532 (letter to Browning, Sept. 9, 1861); Tap, *Over Lincoln's Shoulder*, 17.
122. McPherson, *Negro's Civil War*, 141.
123. Long, *Day by Day*, 114; Patricia L. Faust, ed., *Historical Times Illustrated Encyclopedia of the Civil War* (New York: Harper & Row, 1986), 414–15; Kennett, *Sherman*, 129–30; Maihafer, *General and Journalists*, 75.
124. Maihafer, *General and Journalists*, 76.
125. Ibid., 77.
126. David S. Heidler and Jeanne T. Heidler, eds., *Encyclopedia of the American Civil War: A Political, Social, and Military History* (Santa Barbara, CA: ABC-CLIO, 2000), 1: 418–19 (hereinafter ABC-CLIO *Encyclopedia*); Long, *Day by Day*, 117; Hunter Lesser, "Robert E. Lee's 'Forlorn Hope,'" at http://www.Randolpharts.org/ReleaseHistory/Lecture-RobertELee.html; Joseph Glatthaar, "Profile in Leadership: Generalship and Resistance in Robert E. Lee's First Month in Command of the Army of Northern Virginia," in *Wars Within a War: Controversy and Conflict over the American Civil War*, edited by Joan Waugh and Gary W. Gallagher (Chapel Hill: University of North Carolina Press, 2009), 71.
127. McPherson, *Battle Cry*, 289; Basler, *Collected Works*, 4: 523.
128. McPherson, *Battle Cry*, 370.
129. Axelrod, *Political History of America's Wars*, 161; http://www.emayzine.com/lectures/navajo.htm.
130. John Y. Cole, "Ainsworth Spofford and the 'National Library'" (dissertation, George Washington University, 1971), 68–69, quoting dispatch published in the *Commercial*, Sept. 23, 1861.
131. Kennett, *Sherman*, 132.
132. Long, *Day by Day*, 123.
133. Sidebar sources: J. Cutler Andrews, *The North Reports the Civil War* (Pittsburgh: University of Pittsburgh Press, 1985), esp. 31, 49–50; J. Cutler Andrews, *The South Reports the Civil War* (Princeton, NJ: Princeton University Press, 1970), esp. 55–57; James M. Perry, *A Bohemian Brigade: The Civil War Correspondents—Mostly Rough, Sometimes Ready* (New York: John Wiley & Sons, 2000), esp. 32, 71; Alfred B. McCalmont, *Extracts from Letters Written by Alfred B. McCalmont . . . from the Front During the War of the Rebellion* (privately printed, circa 1908), 24; *CWDR*, 805–58.
134. Sears, *McClellan*, 118; Tap, *Over Lincoln's Shoulder*, 18, 115.
135. Kennett, *Sherman*, 127–36; Long, *Day by Day*, 125.
136. Russell, *Diary*, 256.
137. Kennett, *Sherman*, 136–40.
138. *CWDR*, 248; Tap, *Over Lincoln's Shoulder*, 17–18; Tom Wheeler, *Mr. Lincoln's T-Mails: The Untold Story of How Abraham Lincoln Used the Telegraph to Win the Civil War* (New York: HarperCollins, 2006), 8.
139. Sears, *McClellan*, 122–23; Tap, *Over Lincoln's Shoulder*, 18–19.
140. Sears, *McClellan*, 125.
141. Glatthaar in Waugh and Gallagher, *Wars Within a War*, 71–72; Eicher and Eicher, *Civil War High Commands*, 344.
142. *CWDR*, 146.
143. McPherson, *Battle Cry*, 371; *CWDR*, 248–49.
144. Grant, *Memoirs*, 139–44; National Park Service, Belmont battle summary at http://www.nps.gov/history/hps/abpp/battles/m0009.htm.
145. Kennett, *Sherman*, 142.
146. McPherson, *Battle Cry*, 389–90; Donald, *Liberty and Union*, 107; Wagner, *Civil War: 365*, May 7.
147. Mark E. Neely Jr. *Southern Rights: Political Prisoners and the Myth of Confederate Constitutionalism* (Charlottesville: University Press of Virginia, 1999), 155.
148. James M. McPherson, *Tried by War: Abraham Lincoln as Commander in Chief* (New York: Penguin, 2008), 53; Goodwin, *Team of Rivals*, 383.
149. Tap, *Over Lincoln's Shoulder*, 19.
150. *CWDR*, 12.
151. Ibid., 146; Tap, *Over Lincoln's Shoulder*, 19 (letter to Cameron from T. Reilly, December 7, 1861); Goodwin, *Team of Rivals*, 404–5; McPherson, *Negro's Civil War*, 38, citing *Douglass Monthly* IV (August 1861): 502.
152. *CWDR*, 13; McPherson, *Negro's Civil War*, 89–92; Wagner, *Civil War: 365*, Jan. 5.
153. *CWDR*, 528; Semmes, *The Cruise of the Alabama and the Sumter*, 1: 173–74.
154. Tap, *Over Lincoln's Shoulder*, 24–35.
155. *CWDR*, 13.
156. Ibid., 249.
157. Jones, *Diplomacy*, 106–7; Wagner, *Civil War: 365*, May 7; Frederick W. Seward, *Reminiscences of a War-Time Statesman and Diplomat, 1830–1915* (New York: G. P. Putnam's Sons, 1916), 188–89; Long, *Day by Day*, 151.
158. ABC-CLIO *Encyclopedia*, 1: 518–19; National Park Service battle summary, at http://www.nps.gov/history/hps/abpp/battles/ok003.htm.
159. Tap, *Over Lincoln's Shoulder*, 106.
160. *CWDR*, 528.
161. Basler, *Complete Works*, 5: 95; Goodwin, *Team of Rivals*, 410.
162. Basler, *Complete Works*, 5: 98.
163. Long, *Day by Day*, 160–61.
164. *CWDR*, 528.

165. Long, *Day by Day*, 162; *CWDR*, 251; National Park Service battle summary, at http://www.nps.gov/history/hps/abpp/battles/ky006.htm.

166. Long, *Day by Day*, 163–64; Jeffry D. Wert, *The Sword of Lincoln: The Army of the Potomac* (New York: Simon & Schuster, 2005), 59–60.

167. McPherson, *Battle Cry*, 514; Long, *Day by Day*, 164–65.

168. McPherson, *Battle Cry*, 316.

169. Basler, *Complete Works*, 5: 125–26.

170. Ibid., 396; Faust, *Illustrated Encyclopedia*, 274, 280–81; National Park Service battle summary, at http://www.nps.gov/hps/abpp/battles/tn001.htm.

171. *New York Times*, February 28, 1862; Faust, *Illustrated Encyclopedia*, 636; National Park Service battle summary, at http://www.nps.gov/history/hps/abpp/battles/nc002.htm; *CWDR*, 182.

172. McPherson, *Battle Cry*, 514; Faust, *Illustrated Encyclopedia*, 609–10; *Dictionary of American Biography* (1943), 11: 565–66; Richard N. Current, ed., *The Confederacy: Selections from the Four-Volume Simon & Schuster Encyclopedia of the Confederacy* (New York: Macmillan Reference USA, 1993), 482–85; *CWDR*, 352.

173. McPherson, *Battle Cry*, 400–402; Faust, *Illustrated Encyclopedia*, 272–73; Baker, *Cyclone in Calico*, 77–78.

174. McPherson, *Battle Cry*, 400–402; Faust, *Illustrated Encyclopedia*, 272–73; Maihafer, *General and Journalists*, 97; Baker, *Cyclone in Calico*, 82–83; Grimsley, *Hard Hand of War*, 148.

175. *CWDR*, 147; *New York Times*, February 27, 1862.

176. Wagner, *Civil War: 365*, Feb. 5; Goodwin, *Team of Rivals*, 415–23.

177. *CWDR*, 249; Bascom's death noted at http://www.answers.com/topic/george-n-bascom.

178. McPherson, *Battle Cry*, 403; *Davis, Constitutionalist*, 202; Glatthaar in Waugh and Gallagher, *Wars Within a War*, 73–74.

179. James B. Mitchell Papers, LC.

180. McPherson, *Battle Cry*, 402–3.

181. Ibid., 446–47; McPherson, *Ordeal by Fire*, 204–6; *CWDR*, 147–48.

182. *CWDR*, 528–29.

183. McPherson, *Battle Cry*, 434; Current, *Encyclopedia of the Confederacy*, 2: 727–28; *CWDR*, 148.

184. *CWDR*, 26, 146, 529.

185. Ibid., 255; Wagner, *Civil War: 365*, Apr. 9.

186. McPherson, *Tried by War*, 79.

187. Naval Historical Center, "CSS *Virginia* Destroys USS *Cumberland* and USS *Congress*, 8 March 1862," at http://www.history.navy.mil/photos/events/civilwar/n-at-cst/hr-james/8mar62.htm; Raimondo Luraghi, *A History of the Confederate Navy* (Annapolis: Naval Institute Press, 1996), 140–43.

188. Luraghi, *Confederate Navy*, 143–46; Wagner, *Civil War: 365*, May 8, 9, 10; Catherine Ann Devereux Edmondston, *"Journal of a Secesh Lady": The Diary of Catherine Ann Devereux Edmondston, 1860–1866*, Beth G. Crabtree and James W. Patton, eds. (Raleigh, NC: Division of Archives and History, Department of Cultural Resources, 1979), 132.

189. *CWDR*, 15.

190. Faust, *Illustrated Encyclopedia*, 524; *CWDR*, 445–46 (Brownell); North Carolina Railroad History website, http://www.ncrr.com/ncrr-history.html.

191. *CWDR*, 529.

192. Glatthaar in Waugh and Gallagher, *Wars Within a War*, 72.

193. *CWDR*, 182.

194. Long, *Day by Day*, 187–88; Stephenson, *Civil War Maps*, 1–3; *CWDR*, 345–49.

195. Jedediah Hotchkiss, *Make Me a Map of the Valley: The Civil War Journal of Stonewall Jackson's Topographer*, edited by Archie P. McDonald (Dallas: Southern Methodist University Press, 1973), 10; Jedediah Hotchkiss Papers, LC; *CWDR*, 259–61; Wagner, *Civil War: 365*, Mar. 6.

196. McPherson, *Negro's Civil War*, 437.

197. *CWDR*, 15.

198. McPherson, *Battle Cry*, 437.

199. *CWDR*, 529; ABC-CLIO *Encyclopedia*, 2: 1048; Current, *Encyclopedia of the Confederacy*, 3:1133.

200. Faust, *Illustrated Encyclopedia*, 847; *CWDR*, 256; ABC-CLIO *Encyclopedia*, 4: 2163–66.

201. ABC-CLIO *Encyclopedia*, 4: 1778; McPherson, *Ordeal by Fire*, 226.

202. McPherson, *Battle Cry*, 408–15; McPherson, *Ordeal by Fire*, 226–29; Wagner, *Civil War: 365*, Feb. 25, Sept. 2; Grant, *Memoirs*, 191.

203. McPherson, *Battle Cry*, 498; *CWDR*, 261; Davis, *Look Away*, 37 (slave labor).

204. Herman Hattaway and Richard E. Beringer, *Jefferson Davis, Confederate President* (Lawrence: University Press of Kansas, 2002), 162–63; *CWDR*, 148.

205. Benjamin P. Thomas, *Abraham Lincoln, A Biography* (Carbondale: Southern Illinois University Press, 2008), 126–27; National Archives: Exhibit Hall, Featured Document, The District of Columbia Emancipation Act, at http://www.archives.gov/exhibits/featured_documents/dc_emancipation_act/; McPherson, *Negro's Civil War*, 45.

206. McPherson, *Battle Cry*, 482; *CWDR*, 529.

207. *CWDR*, 448; Current, *Confederacy* (Macmillan), 254

208. *CWDR*, 18

209. *CWDR*, 261–62; Perry, *Bohemian Brigade*, 100–107; Andrews, *The South Reports the Civil War*, 150–51.

210. Andrews, *The South Reports the Civil War*, 150–51; Nevins, *Ordeal of the Union* 3, part 2:100–101.

CHAPTER 2

1. Oliver Willcox Norton, *Army Letters, 1861–1865* (privately printed, 1903), 125–26.

2. Joseph Christmas Ives Papers, LC (Cora Ives letter).

3. Stephen W. Sears, *To the Gates of Richmond: The Peninsula Campaign* (New York: Ticknor & Fields, 1992), 27, 54; James M. Guthrie, *Camp-Fires of the Afro-American* (Philadelphia: Afro-American Pub. Co., 1899; reprinted 1970), 336–41 (Phelps letter); Norton, *Army Letters*, 75; Edmondston, *"Journal of a Secesh Lady,"* 167.

4. John Beatty, *Memoirs of a Volunteer, 1861–1863* (New York: W. W. Norton, 1946), 108.

5. Sears, *Gates of Richmond*, 58–62, 65; Gilbert Thompson Papers, LC.

6. Sears, *Gates of Richmond*, 83–84; Robert Ryal Miller, *Arms Across the Border: United States Aid to Juárez During the French Intervention in Mexico* (Philadelphia: The American Philosophical Society, 1973), 6.

7. Sears, *Gates of Richmond*, 89–90.

8. *CWDR*, 259–61.

9. McPherson, *Battle Cry*, 499; Basler, *Collected Works*, 5: 222.

10. Sears, *Gates of Richmond*, 90–91; ABC-CLIO *Encyclopedia*, 3: 1532–33; Long, *Day by Day*, 210.

11. Sears, *Gates of Richmond*, 91–92.

12. McPherson, *Negro's Civil War*, 154–57, citing Guthrie, *Camp-Fires*, 306–13.

13. McPherson, *Battle Cry*, 551–52; Long, *Day by Day*, 212; *CWDR*, 18–19, 148–49.

14. Basler, *Collected Works*, 5: 222–23.

15. McPherson, *Battle Cry*, 450–51; Donald, *Liberty and Union*, 224.

16. Nevins, *Ordeal of the Union* 3, part 2:118–22.

17. Smith, *Life and Letters of Thomas Kilby Smith*, 206–10.

18. Nevins, *Ordeal of the Union* 3, part 2:122; Sears, *Gates of Richmond*, 120.

19. Sears, *Gates of Richmond*, 124–40; Faust, *Illustrated Encyclopedia*, 668; Bryan Grimes, *Extracts of Letters of Major Gen'l Bryan Grimes to His Wife* (Raleigh, NC: Edwards, Broughton & Co., 1883), 15.

20. McPherson, *Battle Cry*, 460; Glatthaar in Waugh and Gallagher, *Wars Within a War*, 72, 74–76.

21. Nevins, *Ordeal of the Union* 3, part 2:104; McPherson, *Battle Cry*, 417; Long, *Day by Day*, 222–23.

22. Dowdey, *Wartime Papers of R. E. Lee*, 194.

23. Long, *Day by Day*, 230; Dowdey, *Wartime Papers of R. E. Lee*, 197–98; Sears, *Gates of Richmond*, 173; "The Burial of Latane," in *Encyclopedia Virginia*, at http://www.encyclopediavirginia.org/Burial_of_LatanAC._The.

24. Current, *Encyclopedia of the Confederacy*, 1: 149; *CWDR*, 20, 150.

25. Nevins, *Ordeal of the Union* 3, part 2:94.

26. Long, *Day by Day*, 230; McPherson, *Battle Cry*, 599.

27. Virginia Foundation of the Humanities, "Battle of Mechanicsville," in *Encyclopedia Virginia*, at http://www.encyclopediavirginia.org/; James M. McPherson, *Crossroads of Freedom: Antietam* (New York: Oxford University Press, 2002), 44.

28. Basler, *Collected Works*, 5: 287.

29. Faust, *Illustrated Encyclopedia*, 667; *CWDR*, 256–59; Spencer Glasgow Welch, *A Confederate Surgeon's Letters to His Wife* (New York: Neale Publishing Company, 1911), 16; Furgurson, *Freedom Rising*, 191.

30. Wagner, *Civil War: 365*, May 14; McPherson, *Crossroads*, 47, 56–58; Sears, *McClellan*, 231; McPherson, *Battle Cry*, 447–51, 470; Donald, *Liberty and Union*, 137.

31. McPherson, *Battle Cry*, 491; Hyman, *Era of the Oath*, 21; *CWDR*, 149–50.

32. Lester Nurick and Roger W. Barrett, "Legality of Guerrilla Forces Under the Laws of War," *American Journal of International Law* 40, no. 3 (July

1946): 572, citing *17 Official Records of the War of the Rebellion*, Series IV, 1094–95; *CWDR*, 450.

33. Patrick J. Kelly, *Creating a National Home: Building the Veterans' Welfare State* (Cambridge, MA: Harvard University Press, 1997), 32–38; *CWDR*, 699–700; McPherson, *Negro's Civil War*, 46–47.

34. *The War of the Rebellion: A Compilation of the Official Records of the Union and Confederate Armies* (Washington: Government Printing Office, 1880–1902; hereinafter *OR*), series 1, vol. 11, part 1:73 –74; Basler, *Collected Works*, 5: 346.

35. Basler, *Collected Works*, 5: 312–13; Tap, *Over Lincoln's Shoulder*, 122–24; Sears, *McClellan*, 240.

36. Goodwin, *Team of Rivals*, 463, citing Welles Diary, vol. 1 (1960 ed.), 70–71; Long, *Day by Day*, 237; Faust, *Illustrated Encyclopedia*, 270, 510; Charles R. Wilson, "Cincinnati's Reputation During the Civil War," *Journal of Southern History* 2, no. 4 (Nov. 1936): 478.

37. Kelly, *Creating a National Home*, 57; *CWDR*, 745.

38. Ivan Musicant, *Divided Waters: The Naval History of the Civil War* (New York: HarperCollins, 1995), 248–52; Wilson, "Cincinnati's Reputation," 479.

39. Second Confiscation Act, text at http://www.history.umd.edu/ Freedmen/conact2.htm; *CWDR*, 429.

40. *CWDR*, 451.

41. Kennett, *Sherman*, 172–85 (quote, 176).

42. *CWDR*, 596; McPherson, *Battle Cry*, 791–92; Goodwin, *Team of Rivals*, 463–68.

43. McPherson, *Battle Cry*, 516; Long, *Day by Day*, 243.

44. Sears, *McClellan*, 239–41.

45. Long, *Day by Day*, 245; Lisa Tendrich Frank, ed., *Women in the American Civil War* (Santa Barbara, CA: ABC-CLIO, 2008), 1: 137–39, 307–9; *CWDR*, 452, 457–59.

46. *CWDR*, 531.

47. McPherson, *Negro's Civil War*, 47–48.

48. *CWDR*, 531.

49. *CWDR*, 264; Charles Fessenden Morse, *Letters Written During the Civil War* (privately printed, 1898), 77–79; Clara Barton Chronology, at http:// www.nps.gov/clba/forkids/chron2.htm.

50. Davis, *Look Away!*, 268.

51. Sears, *McClellan*, 245–47; Faust, *Illustrated Encyclopedia*, 414; Basler, *Collected Works*, 5: 370–75; McPherson, *Negro's Civil War*, 92–93.

52. Text of "The Prayer of the Twenty Millions," at http://www .civilwarhome.com/lincolngreeley.htm, citing Harlan H. Horner, *Lincoln and Greeley* (Urbana: University of Illinois Press, 1953).

53. McPherson, *Battle Cry*, 566.

54. Basler, *Collected Works*, 5: 388–89; McPherson, *Battle Cry*, 510.

55. Faust, *Illustrated Encyclopedia*, 733; Semmes, *The Cruise of the Alabama and the Sumter*, 1: 264.

56. McPherson, *Negro's Civil War*, 167; *CWDR*, 429; Wagner, *Civil War: 365*, Mar. 11; Long, *Day by Day*, 256.

57. Wagner, *Civil War: 365*, Mar. 11; Sears, *McClellan*, 250–51.

58. McPherson, *Battle Cry*, 528–32; Long, *Day by Day*, 256–58; Wagner, *Civil War: 365*, Mar. 13; Sears, *McClellan*, 257; Faust, *Illustrated Encyclopedia*, 129.

59. Faust, *Illustrated Encyclopedia*, 414; Long, *Day by Day*, 258.

60. Faust, *Illustrated Encyclopedia*, 129–30; Sears, *McClellan*, 259; *CWDR*, 22.

61. McPherson, *Crossroads*, 86–88; Sears, *McClellan*, 267.

62. Dowdey, *Wartime Papers of R. E. Lee*, 299; McPherson, *Crossroads*, 85.

63. Sears, *McClellan*, 270; Dowdey, *Wartime Papers of R. E. Lee*, 301; McPherson, *Crossroads*, 94.

64. Dowdey, *Wartime Papers of R. E. Lee*, 301–2; McPherson, *Crossroads*, 106–7.

65. Sears, *McClellan*, 279; McPherson, *Crossroads*, 105–6; Basler, *Collected Works*, 5: 418.

66. McPherson, *Crossroads*, 112.

67. Ibid., 111–12.

68. Basler, *Collected Works*, 5: 426; McPherson, *Crossroads*, 113.

69. McPherson, *Crossroads*, 115–16.

70. Nevins, *Ordeal of the Union* 3, part 2:224–25; McPherson, *Crossroads*, 117–128 (Welch quote, 119).

71. Nevins, *Ordeal of the Union* 3, part 2:225–27; McPherson, *Crossroads*, 129–30; National Park Service, "Clara Barton at Antietam," http://www .nps.gov/anti/historyculture/clarabarton.htm; John W. Jaques, *Three Years' Campaign of the Ninth, N.Y.S.M., During the Southern Rebellion* (New York: Hilton & Co., 1865), 115; Mercer Green Johnston Papers (letter from James Steptoe Johnston to Mary Green, September 22, 1862), LC.

72. Warren H. Freeman and Eugene H. Freeman, *Letters from Two Brothers Serving in the War for the Union to Their Family at Home in West Cambridge, Mass.* (Cambridge, MA: privately printed, 1871), 52; National Park Service, "Antietam: Casualties of Battle," http://www.nps.gov/anti/ historyculture/casualties.htm.

73. McPherson, *Crossroads*, 138–42 (Palmerston quote, 142); *CWDR*, 23, 211–12.

74. McPherson, *Battle Cry*, 493; Nevins, *Ordeal of the Union* 3, part 2:317–18; *CWDR*, 23; text of proclamation, at http://teachingamericanhistory.org/ library/index.asp?document=425.

75. Long, *Day by Day*, 271–72; *CWDR*, 151, 429–30.

76. Nevins, *Ordeal of the Union* 3, part 2:325.

77. Wagner, *Civil War: 365*, Sept. 5; Basler, *Collected Works*, 5: 450.

78. Wagner, *Civil War: 365*, Apr. 14; Tap, *Over Lincoln's Shoulder*, 152; McPherson, *Battle Cry*, 559; Nevins, *Ordeal of the Union* 3, part 2:325, 329; Basler, *Collected Works*, 5: 474.

79. *CWDR*, 263–64, 405–6; Long, *Day by Day*, 276, 281.

80. Nevins, *Ordeal of the Union* 3, part 2:326; McPherson, *Crossroads*, 150; McPherson, *Battle Cry*, 561.

81. Long, *Day by Day*, 278; McPherson, *Battle Cry*, 611–12.

82. McPherson, *Battle Cry*, 568; Basler, *Collected Works*, 5: 460–61.

83. Long, *Day by Day*, 278–284; McPherson, *Battle Cry*, 560; McPherson, *Crossroads*, 153–54; Tap, *Over Lincoln's Shoulder*, 138–41.

84. "Brady's Photographs; Pictures of the Dead at Antietam," *New York Times*, October 20, 1862.

85. McPherson, *Battle Cry*, 569; Sears, *McClellan*, 336, 339; Nevins, *Ordeal of the Union* 3, part 2:328.

86. *CWDR*, 428.

87. Sears, *McClellan*, 340–43.

88. Basler, *Collected Works*, 5: 493; Wagner, *Civil War: 365*, Apr. 11.

89. Sidebar sources: "Photography at the Seat of War," *Moore's Rural New-Yorker*, October 25, 1862, 8, http://www.libraryweb.org/rochimag/roads/ moores.htm; *CWDR*, 811–15; "William Henry Fox Talbot (1800–1877) and the Invention of Photography," at http://www.metmuseum.org/toah/ hd/tlbt/hd_tlbt.htm; Mary Panzer, *Mathew Brady and the Image of History* (Washington, DC: Smithsonian Institution Press, 1997), 101–11 (reporter quote, 103, from Mathew Brady Scrapbook, Brady/Handy Collection, Library of Congress).

90. Nevins, *Ordeal of the Union* 3, part 2:343–44; Wert, *Sword of Lincoln*, 186.

91. Edmondston, *"Journal of a Secesh Lady,"* 301.

92. Wert, *Sword of Lincoln*, 185–86; Basler, *Collected Works*, 5: 485.

93. Long, *Day by Day*, 288–89; Faust, *Illustrated Encyclopedia*, 664–65.

94. Basler, *Collected Works*, 5: 514; Dowdey, *Wartime Papers of R. E. Lee*, 348–49.

95. Davis, *Look Away!*, 229.

96. Long, *Day by Day*, 293; *CWDR*, 271.

97. Wert, *Sword of Lincoln*, 189–97 (Bowen quote, 192); Dowdey, *Wartime Papers of R. E. Lee*, 339.

98. Kennett, *Sherman*, 188–90.

99. *CWDR*, 271–74, 368; Tap, *Over Lincoln's Shoulder*, 143.

100. Goodwin, *Team of Rivals*, 486–92; Tap, *Over Lincoln's Shoulder*, 148.

101. Davis, *Constitutionalist*, 5: 386–87; Grant, *Personal Memoirs*, 225–27.

102. Kennett, *Sherman*, 194–95.

103. Walt Whitman, *The Wound Dresser: A Series of Letters Written from the Hospitals in Washington During the War of the Rebellion* (Boston: Small, Maynard & Company, 1898), 47–48.

104. *CWDR*, 531.

105. McPherson, *Battle Cry*, 580–83; *CWDR*, 274; James B. Mitchell Papers, LC (letter to his father, January 12–13, 1863); Beatty, *Memoirs of a Volunteer*, 155–56.

106. *CWDR*, 430; McPherson, *Battle Cry*, 563; McPherson, *Negro's Civil War*, 50; Faust, *Illustrated Encyclopedia*, 296–97.

107. *CWDR*, 152.

108. Wagner, *Civil War: 365*, Sept. 5.

109. Semmes, *The Cruise of the Alabama and the Sumter*, 2: 49–58.

110. Davis, *Constitutionalist*, 409; McPherson, *Battle Cry*, 566

111. Norton, *Army Letters*, 133; McPherson, *Battle Cry*, 584; Basler, *Collected Works*, 6: 78.

112. Basler, *Collected Works*, 6: 78–79; Lincoln Papers, LC ; McPherson, *Battle Cry*, 585–86.

113. *CWDR*, 279; Faust, *Illustrated Encyclopedia*, 846.

114. Kate Cumming, *A Journal of Hospital Life in the Confederate Army of Tennessee* (Louisville, KY: John P. Morton, 1866), 59–60.

115. Current, *Encyclopedia of the Confederacy*, 2: 727–28.

116. Frank Freidel, "The Loyal Publication Society: A Pro-Union Propaganda Agency," *Mississippi Valley Historical Review* 26, no. 3 (Dec. 1939): 359–376; *New York Times*, September 24, 1864.

117. A. M. Stewart, *Camp, March and Battle-Field* (Philadelphia: Jas. B. Rodgers, 1865), 295.

118. McPherson, *Battle Cry*, 594; Long, *Day by Day*, 323; *CWDR*, 153.

119. Long, *Day by Day*, 323.

120. *CWDR*, 27, 153; McPherson, *Battle Cry*, 592, 613; Long, *Day by Day*, 325.

121. McPherson, *Negro's Civil War*, 70.

122. Long, *Day by Day*, 327; Faust, *Illustrated Encyclopedia*, 514, 724.

123. *CWDR*, 153; McGinty, *Lincoln and the Court*, 118–43; Kermit L. Hall, *The Oxford Guide to United States Supreme Court Decisions* (New York: Oxford University Press, 1999), 246–47.

124. Long, *Day by Day*, 328; Current, *Confederacy* (Macmillan), 74; Willard Family Papers, LC.

125. Musicant, *Divided Waters*, 277–80 (Steele's Bayou), 280–86 (Port Hudson); George G. Smith, *Leaves from a Soldier's Diary: The Personal Record of Lieutenant George G. Smith* (Putnam, CT: G. G. Smith, 1906), 40–41.

126. *CWDR*, 430–31.

127. *CWDR*, 736, 774; "Final Report of the American Freedmen's Inquiry Commission to the Secretary of War," at http://www.civilwarhome .com/commissionreport.htm.

128. Daniel E. Sutherland, *Fredericksburg and Chancellorsville: The Dare Mark Campaign* (Lincoln: University of Nebraska Press, 1998), 117.

129. Long, *Day by Day*, 316, 329–30; *CWDR*, 204–5

130. *CWDR*, 153–54.

131. McPherson, *Battle Cry*, 617; Current, *Confederacy* (Macmillan), 74; Davis, *Look Away!*, 212–13.

132. Musicant, *Divided Waters*, 387–91 (Rodgers quotes, 389–90); McPherson, *Battle Cry*, 646.

133. *Davis, Constitutionalist*, 5: 472–73.

134. "General Order No. 38," http://www.ohiohistorycentral.org/entry .php?rec=1481; McPherson, *Battle Cry*, 596; Nevins, *Ordeal of the Union* 3, part 2:453–54; Wagner, *Civil War: 365*, Apr. 19.

135. Stewart, *Camp, March and Battle-Field*, 306–7; Basler, *Collected Works*, 6: 164–65.

136. McPherson, *Battle Cry*, 626.

137. Ibid., 628; Long, *Day by Day*, 339; *CWDR*, 280.

138. Dowdey, *Wartime Papers of R. E. Lee*, 437–38.

139. *CWDR*, 28–29, 431, 450–51; McPherson, *Battle Cry*, 615–16.

140. Stewart, *Camp, March and Battle-Field*, 308; Wert, *Sword of Lincoln*, 232.

141. Dowdey, *Wartime Papers of R. E. Lee*, 442; Wert, *Sword of Lincoln*, 232–34; Sutherland, *Fredericksburg and Chancellorsville*, 128.

CHAPTER 3

1. Cumming, *Journal of Hospital Life*, 72.

2. Whitman, *Wound Dresser*, 111.

3. Rufus Dawes, *Service with the Sixth Wisconsin Volunteers* (Marietta, OH: E. R. Alderman & Sons, 1890), 125–26; Sutherland, *Fredericksburg and Chancellorsville*, 141; Kennett, *Sherman*, 201–3 (Grant quote, 202, citing *Personal Memoirs of U.S. Grant*, 2 vols. [New York: Charles L. Webster, 1885], 1:49–50); James M. McPherson, *This Mighty Scourge: Perspectives on the Civil War* (New York: Oxford University Press, 2007), 140.

4. McPherson, *Negro's Civil War*, 174; *CWDR*, 597; Wagner, *Civil War: 365*, Oct. 19; "Historical Document: Journal of a Residence on a Georgian Plantation," http://www.pbs.org.wgbh/aia/part4/4h2922.html; McPherson, *Battle Cry*, 596–97; Frank L. Klement, *The Limits of Dissent: Clement L. Vallandigham and the Civil War* (New York: Fordham University Press, 1998), 161; Sutherland, *Fredericksburg and Chancellorsville*, 141–46 (Williams quote, 144); Long, *Day by Day*, 344–45.

5. Sutherland, *Fredericksburg and Chancellorsville*, 154–57; Stephen W. Sears, *Chancellorsville* (Boston: Houghton Mifflin, 1996), 284 (Parker quote); Long, *Day by Day*, 346.

6. Basler, *Collected Works*, 6: 196; Sutherland, *Fredericksburg and Chancellorsville*, 163–65; Sears, *Chancellorsville*, 336–39, 359–60 (Chancellor quote); Dowdey, *Wartime Papers of R. E. Lee*, 452–53.

7. Sutherland, *Fredericksburg and Chancellorsville*, 178–79; Morse, *Letters Written During the Civil War*, 137–38; *CWDR*, 277–78.

8. Goodwin, *Team of Rivals*, 520.

9. Klement, *Limits of Dissent*, 166–68, 215, 178–79; McPherson, *Battle Cry*, 597.

10. Dowdey, *Wartime Papers of R. E. Lee*, 483; Judith W. McGuire. *Diary of a Southern Refugee During the War* (New York: Arno Press, 1972), 211–12; Wagner, *Civil War: 365*, Mar. 23.

11. Faust, *Illustrated Encyclopedia*, 392–93; National Park Service, "Jackson" battle summary, at http://www.nps.gov.history/hps/abpp/battles /ms008.htm; Grant, *Memoirs*, 265; Nevins, *Ordeal of the Union* 4, part 1:59.

12. McPherson, *Battle Cry*, 647–48.

13. Ibid., 630; Faust, *Illustrated Encyclopedia*, 126; Grant, *Memoirs*, 269–73 (quote, 272–73).

14. McPherson, *Battle Cry*, 630–31; Freeman, *Letters from Two Brothers*, 74.

15. Paul M. Angle and Earl Schenck Miers, *Tragic Years, 1860–1865: A Documentary History of the American Civil War* (New York: Simon & Schuster, 1960), 2: 608–9.

16. Grant, *Memoirs*, 276–77; Paul Mathless, ed. *Voices of the Civil War: Vicksburg* (Richmond, VA: Time-Life Books, 1997), 92–93 (Jones quote).

17. McPherson, *Negro's Civil War*, 173; *CWDR*, 431.

18. Iver Bernstein, *The New York City Draft Riots: Their Significance for American Society and Politics in the Age of the Civil War* (New York: Oxford University Press, 1990), 11; *CWDR*, 432.

19. *New York Times*, June 4, 1863; Bernstein, *Draft Riots*, 11.

20. *CWDR*, 432.

21. McPherson, *Negro's Civil War*, 186–87; McPherson, *Battle Cry*, 634; *CWDR*, 432–33.

22. Faust, *Illustrated Encyclopedia*, 76; Nevins, *Ordeal of the Union* 4, part 1:79–80; McPherson, *Battle Cry*, 649; Andrews, *The South Reports the Civil War*, 303–4.

23. Basler, *Collected Works*, 6: 257.

24. Wert, *Sword of Lincoln*, 263.

25. Long, *Day by Day*, 366.

26. Basler, *Collected Works*, 6: 281, 282.

27. *CWDR*, 533, 553–54; Faust, *Illustrated Encyclopedia*, 200; Angle and Miers, *Tragic Years*, 2: 613–14; Mary Webster Loughborough, *My Cave Life in Vicksburg* (New York: D. Appleton and Company, 1864), 89–90.

28. Fishel, *Secret War*, 459; Wert, *Sword of Lincoln*, 264.

29. Basler, *Collected Works*, 6: 181; *CWDR*, 144; Long, *Day by Day*, 686 (May 9).

30. Robert Garlick Hill Kean, *Inside the Confederate Government: The Diary of Robert Garlick Hill Kean*, edited by Edward Younger (Baton Rouge: Louisiana State University Press, 1993), 75–76.

31. Angle and Miers, *Tragic Years*, 2: 628–29.

32. Faust, *Illustrated Encyclopedia*, 764–65.

33. Wert, *Sword of Lincoln*, 264.

34. Long, *Day by Day*, 371; Angle and Miers, *Tragic Years*, 2: 630–31; McPherson, *Battle Cry*, 646–49.

35. Wert, *Sword of Lincoln*, 265–66.

36. Ibid., 266–69; *CWDR*, 417; McPherson, *Battle Cry*, 652, 636; Nevins, *Ordeal of the Union* 4, part 1:71.

37. Alpheus S. Williams, *From the Cannon's Mouth: The Civil War Letters of General Alpheus S. Williams* (Lincoln: University of Nebraska Press, 1995), 221.

38. Whitman, *Wound Dresser*, 89–91; Wert, *Sword of Lincoln*, 273.

39. Wert, *Sword of Lincoln*, 274–85; Grant, *Memoirs*, 290.

40. *CWDR*, 287–89; Wert, *Sword of Lincoln*, 285–95.

41. McPherson, *Battle Cry*, 650; James Z. Rabun, "Alexander H. Stephens and Jefferson Davis," *American Historical Review* 58, no. 2 (Jan. 1953): 290–321 (esp. 304–6); Grant, *Memoirs*, 291–93; Wert, *Sword of Lincoln*, 295–303.

42. Sophronia Bucklin, *In Hospital and Camp* (Philadelphia: J. E. Potter and Company, 1869), 139; Basler, *Complete Works*, 6: 314; Edward Colimore, "Fresh News from Gettysburg Battleground," *Philadelphia Inquirer*, May 31, 2009, at http://www.philly.com/inquirer/special/20090531_Fresh _news_from_Gettysburg_battleground.html; McPherson, *Battle Cry*, 609, 637–38, 664; Rabun, "Alexander H. Stephens and Jefferson Davis," 306.

43. Long, *Day by Day*, 381–82; Basler, *Complete Works*, 6: 409.

44. Long, *Day by Day*, 382; Faust, *Illustrated Encyclopedia*, 727 (Gen. Strong).

45. McPherson, *Battle Cry*, 609.

46. Basler, *Collected Works*, 6: 326.

47. McPherson, *Battle Cry*, 610; Bernstein, *Draft Riots*, 18; Angle and Miers, *Tragic Years*, 2: 679–82; "The New York City Draft Riots of 1863" (excerpt from Leslie M. Harris, *In the Shadow of Slavery: African Americans in New*

York City, 1626–1863), at http://www.press.uchicago.edu/Misc /Chicago/317749.html.

48. *CWDR*, 533; Basler, *Complete Works*, 7: 39.

49. *CWDR*, 433–34; McPherson, *Negro's Civil War*, 190–91; "The 54th Massachusetts Infantry Regiment (African)" at http://www.mycivilwar .com/regiments/usa-ma/ma_inf_reg_54.htm.

50. Basler, *Collected Works*, 6: 357; McPherson, *Battle Cry*, 794.

51. Davis, *Look Away!*, 178.

52. McPherson, *Negro's Civil War*, 197 et seq.; *CWDR*, 432.

53. McPherson, *Battle Cry*, 786.

54. Ibid., 611; Bernstein, *Draft Riots*, 40.

55. Hotchkiss, *Make Me a Map of the Valley*, 168–69; L. M. (Louisa May) Alcott, *Hospital Sketches* (Boston: J. Redpath, 1863), 33–35.

56. *CWDR*, 289.

57. Ibid., 533, 565–66.

58. David Lane, *A Soldier's Diary: The Story of a Volunteer, 1862–1865* (privately printed, 1905), 88; James B. Mitchell Papers, LC (letter of October 4, 1863).

59. Long, *Day by Day*, 403; McPherson, *Battle Cry*, 670.

60. Donald, *Liberty and Union*, 152; Faust, *Illustrated Encyclopedia*, 423.

61. *CWDR*, 533; "The 54th Massachusetts Infantry Regiment," at http:// www.mycivilwar.com/regiments/usa-ma/ma_inf_reg_54.htm.

62. McPherson, *Battle Cry*, 670–71; Faust, *Illustrated Encyclopedia*, 650; *CWDR*, 533.

63. McPherson, *Battle Cry*, 671, 696–98; *CWDR*, 289, 534.

64. McPherson, *Battle Cry*, 696; *CWDR*, 291.

65. Beatty, *Memoirs of a Volunteer*, 244.

66. Nevins, *Ordeal of the Union* 4, part 1:195–99; McPherson, *Battle Cry*, 672–74; Wagner, *Civil War: 365*, Sept. 19; Beatty, *Memoirs*, 252.

67. John Hay, *Lincoln and the Civil War in the Diaries and Letters of John Hay*, edited by Tyler Dennett (Westport, CT: Negro Universities Press, 1972), 93; *CWDR*, 351; McPherson, *Battle Cry*, 675.

68. Basler, *Collected Works*, 6: 478; Goodwin, *Team of Rivals*, 590.

69. Davis, *Look Away!*, 214–15.

70. Caleb Henry Carlton Papers, LC.

71. Beatty, *Memoirs*, 256–58.

72. *CWDR*, 534; Long, *Day by Day*, 418; Naval Historical Center, "Ships of the Confederate States; CSS *David* (1863–1865?)," at http://www.history .navy.mil/photos/sh-us-cs/csa-sh/csash-ag/david.htm.

73. *CWDR*, 465; Lillian Schlissel, ed., *Conscience in America: A Documentary History of Conscientious Objection in America, 1757–1967* (New York: E. P. Dutton & Co., Inc., 1968), 108–9.

74. Kean, *Inside the Confederate Government*, 108–9; McPherson, *Battle Cry*, 676–77; Long, *Day by Day*, 427.

75. Long, *Day by Day*, 421; McPherson, *Battle Cry*, 684–88, 689–92; Current, *Confederacy* (Macmillan), 186–88; *CWDR*, 33–34.

76. *CWDR*, 534, 566.

77. Long, *Day by Day*, 423–24.

78. Grant, *Memoirs*, 313–15; McPherson, *Battle Cry*, 676.

79. *CWDR*, 34; Chicago Sanitary Commission, "North-Western Fair for the Sanitary Commission" (Chicago: 1863), at http://www.wisconsinhistory .org/turningpoints/search.asp?id=95, 1; "Sanitary Fairs — Civilian Fund-Raisers," at http://civilwar.bluegrass.net/HomeFront/ sanitaryfairs.html; Baker, *Cyclone in Calico*, 169–70; L. P. Brockett, *Woman's Work in the Civil War: A Record of Heroism, Patriotism and Patience* (Philadelphia: Zeigler, McCurdy, 1867), 561; Library of Congress, "The Construction of the Proclamation," at http://www.loc.gov/exhibits/ treasures/trto28.html.

80. Sidebar sources: Cumming, *Journal of Hospital Life*, 128, 112; *CWDR*, 623–24; Whitman, *Wound Dresser*, 123–24.

81. Long, *Day by Day*, 429.

82. Ibid., 430; McPherson, *Battle Cry*, 677.

83. Wagner, *Civil War: 365*, Oct. 21; Carl Nolte, "Russian Warship Makes Rare S.F. Appearance," *San Francisco Chronicle*, June 22, 2010; Silas Ruark, "Russian Sailors Buried on Mare Island (near Vallejo)," at http://www .wadiocese.com/edocs_comments.php?id=97_0_13_0_C68.

84. Lawrence Van Alstyne, *Diary of an Enlisted Man* (New Haven, CT: Tuttle, Morehouse & Taylor, 1910), 213–14.

85. Goodwin, *Team of Rivals*, 583; Dennett, *Lincoln and the Civil War*, 119; "Edward Everett," at http://www.harvardsquarelibrary.org /HVDpresidents/everett.php.

86. Goodwin, *Team of Rivals*, 585–86; Hay, *Lincoln and the Civil War*, 121.

87. Baker, *Cyclone in Calico*, 171–72.

88. *CWDR*, 293.

89. Wagner, *Civil War: 365*, Sept. 22; Baker, *Cyclone in Calico*, 173–74.

90. Charles A. Dana, *Recollections of the Civil War: With the Leaders at Washington and in the Field in the Sixties* (Lincoln: University of Nebraska Press, 1996), 150; McPherson, *Battle Cry*, 678–81 (Clay quote, 681).

91. Davis, *Look Away!*, 167–70; ABC-CLIO *Encyclopedia*, 2: 1, 359–60; *CWDR*, 293.

92. Cooper, *Jefferson Davis, American*, 466–67.

93. *CWDR*, 155; Melinda Lawson, "A Profound National Devotion: The Civil War Union Leagues and the Construction of a New National Patriotism" in *Civil War History* 48, no. 4 (Dec. 2002): 338–62 (Hale material, 338–39).

94. McPherson, *Battle Cry*, 698–701; *CWDR*, 155, 762–63; Basler, *Collected Works*, 7: 53–56.

95. Dowdey, *Wartime Papers of R. E. Lee*, 642; Cooper, *Jefferson Davis, American*, 467.

96. Goodwin, *Team of Rivals*, 590–93; Basler, *Collected Works*, 7: 63–64.

97. Cooper, *Jefferson Davis, American*, 467–68, 364 (lack of trust).

98. Joseph T. Glatthaar, *Forged in Battle: The Civil War Alliance of Black Soldiers and White Officers* (New York: The Free Press, 1990), 45–46; *CWDR*, 434.

99. Dowdey, *Wartime Papers of R. E. Lee*, 645; Beatty, *Memoirs*, 267–68.

100. Long, *Day by Day*, 449.

101. *CWDR*, 155, 408; Davis, *Look Away!*, 157–58.

102. Davis, *Look Away!*, 211.

103. McPherson, *Negro's Civil War*, 278.

104. Howard Jones, *Blue and Gray Diplomacy*, 314–15; Long, *Day by Day*, 453.

105. Glatthaar, *Forged in Battle*, 173; *CWDR*, 434.

106. Goodwin, *Team of Rivals*, 604–5.

107. J. Matthew Gallman, *America's Joan of Arc: The Life of Anna Elizabeth Dickinson* (New York: Oxford University Press, 2006), 36–38; Frank, *Women in the American Civil War*, 1: 210–12.

108. *CWDR*, 295–96.

109. Donald E. Collins, "War Crime or Justice? General George Pickett and the Mass Execution of Deserters in Civil War Kinston, North Carolina," at http://homepages.rootsweb.ancestry.com/~ncuv/kinston1.htm; *New York Times*, March 11, 1864; Davis, *Look Away!*, 273.

110. Goodwin, *Team of Rivals*, 603; Long, *Day by Day*, 463.

111. *CWDR*, 36; McPherson, *Battle Cry*, 763–64.

112. Davis, *Look Away!*, 181–82; McPherson, *Battle Cry*, 693–94; Long, *Day by Day*, 465; *CWDR*, 449, 534, 566.

113. Goodwin, *Team of Rivals*, 606; McPherson, *Battle Cry*, 714–15.

114. *CWDR*, 156; "Constitutional Law. Freedom of Religion. Exemption of Conscientious Objectors from Military Service," *Columbia Law Review* 43, no. 1 (Jan. 1943): 112, n. 5.

115. Long, *Day by Day*, 469; John Ransom, *Andersonville Diary* (Philadelphia: Douglass Bros., 1883), 55; Wagner, *Civil War: 365*, Aug. 22.

116. *CWDR*, 296; Dowdey, *Wartime Papers of R. E. Lee*, 678.

117. Long, *Day by Day*, 471; Basler, *Collected Works*, 235n.

118. *New York Times*, March 11, 1864.

119. "History of the Twenty-Ninth (Colored) Regt. C. V. Infantry," on the Connecticut State Library website, at http://www.cslib.org/wmwebb /History29th.htm ; Frank, *Women in the American Civil War*, 1: 156–57; Basler, *Collected Works*, 7: 234–35.

120. Wagner, *Civil War: 365*, Nov. 13; Willard Family Papers, LC; The American Presidency Project. Text of Lincoln's executive order, at http://www.presidency.ucsb.edu/ws/index.php?pid=70011.

121. *CWDR*, 633; Wagner, *Civil War: 365*, Oct. 13.

122. *CWDR*, 296–98; McPherson, *Negro's Civil War*, 278–80.

123. CWDR, 296–98; Faust, *Illustrated Encyclopedia*, 106–7.

124. Grant, *Memoirs*, 366.

125. CWDR, 296–98.

126. "French Intervention and Maximilian," at http://historicaltextarchive .com/print.php?action=section&artid=747.

127. *CWDR*, 298–99, 435; McPherson, *Battle Cry*, 748; Basler, *Collected Works*, 7: 302–3; Tap, *Over Lincoln's Shoulder*, 195–96 (newspaper quote), 200, 205.

128. McPherson, *Battle Cry*, 793.

129. *CWDR*, 435.

130. Ibid.; Cooper, *Jefferson Davis, American*, 480; Freeman, *Letters from Two Brothers*, 111.

CHAPTER 4

1. McPherson, *Battle Cry*, 731, citing *OR*, series 1, vol. 36, part 2:672.
2. Jean Edward Smith, *Grant* (New York: Simon & Schuster, 2001), 370.
3. McPherson, *Battle Cry*, 809.
4. Cumming, *Hospital Life*, 158 (diary entry for December 31, 1864).
5. Warren Akin, *Letters of Warren Akin, Confederate Congressman*, edited by Bell Irvin Wiley (Athens: University of Georgia Press, 1959), 32.
6. Worthington Chauncey Ford, ed., *A Cycle of Adams Letters, 1861–1865*, 2 vols. (Boston: Houghton Mifflin Company, 1920), 2: 148.
7. Current, *Confederacy* (Macmillan), 186–88.
8. Wert, *Sword of Lincoln*, 333–34; Joseph Glatthaar, *General Lee's Army: From Victory to Collapse* (New York: The Free Press, 2008), 364; *CWDR*, 299.
9. ABC-CLIO *Encyclopedia*, 1: 218–20; Wert, *Sword of Lincoln*, 336–38; Glatthaar, *General Lee's Army*, 365.
10. Wert, *Sword of Lincoln*, 340–42; Glatthaar, *General Lee's Army*, 365–68.
11. ABC-CLIO *Encyclopedia*, 1: 220; Long, *Day by Day*, 495; Wert, *Sword of Lincoln*, 344; McPherson, *Battle Cry*, 726–28; Dana, *Recollections*, 194–95.
12. Wert, *Sword of Lincoln*, 343–47.
13. Long, *Day by Day*, 495, 497; ABC-CLIO *Encyclopedia*, 1: 220; Faust, *Illustrated Encyclopedia*, 57–58, 665; Wert, *Sword of Lincoln*, 347.
14. Wert, *Sword of Lincoln*, 348–50; Stephen E. Ambrose, *Upton and the Army* (Baton Rouge: Louisiana State University Press, 1993), 30–33.
15. Ernest B. Furgurson, *Ashes of Glory: Richmond at War* (New York: Alfred A. Knopf, 1996), 266, 268–69; Wert, *Sword of Lincoln*, 355; McPherson, *Battle Cry*, 728.
16. Wert, *Sword of Lincoln*, 351–54; Welch, *A Confederate Surgeon's Letters*, 96–97; Furgurson, *Ashes of Glory*, 268–69; Dowdey, *Wartime Papers of R. E. Lee*, 736; *CWDR*, 307; Faust, *Illustrated Encyclopedia*, 227.
17. Faust, *Illustrated Encyclopedia*, 228; Whitman, *Wound Dresser*, 181–82.
18. McPherson, *Battle Cry*, 724; Long, *Day by Day*, 501–2, 506.
19. McPherson, *Battle Cry*, 724; Faust, *Illustrated Encyclopedia*, 228.
20. Wert, *Sword of Lincoln*, 356, 358.
21. Ibid., 358–60; Grant, *Personal Memoirs*, 432.
22. Kathryn Abbey Hanna, "Incidents of the Confederate Blockade," *Journal of Southern History* 11, no. 2 (May 1945): 218.
23. Dowdey, *Wartime Papers of R. L. Lee*, 753; Wert, *Sword of Lincoln*, 361; "The Battle of Totopotomoy Creek, May 29–31, 1864," at http://www.nps.gov/rich/historyculture/tcbattlebull.htm.
24. *CWDR*, 156; Goodwin, *Team of Rivals*, 624; "Fremont and the Radical Democracy," on the HarpWeek website, at http://elections.harpweek.com/1864/Overview-1864-2.htm; Wert, *Sword of Lincoln*, 361; "Cold Harbor," battle summary, at http://www.nps.gov/hps/abpp/battles/va062.htm.
25. Wert, *Sword of Lincoln*, 361–63; Faust, *Illustrated Encyclopedia*, 79.
26. Wert, *Sword of Lincoln*, 364–66; Grant, *Memoirs*, 444–45; McPherson, *Battle Cry*, 735.
27. Faust, *Illustrated Encyclopedia*, 79.
28. Long, *Day by Day*, 517; Faust, *Illustrated Encyclopedia*, 763; Wert, *Sword of Lincoln*, 377; Whitman, *Wound Dresser*, 194.
29. Goodwin, *Team of Rivals*, 625–26; McPherson, *Battle Cry*, 716.
30. Faust, *Illustrated Encyclopedia*, 79, 729–30; "Brices Cross Roads National Battlefield Site: The Battle," at http://www.nps.gov/brcr/the-battle.htm; *CWDR*, 426; Long, *Day by Day*, 520; Semmes, *The Cruise of the Alabama and the Sumter*, 2: 274–75.
31. McPherson, *Battle Cry*, 739; Faust, *Illustrated Encyclopedia*, 763; "General David Hunter in the Shenandoah Valley; Operations Report for Period June 6–July 14, 1864," from *OR*, series 1, vol. 37, part 1, at the Virginia Military Institute Archives, http://www.vmi.edu/archives.aspx?id=4765.
32. Wert, *Sword of Lincoln*, 370; John Whiteclay Chambers, ed., *The Oxford Companion to American Military History* (New York: Oxford University Press, 1999), 59.
33. Basler, *Collected Works*, 7: 393; Long, *Day by Day*, 522; Semmes, *The Cruise of the Alabama and the Sumter*, 2: 277–78.
34. McPherson, *Battle Cry*, 706; McPherson, *Negro's Civil War*, 206; Wert, *Sword of Lincoln*, 371–72; *CWDR*, 436.
35. Basler, *Collected Works*, 7: 394–95.
36. "Terrible Calamity at the Washington Arsenal," *Daily National Intelligence*, June 18, 1864, at http://www.mcelfresh.ws/DC_arsenalfire.html; *CWDR*, 27.
37. Wert, *Sword of Lincoln*, 372–73; McPherson, *Battle Cry*, 740–41.

38. Wagner, *Civil War: 365*, May 27; Musicant, *Divided Waters*, 350–53 (Kell quote, 352); Luraghi, *A History of the Confederate Navy*, 319–20; Edmondston, *"Journal of a Secesh Lady,"* 590.
39. Wert, *Sword of Lincoln*, 376–77; Faust, *Illustrated Encyclopedia*, 833; Long, *Day by Day*, 526–27; Hay, *Lincoln and the Civil War*, 195.
40. Long, *Day by Day*, 528; Current, *Encyclopedia of the Confederacy*, 2:504; Glatthaar, *General Lee's Army*, 426.
41. Hay, *Lincoln and the Civil War*, 197.
42. Wert, *Sword of Lincoln*, 380–82.
43. Goodwin, *Team of Rivals*, 631–32; McGinty, *Lincoln and the Court*, 227 (Lincoln quote); McPherson, *Battle Cry*, 749–50; Nevins, *Ordeal of the Union* 4, part 2:55.
44. Long, *Day by Day*, 529–30; Goodwin, *Team of Rivals*, 632; McGinty, *Lincoln and the Court*, 226 (Wade remark).
45. Goodwin, *Team of Rivals*, 632–33; Basler, *Collected Works*, 7: 419; Long, *Day by Day*, 531.
46. Faust, *Illustrated Encyclopedia*, 794–95; Donald, *Liberty and Union*, 159 (manifesto quote).
47. Long, *Day by Day*, 532–33; Peter J. Parish, *The American Civil War* (London: Eyre Methuen, 1975), 142; *New York Times*, August 31, 1864; Furgurson, *Ashes of Glory*, 275; Glatthaar, *General Lee's Army*, 426.
48. McPherson, *Battle Cry*, 748–49; Faust, *Illustrated Encyclopedia*, 765 ; Harlan Hoyt Horner, *Lincoln and Greeley* (Urbana: University of Illinois Press, 1953), 296–98.
49. Mary Deborah Petite, *The Women Will Howl: The Union Army Capture of Roswell and New Manchester, Georgia, and the Forced Relocation of Mill Workers* (Jefferson, NC: McFarland & Company, 2008), 8, 82, 66, 110, 144.
50. McPherson, *Battle Cry*, 752; Nevins, *Ordeal of the Union* 4, part 2:56; Faust, *Illustrated Encyclopedia*, 504; Wert, *Sword of Lincoln*, 386; Wagner, *Civil War: 365*, Nov. 23; Goodwin, *Team of Rivals*, 641–42 (Breckinridge quote).
51. Goodwin, *Team of Rivals*, 642–43; Wert, *Sword of Lincoln*, 386; Nevins, *Ordeal of the Union* 4, part 2:88–89.
52. McPherson, *Battle Cry*, 756; Goodwin, *Team of Rivals*, 643; Nevins, *Ordeal of the Union* 4, part 2:88–89; National Park Service, "Battle Summary: Fort Stevens," at http://www.nps.gov/hps/abpp/battles/dc001.htm.
53. McPherson, *Battle Cry*, 748–49; Faust, *Illustrated Encyclopedia*, 765–66.
54. Long, *Day by Day*, 540–41; McPherson, *Battle Cry*, 753.
55. Long, *Day by Day*, 541; Horner, *Lincoln and Greeley*, 304–11; McPherson, *Battle Cry*, 757–58, 766–67.
56. Faust, *Illustrated Encyclopedia*, 565–66; National Park Service, "Battle Summary: Peachtree Creek," at http://www.nps.gov/hps/abpp/battles/ga016.htm.
57. Faust, *Illustrated Encyclopedia*, 27–28.
58. Wert, *Sword of Lincoln*, 382.
59. Faust, *Illustrated Encyclopedia*, 415–16; Grant, *Memoirs*, 468.
60. Faust, *Illustrated Encyclopedia*, 250–51.
61. *CWDR*, 313–14; Faust, *Illustrated Encyclopedia*, 125; Wert, *Sword of Lincoln*, 383–85; McPherson, *Battle Cry*, 760; Furgurson, *Ashes of Glory*, 274.
62. Current, *Encyclopedia of the Confederacy*, 2: 727–28.
63. Furgurson, *Ashes of Glory*, 275.
64. Wagner, *Civil War: 365*, May 28; McPherson, *Battle Cry*, 761; Long, *Day by Day*, 551–52; Nevins, *Ordeal of the Union* 3, part 2:95.
65. Goodwin, *Team of Rivals*, 650.
66. Ibid., 647–48.
67. McPherson, *Battle Cry*, 765; Nevins, *Ordeal of the Union* 4, part 2:98–101.
68. McPherson, *Battle Cry*, 774–75; Kennett, *Sherman*, 251.
69. Current, *Encyclopedia of the Confederacy*, 3: 1087; Furgurson, *Ashes of Glory*, 280.
70. "Correspondence Pertaining to Sherman's Evacuation of Atlanta," from *OR*, series 1, vol. 39, part 2, at http://www.civilwarhome.com/atlantaevacuation.htm; Kennett, *Sherman*, 251; McPherson, *Battle Cry*, 809.
71. Ransom, *Andersonville Diary*, 133–39; Faust, *Illustrated Encyclopedia*, 837; Long, *Day by Day*, 695.
72. Sears, *McClellan*, 374–75; McPherson, *Battle Cry*, 775–76.
73. Faust, *Illustrated Encyclopedia*, 336–37; Glatthaar, *General Lee's Army*, 383–84.
74. "Archives of Maryland, Historical List, Constitutional Convention, 1864," at http://www.msa.md.gov/msa/speccol/sc2600/sc2685/html/conv1864.html; Lane, *A Soldier's Diary*, 201–2.
75. Frank L. Klement, *Dark Lanterns: Secret Political Societies, Conspiracies, and Treason Trials in the Civil War* (Baton Rouge: Louisiana State University

Press, 1984), 189; Oklahoma Historical Society, "Cabin Creek, battles of," *Encyclopedia of Oklahoma History & Culture*, at http://digital.library .okstate.edu/encyclopedia/entries/C/CA001.html; Current, *Confederacy* (Macmillan), 448; Faust, *Illustrated Encyclopedia*, 602–3; *CWDR*, 314.

76. *CWDR*, 314.

77. Basler, *Collected Works*, 8: 18–19.

78. Cooper, *Jefferson Davis, American*, 489–90; Kennett, *Sherman*, 258; Long, *Day by Day*, 574, 578.

79. McPherson, *Battle Cry*, 786–88; *CWDR*, 315.

80. Glatthaar, *Forged in Battle*, 156; *CWDR*, 315–16, 317.

81. McPherson, *Negro's Civil War*, 286–87.

82. Faust, *Illustrated Encyclopedia*, 264; *CWDR*, 536, 563–64.

83. McGinty, *Lincoln and the Court*, 209, 214 (Hay), 229 (Sumner).

84. *CWDR*, 314–15; McPherson, *Battle Cry*, 779–80; Long, *Day by Day*, 585–86; Habersham Family Papers, LC.

85. Long, *Day by Day*, 585–86; Faust, *Illustrated Encyclopedia*, 780, 793–94; *ABC-CLIO Encyclopedia*, 4: 2041–42.

86. Kennett, *Sherman*, 258–59.

87. Luraghi, *History of the Confederate Navy*, 330–31; Naval Historical Center, "CSS *Albemarle* (1864–1864)," at http://www.history.navy.mil/photos /sh-us-cs/csa-sh/csash-ag/albmrl.htm, and "Report of Lieutenant William Barker Cushing, U.S. Navy," at http://www.history.navy.mil /docs/civilwar/64-10-30.htm.

88. Jacqueline Bernard, *Journey Toward Freedom: The Story of Sojourner Truth* (New York: Feminist Press at the City University of New York, 1990), 202–3, 215–16; Wagner, *Civil War: 365*, June 21; Mr. Lincoln's White House, "Sojourner Truth (1797–1883)," at http://www .mrlincolnswhitehouse.org/inside.asp?ID=671&subjectID=2.

89. McPherson, *Battle Cry*, 833–34.

90. Ibid., 804–5; Long, *Day by Day*, 594; Sears, *McClellan*, 386; Lane, *Soldier's Diary*, 226; John Wilkes Booth, *"Right or Wrong, God Judge Me": The Writings of John Wilkes Booth*, edited by John Rhodehamel and Louise Taper (Urbana: University of Illinois Press, 1997), 124.

91. *CWDR*, 316; Long, *Day by Day*, 597; Kennett, *Sherman*, 260–62.

92. *New York Times*, Nov. 17, 1864.

93. *CWDR*, 317; McPherson, *Battle Cry*, 812–13.

94. *CWDR*, 319; Faust, *Illustrated Encyclopedia*, 722.

95. Faust, *Illustrated Encyclopedia*, 810.

96. McGinty, *Lincoln and the Court*, 232; Basler, *Collected Works*, 8: 151–52.

97. Wert, *Sword of Lincoln*, 394; *CWDR*, 316; Wagner, *Civil War: 365*, Sept. 24; McPherson, *Negro's Civil War*, 299.

98. *CWDR*, 319; McPherson, *Battle Cry*, 813–15; Wagner, *Civil War: 365*, Sept. 23 and 28; McPherson, *Negro's Civil War*, 229–33.

99. Faust, *Illustrated Encyclopedia*, 99–100; *CWDR*, 321; Grant, *Memoirs*, 509; Musicant, *Divided Waters*, 423–24.

100. Kennett, *Sherman*, 265; McPherson, *Battle Cry*, 811; Long, *Day by Day*, 613–14.

101. *CWDR*, 321; Faust, *Illustrated Encyclopedia*, 99–100; Wagner, *Civil War: 365*, Nov. 27; Grant, *Memoirs*, 510.

102. Davis, *Look Away!*, 217.

103. Goodwin, *Team of Rivals*, 690–91; Basler, *Collected Works*, 8: 220–21; Freedmen & Southern Society Project, "Chronology of Emancipation During the Civil War," at http://www.history.umd.edu/Freedmen /chronol.htm.

104. McPherson, *Battle Cry*, 820–21, 841; McPherson, *Negro's Civil War*, 299; Freedmen & Southern Society Project, "Newspaper Account of a Meeting Between Black Religious Leaders and Union Military Authorities," at http://www.history.umd.edu/Freedmen/savmtg.htm; Faust, *Illustrated Encyclopedia*, 273, 574; Musicant, *Divided Waters*, 427–29.

105. McPherson, *Negro's Civil War*, 299–300; text of Special Field Orders, No. 15, at the Freedmen & Southern Society Project website, http://www .history.umd.edu/Freedmen/sfo15.htm.

106. Kelly, *Creating a National Home*, 45.

107. Cooper, *Jefferson Davis, American*, 513–15; Craig A. Bauer, "The Last Effort: The Secret Mission of the Confederate Diplomat Duncan F. Kenner," *Louisiana History: The Journal of the Louisiana Historical Association* 22, no. 1 (Winter 1981): 67–95 (departure date, 80).

108. Long, *Day by Day*, 628; McPherson, *Battle Cry*, 821; Douglas J. and Rufus W. Cater Papers, LC (Douglas Cater to his cousin Fanny, Feb. 3, 1863).

109. Goodwin, *Team of Rivals*, 691–92.

110. McPherson, *Battle Cry*, 839–40; Goodwin, *Team of Rivals*, 688–90; Long, *Day by Day*, 630.

111. McPherson, *Battle Cry*, 825–26; *CWDR*, 323–24; McGinty, *Lincoln and the Court*, 243–44.

112. Basler, *Collected Works*, 8: 256, 282; Goodwin, *Team of Rivals*, 692–94; McPherson, *Battle Cry*, 822; Josiah Gorgas, *The Journals of Josiah Gorgas, 1857–1878*, edited by Sarah W. Wiggins (Tuscaloosa: University of Alabama Press, 1995), 151 (diary entries for Feb. 8, 10, 1865).

113. *CWDR*, 322; Wert, *Sword of Lincoln*, 396.

114. Cooper, *Jefferson Davis, American*, 512–13.

115. Long, *Day by Day*, 637, 639.

116. Ibid., 639–40.

117. McPherson, *Battle Cry*, 828–29; Long, *Day by Day*, 640; *CWDR*, 437; Susie King Taylor, *Reminiscences of My Life in Camp* (New York: Arno Press, 1968), 42.

118. Long, *Day by Day*, 642–43.

119. *CWDR*, 436, 737, 774–78; Freedmen & Southern Society website, at http://www.history.umd.edu/Freedmen/fbact.htm (act establishing Freedmen's Bureau) and http://www.history.umd.edu/Freedmen /soldfam.htm (resolution); Kelly, *Creating a National Home*, 46–47.

120. Goodwin, *Team of Rivals*, 697–99; Long, *Day by Day*, 647; Basler, *Collected Works*, 8: 332–33; Mr. Lincoln's White House, "Frederick Douglass (1817–1895)," at http://www.mrlincolnswhitehouse.org/inside .asp?ID=38&subjectID=2.

121. Long, *Day by Day*, 648; McPherson, *Battle Cry*, 826.

122. Cooper, *Jefferson Davis, American*, 517–18.

123. Bauer, "The Last Effort," 91–94; McPherson, *Battle Cry*, 837–38.

124. *CWDR*, 324.

125. Ibid., 324–25.

126. Goodwin, *Team of Rivals*, 708–9.

127. *CWDR*, 322; Wert, *Sword of Lincoln*, 397–98; Goodwin, *Team of Rivals*, 710; Basler, *Collected Works*, 8: 374.

128. Wert, *Sword of Lincoln*, 399; Goodwin, *Team of Rivals*, 712–13.

129. Basler, *Collected Works*, 8: 377–78.

130. *CWDR*, 322–23; Wert, *Sword of Lincoln*, 400; Goodwin, *Team of Rivals*, 715.

131. Wert, *Sword of Lincoln*, 403–4; McPherson, *Battle Cry*, 845–47; Wagner, *Civil War: 365*, Dec. 3; *CWDR*, 324–25.

132. Goodwin, *Team of Rivals*, 716, 718–19; McPherson, *Battle Cry*, 846–47; *CWDR*, 159.

133. Cooper, *Jefferson Davis, American*, 524; McPherson, *Battle Cry*, 847.

134. *CWDR*, 326.

135. Ibid., 326–27.

136. Ibid., 326–28; Goodwin, *Team of Rivals*, 725–27; Gary W. Gallagher, *The Confederate War* (Cambridge, MA: Harvard University Press, 1997), 96.

137. Basler, *Collected Works*, 8: 399–405 (Louisiana quote, 403); Goodwin, *Team of Rivals*, 727–28; Wagner, *Civil War: 365*, Apr. 28.

138. Wagner, *Civil War: 365*, Dec. 9, 10, 11; *CWDR*, 231; Abraham Lincoln Papers, LC (Letter from James S. Knox to his father, Apr. 15, 1865).

139. Wagner, *Civil War: 365*, Dec.11; Goodwin, *Team of Rivals*, 744; *CWDR*, 231.

140. *CWDR*, 324.

141. Long, *Day by Day*, 679–80; J. D. G. Shea, ed., *The Lincoln Memorial: A Record of the Life, Assassination, and Obsequies of the Martyred President* (New York: Bunce & Huntington, 1865), 168; Wagner, *Civil War: 365*, Dec. 12.

142. *CWDR*, 50, 231, 324.

143. Wagner, *Civil War: 365*, May 30.

144. Ibid., Sept. 30; Grant. *Memoirs*, 573; *CWDR*, 232; Long, *Day by Day*, 687.

145. Wagner, *Civil War: 365*, Dec. 15; Long, *Day by Day*, 689–91.

EPILOGUE

146. McPherson, *Battle Cry*, 854.

147. *CWDR*, 731–804; Wagner, *Civil War: 365*, Dec. 26, 27.

148. William Salter, *The Life of James W. Grimes, Governor of Iowa, 1854–1858; A Senator of the United States, 1859–1869* (New York: D. Appleton and Company, 1876), 135–36 (letter to Samuel J. Kirkwood, Jan. 28, 1861).

BIBLIOGRAPHY

Tens of thousands of volumes have been written about the Civil War, from general overviews to personal memoirs and detailed accounts of individual battles. Most of these works are in the collections of the Library of Congress, along with well over a thousand Civil War–related manuscript collections and much other material, such as maps, photographs, and drawings (see "Civil War Collections in the Library of Congress," page 244). The materials listed below are among the principal published and manuscript resources from which the information in *The Library of Congress Illustrated Timeline of the Civil War* was drawn.

REFERENCE WORKS AND GENERAL HISTORIES

Angle, Paul M., and Earl Schenck Miers. *Tragic Years, 1860–1865: A Documentary History of the American Civil War.* New York: Simon & Schuster, 1960.

Basler, Roy P., ed. *The Collected Works of Abraham Lincoln.* Vols. 4–8. New Brunswick, NJ: Rutgers University Press, 1953.

Current, Richard N., ed. in chief. *The Confederacy: Selections from the Four-Volume Simon & Schuster Encyclopedia of the Confederacy.* New York: Macmillan Reference, 1998.

———. *Encyclopedia of the Confederacy.* 4 vols. New York: Simon & Schuster, 1993.

Davis, William C. *Look Away! A History of the Confederate States of America.* New York: The Free Press, 2002.

Donald, David Herbert. *Liberty and Union.* Lexington, MA: D. C. Heath and Company, 1978.

Donald, David Herbert, Jean Harvey Baker, and Michael F. Holt. *The Civil War and Reconstruction.* New York: W. W. Norton, 2001.

Faust, Patricia L., ed. *Historical Times Illustrated Encyclopedia of the Civil War.* New York: Harper & Row, 1986.

Frank, Lisa Tendrich, ed. *Women in the American Civil War.* 2 vols. Santa Barbara, CA: ABC-CLIO, 2008.

Gallagher, Gary W. *The Confederate War.* Cambridge, MA: Harvard University Press, 1997.

Heidler, David S., and Jeanne T. Heidler, eds. *Encyclopedia of the American Civil War: A Political, Social, and Military History.* 5 vols. Santa Barbara, CA: ABC-CLIO, 2000.

Long, E. B., with Barbara Long. *The Civil War Day by Day: An Almanac, 1861–1865.* Garden City, NY: Doubleday & Company, 1971.

McPherson, James M. *Battle Cry of Freedom: The Civil War Era.* New York: Oxford University Press, 1988.

———. *Ordeal by Fire: The Civil War and Reconstruction.* 2nd ed. New York: McGraw-Hill, 1992.

———. *This Mighty Scourge: Perspectives on the Civil War.* New York: Oxford University Press, 2007.

Nevins, Allan. *Ordeal of the Union.* 4 vols. New York: Macmillan, 1992.

Parish, Peter J. *The American Civil War.* London: Eyre Methuen, 1975.

Rowland, Dunbar, ed. *Jefferson Davis, Constitutionalist: His Letters, Papers, and Speeches.* 10 vols. Jackson, MS: Mississippi Department of Archives and History, 1923.

Stephenson, Richard W. *Civil War Maps: An Annotated List of Maps and Atlases in the Library of Congress.* Washington, DC: Library of Congress, 1989. See, especially, the introductory essay on Civil War mapping.

Wagner, Margaret E. *The American Civil War: 365 Days.* New York: Harry N. Abrams, 2006.

Wagner, Margaret E., Gary W. Gallagher, and Paul Finkelman, eds. *The Library of Congress Civil War Desk Reference.* New York: Simon & Schuster, 2002.

Waugh, Joan, and Gary W. Gallagher, eds. *Wars Within a War: Controversy and Conflict over the American Civil War.* Chapel Hill: University of North Carolina Press, 2009.

BATTLEFIELDS AND THE MILITARY

Dowdey, Clifford, ed. *The Wartime Papers of R. E. Lee.* Boston: Little, Brown, 1961.

Eicher, John H., and David J. Eicher. *Civil War High Commands.* Stanford, CA: Stanford University Press, 2001.

Fishel, Edwin C. *The Secret War for the Union: The Untold Story of Military Intelligence in the Civil War.* Boston: Houghton Mifflin, 1996.

Glatthaar, Joseph. *Forged in Battle: The Civil War Alliance of Black Soldiers and White Officers.* New York: The Free Press, 1990.

———. *General Lee's Army: From Victory to Collapse.* New York: The Free Press, 2008.

———. "Profile in Leadership: Generalship and Resistance in Robert E. Lee's First Month in Command of the Army of Northern Virginia." In *Wars Within a War: Controversy and Conflict over the American Civil War*, edited by Joan Waugh and Gary W. Gallagher, 68–86. Chapel Hill: University of North Carolina Press, 2009.

Guthrie, James M. *Campfires of the Afro-American, or The Colored Man as a Patriot.* 1899. New York: Johnson Reprint Corporation, 1970.

Hanna, Kathryn Abbey. "Incidents of the Confederate Blockade." *The Journal of Southern History* 11, no. 2 (May 1945): 214–29.

Hattaway, Herman, and Archer Jones. *How the North Won: A Military History of the Civil War.* Urbana: University of Illinois Press, 1983.

Luraghi, Raimondo. *A History of the Confederate Navy.* Annapolis: Naval Institute Press, 1996.

Mathless, Paul, ed. *Voices of the Civil War: Vicksburg.* Richmond, VA: Time-Life Books, 1997.

McPherson, James M. *Crossroads of Freedom: Antietam.* New York: Oxford University Press, 2002.

———. *Tried by War: Abraham Lincoln as Commander in Chief.* New York: Penguin, 2008.

Musicant, Ivan. *Divided Waters: The Naval History of the Civil War.* New York: HarperCollins, 1995.

Nurick, Lester, and Roger W. Barrett. "Legality of Guerrilla Forces Under the Laws of War." *American Journal of International Law* 40, no. 3 (July 1946): 563–83.

Petite, Mary Deborah. *The Women Will Howl: The Union Army Capture of Roswell and New Manchester, Georgia, and the Forced Relocation of Mill Workers.* Jefferson, NC: McFarland & Company, 2008.

Sears, Stephen W. *Chancellorsville.* Boston: Houghton Mifflin, 1996.

———. *To the Gates of Richmond: The Peninsula Campaign.* New York: Ticknor & Fields, 1992.

Sutherland, Daniel E. *Fredericksburg and Chancellorsville: The Dare Mark Campaign.* Lincoln: University of Nebraska Press, 1998.

United States War Department. *The War of the Rebellion: A Compilation of the Official Records of the Union and Confederate Armies.* Also known as "Official Records," or OR. 70 vols. in 128 books. Washington, DC: Government Printing Office, 1880–1900.

Wert, Jeffry D. *The Sword of Lincoln: The Army of the Potomac.* New York: Simon & Schuster, 2005.

POLITICS, DIPLOMACY, AND THE HOME FRONTS

Andrews, J. Cutler. *The North Reports the Civil War.* Pittsburgh: University of Pittsburgh Press, 1985.

———. *The South Reports the Civil War.* Princeton, NJ: Princeton University Press, 1970.

Bauer, Craig A. "The Last Effort: The Secret Mission of the Confederate Diplomat, Duncan F. Kenner." *Louisiana History: The Journal of the Louisiana Historical Association* 22, no. 1 (Winter 1981): 67–95.

Bernstein, Iver. *The New York City Draft Riots: Their Significance for American Society and Politics in the Age of the Civil War.* New York: Oxford University Press, 1990.

Brockett, L. P. *Woman's Work in the Civil War: A Record of Heroism, Patriotism and Patience.* Philadelphia: Zeigler, McCurdy, 1867.

Freidel, Frank. "The Loyal Publication Society: A Pro-Union Propaganda Agency." *Mississippi Valley Historical Review* 26, no. 3 (Dec. 1939): 359–76.

Furgurson, Ernest B. *Ashes of Glory: Richmond at War.* New York: Alfred A. Knopf, 1996.

———. *Freedom Rising: Washington in the Civil War.* New York: Alfred A. Knopf, 2004.

Goodwin, Doris Kearns. *Team of Rivals: The Political Genius of Abraham Lincoln.* New York: Simon & Schuster, 2005.

Grimsley, Mark. *The Hard Hand of War: Union Military Policy Toward Southern Civilians, 1861–1865.* New York: Cambridge University Press, 1996.

Hoole, W. Stanley. *Vizetelly Covers the Confederacy.* Tuscaloosa, AL: Confederate Publishing Company, 1957.

Hyman, Harold Melvin. *Era of the Oath: Northern Loyalty Tests During the Civil War and Reconstruction.* Philadelphia: University of Pennsylvania Press, 1954.

Jones, Howard. *Blue and Gray Diplomacy: A History of Union and Confederate Foreign Relations.* Chapel Hill: University of North Carolina Press, 2010.

Kelly, Patrick J. *Creating a National Home: Building the Veterans' Welfare State.* Cambridge, MA: Harvard University Press, 1997.

Klein, Maury. *Days of Defiance: Sumter, Secession, and the Coming of the Civil War.* New York: Alfred A. Knopf, 1997.

Klement, Frank L. *Dark Lanterns: Secret Political Societies, Conspiracies, and Treason Trials in the Civil War.* Baton Rouge: Louisiana State University Press, 1984.

———. *The Limits of Dissent: Clement L. Vallandigham and the Civil War.* New York: Fordham University Press, 1998.

Lawson, Melinda. "'A Profound National Devotion': The Civil War Union Leagues and the Construction of a New National Patriotism." *Civil War History* 48, no. 4 (Dec. 2002): 338–62.

Maihafer, Harry J. *The General and the Journalists: Ulysses S. Grant, Horace Greeley, and Charles Dana.* Washington, DC: Brassey's Books, 2001.

Maxwell, William Quentin. *Lincoln's Fifth Wheel: The Political History of the United States Sanitary Commission.* New York: Longmans, Green & Co., 1956.

McGinty, Brian. *Lincoln and the Court.* Cambridge, MA: Harvard University Press, 2009.

McPherson, James M. *The Negro's Civil War: How American Negroes Felt and Acted During the War for the Union.* New York: Pantheon, 1965.

Miller, Robert Ryal. *Arms Across the Border: United States Aid to Juárez during the French Intervention in Mexico.* Philadelphia: The American Philosophical Society, 1973.

Neely, Mark E., Jr. *Southern Rights: Political Prisoners and the Myth of Confederate Constitutionalism.* Charlottesville: University Press of Virginia, 1999.

Perry, James M. *A Bohemian Brigade: The Civil War Correspondents—Mostly Rough, Sometimes Ready.* New York: John Wiley & Sons, 2000.

Schlissel, Lillian, ed. *Conscience in America: A Documentary History of Conscientious Objection in America, 1757–1967.* New York: E. P. Dutton & Co., 1968.

Tap, Bruce. *Over Lincoln's Shoulder: The Committee on the Conduct of the War.* Lawrence: University Press of Kansas, 1998.

Wheeler, Tom. *Mr. Lincoln's T-Mails: The Untold Story of How Abraham Lincoln Used the Telegraph to Win the Civil War.* New York: HarperCollins, 2006.

Wilson, Charles R. "Cincinnati's Reputation During the Civil War." *Journal of Southern History* 2, no. 4 (Nov. 1936): 468–79.

BIOGRAPHIES AND MEMOIRS

Akin, Warren. *Letters of Warren Akin, Confederate Congressman.* Edited by Bell Irvin Wiley. Athens: University of Georgia Press, 1959.

Alcott, Louisa May. *Hospital Sketches.* Boston: J. Redpath, 1863. Available online at http://digital.library.upenn.edu/women/alcott/sketches/sketches.html#31. Several newer print editions are also available.

Ambrose, Stephen E. *Upton and the Army.* Baton Rouge: Louisiana State University Press, 1993.

Baker, Nina Brown. *Cyclone in Calico: The Story of Mary Ann Bickerdyke.* Boston: Little, Brown, 1952.

Beatty, John. *Memoirs of a Volunteer, 1861–1863.* New York: W. W. Norton, 1946.

Bernard, Jacqueline. *Journey Toward Freedom: The Story of Sojourner Truth.* New York: Feminist Press at the City University of New York, 1990.

Booth, John Wilkes. *"Right or Wrong, God Judge Me": The Writings of John Wilkes Booth.* Edited by John Rhodehamel and Louise Taper. Urbana: University of Illinois Press, 1997.

Bucklin, Sophronia. *In Hospital and Camp.* Philadelphia: J. E. Potter and Company, 1869. Available online at http://www.archive.org/details/inhospitalcampwo00buck.

Cooper, William J., Jr. *Jefferson Davis, American.* New York: Alfred A. Knopf, 2000.

Cumming, Kate. *A Journal of Hospital Life in the Confederate Army of Tennessee.* Louisville, KY: John P. Morton, 1866. Available online via Google Books, and reprinted as *Kate: The Journal of a Confederate Nurse* (Baton Rouge: Louisiana State University Press, 1959, 1998).

Dana, Charles A. *Recollections of the Civil War: With the Leaders at Washington and in the Field in the Sixties.* Lincoln: University of Nebraska Press, 1996.

Davis, Varina. *Jefferson Davis, Ex-president of the Confederate States of America: A Memoir by His Wife.* New York: Belford Company, 1890. Reprinted in 1990 by the Nautical & Aviation Pub. Co. of America.

Dawes, Rufus. *Service with the Sixth Wisconsin Volunteers.* Marietta, OH: E. R. Alderman & Sons, 1890. Reprinted as *A Full Blown Yankee of the Iron Brigade: Service with the Sixth Wisconsin Volunteers.* Lincoln: University of Nebraska Press, 1999.

Edmondston, Catherine Ann Devereux. *"Journal of a Secesh Lady": The Journal of Catherine Ann Devereux Edmondston, 1860–1866.* Edited by Beth G. Crabtree and James W. Patton. Raleigh, NC: Division of Archives and History, Department of Cultural Resources, 1979.

Ford, Worthington Chauncey, ed. *A Cycle of Adams Letters, 1861–1865.* 2 vols. Boston: Houghton Mifflin, 1920. Available online at http://www.archive.org/details/cycleadamsletters01fordrich.

Freeman, Warren H., and Eugene H. Freeman. *Letters from Two Brothers Serving in the War for the Union to Their Family at Home in West Cambridge, Mass.* Cambridge, MA: Privately printed, 1871. Available online at http://lcweb2.loc.gov/service/gdc/scd0001/2005/20051129001le/20051129001le.pdf and via Google Books.

Gallman, J. Matthew. *America's Joan of Arc: The Life of Anna Elizabeth Dickinson.* New York: Oxford University Press, 2006.

Gorgas, Josiah. *The Journals of Josiah Gorgas, 1857–1878.* Edited by Sarah W. Wiggins. Tuscaloosa: University of Alabama Press, 1995.

Grant, Ulysses S. *Personal Memoirs of U. S. Grant.* New York: Da Capo Press, 1982.

Grimes, Bryan. *Extracts of Letters of Major Gen'l Bryan Grimes to His Wife.* Raleigh, NC: Edwards, Broughton & Co., 1883. Available online at http://docsouth.unc.edu/fpn/grimes/grimes.html.

Hattaway, Herman, and Richard E. Beringer. *Jefferson Davis, Confederate President.* Lawrence: University Press of Kansas, 2002.

Hay, John. *Lincoln and the Civil War in the Diaries and Letters of John Hay.* Edited by Tyler Dennett. Westport, CT: Negro Universities Press, 1972.

Hoptak, John David. "A Forgotten Hero of the Civil War" [Nicholas Biddle]. Online at http://www.portal.state.pa.us/portal/server.pt/community/beginnings/18088/nick_biddle/689875. Originally published in *Pennsylvania Heritage*, Spring 2010.

Horner, Harlan Hoyt. *Lincoln and Greeley.* Urbana: University of Illinois Press, 1953.

Hotchkiss, Jedediah. *Make Me a Map of the Valley: The Civil War Journal of Stonewall Jackson's Topographer.* Edited by Archie P. McDonald. Dallas: Southern Methodist University Press, 1973.

Jaques, John W. *Three Years' Campaign of the Ninth, N.Y.S.M., During the Southern Rebellion.* New York: Hilton & Co., 1865. Available online at http://www.fauquiercivilwar.com/Assets/downloads/book_Three-years-Campaign-of-the-Ninth-NY.pdf.

Kean, Robert Garlick Hill. *Inside the Confederate Government: The Diary of Robert Garlick Hill Kean.* Edited by Edward Younger. Baton Rouge: Louisiana State University Press, 1993.

Kennett, Lee B. *Sherman: A Soldier's Life.* New York: HarperCollins, 2001.

Lane, David. *A Soldier's Diary: The Story of a Volunteer, 1862–1865.* Privately printed, 1905. Available online at http://www.archive.org/details/soldiersdiarysto00lane.

Lewis, Richard. *Camp Life of a Confederate Boy, of Bratton's Brigade, Longstreet's Corps, C.S.A.* Charleston, SC: The News and Courier Book Presses, 1883.

Loughborough, Mary Webster. *My Cave Life in Vicksburg.* New York: D. Appleton and Company, 1864. Reprinted in 1976 by the Spartanburg, SC, Reprint Co.

McCalmont, Alfred B. *Extracts from Letters Written by Alfred B. McCalmont . . . from the Front during the War of the Rebellion.* Privately printed, circa 1908.

McGuire, Judith W. *Diary of a Southern Refugee During the War.* New York: Arno Press, 1972.

Morse, Charles Fessenden. *Letters Written During the Civil War.* Privately printed, 1898. Available online via Google Books.

Norton, O. W. (Oliver Willcox, or Wilcox). *Army Letters, 1861–1865.* Privately printed, 1903. Available online via Google Books.

Panzer, Mary. *Mathew Brady and the Image of History.* Washington, DC: Smithsonian Institution Press, 1997.

Perkins, George Hamilton. *Letters of Capt. Geo. Hamilton Perkins, U.S.N.* Concord, NH: I. C. Evans, 1886. Reprinted in 1970 by Books for Libraries Press.

Rabun, James Z. "Alexander H. Stephens and Jefferson Davis." *American Historical Review* 58, no. 2 (Jan. 1953): 290–321.

Ransom, John. *Andersonville Diary.* Philadelphia: Douglass Bros., 1883. Reprinted as *John Ransom's Andersonville Diary.* New York: Berkley Books, 1994.

Russell, William Howard. *My Diary North and South.* New York: Harper & Brothers, 1954.

Salter, William. *The Life of James W. Grimes, Governor of Iowa, 1854–1858; A Senator of the United States, 1859–1869.* New York: D. Appleton and Company, 1876. Available online at http://quod.lib.umich.edu/cgi/t/text/text-idx?c=moa;idno=ABJ6736.

Sears, Stephen W. *George McClellan: The Young Napoleon*. New York: Da Capo Press, 1999.

Semmes, Raphael. *The Cruise of the Alabama and the Sumter*. 2 vols. London: Saunders, Otley, and Co., 1864. Available online at http://www .gutenberg.org/ebooks/13163.

Seward, Frederick W. *Reminiscences of a War-time Statesman and Diplomat, 1830–1915*. New York: G. P. Putnam's Sons, 1916. Available online at http://www.archive.org/details/reminiscencesofwoosew.

Shea, J. D. G., ed. *The Lincoln Memorial: A Record of the Life, Assassination, and Obsequies of the Martyred President*. New York: Bunce & Huntington, 1865. Available online at http://quod.lib.umich.edu/cgi/t/text/text-idx?c=moa;idno=ACK8359.

Smith, George G. *Leaves from a Soldier's Diary: The Personal Record of Lieutenant George G. Smith*. Putnam, CT: G. G. Smith, 1906.

Smith, Jean Edward. *Grant*. New York: Simon & Schuster, 2001.

Smith, Walter George. *Life and Letters of Thomas Kilby Smith*. New York: G. P. Putnam's Sons, 1898. Available online at http://www.archive.org/details/lifelettersofthooosmit.

Stewart, A. M. *Camp, March and Battle-Field*. Philadelphia: Jas. B. Rodgers, 1865.

Taylor, Susie King. *Reminiscences of My Life in Camp*. New York: Arno Press, 1968.

Thomas, Benjamin P. *Abraham Lincoln, A Biography*. Carbondale: Southern Illinois University Press, 2008.

Van Alstyne, Lawrence. *Diary of an Enlisted Man*. New Haven, CT: Tuttle, Morehouse & Taylor, 1910.

Welch, Spencer Glasgow. *A Confederate Surgeon's Letters to His Wife*. New York: Neale Publishing Company, 1911. Reprinted in 1954 by Continental Book Co.

Whitman, Walt. *The Wound Dresser: A Series of Letters Written from the Hospitals in Washington during the War of the Rebellion*. Boston: Small, Maynard & Co., 1898. Reprinted in 1978 by Norwood Editions. Also available online via Google Books.

Williams, Alpheus S. *From the Cannon's Mouth: The Civil War Letters of General Alpheus S. Williams*. Lincoln: University of Nebraska Press, 1995.

LIBRARY OF CONGRESS MANUSCRIPT COLLECTIONS USED IN THIS BOOK

Bickerdyke, Mary Ann Ball
Bourne, William Oland
Carlton, Caleb Henry
Carman, Ezra Ayers
Cater, Douglas J. and Rufus W.
Confederate States of America
Early, Jubal Anderson
Ewing, Thomas
Gladstone Collection
Habersham Family (Richard W. Habersham)
Harrison, Burton
Hotchkiss, Jedediah
Johnston, Mercer Green
Lincoln, Abraham
Mitchell, James B. (Billingslea)
Reichhelm, Edward Paul
Shiner, Michael
Thompson, Gilbert
Willard Family

CIVIL WAR COLLECTIONS IN THE LIBRARY OF CONGRESS

The largest library in the world and an institution known both as "America's Library" and the "Nation's Memory," the Library of Congress is located in three large buildings on Capitol Hill in Washington, DC, and the Packard Campus for Audio-Visual Conservation in Culpeper, Virginia, which houses 6.2 million moving images, sound recordings, and related documents. (Materials in Culpeper can be called to or accessed from the Library's Washington facilities.) From 740 volumes and 3 maps in 1801, the Library's collections increased, by 2011, to more than 145 million items — on all subjects and in almost all media. Reflecting America's membership in the community of nations and the diverse origins of its people, the Library's collections are international in scope, including material in more than 460 languages. Yet the heart of the Library is found in its vast collections of written, visual, recorded, and electronic materials that chronicle the origins and development of the United States of America. Its matchless array of materials pertaining to the American Civil War, preserved within several specialized divisions, constitutes an unparalleled resource for the study of this defining era in the history of the United States. Below are some of the highlights of each division's Civil War holdings.

American Folklife Center (AFC), http://www.loc.gov/folklife/
AFC's Civil War–related materials include recordings of reminiscences of former slaves collected during the Depression era by the Works Projects Administration Federal Writers' Project; tales of the Confederate Army recorded by Julius Franklin Howell (1846–1948), veteran of the Twenty-fourth Virginia Cavalry and throughout his long life devoted to preservation of the memories of Confederate soldiers; recordings from the Blue Ridge Parkway Folklife Project Collection and the Vaughn and Kay Brewer Ozark Mountain Collection, in which people describe their grandparents' wartime service; a recording of *The Adam and Eve Wedding Song*, a composition attributed to Abraham Lincoln, and recordings of other Civil War–era music; a recording of a 1940 celebration of the Emancipation Proclamation held at the Library of Congress; and a 1954 recording of the Sons of the Union Veterans of the Civil War program honoring Minnesotan Albert Woolson, then 107 and the last surviving Union Army veteran.

General Collections (Humanities and Social Sciences Division, HSS), http://www.loc.gov/rr/main/
The General Collections include thousands of volumes pertaining to the war, from memoirs, diaries, and letters published during the conflict to present-day histories. These collections include accounts and analyses of individual Civil War battles; treatments of various aspects of the war (for example, naval warfare, guerrilla warfare, cavalry operations, weaponry,

intelligence gathering, politics, government, and diplomacy); books on slavery and African American wartime experiences; books on camp life and Civil War humor; Civil War–related fiction and poetry; regimental histories and bound volumes of the newsletters and magazines of veterans' groups; and Civil War almanacs, chronologies, and encyclopedias. To browse items in the General Collections, go to the Library's main webpage, www.loc.gov, click on "Library Catalogs" at the top of the page, and select either "Basic Search" or "Guided Search." Under "Basic Search," choose "Subject Browse" and type in, as the subject, United States-History-Civil War, 1861–1865.

Geography and Map Division (G&M), http://www.loc.gov/rr/geogmap/
The Library's cartographic collections, the largest in the world, include more than 2,240 printed maps, manuscript maps, and sketch or reconnaissance maps made by both Union and Confederate forces immediately prior to, during, or in the immediate aftermath of the Civil War. G&M collections also include more than seventy-five atlases prepared by both Union and Confederate troops as "after action reports" regarding specific battles and campaigns. Among the reconnaissance, sketch, and theater-of-war maps are detailed battle maps made by Major Jedediah Hotchkiss for Generals Robert E. Lee and Stonewall Jackson; maps of General William Tecumseh Sherman's Southern military campaigns; and maps taken from newspapers, diaries, scrapbooks, and manuscripts compiled by individual soldiers. These materials are accessible online through the Library of Congress American Memory webpage, at http://memory.loc.gov/ammem/collections/civil_war_maps/.

Also accessible via this webpage are Civil War cartographic materials from the Virginia Historical Society and the Library of Virginia.

Law Library (Law), http://www.loc.gov/law/about/
The world's largest law library, the Library of Congress Law Library holds more than 2.65 million volumes. Included within its collections are records of military trials/court-martial proceedings conducted by the departmental commands of the United States Army during and after the Civil War against Union army personnel, civilians, and, in rare instances, members of the Confederate army. Law also holds state session laws for the Civil War period; bills from the Thirty-seventh and Thirty-eighth Congresses (1861–1865); and *A Digest of the Military and Naval Laws of the Confederate States, from the Commencement of the Provisional Congress to the End of the First Congress Under the Permanent Constitution* (Columbia, SC, 1864).

Manuscript Division (MSS), http://www.loc.gov/rr/mss/
An especially rich repository of Civil War materials, the Manuscript Division holds the nation's premier collection of original Abraham Lincoln

BIBLIOGRAPHY

documents, which may be accessed online, at http://memory.loc.gov/ammem/alhtml/malhome.html. The division also holds the papers of Lincoln's private secretaries and biographers John George Nicolay and John Hay and those of most of his cabinet, including Postmaster General Montgomery Blair (in the Blair Family Papers), Secretary of the Treasury Salmon P. Chase, Secretary of War Edwin M. Stanton, and Secretary of the Navy Gideon Welles. MSS is also the principal repository for the papers of Generals Nathaniel P. Banks, P. G. T. Beauregard, Benjamin F. Butler, Joshua Lawrence Chamberlain, Jubal A. Early, Charles and Thomas Ewing Jr., James A. Garfield, Ulysses S. Grant, Samuel P. Heintzelman, Henry J. Hunt, Joseph W. Keifer, George B. McClellan, Montgomery C. Meigs, Carl Schurz, Philip H. Sheridan, and William T. Sherman.

Admirals Andrew H. Foote, Louis M. Goldsborough, Samuel P. Lee, and Matthew Fontaine Maury are also represented by collections, as are hundreds of noncommissioned officers and enlisted personnel. The Confederate States of America Collection and the papers of war correspondent Whitelaw Reid (*Cincinnati Gazette*), newspaper editors Horace Greeley (*New York Tribune*) and Manton Marble (*New York World*), nurse and American Red Cross founder Clara Barton, Burton N. Harrison (secretary to Jefferson Davis), and poet and Civil War nurse Walt Whitman are noteworthy among the more than one thousand discrete collections in the division that relate to the Civil War.

Notable individual items within these manuscript collections include: drafts of Abraham Lincoln's Gettysburg Address, Emancipation Proclamation, and first and second inaugural addresses; Ulysses S. Grant's commission as lieutenant general; Varina Davis's letter to Montgomery Blair describing the capture of her husband, Jefferson Davis; Clara Barton's war lectures; the letters of artist and soldier Charles Wellington Reed (many decorated with scenes of army life); Jubal Early's postwar scrapbook (see page 232); and, in the Gladstone Collection, a letter from African American activist, orator, dentist, and lawyer John Rock seeking a Washington attorney's assistance in Rock's successful bid to become the first African American to be admitted to practice before the U.S. Supreme Court (see pages 45 and 218).

In sum, Manuscript Division Civil War collections provide an abundance of information on virtually every aspect of the war, from the experiences and contributions of women and African Americans through the motivations of volunteer soldiers and the treatment of prisoners, to the financing of the war and wartime diplomacy.

A more detailed listing of MSS Civil War Collections can be accessed by going to the division's "Catalogs, Bibliographies, and Guides" webpage, at http://www.loc.gov/rr/mss/findaid.html, and activating the "Civil War Guide" link. (To peruse all MSS online finding aids, go to the Finding Aids home page at http://www.loc.gov/rr/mss/f-aids/mssfa.html.)

Motion Picture, Broadcasting, and Recorded Sound Division (MBRS), http://www.loc.gov/rr/mopic/

Repository of the world's largest film collection and the nation's largest public collection of sound recordings, MBRS holds Civil War materials ranging from ten minutes of raw, unedited footage of a 1930 Confederate reunion through modern documentaries exploring the entire war, individual battles, and leading figures (including Ulysses S. Grant, Robert E. Lee, Abraham Lincoln, Clara Barton, and Harriet Tubman); the African American wartime experience; guerrilla warfare; and Civil War music. Fictional films held in the division run from silent film–era director D. W. Griffith's groundbreaking — if ideologically indefensible — *Birth of a Nation* through the 1939 Clark Gable–Vivien Leigh epic *Gone with the Wind* to 1989's *Glory* and the 2003 film version of Charles Frazier's National Book Award–winning novel *Cold Mountain*.

Recorded sound collections include recordings of interviews with people who were living during the Civil War — for example, a series of interviews with seven Union veterans conducted in the 1940s by the Sons of Union Veterans of the Civil War. The NBC Radio Collection includes broadcasts from Gettysburg, Pennsylvania, between June 30 and July 3, 1938, relating to the commemoration of the seventy-fifth anniversary of the battle. These broadcasts feature brief interviews with both Union and Confederate veterans; a short radio drama about the battle, *That a Nation Might Live;* a description of the seventy-fifth anniversary parade; a memorial service; and selections played by the U.S. Marine Band. The recorded sound collections also contain recordings of Civil War songs and such dramatizations as MacKinlay Kantor's *Lee and Grant at Appomattox,* and a *You Are There* dramatization of "The Battle of Gettysburg," as well as a recording of the radio broadcast of Stephen Vincent Benét's epic narrative poem *John Brown's Body* featuring Tyrone Power, Dame Judith Anderson, and Raymond Massey.

Music Division (MUS), http://www.loc.gov/rr/perform/

Holding more than 20.5 million items covering a thousand years of music history, the Music Division collections are particularly strong in material related to American music, including manuscripts, correspondence, and papers of every notable American composer and musician. The division holds more than 2,500 Civil War sheet-music titles, which can be browsed online via the Performing Arts Encyclopedia webpage, at http://www.loc.gov/performingarts/ (see the list of "Special Presentations," and follow the "Civil War Sheet Music" link). The division also holds band books used by Civil War army bands, important morale-boosting components on both sides of the conflict. A presentation, "Band Music from the Civil War Era," is available on the Library's American Memory website, at http://memory.loc.gov/ammem/cwmhtml/cwmhome.html. The Francis Maria Scala Collection contains the music manuscripts and papers of noted bandleader Francis Scala, who was the director of the U.S. Marine Band from 1855 to 1871.

Prints and Photographs Division (P&P), http://www.loc.gov/rr/print/

Another particularly rich repository of Civil War materials, the Prints and Photographs Division holds thousands of Civil War–related materials in a variety of formats, including:

Photographs by such masters as Mathew Brady, Alexander Gardner, and Timothy O'Sullivan, as well as many less well-known photographers. Portraits of leading figures on both sides, photos showing life in army camps and the grim aftermath of battle, and haunting images of "ordinary" soldiers and sailors are included in this photographic record. In 2010, the division received the Liljenquist Family Collection of Civil War Photographs, more than 700 ambrotype and tintype photographs of Union and Confederate soldiers (plus other war-related artifacts) collected and donated by Tom Liljenquist and his sons, Jason, Brandon, and Christian. A number of photographs from the Liljenquist Collection are included in this volume, their first appearance in a major print publication.

Drawings including both rough sketches and finished documentary drawings by Alfred R. Waud; his brother, William; Edwin Forbes; and other artist-correspondents for the Union's illustrated newspapers, as well as British artist-correspondent Frank Vizetelly, plus watercolor drawings by artist-soldiers William McIlvaine and James Fuller Queen.

Popular graphic arts including both color and black-and-white lithographs and woodcuts depicting wartime leaders, battle scenes, fortifications and hospitals, and sentimental vignettes, as well as political banners and cartoons.

Miscellaneous materials including patriotic envelopes, advertisements featuring battle scenes and depictions of war leaders, illustrated sheet-music covers, illustrated pamphlets, and illustrated books and bound portfolios such as Alexander Gardner's *Photographic Sketchbook of the Civil War* and George N. Barnard's *Photographic Views of Sherman's Campaign.*

Thousands of the division's Civil War–related items have been digitized and made available via the Prints and Photographs Online Catalog, at http://www.loc.gov/pictures/.

Rare Book and Special Collections Division (RBSC), http://www.loc.gov/rr/rarebook/

Among the Rare Book Division's many Civil War treasures are the Walt Whitman Collection and the Alfred Whital Stern Collection of publications, manuscripts, prints, and other material related to Abraham Lincoln; unusual Lincolniana held by the division include the contents of Lincoln's pockets on the night of his assassination and a few pieces of Mary Todd Lincoln's jewelry. Rare Book's Confederate States of America (CSA) Collection consists of 1,812 volumes, including a rich selection pertaining to the CSA national and state governments and 158 broadsides featuring ballads relating to the war, as well as almanacs, textbooks, volumes of history, prayer books, and other works produced in the wartime South. The Broadside Collection includes Union and some Confederate recruiting posters, special orders by military commanders, and such interesting ephemera as a poem by General Lew Wallace that may have been published to help raise funds for the U.S. Sanitary Commission. The division also holds a collection of illustrated Civil War envelopes and such unusual items as the Myriopticon (see page 200) and a game, The Campaigns in Virginia (see page 67).

Rare Book's African American Pamphlet Collection contains 396 pamphlets on topics such as slavery, colonization, emancipation, and reconstruction, and the Daniel P. Murray Pamphlet Collection contains an additional 184 pamphlets pertaining chiefly to slavery and abolition. A majority of the pamphlets in the Congressional Speech Collection (consisting of speeches delivered by members of Congress between 1826 and 1940) date from the last six decades of the nineteenth century. Other special Rare Book collections that include materials on the war and its causes include the Dime Novel Collection and the juvenile collections (children's books dating from the early eighteenth century to the present, encompassing such titles as *The Anti-Slavery Alphabet,* published in 1847).

Serial and Government Publications Division (SER), http://www.loc.gov/rr/news/
This division's newspaper collection includes many papers from the Civil War era representing both Confederate and Union perspectives as well as titles that best document the military aspects of the war, many of which are illustrated with battlefield maps. In all, the Library holds more than 790 original bound newspaper volumes covering the period 1861–1865. It also holds a collection of separate newspaper issues containing illustrated battle maps. Selected items in the division's Historic Events Newspaper Collection document landmark battles and other important occurrences as covered in such papers as the *New York Herald,* the *New York Times,* the *Vicksburg Citizen,* and others. Postwar papers sometimes feature veterans' recollections.

Online Exhibitions, http://www.loc.gov/exhibits/all/
Selected materials from the Library of Congress collections are always available to in-person visitors through both permanent and temporary exhibitions in the Thomas Jefferson Building and smaller exhibition spaces in the James Madison Memorial Building. Online versions of all major Library exhibitions are available through the Library's website. Those pertaining to the Civil War include:

The Gettysburg Address, featuring the Library's two manuscript copies of the address (given by Lincoln to his two private secretaries, John Hay and John Nicolay; see the earliest known copy, given to Nicolay, on page 159) and other documents relating to the address, including the invitation sent to Lincoln to make some remarks at the opening of the national cemetery at Gettysburg.

The Last Full Measure: Civil War Photographs from the Liljenquist Family Collection, featuring 379 Civil War–era ambrotypes and tintypes of enlisted Union and Confederate soldiers; it provides a poignant reminder of the human cost of the conflict.

With Malice Toward None: The Abraham Lincoln Bicentennial Exhibition. Created to commemorate the 200th anniversary of the 1809 birth of the nation's most revered president, this exhibition reveals Lincoln the man, whose thoughts, words, and actions were deeply affected by personal experiences and pivotal historic events.

Civil War materials are also included in the following exhibitions:

American Treasures in the Library of Congress

The African-American Mosaic: African-American Culture and History

The African-American Odyssey: A Quest for Full Citizenship

"I Do Solemnly Swear . . ." Inaugural Materials from the Collections of the Library of Congress

Library of Congress Webcasts, http://www.loc.gov/today/cyberlc/index.php
Included in the large and constantly growing collection of video recordings of programs presented at the Library is coverage of the Lincoln Bicentennial Symposium, featuring many noted scholars of the Civil War era. Webcasts of author talks include considerations of the entire span of the war as well as many of its individual aspects, including Washington during the Civil War; the African American journey from slavery to freedom; Robert E. Lee, as discovered through his letters and papers; and the "parallel lives" of Abraham Lincoln and Walt Whitman in wartime Washington.

To access webcasts pertaining to the Civil War, go to the Internet address given above and type "Civil War" into the Webcast Pages "Search" module at the top of the main Webcast page.

Information about and artifacts from the Library of Congress are also available on Facebook, Twitter, YouTube, and Flickr (where photographs of Civil War soldiers from the Liljenquist Family Collection are available, as well as nearly two dozen photographs of Abraham Lincoln).

INFORMATION ABOUT IMAGES

To acquire reproductions of images in this book, note the negative or digital ID numbers that follow page numbers in the chapter lists below. Many images in this book are from the Library's Prints & Photographs Division and can be viewed or downloaded from http://www.loc.gov/pictures/. Items from other divisions are noted using the abbreviations listed below. Contact the appropriate custodial division or Duplication Services of the Library of Congress, http://www.loc.gov/duplicationservices/, (202) 707-5640, to obtain copies of these items. Some of these are also available online; see "Civil War Collections in the Library of Congress," page 244.

Images that were cropped or restored for use in this book are noted with an asterisk.

ABBREVIATIONS FOR CUSTODIAL DIVISIONS
GC   General Collections
G&M Geography and Map Division
MSS Manuscript Division
MUS Music Division
RBSC Rare Book and Special Collections
SER Serial and Government Publications Division

i: GC. ii–iii: LC-DIG-pga-19554. iv–v: G&M, cw0024000. vi: LC-DIG-cwpb-02942.

Chapter One: Torn Asunder: February 1861–April 1862
1: LC-USZ62-133797. 2–3: LC-USZC4-1736. 4–5: LC DIG-ppmsca-07636. 6: G&M, cw0024000. 7: left LC-DIG-ds-00121, right LC-DIG-ppmsca-26716. 8: LC-DIG-pga-02817. 10: LC-USZ62-6854. 11: LC-USZ62-16832. 12: left MSS Abraham Lincoln Papers, right LC-DIG-ppmsca-19482. 13: left LC-USZ62-132563, right LC-USZC4-9183. 14: LC-USZC2-2353. 15: left GC, center LC-DIG-ds-00120, right LC-USZ62-16831. 16: left LC-USZ62-126417. 17: LC-USZC4-1736. 18: left LC-USZ62-44000, right LC-USZ62-132138. 19: left MSS LC-MS-12880-13, right GC. 20: left LC-USZ62-137051*, right LC-DIG-cwpbh-01728. 21: left LC-DIG-pga-03087, right LC-DIG-cwpbh-04523. 22: left LC-USZC2-2231, right LC-USZ62-36161. 23: left LC-USZC4-13450, center LC-USZ62-85746, right LC-USZ62-104937. 24: left MSS Samuel P. Heintzelman Papers, right MSS Michael Shiner Diary. 25: left G&M, right GC. 26: left G&M, right LC-USZ62-9797. 27: LC-USZ62-40070. 28: GC. 29: left LC-DIG-ppmsca-26834, right LC-DIG-ppmsca-21460. 30: left LC-USZ62-38480, right MSS Ezra Carman Papers.

31: left G&M, right GC. 32: left LC-DIG-cwpb-05665, right LC-USZC4-4773. 33: LC-DIG-pga-01861. 34: LC-DIG-ds-00118. 35: LC-DIG-pga-00431. 36: LC-DIG-ppmsca-21215. 37: GC. 38–39: LC-USZ62-123476. 40: LC-DIG-ppmsca-20874. 41: left LC-DIG-ppmsca-08348, right LC-USZ62-99838. 42: left LC-DIG-cwpbh-03078, center LC-USZ62-15450, right LC-DIG-ppmsca-04324. 43: LC-DIG-ppmsca-19421. 44: left LC-USZ62-24165, right LC-DIG-ppmsca-20701. 45: left LC-USZC4-4908, right LC-USZ62-110530*. 46: G&M. 47: left LC-DIG-ppmsca-20778, right MSS Abraham Lincoln Papers. 48: LC-DIG-pga-03975. 49: left LC-DIG-ds-00119, right LC-DIG-cwpb-05905. 50: LC-DIG-pga-01849. 51: left LC-USZ62-76968, right LC-DIG-ppmsca-19235. 52: left MSS James B. Mitchell Papers, right LC-USZC4-10799. 53: left LC-DIG-pga-01888, right LC-DIG-cwpb-04943. 54: left LC-DIG-pga-01850, right LC-DIG-cwpbh-03896. 55: left LC-USZ62-110631, right LC-USZ62-14015. 56: LC-USZ62-67468. 57: LC-DIG-pga-00540. 58: HABS GA, 26-SAV.V (2-87). 59: Law Library — Rare Book Room. 60: left LC-DIG-cwpb-05227, right SER. 61: GC.

Chapter Two: Toward a New Birth of Freedom: May 1862–April 1863
62–63: LC-USZC4-12604. 64–65: LC-DIG-cwpbh-03384. 66: left GC, right LC-DIG-36456*. 67: upper RBSC, photographed by Lee Ewing, lower RBSC. 68: GC. 70: left LC-DIG-ppmsca-21417, right LC-DIG-ppmsca-08362. 71: LC-DIG-ds-00358. 72: left LC-DIG-ds-00290, right LC-DIG-ds-00287. 73: left LC-DIG-ppmsca-20014, right LC-DIG-ppmsca-21081. 74: upper left MSS Douglas & Rufus Cater Papers, lower left GC, right LC-USZ62-42856. 75: GC. 76: left LC-USZC4-2462, right LC-DIG-pga-00456. 77: LC-DIG-ppmsca-21142. 78: RBSC. 79: left LC-B8184-10037, right LC-USZC2-3799. 80: LC-DIG-ppmsca-20033. 81: left RBSC, right LC-DIG-cwpb-06956. 82: left GC, right LC-USZ62-99327. 83: G&M cw0245390. 84: left RBSC, right LC-DIG-cwpbh-01988. 85: LC-DIG-ds-00359. 86: LC-DIG-ppmsca-20792. 87: LC-DIG-ppmsca-21302. 88: left LC-DIG-pga-00057, right LC-DIG-ppmsca-19243. 89: GC. 90: left LC-USZC4-12604, right MUS M1642.C. 91: left GC, right LC-DIG-pga-02157. 92: LC-USZC4-3132. 93: left G&M cw0246300, right LC-USZC4-6307. 94: RBSC. 95: left LC-USZ6-704, right LC-USZ62-105562. 96: LC-DIG-cwpb-04339. 97: left LC-USZ62-80740, right RBSC. 98: left RBSC rbpe.15703600, right LC-DIG-ppmsca-26730. 99: LC-DIG-ppmsca-22477. 100: left LC-DIG-ppmsca-27159, right LC-DIG-ppmsca-26863. 101: upper right LC-DIG-cwpbh-05229, left LC-DIG-cwpb-03518, lower right LC-BH8277- 550. 102: left LC-DIG-ppmsca-21411, right LC-DIG-cwpb-04578*. 103: LC-DIG-ppmsca-20777. 104: LC-DIG-ppmsca-20787. 105: left Dietrich Hecht Collection, right LC-DIG-ppmsca-21123. 106: left LC-DIG-

ppmsca-21003, right LC-DIG-ppmsca-08541. 107: left LC-DIG-ppmsca-07385, right MSS E. Paul Reichhelm Papers. 108: LC-DIG-pga-01858. 109: left LC-USZ62-88808, right LC-USZ62-6858. 110: left LC-DIG-ppmsca-21006, right G&M cw0280000. 111: left and center RBSC Stern Collection, right GC. 112: left RBSC, right LC-DIG-cwpb-07587. 113: LC-USZ62-100253. 114: MSS David Dixon Porter Papers 115: left LC-DIG-cwpb-07616*, center LC-DIG-cwpb-05434, right MSS CSA Collection. 116–117: GC. 118: LC-DIG-ppmsca-22450. 119: left LC-USZ62-60562, right LC-DIG-ppmsca-20603.

Chapter Three: The Hard Hand of War: May 1863–April 1864
120–121: LC-DIG-ppmsca-08297. 122–123: LC-DIG-ppmsca-20527. 124: left GC, right LC-DIG-ppmsca-19395. 125: MUS M20.C61E. 126: LC-USZC4-2525. 128: left LC-USZ62-3646, right LC-DIG-pga-01844. 129: left LC-DIG-ds-00288, right LC-DIG-ppmsca-22953. 130: LC-DIG-pga-02196. 131: left LC-USZ62-130838, right LC-DIG-ppmsca-21299. 132: LC-DIG-ppmsca-36454. 133: LC-USZ62-131137*. 134: left LC-DIG-ppmsca-22921, center LC-DIG-cwpb-07436, right LC-DIG-cwpbh-03184. 135: left LC-DIG-ggbain-03110, right LC-USZ62-100070. 136: left LC-DIG-cwpb-05423, right LC-DIG-ds-00294. 137: left RBSC, right GC. 138: left LC-DIG-cwpb-03981, right RBSC. 139: left LC-USZ62-132854, right RBSC. 140: LC-USZC4-3269. 141: G&M cw0347000. 142: left LC-DIG-ppmsca-21219, right LC-DIG-ds-00293. 143: LC-DIG-pga-03266. 144: left LC-DIG-ds-00289, right LC-DIG-ds-00292. 145: left GC, right LC-USZ62-113909. 146: left LC-DIG-ppmsca-10884, right GC. 147: left RBSC Photographed by Lee Ewing, right LC-USZ62-75860. 148: LC-USZ62-134452. 149: left LC-DIG-ppmsca-21422, right MSS Burton Harrison Papers. 150: left LC-USZ62-61447, right LC-DIG-ppmsca-21293. 151: left LC-DIG-ds-00297, right LC-DIG-cwpbh-01069. 152: left LC-B8184-10702, right GC. 153: left LC-USZ62-10073, right LC-DIG-ppmsca-26955. 154: G&M cw0398200r. 155: left LC-USZ62-12959, right LC-DIG-ds-00296. 156: upper LC-USZ62-42772, lower RBSC. 157: LC-DIG-ds-00295. 158: left LC-USZ62-77747, right LC-DIG-pga-04158. 159: MSS Abraham Lincoln Papers. 160: LC-DIG-ds-00298. 161: left GC, right LC-DIG-ppmsca-22939. 162: left RBSC, right LC-DIG-ppmsca-20861. 163: MSS Abraham Lincoln Papers. 164: left LC-USZC4-1841, right LC-DIG-ppmsca-20629. 165: left LC-USZ62-107446, right LC-USZ62-42028. 166: left LC-DIG-cwpbh-02348, right LC-DIG-ppmsca-21139. 167: left MSS Rose Bell Knox Papers, right LC-DIG-cwpbh-00682. 168: left LC-DIG-cwpb-01544, right LC-DIG-ppmsca-10762. 169: LC-DIG-ppmsca-21035. 170: left LC-USZ62-51046, right MSS Willard Family Papers. 171: LC-USZ62-39604. 172: left LC-USZ62-14618, right LC-USZ62-33811. 173: LC-DIG-cwpb-01401.

Chapter Four: "The Heavens Are Hung in Black": May 1864–May 1865
174–175: LC-DIG-pga-04038. 176–177: LC-DIG-ppmsca-21750. 178: GC. 179: MSS Jubal Anderson Early Papers, Photographed by Lee Ewing. 180: LC-DIG-ppmsca-19215. 182: LC-DIG-ppmsca-21457. 183: left RBSC, center LC-DIG-cwpb-04579, right LC-DIG-cwpb-01697. 184: left LC-DIG-cwpb-04402, right LC-DIG-cwpb-06381. 185: left LC-DIG-cwpb-05761, right LC-DIG-cwpb-07546. 186: left LC-DIG-ppmsca-08359, center LC-DIG-ppmsca-26873, right LC-DIG-ppmsca-26874. 187: G&M cw0396350. 188: left LC-USZC2-3251, center LC-DIG-ppmsca-19440, right LC-DIG-ppmsca-19433. 189: LC-DIG-cwpb-01276. 190: left LC-DIG-ppmscd-00082, right LC-DIG-cwpb-01896. 191: LC-USZ62-111179. 192: left E632.B88 Case X, right LC-USZ62-132749. 193: LC-DIG-pga-04041. 194: left: RBSC, right MUS M1642.S. 195: left LC-DIG-ppmsca-21083, center LC-DIG-cwpbh-02996, right LC-DIG-cwpb-05620. 196: GC. 197: left LC-DIG-ppmsca-36964, center G&M g3881sm.gcwh0008, right LC-DIG-cwpbh-00934. 198: LC-DIG-cwpb-01948. 199: left MSS Montgomery C. Meigs Papers, right LC-DIG-ppmsca-20280. 200: left RBSC, Photographed by Lee Ewing, center GC, right LC-USZ62-64034. 201: GC. 202: left LC-DIG-pga-02396, right MSS Abraham Lincoln Papers. 203: left LC-DIG-ppmsca-17561, right LC-DIG-cwpb-03467*. 204: upper left GC, lower LC-DIG-ppmsca-22447*, right RBSC, Photographed by Lee Ewing. 205: left LC-DIG-cwpb-07540, center G&M cwh00185, right LC-DIG-cwpbh-02637. 206: RBSC, Photographed by Lee Ewing. 207: LC-DIG-pga-04047. 208: left LC-B8184-10672, right MUS M20.C59S. 209: LC-DIG-pga-02834. 210: left LC-DIG-ppmsca-19233, center LC-DIG-cwpb-05987, right LC-DIG-cwpb-02226. 211: left LC-DIG-ppmsca-21298, right LC-USZ62-111947. 212: left LC-DIG-pga-03676, right LC-DIG-cwpb-03898. 213: LC-DIG-pga-01886. 214: LC-DIG-ppmsca-19925. 215 left: GC, right & 216: MSS William O. Bourne Papers, Photographed by Lee Ewing. 217: GC. 218: MSS William A. Gladstone Collection, Photographed by Lee Ewing. 219: LC-USZ62-133068. 220: left LC-USZ61-1863, right MSS Abraham Lincoln Papers. 221: LC-DIG-ppmsca-23718. 222: left LC-DIG-cwpb-06208, center LC-DIG-ppmsca-19229, right LC-USZ62-67405. 223: GC. 224: LC-DIG-pga-03629. 225: LC-USZ62-6931. 226: LC-DIG-pga-02091. 227: left LC-DIG-highsm-04710, center RBSC Photographed by Lee Ewing, right LC-DIG-cwpb-02464. 228: left LC-USZC4-1621, right LC-DIG-ppmsca-13487. 229: left MUS M1640.T, right LC-DIG-ppmsca-21144. 230: LC-DIG-ppmsca-23873*. 231: left LC-DIG-cwpb-04230, right LC-DIG-ppmsca-05704. 232: MSS Jubal Anderson Early Papers. 233: RBSC.

ACKNOWLEDGMENTS

Creating *The Library of Congress Illustrated Timeline of the Civil War* was a labor of love and, as with every new Library project, even those on familiar topics, an exciting voyage of discovery. Drawing on the massive Civil War collections of the Library of Congress, the *Timeline* was also very much a collaborative effort.

The book has benefited most especially from the dedication, knowledge, artistic eye, sleuthing abilities, and organizational skills of its incomparable picture editor, Athena Angelos. Her research acumen and sage advice have resulted in a nourishing visual feast that grandly complements the text.

In addition to writing an eloquent and informed introduction to the book and the Civil War era, Gary W. Gallagher reviewed the *Timeline* text; his comments, corrections, and suggestions — given with characteristic consideration, zest, and good humor — have made this a stronger book.

It has been a great pleasure to work with our colleagues at Little, Brown and Company, where executive editor Michael Sand guided the book to completion with excellent editorial suggestions while exhibiting much-appreciated patience. At the crucial intersection of several streams of production requirements, Melissa Caminneci was a perfect diplomat and traffic officer and helped keep the book on track. Designer Laura Lindgren has taken hundreds of elements and transformed them with skill and artistry into a stunning volume. And I offer a special tip of my cap to the excellent copyediting team of Peggy Freudenthal, Janet Byrne, and Pamela Marshall, for whose careful attention to telling details I am most grateful.

Several members of the talented and dedicated staff of the Library of Congress are due special thanks for their assistance on this book. Prints and Photographs Division chief Helena Zinkham provided guidance and excellent suggestions for exploration and methods of operation, while Sara Duke, curator of popular and applied graphic arts, and Carol Johnson, curator of photography, introduced us to thrilling material in their P&P domains. Clark Evans, head of reference in the Rare Book and Special Collections Division, and that division's Civil War–era specialist, was a most excellent guide to the treasures there. In the Manuscript Division thanks go to assistant chief Janice Ruth and to Civil War and Reconstruction specialist Michelle Krowl, who led us enthusiastically through the wealth of material there. Thanks, too, to Cheryl Regan, exhibition director in the Interpretive Programs Office; Ed Redmond, in the Geography and Map Division; James Martin, in the Law Division; Domenico Sergi, in the Information Technology Service; Margaret Kiekhefer, Georgia Zola, and Paul Hogroian in Duplication Services; Beatriz BM Haspo, in the Loan Division; consultant Lee Ewing, for his excellent special photography; and to Publishing Office interns Ariel Moore and Julie Thompson, whose research and fact checking contributed much to the development of the *Timeline*. All those named above have made this a richer book; the flaws that remain in the text are my own.

Finally, and especially, I salute my dauntless colleagues in the Publishing Office at the Library of Congress: Director of Publishing Ralph Eubanks, fellow writer-editors Linda Osborne, Susan Reyburn, and Aimee Hess, and administrative wizard Myint San. Their love of history and the making of good books, their integrity and devotion to producing work of the highest quality, their wisecracks and wise counsel are ever a joy and an inspiration.

M.E.W.

INDEX